# DESIGNING SERVICES AND PROGRAMS
## fOR HIGH-ABILITY LEARNERS

This book is dedicated to all the teachers, coordinators,
administrators, and state directors who persevere and pioneer on
behalf of all students, especially those who are gifted and talented:
*
Sandra N. Kaplan for her vision and voice. We stand proudly on your shoulders;
*
Deborah for her courage and persistence;
*
Jeffrey C. Anderson, who taught me everything
I know about teaching gifted and talented students; and
*
Janet and Joe, who are indeed my favorite teammates.

# DESIGNING SERVICES AND PROGRAMS
## for HIGH-ABILITY LEARNERS

## A GUIDEBOOK FOR GIFTED EDUCATION

Jeanne H.
Purcell
EDITOR

Rebecca D.
Eckert
EDITOR

A JOINT PUBLICATION

NATIONAL ASSOCIATION FOR
Gifted Children

CORWIN PRESS
A SAGE Publications Company
Thousand Oaks, California

*For information:*

Corwin Press
A Sage Publications Company
2455 Teller Road
Thousand Oaks, California 91320
www.corwinpress.com

Sage Publications Ltd.
1 Oliver's Yard
55 City Road
London EC1Y 1SP
United Kingdom

Sage Publications India Pvt. Ltd.
B-42, Panchsheel Enclave
Post Box 4109
New Delhi 110 017 India

Printed in the United States of America

Library of Congress Cataloging-in-Publication Data

Purcell, Jeanne H.
Designing services and programs for high-ability learners: A guidebook for gifted education/Jeanne H. Purcell and Rebecca D. Eckert.
        p. cm.
"Joint publication of the National Association for Gifted Children and Corwin Press."
Includes bibliographical references and index.
ISBN 1–4129–2616–5 (cloth)—ISBN 1–4129–2617–3 (pbk.)
    1. Gifted children—Education—United States. 2. Educational planning—United States.
I. Eckert, Rebecca D. II. National Association for Gifted Children (U.S.) III. Title.
LC3993.9.P87 2006        371.95—dc22

This book is printed on acid-free paper.

05   06   07   08   09   10   9   8   7   6   5   4   3   2   1

| | |
|---|---|
| *Acquisitions Editor:* | Kylee Liegl |
| *Production Editor:* | Beth A. Bernstein |
| *Copy Editor:* | Freelance Editorial Services |
| *Typesetter:* | C&M Digitals (P) Ltd. |
| *Proofreader:* | Dennis W. Webb |
| *Indexer:* | Rick Hurd |
| *Cover Designer:* | Rose Storey |
| *Graphic Designer:* | Scott Van Atta |
| *NAGC Publications Coordinator:* | Jane Clarenbach |

# Contents

# Foreword

It has been more than 10 years since the last national report on the status of programs for gifted and talented students in the United States. *National Excellence: A Case for Developing America's Talent* gave a portrait of where we were as a nation in our efforts to develop students' talents to exceptionally high levels, and it made recommendations on how we should move forward to improve our overall system in a way that supports these students. In many ways, services for gifted and talented students have evolved since this report was published and are poised now to make an even greater contribution to American education.

We understand that there are twin goals for programs that serve gifted and talented students. We must develop the potential in students who, for whatever reason, have not had access to enriching educational opportunities that would allow their talents to blossom. We must also make sure that we provide a challenging education to students who excel and make sure that we nurture and accommodate their advanced abilities. In many cases, programs have addressed one of these goals and neglected the other. Our challenge, as we move forward, is to work toward a system of educational opportunities that seamlessly addresses both of these goals.

This guidebook provides sensible advice on many aspects of gifted and talented education. It deals with a number of critical issues, such as addressing special populations, successful strategies for program administration, and research summaries on many areas of particular interest. Its "models for excellence," included in every chapter, place renewed emphasis on the need for the highest quality educational opportunities for all students.

—Pat O'Connell Ross
Team Leader
Javits Gifted and Talented Students Education Program
United States Department of Education

# Guest Foreword

As an educator with more than 30 years of experience, I strongly believe that we must provide opportunities for all learners to reach for excellence. There are gifted children everywhere, and our responsibility is to find them and ensure that they have access to programs that are challenging and rigorous.

I also have learned that the business of education is a complex undertaking, and programs to support accelerated academic achievement take many forms. This guidebook is an excellent tool for school personnel as they design programs, procedures, and services to meet the needs of highly able students. It will also assist districts in developing a strong foundation for high-quality services.

Because no *one* gifted experience or gifted education program suffices, the guidebook identifies and discusses the key components of a quality gifted education program. Many of the issues surrounding advanced learners, including testing, identification, and evaluation, are often misunderstood. The guidebook offers solid advice on these issues and provides essential criteria to help practitioners and planners make informed decisions that will be useful even to those with long-standing programs.

The guidebook is a collaborative product of professionals experienced with high-potential students, born of their shared commitment to ensuring that all children have a chance to develop their abilities to the fullest. All readers, from those with little exposure to the field of gifted and talented education, to those who have been immersed for decades in serving the needs of these children, will find this book a welcome and useful resource.

—Eric J. Smith, Ed.D.
Superintendent of Schools
Anne Arundel County Public Schools
Annapolis, Maryland

# Preface

## HOW WE GOT HERE

More than five years ago, we began searching for a publication that explained how to set up high-quality services and programs for gifted and talented students. We Googled and searched using a variety of terms, including *guidebook* and *handbook*. We queried university personnel for the name of manuals, texts, or articles that included explanations for how to set up educational programs for gifted and talented students. We sent out e-mail messages to all state directors of gifted and talented programs requesting copies of how-to manuals. Although directors responded with publications that dealt with some of the components of programs and services, none was comprehensive enough or generic enough to transcend the policies and legislation of an individual state.

We tried another avenue and searched for the lineage of such a handbook or guidebook. One day we stumbled across Sandra Kaplan's *Providing Programs for the Gifted and Talented: A Handbook*, published in 1974. We knew we had discovered the first generation of the volume we were seeking. To our amazement, nothing preceded Kaplan's publication, and no other publication came after her much needed guidebook.

Having exhausted our possibilities, only one course of action appeared possible: Write a new guidebook for practitioners that addressed the complex task of developing programs and services for high-achieving students. As they say, the rest is history.

## WHY NOW?

There are three reasons why this book is so necessary now. The first and most obvious reason is that Kaplan's original guidebook was written more than 30 years ago, and much has changed in the field. There are new theories, new models, more inclusive definitions of the words *gifted* and *talented*, and more sophisticated research techniques that can reveal a great deal about what constitutes best practices. Quite simply, the field is vastly more complex than it was 30 years ago.

The second reason why this guidebook is so important is because of the recent avalanche of literature, research, and publications related to all aspects of programming and services for gifted and talented students. Many practitioners and administrators have shared openly that they are overwhelmed and need guidelines to direct the provision of educational opportunities for high-achieving students.

Finally, this guidebook comes at a critical time in educational history. Some would argue that we have entered into a time when equity, rather than excellence, is viewed as a higher priority. In times such as these, programs for the gifted and talented are easily compromised, especially in states without mandates to identify or serve these young people.

High-quality programs that can demonstrate increases in student achievement are not only more likely to survive budget cuts, but can also serve as a beacon for those who seek the twin goals of equity and excellence for all. In this time of No Child Left Behind, we have the rare opportunity to demonstrate that the field of gifted education is also deeply concerned about students who have been inadvertently left behind from achieving their fullest potential. It is our hope that this guidebook will help us to demonstrate the power of gifted education pedagogy.

## HOW THIS BOOK IS DIFFERENT

Much has been written about gifted education, and what we know is contained in countless monographs, journal articles, doctoral dissertations, videos, and books; however, there is no consolidated and comprehensive discussion of the practical issues related to services and programs for high-achieving students. Although we have standards for the field, and a text that illuminates those standards, *Aiming for Excellence: Gifted Program Standards: Annotations to the NAGC Pre-K–Grade 12 Gifted Program Standards,* by Landrum, Callahan, and Shaklee, published in 2001, there are very few publications that provide detailed guidelines to help new or experienced practitioners create and sustain these programs and services. This guidebook does both. We hope it provides a comprehensive discussion of the key features that characterize programs and services for the gifted. In addition, we provide guidelines, practical tips, templates, and suggestions to help practitioners determine where they are now, where they are going, and how they are doing along the way.

## FOR WHOM IS THIS BOOK WRITTEN?

A wide variety of audiences will find this guidebook helpful. Teachers of the gifted and talented, who have major responsibilities for program delivery, will be able to use this book as a reference to develop their services. District administrators, charged with monitoring the development of services for high-achieving students, will be able to use this book as a roadmap to help identify the services that currently exist and as a compass to identify how services can be enhanced. Superintendents of school systems can use this book as a reference for exemplar programs and services. State directors for the gifted and talented, who play leadership roles in their respective states, can use this publication as a manual to support their work with many school districts. This guidebook can be readily understood by those who are new to the field as well as those who have years of experience in gifted education. In these times of turnover in district positions, the guidebook can provide continuity when leadership changes. Finally, this publication can be used by university personnel who teach introductory courses in gifted education. The book contains useful information about the key features of successful programs and services.

## THE BOOK'S STRUCTURE

We have, from the beginning, conceived of *Designing Services and Programs for High-Ability Learners: A Guidebook for Gifted Education* as a working book. It is designed to be useful, and we hope that readers will make lots of notes in the margins, dog-ear pages, and attach sticky notes that pinpoint especially noteworthy passages and chapters.

The book contains 21 chapters that address key features of gifted education programs and services. Readers will recognize many of the key features that are included such as a definition of gifted and talented students, program models, and program evaluation, for example. Other key features, reflecting the times in which we live, may be a surprise: alignment with regular education, state policies on gifted education, and research-based practices.

All chapters in this guidebook begin with an introduction and overview of the importance of a particular aspect of gifted education programming or service delivery written by the editors. Additionally, Chapters 2-21 share parallel components that were purposefully included to guide your reading:

**Definition.** A definition is provided to ensure a common understanding of the key feature under consideration.

**Rationale.** The rationale section includes an explanation about the critical importance of the key feature. Oftentimes, this part of each chapter includes current research.

**Guiding Principles.** This section contains a brief list of the assumptions that form the foundation for each key feature of gifted education programs and services.

**Attributes That Define High Quality.** Chapter authors provide a parsimonious list of high-quality markers that determine the effective implementation of an aspect of programming so that those charged with programs and services can assess the overall effectiveness of each key feature.

**An Example in Need of Revision.** We asked all of our authors to reflect on their experiences in the field and to generate a carefully crafted example of the key feature gone awry. Examples, as well as exemplars, help us to clearly understand what we are seeking.

**Strategies for Improving the Example.** Each chapter includes a description of what is wrong with the lackluster example, as well as strategies for improving it. The diagnosis makes the weaknesses explicit. The strategies highlight how typical weaknesses can be eliminated.

**Makeover Example.** The revised example in each chapter serves as a contrast to the lackluster example and makes explicit the differences between a less-than-satisfactory example and one that is of high quality. The lackluster example and the exemplar provide readers with bookends, so to speak, to help them better understand the continuum of quality in the field and to keep us aiming for excellence.

**Strategic Plan for Designing or Remodeling the Key Feature.** Too often we underestimate the amount of time and effort that will be required to create or remodel a key feature of gifted education programs or services. The strategic plan provided by each author uncovers the complex process that is required to develop high-quality features of programs and services.

**Template for Getting Started.** Many of the chapters contain a graphic organizer for getting started with the evaluation and/or retooling of the key feature under consideration. For those in leadership positions, it has been designed to help jump-start the creation or remodeling process.

**Resources.** Authors for each chapter were selected for their expertise related to the key feature, and they have a working knowledge of resources that deal with their key feature. We asked them to select a few key resources that would be most beneficial to practitioners.

## NEXT STEPS

While we were writing and editing the guidebook, many ideas surfaced from reviewers to extend the publication and make it more interactive. We invite readers, accompanying us on this journey, to create these new pieces. One idea includes developing a series of questions for each chapter that can be used to guide readers through each key feature. Another suggestion is to create an interactive Web site through which readers can look at and join in conversations about the contents of the guidebook; submit ideas, plans, or problems; and ask and respond to questions. It would be one more way to support the development of high-quality educational services for all students including those with gifts and talents. We look forward to opportunities to discuss this guidebook with you. We also urge you to take this base and expand upon it, providing up-to-date information for your schools and classrooms for years to come. These continued efforts and further collaboration will provide the gateway to the future of gifted education.

# Acknowledgments

This book has been a long time in the making, and it has not been a solo voyage by any means. As it has evolved over the last five years, many people have contributed their ideas, time, and suggestions to make it what it is today. We have had the privilege of working collaboratively with a number of people and professional groups.

First, we would like to thank the chapter authors whose scholarly ideas, experiences, and research interests have shaped this publication. Their generous contributions of time and effort are a clear demonstration of their commitment to high-quality education for gifted students.

Members of the Publications Committee of National Association for Gifted Children (NAGC) have been involved with us since we started writing this guidebook. They reviewed our original prospectus and asked us many tough but critical questions about the intended publication. They helped us to define, with great clarity, just how the publication would be different from others, and how it would assist practitioners at all levels across the country. Furthermore, they reviewed the manuscript when it was completed. Once again, each member gave it thoughtful consideration. The questions and points they raised helped us to deliver a much more powerful contribution to the field. We appreciate the time they took to provide their feedback.

Other colleagues reviewed each chapter as it was written. In this review process, we asked for the help of state directors, division chairs, and other experts within and outside of the field of gifted education. It was our goal to have each chapter reviewed by at least three individuals. We asked these colleagues to help us ensure that the content of each chapter was up to date, comprehensive, and that it transcended the idiosyncratic policies and legislation of each state. Each of these reviewers, listed below, provided individual author's with a carefully crafted set of recommendations and thoughts. We want to thank each of them:

Ann Biggers, Arkansas Department of Education; Oretha Bridgwaters, Elementary Principal, Glenarden, MD; Elissa Brown, Center for Gifted Education, College of William and Mary; Katherine M. Brown, Project Director of the Javits C.H.A.M.P.S. Project; Deborah L. Carpenter, North Carolina Association for the Gifted and Talented; Kimberley L. Chandler, Center for Gifted Education, College of William and Mary; Carolyn R. Cooper, Maryland Department of Education Tracy Cross, Indiana Academy, Ball State University; Mary Duffy, Nebraska Department of Education; Donald C. Eckert, Elementary Principal, Wrightsville, PA; David Ehle, Ohio Department of Education; Kristy Ehlers, Oklahoma State Department of Education; Tamara J. Fisher, Gifted Education Coordinator, Polson School District, MT; Sandra Frank, California State Department of Education; Lynn

Gatehouse, Gifted Education Specialist, Pleasanton, CA; Jeanie Goertz, Ohio Department of Education; Michael Hall, Montana Office of Public Instruction; Gail P. Hammond, Mississippi Association for Gifted Education; Debora Hansen, Delaware Department of Education; Valorie Hargett, North Carolina Department of Instruction; Thomas Hébert, University of Georgia; Tillie Hickman, Middle School Principal, Beaumont, TX; Christine L. Hill, Supervisor of Gifted Services, Newport News Public Schools, VA; Timothy R. Jenney, Superintendent of Schools, Virginia Beach City Public Schools, VA; Terri Knapp, Guam Department of Education; Jonna Kwiatkowski, Yale University; Wayne Lord, South Carolina Department of Education; Jay McIntire, Waterville, ME; Judy McIntyre, Louisiana Department of Education; Wanda Monthey, Maine Department of Education; Rebecca Odoardi, Gifted Education Coordinator, Farmington, UT; Iris Palazesi, Florida Department of Education; Rebecca L. Pierce, Ball State University; Barbara Post, Gifted Facilitator, Washington School District, AZ; Donnajo Smith, Florida Department of Education; Pamela Sutcliffe, New Mexico Public Education Department; Bruce Thaler, The Gifted Child Society, NJ; Michael Thew, Superintendent of Schools, Eastern York School District, PA; Sally Y. Walker, Illinois Association for Gifted Children; David Welch, Missouri Department of Elementary and Secondary Education; Ann Wink, International Baccalaureate North America; Karen Zaleski, Gifted Education Specialist, West Geauga School District, OH.

Jane Clarenbach has been a constant companion. In fact, we talked with Jane about the possibility of the guidebook even before we had a vision of the final product. She has been a willing, energetic, thoughtful, and steady companion. She cheered us on when all seemed impossible; she reminded us about deadlines; she read every word of the manuscript and offered her counsel as a newcomer to the field; and she helped us to find a publisher who was willing to work with us on the final formatting and dissemination. We are indebted to her as a critical friend.

Publishing with Corwin Press has been a pleasure. The editors offer options and suggestions from their vast array of experiences in the publishing world. They have an eye for what is appealing as well as practical. And they know, understand, and support teachers. We would specially like to recognize our editor, Kylee Liegl.

Finally, we would like to thank family and friends who have offered support and encouragement. In all honesty, there were difficult moments when we were filled with doubts about the publication and times when we worked Saturdays, Sundays, and holidays to write and rework many passages. We know that our families and friends made personal sacrifices. We hope that we have grown as a result of their sacrifices.

—Jeanne H. Purcell

—Rebecca D. Eckert

# Introduction

Time has a way of slipping through our fingers. It seems only yesterday that we read Sandra Kaplan's new book, *Providing Programs for the Gifted and Talented: A Handbook*. In actuality, it was published in 1974 when no one knew about multiple intelligences, the Javits legislation, what a National Research Center on the Gifted and Talented might do, or what a second national report on gifted education, *National Excellence: A Case for Developing America's Talent*, might look like. No Child Left Behind was nonexistent, not even on the distant horizon.

Much has changed since that first handbook. All 50 states have adopted definitions of giftedness and a large percentage of states have legislated that talented and gifted students receive special services. We have federal dollars available for competitive grants to forward the field and for funding a National Research Center on the Gifted and Talented that has, for the last 15 years, provided the field with research on all topics related to the field and best practices for providing programs and services. The National Association for Gifted Children (NAGC) continues to evolve and grow. There is now a Council of State Directors of Programs for the Gifted that meets regularly, exchanges practices and legislation, and with the NAGC, publishes a biannual *State of the States* report about the status of gifted education. Theories, program models, and strategies for teaching high-achieving students have become more numerous, sophisticated, and sound.

These new theories, research, identification and programming models, and legislation provide new challenges for those responsible for implementing programs and services for gifted and talented students. In these complex times of accountability and standards, practitioners need practical information and advice that translates theory and research into practice. We delight in writing the introduction to this updated guidebook, *Designing Services and Programs for High-Ability Learners: A Guidebook for Gifted Education*, because it offers much to a broad array of practitioners: teachers of the gifted, coordinators of district programs, state directors of gifted education, university faculty, and others. We believe that three of its features are especially noteworthy: its comprehensiveness, its practicality, and its many models for excellence.

This guidebook contains 21 chapters, each dealing with critical aspects of programming and services for high-achieving students in the 21st century. Although many publications about the gifted and gifted education have been written in recent years, this guidebook is one of the most comprehensive. The authors, purposefully selected for their content-area expertise, provide readers with the most up-to-date information, readings, and research related to their respective topics.

Equally important, this guidebook is designed for those who want practical advice and strategies. The format, common to all chapters, includes 10 elements: a definition, a rationale, guiding principles, traits or attributes that define high quality, an example in need of revision, strategies for improving the example, a revised example, a strategic plan for designing or remodeling the key feature, resources, and references. These common elements uncover what we have known for a long time—that the process of creating programs and services is, indeed, complex. To uncover the intricate workings of program and service development, the authors provide practical wisdom related to each of the chapter elements. Finally, each chapter contains a special paragraph designed for those who are sole practitioners. Recognizing the limitations of those who go it alone, each author has crafted specific, practical advice for the sole practitioner.

Finally, this guidebook includes two examples in every chapter. The first example represents what some might describe as a less-than-satisfactory illustration of the key feature under consideration. For example, in the chapter on creating a definition, Sidney Moon provides readers with a definition of gifted and talented children that may not be comprehensive or research based. Continuing on, Moon pinpoints the specific weaknesses of the first definition, explains how to remodel each weakness, and provides readers with a second example so that the chapter includes an exemplary definition.

This guidebook, then, serves as a detailed roadmap for all those who strive for excellence in gifted education in these complex times. In this new age of accountability, we must refuse to accept mediocrity from ourselves and our students. Quality must become a way of life. We encourage you to read the book thoughtfully and to continue to exchange ideas with colleagues in the field and in the larger arena of general education.

—Sandra N. Kaplan
University of Southern California

—Joseph S. Renzulli
University of Connecticut

# About the Authors

**Jeanne H. Purcell**, Ph.D., editor, is the consultant to the Connecticut State Department of Education for gifted and talented education. She is the author of several books and has published numerous articles that have appeared in *Educational Leadership, Gifted Child Quarterly, Roeper Review, Educational and Psychological Measurement*, National Association of Secondary School Principals' Bulletin, *Our Children: The National PTA Magazine, Parenting for High Potential*, and *Journal for the Education of the Gifted*. Dr. Purcell is active in the National Association for Gifted Children (NAGC) and was recently elected secretary. She serves or has served as a member of the NAGC Board of Directors and the Awards Committee and cochaired the annual Curriculum Awards Competition sponsored by the Curriculum Division, as well as the Education Committee and the Governance Task Force.

**Rebecca D. Eckert**, Ph.D., editor, is the gifted resource specialist for the National Association for Gifted Children. Her previous work at the National Research Center on the Gifted and Talented included participation on the research team that developed and implemented the Schoolwide Enrichment Reading Model. Her research interests include talented readers, recruitment and preparation of new teachers, university and community partnerships, and public policy and gifted education. She is a former middle school teacher with experience in geography, history, and theatre arts.

**Cheryll M. Adams**, Ph.D., is the director of the Center for Gifted Studies and Talent Development at Ball State University. Her areas of teaching and research specialization are gifted education and curriculum development and she has published articles and book chapters in both areas. She teaches graduate-level courses for licensure in gifted education. She has coauthored and received several grants from both the state and federal governments for identifying and serving gifted children. She received her doctorate degree from the University of Virginia.

**Susan Baum**, Ph.D., is a professor at the College of New Rochelle, where she teaches graduate courses in elementary education and the education of gifted and talented students. Her professional activities include consulting both nationally and internationally, writing and researching in many areas of education including differentiated curriculum and instruction, emotional needs of children, gifted learning-disabled students, primary-aged gifted youngsters, gifted underachieving students, and economically disadvantaged students. Dr. Baum has served on the Board of Directors of the National Association for Gifted Children and as secretary for the organization. She is the past president and founder of the Association for the Education of Gifted Underachieving Students (AEGUS).

**Christine J. Briggs**, Ph.D., is an assistant professor in curriculum and instruction at the University of Louisiana at Lafayette. She received her doctorate from the University of Connecticut, specializing in gifted education and talent development and multicultural education. Her research interests include talent development in diverse populations and curriculum development.

**Deborah E. Burns**, Ph.D., is a central office curriculum coordinator for the Cheshire Public Schools in Connecticut. Prior to that position, she served for 15 years as an associate professor in residence, program director, and research scientist at the University of Connecticut's School of Education. Dr. Burns is a coauthor of two books about how to develop and write differentiated curriculum. In addition, she has written grants, assessments, program evaluations, curriculum units, professional development modules, and journal articles about teaching methods, curriculum development, professional development strategies, differentiation, and assessment techniques. She earned a bachelor's degree in elementary education from Michigan State University, a MEd from Ashland University in reading, and a Ph.D. from the University of Connecticut in educational psychology.

**Carolyn M. Callahan**, Ph.D., received her doctorate degree in the area of educational psychology with an emphasis in gifted education from the University of Connecticut. Since that time, she has been on the faculty of the University of Virginia, where she has developed the graduate program in gifted education, the Summer and Saturday Enrichment Programs for gifted students, and for the past 13 years has been the director of the University of Virginia National Research Center on the Gifted and Talented. She has done research across a broad range of topics in gifted education including identification of gifted students, the evaluation of gifted education programs, the development of performance assessments, and gifted program options. Dr. Callahan has received numerous awards in the field including the Distinguished Scholar and Distinguished Service Awards from the National Association for Gifted Children. She is a past president of the Association for the Gifted and the National Association for Gifted Children. She also sits on the editorial boards of *Gifted Child Quarterly, Journal for the Education of the Gifted,* and *Roeper Review.*

**Marla Read Capper** is a doctoral student at the University of Virginia studying educational psychology with an emphasis in gifted education. With eight years of teaching, designing, and implementing gifted programming in middle school classrooms, Marla has a special interest in gifted adolescents, especially girls, and curriculum and instruction. She has participated in research at the National Research Center on the Gifted and Talented, analyzing the influence of differentiated instruction on middle school classroom practices and student achievement, and exploring talent development in primary learners using a case-based approach. Currently, Marla facilitates curriculum development and program administration with the University of Virginia Summer and Saturday Enrichment Programs and trains preservice teachers.

**Carolyn R. Cooper**, Ph.D., is a seasoned district-level administrator who has coordinated programs for gifted and talented students in Baltimore County, Maryland, as well as in Wichita; Kansas, and suburban St. Louis. As an assistant superintendent for four small school districts in Massachusetts and earlier, as an assistant to the superintendent of a Connecticut school district, she was responsible for budget oversight and streamlining the annual school budget development process. She is an active volunteer leader at the National Association for Gifted Children and has served on the Board of Directors and the Finance Committee. Dr. Cooper earned her doctorate from the University of Connecticut and works in the Accelerated Schools Program.

**Kristina J. Doubet** is a doctoral student at the University of Virginia, pursuing her degree in curriculum and instruction with an emphasis in gifted education. A former English teacher, she currently trains preservice and practicing teachers, while working with a talent development program to develop high-quality challenging curriculum for traditionally underserved low-economic and minority populations. Kristina has also participated in long-term investigations into the impact of differentiated instruction on middle school classroom practices and student achievement, as well as talent identification in primary grades.

**E. Jean Gubbins**, Ph.D., is associate director of the National Research Center on the Gifted and Talented and associate professor of educational psychology at the University of Connecticut in Storrs. Dr. Gubbins is involved in research studies focusing on professional development and using gifted education pedagogy with all students, with a special emphasis on students with high abilities. Her research interests stem from prior involvement as a classroom teacher, teacher of gifted and talented students, evaluator, educational consultant, and professional developer. She teaches graduate-level courses in gifted education and talent development related to identification, programming, curriculum development, and program evaluation.

**Kelly A. Hedrick** is coordinator of gifted programs with Virginia Beach City Public Schools. Her primary responsibilities include the development of differentiated curriculum and instruction, staff development, resource teacher mentoring, and program communication. She holds a B.S. in elementary education from Longwood College, an MS in educational psychology, gifted, from the University of Virginia, and is currently a doctoral student in educational psychology, gifted, at the University of Virginia.

**Holly Hertberg**, Ph.D., is an assistant professor at the University of Virginia's Curry School of Education and a principal investigator for the National Research Center on the Gifted and Talented. Holly received her Ph.D. in Education and Psychology of the Gifted and her M.A. in English literature from the University of Virginia. Her research interests include research on writing and secondary students, differentiation of instruction, teacher change, and the Advanced Placement and International Baccalaureate programs.

**Marcia B. Imbeau**, Ph.D., is an associate professor at the University of Arkansas, Fayetteville, where she teaches graduate courses in gifted education and elementary education. She is actively involved with University/Public School Partnerships and teaches in a local elementary school as a university liaison. Her experience includes serving as a field researcher for the National Research Center on the Gifted and Talented, an elementary teacher in the regular classroom, a teacher in programs for the gifted, and a coordinator of university-based and Saturday programs for advanced learners. Dr. Imbeau has been a board member for the National Association for Gifted Children and a governor-at-large for the Council for Exceptional Children—The Association for the Gifted Division. She is also a past president of Arkansans for Gifted and Talented Education. She has coauthored a text on differentiated instruction for students with disabilities in the regular classroom and is a member of Association for Supervision and Curriculum Development's (ASCD's) Differentiated Instruction Cadre, which provides support and training to schools interested in improving their efforts to meet the academically diverse learning needs of their students.

**Mary S. Landrum**, Ph.D., has taught in higher education for more than 15 years. Currently, she works in teacher education and gifted education in the College of Education at James Madison University. Previously, she was an elementary and middle school teacher in both English and gifted education positions. Dr. Landrum is a member of the Board of Directors of the National Association for Gifted Children and received the Early Leader Award from that organization in 1997. She is the coauthor of two books on staff development and on standards in gifted education, and she has presented more than 225 inservices to teachers, administrators, and parents as well as more than 150 professional presentations and papers. Dr. Landrum's research and teaching interests are in gifted education, differentiation, collaboration, professional development, distance learning (especially Web-based teaching), and disadvantaged learners.

**Jann H. Leppien**, Ph.D., is an associate professor at the University of Great Falls in Great Falls, Montana, where she teaches coursework in curriculum and instruction, gifted education, assessment and learning, educational research, and methods in social sciences. In addition, she teaches curriculum courses and thinking-skills courses online and in the Three Summers Program at the University of Connecticut. Before joining the faculty at the University of Great Falls, she worked as a research assistant for the National Research Center on the Gifted and Talented. She has been a classroom teacher, enrichment specialist, and coordinator of a gifted education program in Montana. She is the coauthor of *The Multiple Menu Model: A Practical Guide for Developing Differentiated Curriculum* and *The Parallel Curriculum: A Design to Develop High Potential and Challenge High-Ability Students*. She conducts workshops for teachers and is interested in differentiated instruction, curriculum design and assessment, thinking skills, program development, cultural manifestations of giftedness, and underachievement.

**C. June Maker**, Ph.D., is a professor of education of the gifted in the Department of Special Education, Rehabilitation, and School Psychology at the University of Arizona, where she has developed a graduate program and a research and development center in gifted education called DISCOVER Projects. Her major research interests are curriculum development and performance-based assessment of giftedness.

**Sidney M. Moon**, Ph.D., is associate dean for Learning and Engagement in the College of Education, Professor of Educational Studies, and director of the Gifted Education Resource Institute at Purdue University. She has been active in the field of gifted education for 30 years as a parent, counselor, teacher, administrator, and researcher. In that time, she has contributed more than 60 books, articles, and chapters to the field. Dr. Moon is active in the National Association for Gifted Children and has served or is serving on the Board of Directors, the Publications Committee, and the Governance Task Force.

Her research interests include talent development in the STEM disciplines (science, technology, engineering, and mathematics), secondary gifted education, underserved populations of gifted students, differentiated counseling services, and personal talent development.

**Tonya R. Moon**, Ph.D., is associate professor of educational leadership, foundations, and policy at the University of Virginia's Curry School of Education. She is a principal investigator for the National Research Center on the Gifted and Talented, a codirector of the University of Virginia's Summer Institute on Academic Diversity, state director of the Virginia Reading First initiative, and a past president of the Virginia Educational Research Association. Her primary areas of interest include the identification of gifted students and program evaluation. She is active in the National Association for Gifted Children (NAGC) and was awarded the Early Scholar Award by NAGC in 2003.

**Maureen Neihart**, Psy.D., is a licensed clinical child psychologist and educational consultant. She is a former science teacher, school counselor, and board member of the National Association for Gifted Children (NAGC). She lives in Laurel, Montana, with her husband Doug, a high school principal.

**Sally M. Reis**, Ph.D., is a professor and the department head of the Educational Psychology Department in the Neag School of Education at the University of Connecticut where she also serves as principal investigator of the National Research Center on the Gifted and Talented. She was a classroom teacher in public education, as well as an administrator before coming to the University of Connecticut. She has authored and coauthored more than 140 articles, 12 books, 50 book chapters, and numerous monographs and technical reports. Her research interests are related to talent development in all children as well as special populations of gifted and talented students, including students with learning disabilities, gifted females, and diverse groups of talented students who are often underserved. Sally serves on several editorial boards and is a past president of the National Association for Gifted Children (NAGC). She has won several professional awards, including the Distinguished Service Award for outstanding service from NAGC, and most recently, she was named the Distinguished Scholar by NAGC, for her scholarly contributions to the field.

**Julia Link Roberts**, Ed.D., is Mahurin Professor of Gifted Studies and Director of the Center for Gifted Studies at Western Kentucky University. In 1998, Dr. Roberts was named a Distinguished Professor at Western Kentucky University. She was honored in 2001 as the first recipient of the National Association for Gifted Children's David W. Belin Advocacy Award, and she was selected for inclusion in *Profiles of Influence in Gifted Education: Historical Perspectives and Future Directions* (2003). Dr. Roberts is active in the National Association for Gifted Children and is serving, or has served, on its board of directors, awards committee, and legislative committee. She is a board member of the Kentucky Association for Gifted Education and *Gifted Child Today.* She also is a member of the Governor's Advisory Council for the Gifted and Talented in Kentucky. She received her bachelor's degree at the University of Missouri and her doctorate at Oklahoma State University.

**Karen B. Rogers**, Ph.D., is the newly appointed director of research for the University of New South Wales, GERRIC Centre, after 20 years as head of the Gifted Studies Program and department chair of Curriculum and Instruction at the University of St. Thomas. She received her Ph.D. in gifted curriculum and instructional systems at the University of

Minnesota. Her research interests are in research synthesis, gifted program development and evaluation, gifted cognition, arts education, gifted adults, and creativity.

**Ugur Sak**, Ph.D., is an assistant professor in the Department of Special Education at Anadolu University in Turkey. His major research interests include psychological measurements of cognitive aspects of giftedness, expertise and creativity, and the development of teaching models for mathematically talented students.

**Linda Smith**, Ph.D., is director of the Rockwood Gifted Program in St. Louis County, Missouri. She oversees the Center for Creative Learning, Rockwood's elementary campus for gifted education, and supervises programming for gifted students at the middle school and high school levels. Dr. Smith began her career as a public school teacher in Cambridge, Massachusetts, and received her doctorate in gifted child education from the University of Connecticut. Over the years, Dr. Smith has taught gifted education courses at the graduate level; has published articles and conducted workshops on program development, curriculum, and evaluation; and has served on her community's Board of Education.

**Carol Ann Tomlinson**, Ed.D., is professor of educational leadership, foundations, and policy at the University of Virginia, where she is codirector of the Curry Summer Institute on Academic Diversity and a principal investigator for the National Research Center on the Gifted and Talented. Prior to her work at the university, Dr. Tomlinson was a public school teacher and administrator for 21 years. Her research interests include teaching in academically diverse settings and effective instruction of ethnically diverse learners. She is a past president of the National Association for Gifted Children.

**Joyce VanTassel-Baska**, Ed.D., is the Jody and Layton Smith Professor of Education and executive director of the Center for Gifted Education at the College of William and Mary, where she has developed a graduate program and a research and development center in gifted education. Formerly, she initiated and directed the Center for Talent Development at Northwestern University. She has also served as the state director of gifted programs for Illinois, as a regional director of a gifted service center in the Chicago area, as coordinator of gifted programs for the Toledo, Ohio, public school system, and as a teacher of gifted high school students in English and Latin. She is currently president of the National Association for Gifted Children. Dr. VanTassel-Baska has published widely including 15 books and more than 300 refereed journal articles, book chapters, and scholarly reports. She has received numerous awards for her work, including the State Council of Higher Education in Virginia Outstanding Faculty Award in 1993, the Phi Beta Kappa Faculty Award in 1995, and the National Association of Gifted Children Distinguished Scholar Award in 1997. Her major research interests are on the talent development process and effective curricular interventions with the gifted.

**Karen L. Westberg**, Ph.D., is an associate professor in the Gifted, Creative, and Talented program at the University of St. Thomas. She began her career as a classroom teacher and gifted education specialist in Minnesota and was a faculty member at the University of Connecticut, where she was a principal investigator at the National Research Center on the Gifted and Talented. Her research interests include classroom practices, gifted education program development, and creativity.

1

# Identifying Student Cognitive and Affective Needs

*Mary S. Landrum*

It is appropriate that the first chapter of this guidebook focuses on the children we teach. Specifically, this opening chapter focuses on the unique cognitive and affective learning needs of gifted and talented students that have been documented in long lines of research over the past century (Hollingworth, 1926, 1942; Terman, 1930; Gertzel & Gertzel, 1962). All aspects of gifted education programming and services—which are the subject of the remaining chapters in this guidebook—must emanate from highly able students' recognizable educational needs that manifest themselves in their cognitive, psychosocial, and physiological development.

Various characteristics may indicate latent or emergent talent in gifted learners. Early and enduring traits of advanced cognitive ability may be evident in above-average logical thinking, questioning, and problem solving (Cox, 1926; Walberg et al., 1981). Students may also be developmentally advanced in language, thought, and comprehension; learn swiftly; grasp and manipulate sophisticated and abstract concepts at an earlier age; reason accurately, swiftly, and logically; reason mathematically at an advanced, abstract level; and/or demonstrate beyond-grade-level cognitive functioning in music or art (Clark, 2001; Colangelo & Davis, 2003; Davis & Rimm, 2004; VanTassel-Baska, 1998).

Other traits of gifted students may include motivation and persistence in learning, especially when pursuing their advanced interests (Davis & Rimm, 2004; Renzulli, 1978). Silverman (1980) calls these students "immersion learners" who delve into advanced interests with intense curiosity and determination to discover the unknown. Similarly, self-confidence and independence in learning may lead these students to set high goals. Frequently these students attribute their academic success to ability and failure to something other than a lack of ability (Milgram & Milgram, 1976). Creatively gifted individuals differ somewhat from their counterparts who have high potential in academics. In particular, they have a greater tolerance for ambiguity, confidence and risk taking in learning and creative production, high energy, and curiosity and playfulness of ideas (Amabile, 1987; Davis, 1999; Getzels & Jackson, 1962; MacKinnon, 1961; Sternberg, 1988; Torrance, 1987; Wallach & Kogan, 1965).

In addition to advanced cognitive and academic aptitudes, the high-potential learner usually possesses healthy psychological development. Many experts and researchers suggest that affective development of gifted students differs from that of their same-age peers by intensity or degree. Many gifted learners are more self-confident about their ability to succeed and are more intrinsically motivated to succeed. Moral development and extreme sensitivity also mark the emotional intensity of the gifted child (Terman, 1930; Hollingworth, 1942; Neihart, Reis, Robinson, & Moon, 2002).

## CASE STUDIES

The following case studies, which illustrate many of the traits discussed above, have been selected for three reasons. First, they are real. Although some of the students' names have been changed, the stories reveal true portraits of gifted and talented children in the 21st century. Second, the cases have been purposefully selected to illustrate the extraordinary diversity among gifted and talented students, K–12. Although they share similarities, the students presented here are markedly different from each other in their learning profile, learning needs, and the life circumstances that have shaped their development. Third, they have been selected to showcase the many varied programs and services that have been provided to meet their unique learning needs. The narrative that follows each case study highlights educational programs and services that have been selected to address each student's educational needs. These varied interventions underscore the continuing importance of recognizing, understanding, and responding to the characteristics of giftedness and high potential.

### Evan Feinberg

Evan Feinberg was the state and national winner of the National Association for Gifted Children (NAGC) Nicolas Green Award in 2000 when he was in fourth grade. Here is a portion of the essay that he wrote for this competition at age 9:

> Ever since I can remember, I have had a passion for science & astronomy, and mathematics. In my past, I focused on the solar system. Presently, I am fascinated by the field of cosmology, physics, and particle physics. Cosmology is the study of the universe's past, present, future, celestial objects, and the theoretical multiverse which is a web of different universes linked by black holes; particle physics is the opposite of cosmology, it is the study of the small such as elementary particles to superstrings. The cosmologist, Stephen Hawking, and especially the physicist, Albert Einstein inspired me to study these subjects and generate and spawn

theories of my own concerning the universe and the multiverse. Stephen Hawking's discoveries of properties of black holes plus his creativeness of merging quantum mechanics (the study of the small and particles) and the theories of relativity (the theories of large scale) really made me more and more interested in this field. Albert Einstein's biography, his theories of relativity (which are the special and general), and his contributions to the photoelectric effect has also had a great impact on my perspective of life and the universe around us. On a daily basis, I am lucky to have my teacher, Mr. Carbone, because he really inspired me in this subject. For example, he let me take the 4th grade telescope home to stargaze and look for celestial objects and constellations. In addition, he gave me a special research project to study a particular constellation, Bootes. His enthusiasm and love of learning has encouraged me to 'reach for the stars.'

My deep thirst for knowledge has led me to pursue my research of astronomy and even create my own books to share with my family and classmates. I have written a comprehensive, beginner's guide to cosmology, *The Eight Books of Space-Time,* and [another book] *Space Bends While Time Warps: Play with Einstein's Gravity.* It is very rewarding when a classmate asks for a copy of one of these two books! It gives me great joy to share my books and information with my classmates and to know that I have helped to spark their interest. I was even inspired by my research to write poetry which reflects upon my questions of the universe. This poem is called "A Moonless Night." Some of the fantastic books that I have read that seemed to almost quench my thirst for knowledge are, *Albert Einstein and the Theory of Relativity* by the *Solutions* series, *Before the Beginning, Just Six Numbers,* both by Martin Rees. Actually, these books only make me want to learn more and make me so inquisitive that my questions seem infinite.

This study and research triggered new life goals for me such as being a physicist or a cosmologist, proposing new theories, and aspiring to be like my role models, Stephen Hawking and Albert Einstein. My dream one day is to unlock the ultimate theory of the universe, called the theory of everything, and the ultimate question: the mind of G-D. Just as the very fabric of space-time expands and stretches since the big bang, so does my quest for grasping the ultimate theory; the theory of everything.

## Educational Interventions Provided for Evan

Evan was identified as having unique abilities in Grade 3. Throughout the remainder of that year, he participated in enrichment activities in mathematics in his regular classroom. In Grade 4, Evan was identified formally as gifted and talented, and his teachers realized that enrichment was only one of the learning options that he needed to fulfill his potential. They collaborated and recommended two different learning options for his remaining two years in elementary school. In Grades 4 and 5, he participated in a pull-out enrichment class in language arts and mathematics. In addition, he worked on accelerated content in mathematics through the Johns Hopkins Center for Talented Youth (CTY) program.

In middle school, Evan's teachers provided him with additional acceleration options. He was advanced to eighth-grade mathematics and seventh-grade science. In Grade 7, he was subsequently placed in ninth-grade math and eighth-grade science. In addition, a high school teacher traveled to the middle school every day to work with Evan and a small group of 10 eighth graders as they investigated mathematical topics aligned with the eighth-grade curriculum, in more depth.

Evan is currently in eighth grade. Although he was given the option to skip a grade, he decided to stay with his friends. He goes to the high school in the morning, where he takes honors biology with 9th and 10th graders and Algebra II with 10th and 11th graders. His English teacher nurtures his love of nonfiction and, at the same time, challenges him to explore fiction as well. He volunteers as a mathematics tutor and mentor to students in Grades 6, 7, and 10. He continues to love physics and, according to Evan, "It is the year of Einstein."

## Julia

Almost three years ago, at age 9, Julia and her family arrived in North Carolina from the Ukraine. There she had been recognized as a rising young musician. Her parents remember that, even as a baby, Julia hummed, tapped, waved, and spun her way through the days. When she was four, teachers in her preschool noted her perfect pitch and strong sense of rhythm. Her subsequent evaluation by the school's director of music confirmed Julia's exceptional abilities, which then led to twice-weekly, short piano lessons. Rather than shrink from the attention and work in the following months, Julia needed to be "pulled from the piano," her mother said. At her first small recital, Julia surprised (no, shocked) her teacher and her mother by substituting one of her own secret compositions for the piece printed in the program. There was no doubt then that her gift needed to be nurtured.

Fortunately, Julia was also a good student. While not always the top of her class, she easily, and without effort, received excellent marks. By second grade, she was practicing an hour before school and two hours after. In third grade, just months before emigrating, she was selected to solo in a youth festival with a small community chamber orchestra.

### Educational Interventions for Julia

Once Julia's parents settled their family into their new, small apartment, they enrolled Julia and her brother in the neighborhood school. Their almost nonexistent English made the process slow and uncomfortable, but they trusted that school officials would help balance Julia's academic requirements with her driving need to spend time at the piano. In the first weeks, Julia was mourning not only the loss of her treasured piano teacher, but also her grandparents, her friends, and, most of all, her piano: the apartment was too small and the cost too great. Immediately the focus at school was on helping Julia become fluent in English and guiding her in the assimilation process. Julia began to shrink back into herself. She found a piano in the back of the school gym and gravitated to it whenever possible, yet, despite the magical sounds coming from that poorly tuned piano, the gym teacher constantly shooed her away. This teacher stated that Julia needed to socialize with others on the playground, not hide behind music.

Within a month, Julia refused to go to school. She first faked headaches, and then began to throw up, but her parents insisted she attend. The classroom teacher sent notes of concern home and then called for a meeting with the principal. Julia, they said, was emotionally disturbed and required assessment by the school psychologist. The report, while outlining a number of problems and subsequent recommendations for intervention, did not mention music.

Fortunately, Julia's family attended an evening concert at the church that sponsored their move. The moment the last note sounded, Julia was at the side of the pianist, begging to play. That pianist taught at the community music school and instantly recognized the child's amazing potential. She not only offered free lessons, but also arranged travel to and from the center. In addition, her husband, a teacher in a neighboring district, began to unravel Julia's school problems. He arranged for the gym piano to be tuned and moved into a room next to the library. Through a series of creative programming options, Julia was able to practice whenever she completed her class work. She was also allowed to stay indoors during breaks. Far from serving to ostracize her socially, peers were awed by her dedication and skill. Several girls befriended her and banded together to sing fun show tunes together, a far cry from Julia's regular classical repertoire.

Now, in middle school, Julia is once again rising to the challenge in both academics and music. Her English-language skills are excellent, she is the top student in science, and she represented her school in the citywide, creative writing contest. At school, she is able to squeeze in at least one hour of practice a day. This summer she will be on full scholarship at a residential performing arts program in Canada.

## Leron

In 2001, Leron Johnson was one of 10,700 students in a large school district that had a very diverse student population. When Leron attended school in the district, 2% of students were Asian American, 17% were Black, 53% were Hispanic, and 28% were White. Sixty-five percent of the student body was eligible for free or reduced price meals, and 40% of the students, K–12, lived in homes where English was not the primary language. The average per capita income in this urban district was $18,000.

Leron lived with his parents and, as long as he could remember, his mother was his best advocate and a primary support for the family. Many of his friends moved from school to school. Leron's mother worked hard to keep her son in the same school system because she understood that his education was very important to his future. Leron was a very capable student and, although he was never at the top of his class, his grades were always above average.

### Educational Interventions Provided for Leron

Leron was in fourth grade when he was identified for the district's gifted and talented program that provided him with challenge and enrichment one morning a week. His teachers came to know his many interests. He was especially interested in sports, video games, and technology of all kinds. He was also involved with the Boys Club of America, and adults within the organization encouraged Leron to get involved in leadership and community-based projects. In spite of his many outside activities, Leron's academic performance was always B or better.

In middle school, Leron attended a pull-out resource room gifted program one day a week. All his teachers, including his gifted education teacher, encouraged him to maintain his academic pursuits in spite of some negative peer pressure to lead him astray. They also encouraged him to develop his skills as an athlete.

In high school, Leron's passion for sports grew stronger. He played basketball for two years and participated in track. His real love, however, was football, and his coach, who supported his athletic abilities. He became one of the stars on the team by his sophomore year. Leron played on the team all four years, including his last year when he was elected captain. He was recognized by the state interscholastic athletic organization as a scholar athlete.

Other teachers propelled Leron forward in his academics. Mr. Robert Owens, technology coordinator in the district, developed a strong liking for Leron and his constant desire to learn more about technology, especially video production. During his four years in high school, Leron completed several independent video projects including one documentary on local arts. While Mr. Owens was in the background to support him, Leron always took the lead on these investigations. All of the gifted education staff enjoyed having Leron in the program because of his intellectual curiosity and exceptional interpersonal skills.

During his junior year, Leron developed an early interest in attending Yale University. He made a point to attend the Yale summer football camp, where Yale scouts saw him play. The scouts talked to Leron about his passion for football and his grades and followed his progress in high school throughout the first semester of his senior year. Leron's high school counselors made sure he was enrolled in honors and Advanced Placement courses and lined up important letters of recommendation. They made sure he had complete information about a wide variety of colleges and universities. Late in the fall of 2001, Yale offered Leron a full, four-year scholarship to the university.

Leron graduated from Yale in May 2005. He majored in business and finance, and he has already been offered a job in investment banking on Wall Street. Leron returns to his high school on a regular basis. He finds great satisfaction visiting his former teachers and mentoring members of the high school football team.

## Gail

Gail was taller than the average 5-year-old when she entered the K/1 classroom in the fall of 2003. She was the older of two children; her brother was three years younger. Her mother was an assistant professor with a demanding work schedule, so her father assumed responsibilities as the primary caregiver in the family. He transported Gail to and from school and frequently volunteered in the classroom. He was actively involved in both children's activities.

Gail was a highly verbal and social child who did not enjoy learning alone. She thrived in an interactive social environment with peers who were at similar academic and social levels.

Although she enjoyed interactions with other girls, she thrived in competitive activities and played sports and games with boys. She worked well with children of either sex, but her best friends were boys. She had a unique (and irreverent) sense of humor and loved the book series *Captain Underpants* by Dave Pilkey. Her parents valued and supported her strong sense of self, her assertiveness, and her competitive nature.

When the teacher met Gail, she was reading elementary chapter books fluently at the second-grade level. She loved reading and discussing books with her friends. By the end of first grade, she moved through six grade levels, reading with comprehension at the eighth-grade level. She was an avid reader throughout her time in the K/1 classroom and often read books with content well beyond her emotional level.

Gail was not one to sit quietly. She was an exceptionally active child. Sitting in large-group time was difficult for her. She needed an environment where she could be actively involved with learning tools and other children. Gail was a very talented child who did not fit the stereotype of a quiet, calm kindergarten girl. Indeed, she may not have been accepted in a typical kindergarten classroom.

## Educational Interventions for Gail

Because of her precocity, Gail's parents chose an early childhood program with peers and reading materials available beyond her chronological age level. Nevertheless, the teacher found it challenging to provide appropriate literature that matched her social and emotional needs and yet was difficult enough to extend her growth in reading, a common problem for many early readers. By the end of first grade, she was reading the *Narnia* series by C. S. Lewis.

It was important to provide her with peers who were at similar reading and math levels, but also time to engage in in-depth investigation. The curriculum of the early childhood program enabled her to explore a wide variety of interests and pursue challenging investigations that promoted growth in her reading, math, and social skills. The program dedicated one hour each day to a free-choice activity that encouraged students to stay engaged in a single activity such as reading or a long-term project. If Gail wanted to read for an hour, she had the flexibility to do so.

The teacher worked hard to help Gail fit in socially with the rest of the class. Although he recognized Gail and others' competitive spirits, the teacher emphasized cooperative learning and tried to maintain a noncompetitive environment. To prevent gender bias in the classroom, he encouraged cross-gender interaction. He provided an environment that allowed Gail to work with students of either sex. The teacher stressed with the whole class how important it was to have a school experience where they learned how to work and get along with everyone. Through discussions, arrangements of groups, and requests to continually try working with different students, the teacher developed flexible social groups. In doing so, the teacher created a safe environment where students could take emotional and social risks and engage in nonstereotypical behaviors.

## Bao

Bao is a 10-year-old, fifth-grade student who lives in Iowa. He was born in Hong Kong, but identifies himself as Vietnamese. He believes that his parents moved to Hong Kong from North Vietnam so that it would be easier for them to immigrate to the United States. Bao lives with his parents, his 12-year-old sister, and his 5-year-old brother.

Bao moved to the United States with his family when he was four. He has no memories of living in Hong Kong, but has some memories of his first home in Kansas City, Missouri. His mother worked in the home and his father worked two jobs—"one with glass and one making clothes."

When Bao was five, his family moved to Iowa and his parents began working for a meat processing plant. His parents work each afternoon until midnight, so Bao mainly sees them on weekday mornings and on weekends.

When he first began school, Bao stated that he was "scared to make friends" because his English-language skills were limited. He didn't want to raise his hand and felt frustrated in class. Bao received English as a second language (ESL) services for kindergarten and first grade, which helped him to learn English faster and "feel the same as other kids." In ESL classes, Bao felt that he "sort of" was able to show his true abilities. "I knew to read and write to show how smart I was. I learned English faster than the other kids and got them mostly all right so I sort of knew I was smart then."

Learning English rapidly had many positive effects. He has become more comfortable participating actively in classroom discussions and interacting with his classmates—resulting in new friends who provide Bao with a support system at school. He also reports an increased sense of responsibility about helping his parents, who are not yet conversant in English, communicate in the community.

After scoring at the superior level on several standardized tests in third and fourth grade, Bao qualified for the fifth-grade Talented and Gifted (TAG) pull-out and the math mentoring program. The formal identification as a gifted learner increased Bao's self-efficacy, but his comments also provide some insight into his needs as a learner. He explained that he wished he had been told that he was gifted prior to fifth grade. "I did not know how smart I was." Now, he stated that he knows he is talented because "I think fast and I read fast!"

In the future, Bao wants to be an orthodontist or join the U.S. Marine Corps. "I want to serve our country because they gave us a place to live and my parents a job and I want to give something back."

## Educational Interventions for Bao

As previously mentioned, the gifted and talented program in Bao's school begins in the fifth grade for all identified students. Bao qualified for two different components: math mentoring and pull-out enrichment. The math mentoring component consisted of weekly meetings with a mentor to discuss and work on mathematics problems that were either extensions of Bao's regular classroom work or problems that were of particular interest to him. The pull-out enrichment component involved four different units that spanned the academic year: Orientation, Thinking Skills, Career Exploration, and Independent Study. In the orientation unit, Bao learned about giftedness, his unique learning profile, group dynamics, and communication skills. In the thinking skills unit, he was provided with explicit instruction about critical thinking, creative thinking, how to reflect on and regulate his own thinking, and problem-solving strategies. Bao had the opportunity to explore careers in the third unit and, not surprisingly, Bao elected to learn more about careers in mathematics. Finally, he had the opportunity to pursue an independent project of his choice.

## Daquanna

When Daquanna was 3 years old, she entered an early childhood program that her older brother was already attending. She was petite and reluctant to interact with unfamiliar adults, but she loved to draw and sculpt images of people. She would spend hours every day quietly working at her art desk set up for her by her grandparents at home. Daquanna's mother often volunteered in the classroom, and she was concerned about Daquanna's physical health and verbal development due to a hearing impairment caused by frequent childhood ear infections, which necessitated that she wear a hearing aid.

As Daquanna entered elementary school, her mother often shared information with her teachers about her own experiences in school and how she felt unchallenged. She was keenly interested in providing challenging academic experiences for her children and concerned about Daquanna's reluctance to actively engage in educational settings. So, Daquanna and her brother were highly scheduled in afterschool enrichment activities such as Kumon math, dance, gymnastics, art, and violin lessons.

Due in most part to her disability, Daquanna was an extremely shy and quiet child. When she talked, she almost whispered. Her teachers described her as highly sensitive, insightful, and caring and noted that Daquanna was always concerned about her own achievement level and frequently sought approval when she tried new things. Furthermore, she rarely took risks until she was familiar with all aspects of a learning experience. She worked best with constant individual support. She frequently asked, "Is this right?" and she constantly questioned herself and her skills. She typically avoided academics, but enjoyed the creative activities that were available in her school. She especially liked drawing, art, and music. The one class each week where she worked independently and was willing to take risks was art. Her artistic skill became especially apparent when she received a first-place ribbon in a districtwide competition for a sculpture of herself, which included details that reflected her cultural heritage and ethnicity.

Despite her success in art and her family's continued support, Daquanna's teachers suspected that she was still not working up to her full potential. Based on her family history and her reluctance to pursue academics, they feared that without needed support, Daquanna had the potential for being an underachiever.

## Educational Interventions for Daquanna

As she entered elementary school, the main intervention for Daquanna was to increase her self-efficacy and provide her with some additional tools for interacting with peers and adults. In grades K–2, a speech pathologist worked with Daquanna twice each week to help her feel less self-conscious about communicating with others and more confident about her verbal skills. The speech pathologist also met with Daquanna's family to discuss how they could support her progress at home and in the community while at the same time encouraging her interests in art.

In the regular classroom, Daquanna's second-grade teacher tried to nurture independent-learning skills and carefully chose materials that provided the right amount of challenge and a high level of interest. He especially chose to include activities that capitalized on Daquanna's creativity and artistic skills. Throughout the school day, he provided her with a safe environment where she could take risks and make mistakes. He focused on positive social supports to develop appropriate assertiveness and negotiation skills. The teacher also talked her through tasks and then asked her to work independently through those same activities. Gradually, he was able to work with her in a small-group setting when new skills were presented. He then asked Daquanna if she would like more support, and reinforced those skills with the small group before leaving her to work in the larger group with others or on her own.

While the curriculum itself was not changed for Daquanna, the pacing and degree of support was. These adjustments allowed Daquanna to progress at her own rate and provided her with opportunities to work in her strength areas of art and music.

Currently, her performance on assessments still varies according to her level of confidence. Her newfound comfort in unfamiliar learning environments was apparent as she successfully transitioned to an intermediate school last fall. Daquanna's interest in the arts remains strong and additional exploration and enrichment activities are planned for her in the upcoming year.

## Todd

Todd is a very bright high school junior. As he looks back at his childhood, he recognizes that it was complicated by many factors. His parents separated when he was young, and he has not been in touch with his father since before kindergarten. In addition, as much as he looks up to his siblings and receives positive encouragement from them, Todd mentions that one older sibling has a physical disability and another struggles with bipolar disorder. Dealing with such physical and psychological difficulties significantly contributes to the stress his family experiences at home. He says that he has experienced a lot of turmoil and has had to grow up quickly as a result.

Todd was identified as gifted and talented in elementary school. As he reflects on that time, he remembers enjoying these programs because he felt more challenged and because he remembers being with students of similar ability levels. Through junior high and high school, he took advantage of course acceleration and honors courses and now says that he had good teachers at the schools he has attended.

However, things changed for Todd early in his high school career when he got into a fight and subsequently felt he was no longer welcome at school. Complicating the situation, two of Todd's older siblings had been expelled from the same high school. This only furthered Todd's feeling of alienation, especially by the school's administration. Looking to escape his seeming negative reputation, Todd decided to seek a fresh start at the alternative school in his town.

### Educational Interventions for Todd

When Todd relocated to an alternative high school for the remainder of his public school career, teachers and other professionals provided him with five different interventions. First, the alternative high school environment provided a much smaller teacher-student ratio. His teachers had a genuine interest in young people. Second, teachers at the school were provided with learning profiles of each of the students involved in the Iowa Alternative Schools Project. Although many knew that Todd was a very capable young man, they were provided with his ability-based assessment results. These scores provided a unique learning profile that highlighted his reasoning ability strengths, as well as his learning gaps. Third, and based on his learning profile, Todd was provided with additional academic challenges in his interest areas. One offering that was especially meaningful to Todd was an online Advanced Placement (AP) psychology course. Todd had always been interested in people and he took on the distance learning opportunity with great enthusiasm. Todd also had a mentor, selected for him by the school principal. His mentor turned out to be his AP psychology course facilitator. The last intervention was continuous professional development for the entire staff at the alternative high school. As part of the Iowa Alternative Schools Project, funded by the federal Jacob K. Javits Gifted and Talented Students Education Program, staff have been offered the opportunity to attend three days of summer training on issues related to gifted and talented learners, such as underachievement, socio-emotional needs of gifted students, and classroom differentiation strategies.

## Maria

In her acceptance speech as a recipient of a nationally sponsored award for gifted high school students, Maria, a senior at Rolling Hills High School in California, spoke eloquently of the challenges that many gifted students in isolated areas face:

> Living on an Indian Reservation, one is constantly exposed to negativity, violence, and drug abuse. I am not like anyone in my neighborhood and not even like the rest of my family. I am determined to make something of my life, not flipping burgers or picking fruits in someone else's field. I won't mimic my cousins who married young and got pregnant. I am very different! I have always taken the harder path to improve myself. I work hard so I will be able to give my parents all the things they never had. . . . My father always tells me, "Trabaja duro y así vas a poder llegar muy alto y realizar tus sueños." [If you work hard, you will go far and will be able to realize your dreams.] My father's words guide me to achieve my aspirations, even though I sometimes feel insecure, frightened by where my life will lead. I will succeed!

Maria's drive and determination to attend college and become a pediatrician or a psychologist are matched only by her academic talents and interest in learning. Her science teacher commented that, "to say she is a fantastic student is to say Joe Montana was just a good football player." Her quest for knowledge became even more apparent when her home was destroyed by a raging wildfire in the fall of her senior year. Rushing with her family out of the building to safety, Maria grabbed her books because she didn't want to fall behind in school.

### Educational Interventions for Maria

Even though Maria's small, rural school did not have a formal gifted program, her connection with her school community and parental support and encouragement helped her overcome many obstacles. As a Mexican American immigrant, she began school with a stronger grasp of Spanish than English, which often led teachers to see her as a shy and reluctant learner. Nevertheless, she worked diligently to perfect her English, and with the encouragement of her junior high teachers, she found her voice and her gift for leadership. Maria participated in soccer and softball after school; but her real passion was her involvement and leadership in service organizations. While maintaining a 4.10 GPA and taking Advanced Placement (AP) courses in government, anatomy and physiology, and Spanish, Maria also served as president of the Key Club, vice president of the National Honor Society, and as a four-year member of the

California Scholarship Federation and the AVID Leadership Conference. When a wildfire ripped through her community in the late fall of her senior year, Maria stepped forward to volunteer with the Red Cross to translate for non-English-speaking fire victims at FEMA (Federal Emergency Management Agency) meetings. She acknowledges that her involvement was an inspiration to others, but that she really got involved so that she could be part of the solution and feel like she was helping to reassemble all of the lives that were disrupted by the fire.

Despite all of the odds against her, Maria started college at the University of San Diego in the fall of 2004. Her school counselor and AP science teacher, who both played an integral role in helping Maria with her college planning and finding a variety of funding sources, anticipate her continued success because of her hard work and persistence. As the first member of her family to attend college, she is dedicated to making her dreams of becoming a doctor come true.

## SUMMARY

The case studies presented here serve three purposes. First, they help to remind us of the joyful reasons we all entered the teaching profession: our love for all children, our interest in sharing part of their life's journey, and our desire to help young people find affinity and fulfillment in a field that interests them.

Second, they remind us about the diversity among children with whom we will engage in the 21st century. The case studies have been selected to illustrate the variety of students and the range of education needs in our classrooms and programs. Although they have all found success in school, these students do not represent *showcase* portraits, the kind that dazzle. Rather, they are solid portraits: real, familiar, and illustrative of the key role practitioners play in finding and developing student talent.

Finally, the case studies serve as a unique foundation for this guidebook. Together, they illustrate some of its most important principles:

- Gifted and talented students are a very diverse group of students. They sit in every classroom, pre-K–12, in America and come from all ethnicities, socioeconomic backgrounds, and cultures.
- Gifts and talents may be obvious, latent, or emergent, which underscores the need for careful development and maintenance of all aspects of gifted programming and service components.
- High-achieving young people have a unique set of learning needs that set them apart from others, including prior knowledge, readiness to learn, interests, learning-style preference, and a propensity for a particular expression style. As a result, learning opportunities for gifted learners must be designed with the child's specific needs in mind and consist of a continuum of differentiated curricular options, instructional approaches, and resource materials.
- Appropriate gifted education programs and services must be provided both in the regular classroom and in special programs. Gifted and talented students need well-trained and appropriately qualified educators who can provide ongoing levels of challenge every day of the students' school career.

Readers will see these principles emerge as touchstones in slightly different ways and forms in each of the remaining chapters in this guidebook. It is our hope that the cases—and their common, underlying principles—will serve as an additional catalyst to help readers grapple more effectively and efficiently with the content presented here.

## MUST-READ RESOURCES

Brimijoin, K., Marquissee, E., & Tomlinson, C. A. (2003). Using data to differentiate instruction. *Educational Leadership, 6*(5), 70–73.

Callahan, C. M., Tomlinson, C. A., & Pizzat, P. M. (1997). *Contexts for promise: Noteworthy practices and innovations in the identification of gifted students.* Charlottesville, VA: University of Virginia, National Research Center for the Gifted and Talented.

Clark, B. (2001). *Growing up gifted* (6th ed.). New York: Prentice Hall.

Colangelo, N., & Davis, G. A. (2003). *Handbook of gifted education* (3rd ed.). Boston: Allyn & Bacon.

Dunn, R., Denig, S., & Lovelace, M. K. (2001). Multiple intelligences and learning styles: Two sides of the same coin or different strokes for different folks? *Teacher Librarian, 28*(3), 9–15.

Renzulli, J. S., & Purcell, J. H. (1995). Total school improvement. *Our Children. 1*(1), 30–31.

Seagoe, M. (1974). Some learning characteristics of gifted children. In R. Martinson (Ed.), *The identification of the gifted and talented.* Ventura, CA: Office of the Ventura County Superintendent of Schools.

VanTassel-Baska, J. (1998). *Excellence in educating gifted and talented learners* (3rd ed.). Denver, CO: Love.

## REFERENCES

Amabile, T. (1987). The motivation to create. In S. G. Isaksen (Ed.), *Frontiers of creativity research: Beyond the basics* (pp. 223–254). Buffalo, NY: Bearly Limited.

Clark, B. (2001). *Growing up gifted* (6th ed.). New York: Prentice Hall.

Colangelo, N., & Davis, G. A. (2003). *Handbook of gifted education* (3rd ed.). Boston: Allyn & Bacon.

Cox, C. M. (1926). *The early mental traits of 300 geniuses. Vol. 2: Genetic study of genius.* Stanford, CA: Stanford University Press.

Davis, G. A. (1999). *Creativity is forever* (4th ed.). Dubuque, IA: Kendall/Hunt.

Davis, G. A., & Rimm, S. B. (2004). *Education of the gifted and talented* (5th ed.). Boston: Allyn & Bacon.

Gertzel, V., & Gertzel, M. G. (1962). *Cradles of eminence.* Boston: Little, Brown & Company.

Getzels, J. W., & Jackson, P. W. (1962). *Creativity and intelligence.* New York: Wiley.

Hollingworth, L. S. (1926). *Gifted children: Their nature and nurture.* New York: Macmillan.

Hollingworth, L. S. (1942). *Children above 180 IQ Stanford-Binet: Origin and development.* New York: World Book Company.

MacKinnon, D. W. (1961). Creativity in architects. In D. W. MacKinnon (Ed.), *The creative person* (pp. 291–320). Berkeley: University of California, Institute of Personality Assessment Research.

Milgram, R. M., & Milgram, M. A. (1976). Self concept as a function of intelligence and creativity in gifted Israeli children. *Psychology in the Schools, 13,* 91–96.

Neihart, M., Reis, S. M., Robinson, N. M., & Moon, S. M. (Eds.). (2002). *The social and emotional development of gifted children: What do we know?* Waco, TX: Prufrock Press.

Renzulli, J. S. (1978). What makes giftedness: Reexamining a definition. *Phi Delta Kappan, 60,* 180–184.

Silverman, L. K. (Ed.). (1980). *Counseling the gifted and talented.* Denver, CO: Love.

Sternberg, R. J. (1988). *The nature of creativity.* New York: Cambridge University Press.

Terman, L. M. (1930). *Genetic studies of genius.* Palo Alto, CA: Stanford University Press.

Torrance, E. P. (1987). Teaching for creativity. In S. G. Isaksen (Ed.), *Frontiers of creativity research: Beyond the basics* (pp. 189–215). Buffalo, NY: Bearly Limited.

VanTassel-Baska, J. (1998). *Excellence in educating gifted and talented learners* (3rd ed.). Denver, CO: Love.

Walberg, H. J., Tsai, S., Weinstein, T., Gabriel, C. L., Rasher, S. P., Rosecrans, et al. (1981). Childhood traits and environmental conditions of highly eminent adults. *Gifted Child Quarterly, 25,* 103–107.

Wallach, M. A., & Kogan, N. (1965). *Modes of thinking in young children.* New York: Holt.

Editors' Note: The editors would like to thank the following for their contributions to this chapter: Elaine Zottola, New Britain, CT; Rosanne Malek, Iowa Department of Education, Des Moines, IA; Robin Schader, Storrs, CT; Nancy Hertzog, Champaign, IL; David Rogers and Megan Foley Nicpon, Ph.D., Belin-Blank Center at the University of Iowa. The Iowa case examples were developed as part of two initiatives funded in part by the U.S. Department of Education: The Iowa Alternative Schools Project, a collaboration of the Iowa Department of Education, seven local education agencies, the Iowa Association of Alternative Education, and the Belin-Blank Center to serve academically talented students in alternative programs as well as their teachers, and a special project within Iowa's ESL Training Grant: "Our Kids," which provides additional support to the rapidly growing number of English language learning (ELL) students in Iowa's schools.

# 2

# Developing a Mission Statement on the Educational Needs of Gifted and Talented Students

*Rebecca D. Eckert*

> The young sailor at sea was ordered to climb a mast to adjust a sail during a violent storm. He got halfway up, looked down, got dizzy and sick. An old sailor on deck shouted up to him: 'Look up, son. Look up.' The young sailor looked up, regained his composure, and completed his mission. Moral: Look ahead, not back.
>
> —Author Unknown

Looking ahead is not always easy to do when you are caught in the everyday management of programs and services for gifted and talented students. Nevertheless, to chart our journey efficiently and effectively, we must have a destination in mind. What is our program's mission? How can we ensure the success of our gifted programs? How is our mission integral to the success of programs and services for high-achieving students?

Rebecca Eckert reminds us in this chapter that the creation of a mission statement is a critical task of those charged with delivering or coordinating educational services for gifted education students. The process of developing a mission statement starts by asking the big questions of gifted programming and seeking the best possible answers within your context. What is this service? Whom does it serve? Why are the services important? The answers to these questions will establish a foundation for any gifted education teacher or coordinator because all other program activities will refer back to the program's mission in some way. It is the justification for the educational services. In many ways, the mission statement is like an anchor; it grounds and secures services for high-achieving students.

This chapter is a foundational one. As such, it is related to all the other chapters in this guidebook. It is most closely aligned, however, with three chapters that are critical for any gifted education program: Developing a Definition of Giftedness, 3; Articulating Gifted Education Program Goals, 6; and Strategic Planning and Gifted Programs, 21.

## DEFINITION

A mission statement is a short, written passage that clarifies the beliefs of a school district about the nature of giftedness and the need for educational services to meet the learning needs of gifted and talented students. In general, mission statements illuminate who gifted and talented children are, why educational services for them are necessary, one or two overarching program goals, and a clear message about the district's commitment to meeting the learning needs of these students. The statements may be presented in paragraph or bulleted form, or a combination of both formats.

## RATIONALE

Like successful businesses, successful schools invest resources in crafting a vision and fostering values because they recognize that community culture determines how and why people work together toward excellence. According to Knowling (2002), "Most leaders love to make strategy, but it is vision and values that spawn strategic action. The absence of a vision will doom any strategy—especially a strategy for change" (p. 129). Essentially, a mission statement helps community members understand what is crucial to the success of any organization or program, including gifted education.

There are several important reasons for developing a clear and cogent mission statement. Thoughtfully crafted mission statements inform and shape the educational programming available for gifted students within a school district and community. With a coherent set of statements that set forth beliefs about gifted students and their educational needs, educators, parents, and other community members will also gain an understanding of how gifted education is viewed by policymakers (Berg, Csikszentmihalyi, & Nakamura, 2003; Starratt, 1995). Equally important, a clear mission statement provides constituents with a solid reference point to understand the reasons for decisions and actions related to gifted and talented education (Knowling, 2002; Raynor, 1998). Finally, the mission statement is the foundation for all other tasks described in this guidebook (Lawrence, 2002); it supports and is the rationale for the remaining key features.

## GUIDING PRINCIPLES OR ASSUMPTIONS

- Mission statements express beliefs about how giftedness and talents develop.
- Mission statements explain why educational services for students are necessary.
- Mission statements align philosophically with the broad educational goals of the school system.

- Mission statements reflect an understanding of state laws and policies.
- Mission statements are clear and easily understood.

# TRAITS OF A HIGH-QUALITY MISSION STATEMENT

## Comprehensiveness

- Does the statement define, in general, the word "gifted" for the district?
- Does it express how children come to be gifted?
- Does it address broadly the intellectual, social, and emotional needs of students identified as gifted and talented in the school district?
- Does it specify one or two overarching, long-term outcomes that will result from programs and services?
- Does it address the issue of responsibility; in other words, who is responsible for meeting the needs of high-achieving students?

## Rationale

- Does it include solid justification for providing educational programs and services for gifted and talented students?
- Is it grounded in tested theories and supported by research?

## Consistency

- Does the educational vision for gifted and talented students align with the district's general goals for education as stated in the strategic plan?

## Clarity

- Is it written clearly, avoiding educational jargon, so that users (e.g., teachers, administrators, parents, students, and lay persons) will understand its intent?

# EXAMPLE IN NEED OF REVISION

Academically talented children in Jonesville may possess characteristics that necessitate qualitatively different instruction. Our program is designed to provide the atmosphere for stimulating above-average-ability students.

| Trait | 1<br>*No*<br>*Evidence* | 2<br>*Little*<br>*Evidence* | 3<br>*Some*<br>*Evidence* | 4<br>*Considerable*<br>*Evidence* | 5<br>*Powerful* |
|---|---|---|---|---|---|
| Comprehensiveness | | X | | | |
| Rationale | X | | | | |
| Consistency | X | | | | |
| Clarity | | X | | | |

# PROCEDURES FOR ENHANCING OR IMPROVING A MISSION STATEMENT

Often, statements of goals and beliefs are most meaningful when developed in collaboration with a team of individuals with an interest in the project (Richardson, 1996). Therefore, the first recommended step in the revision process is to assemble a task force to critically examine the four defined traits of a high-quality mission statement. (See Step 4.)

1. Although the Jonesville School District's mission statement explicitly states that academically talented students may need qualitatively different instruction, the statement shows little evidence of comprehensiveness. In their revision, the task force plans to address or elaborate on the following:
   - What giftedness looks like in Jonesville and areas of potential gifts and talents that the current mission statement overlooks (e.g., creativity)
   - How children develop giftedness and what the school district can do to uncover hidden talents
   - One or two broad goals for the services to gifted and talented students
   - The responsibility of the school and larger community to meet the learning needs of this population

2. The original mission statement did not provide a rationale explaining why it was necessary to provide an atmosphere that will stimulate students of above-average abilities. The task force needs to explain why educational services are necessary to meet the learning needs of this population. Even though it may not become part of the final polished mission statement, the task force also plans to collect research-based evidence to support their statements.

3. As originally written, the Jonesville mission statement showed no evidence of consistency with other goals and programs within the school district. To successfully shape future programming and positively influence district decisions, the mission statement must reflect the linkages between the broad educational goals for the school district and the broad goals for the services provided to gifted and talented children.

4. Finally, the brevity and use of educational terms (e.g., qualitatively different) in the original mission statement limited the clarity of the document. After all other concerns have been addressed, the task force plans to ask a broad sample of individuals to read the document. Based on their feedback, they will simplify and/or modify the language and detail to ensure that all constituents can understand its intent.

# MAKEOVER EXAMPLE

The mission of the Jonesville School District is to ensure that each child has equal opportunity to receive a suitable program of educational experiences. The school board recognizes that some students possess, or are capable of possessing, extraordinary learning ability and/or outstanding talent. These students come from all socioeconomic, cultural, and ethnic backgrounds. The school board affirms the following:

- Curricular modifications as described in our comprehensive program design will occur in the regular classroom to provide continuous levels of challenge for all students, including those with unique gifts and talents. (See Chapters 7, 8, 17)
- In addition to the regular classroom, a range of instructional settings, both within the school as well as the community, will be available for specialized instruction that is integrated with the regular curriculum and the intellectual and social and emotional needs of gifted and talented children.
- It is the responsibility of the school district and the larger community to ensure the following:
  - Ongoing identification of gifted and talented children
  - Provision of appropriate and systematic educational services to meet the unique learning needs of gifted and talented children

The Jonesville task force designed the mission statement above as a mixture of narrative and bulleted items. They could have also conveyed the same information in one or two paragraphs, as in the following example:

The Smithville Board of Education believes that there are gifted students whose intellectual capacity, rate of learning, and potential for creative contributions demand experiences apart from, but connected to, the regular classroom. These students exhibit high performance, or the potential to achieve, in intellectual, creative, or artistic areas; possess strong leadership capacity; or excel in specific academic fields. It is essential to provide diverse, appropriate, and ongoing learning experiences and environments that incorporate the academic, psychological, and social needs of students. It is our responsibility to provide students with educational alternatives that teach, challenge, and expand their knowledge, while simultaneously stressing the development of independent and self-directed learners who continuously generate questions, analyze, synthesize, and evaluate information and ideas.

We are committed to the belief that gifted students are individuals with potential who require guidance in discovering, developing, and realizing their potentials as individuals and as members of society. Under this philosophy, it becomes the responsibility of the entire staff to meet the needs of gifted students by identifying their gifts and talents and developing those areas. This philosophy also requires a strong partnership between the school system and community.

When comparing the two different formats, note that both mission statements begin with a clear definition of giftedness. In addition, both statements describe program services that address the cognitive and affective needs of students as well as services that can be made available in the larger community. Finally, the mission statements address the responsibility of the school district to provide ongoing levels of challenge for all students, including those who are gifted and talented.

## A STRATEGIC PLAN TO ADDRESS THE CREATION OR REVISION OF A MISSION STATEMENT ON THE EDUCATION OF GIFTED AND TALENTED STUDENTS

*Objective:* To create or revise a mission statement on the education of gifted and talented students

*Evidence:*   A completed mission statement on the education of gifted and talented students

*Tasks:*   Create a mission statement or revise an existing mission statement

---

*Timeline:*   April 23—Convene a meeting of the task force on gifted education to create or revise a mission statement. (The task force may be a subcommittee of the school district's strategic planning committee.)

May 8—Send a working draft of the document to task force members for review and edits.

May 20—Distribute to a broad sample of individuals for review.

May 27—Present completed mission statement to the school board and superintendent for final approval.

---

## TEMPLATE TO BEGIN THE PROCESS OF DESIGNING OR REVISING MISSION STATEMENTS

The material in this section is summarized in the accompanying table.

| Trait | Focusing Question | Our Thinking |
|---|---|---|
| **Comprehensiveness** | What is giftedness? | |
| | Does giftedness develop? Is giftedness an inherited trait? | |
| | Broadly speaking, how do the intellectual and social and emotional needs of gifted and talented students differ from their chronological peers? | |
| | Why is it important that these unique learning needs are met? | |
| **Rationale** | What is the justification or motivation for providing educational services to gifted and talented students? | |
| | Are the policies based on an understanding of state policies and regulations regarding gifted education? | |
| | What is the research base that supports our conclusions? | |

| Trait | Focusing Question | Our Thinking |
|---|---|---|
| **Internal Consistency** | What is the linkage between the broad learning goals for gifted and talented students and the learning goals for all students in the district or system? | |
| **Clarity** | Is the language clear and free of educational jargon?<br><br>Is it written so that all readers will understand the intent of the document? | |

## Checking Our Work

As you begin to craft your own mission statement, remember that "a vision is usually formed by looking both inward and outward—looking inside the school at the people there and looking outside the school at the challenges society and individuals are facing, the challenges schools are supposed to prepare youngsters to deal with" (Starratt, 1995, p. 16). The following questions are provided so that you can reflect on the process of crafting a mission statement as well as the final product:

- Is our mission statement comprehensive?
- Does our mission statement include justification or a rationale for providing educational services for gifted and talented children?
- Does our mission statement align with the broad educational goals for all students in the system or district?
- Have we specified who is responsible for meeting the learning needs of these students?
- Is our mission statement written with familiar words?
- Is the intent of the mission statement clear to all readers?

Although this chapter is about how to create a mission statement, it is important to consider what will happen once it is completed. How will your finely crafted statement of vision and values be used to guide program and service development for gifted students? Ultimately, it will be the responsibility of the gifted education coordinator, task force members, and administrators to ensure that the mission statement comes to life.

## ADVICE FOR THE SOLE PRACTITIONER

Although consensus building is one of the most important side benefits of crafting a mission statement, the sole practitioner can still reap positive rewards from clarifying and sharing an ideal vision of education for the gifted and talented students within his or her district. Begin by assembling district and school goals and mission statements as well as policies and decisions that relate to the gifted education program. Then, seek out examples of mission statements online or from neighboring school districts to help guide your thinking. If you are unable to assemble a task force to assist you in crafting a mission statement, try to elicit feedback from a few stakeholders familiar with your students and your school system. Once you are satisfied with your polished and thoughtful mission statement, you are prepared to share your vision with your school community and get down to work!

## REFERENCES

Berg, G. A., Csikszentmihalyi, M., & Nakamura, J. (2003). A mission possible? Enabling good work in higher education. *Change,* September–October, 41–47.

Knowling, R. (2002). Why vision matters. In F. Hesselbein & R. Johnston (Eds.), *On mission and leadership* (pp. 128–140). San Francisco: Jossey-Bass.

Lawrence, D. M. (2002). Maintaining a mission: Lessons from the marketplace. In F. Hesselbein & R. Johnston (Eds.), *On mission and leadership* (pp. 89–101). San Francisco: Jossey-Bass.

Raynor, M. E. (1998). That vision thing: Do we need it? *Long Range Planning, 31,* 368–376.

Richardson, J. (1996). If you don't know where you're going, how will you know when you arrive? *School Team Innovator,* September. Retrieved September 5, 2004, from www.nsdc.org

Starratt, R. J. (1995). *Leaders with vision: The quest for school renewal.* Thousand Oaks, CA: Corwin.

# 3

# Developing a Definition of Giftedness

*Sidney M. Moon*

Definitions either prevent or put an end to a dispute.

—Nathanial Emmons,
18th-century American theologian

In his quotation, Emmons alerts us to the importance of definitions. Clear definitions support common understandings and foster progress toward a specific goal. They also prevent multiple or incomplete definitions that can lead to misunderstandings, disagreements, or at best, sporadic progress.

For over a century, researchers and theorists in gifted education have grappled with a clear definition of the concept of giftedness. Part of the difficulty related to a clear definition of the term is that our understanding of giftedness has changed substantially in the last 125 years. Originally thought to be a strict function of intelligence, today we understand that intelligence—and its cousins, giftedness and talent—may be related to a set of behaviors, (Renzulli, 1978), and domain-specific skills and abilities (Bamberger, 1986), and have multiple forms (Gardner, 1983; Sternberg, 1985).

The Marland Report (1972) and the more recent federal report, *National Excellence: The Case for Developing America's Talent* (U.S. Department of Education, 1993), contain definitions of the terms *gifted* and *talented*. The federal definition, forwarded in the most recent federal report, dominates the definitions adopted by most states. General intellectual giftedness is the most common area of giftedness identified by 35 states, or 70% of the states in the country (Council of State Directors and the National Association for Gifted Children, 2002). Many states also identify specific academic aptitude, creative thinking, advanced ability in the fine/creative arts, and leadership ability.

In this chapter, Sidney Moon explores the differences between conceptual and operational definitions of giftedness and the need for forging a link between the two within a school district. As teachers and coordinators of gifted education programs craft their district's definition of giftedness, they must be ever mindful of Emmons's admonition, social and political contexts, the demographics of their district's learners, and the importance of the definition they create. Much will depend on it, including identification procedures, program goals, program design, curriculum, budget, learning resources, policies, and strategic planning. In short, this section has strong links with most of the sections in this guidebook.

## DEFINITION

There are two types of definitions of giftedness: conceptual and operational. Conceptual definitions are based on theories of giftedness and are incorporated into a school district's mission statement on the gifted and talented. They define the construct of giftedness and the nature of gifted students in the abstract. Operational definitions provide specific concrete guidance on how a conception of giftedness will be assessed and identified in a particular context, for a specific purpose. Operational definitions are specific instances of more general conceptual definitions and are closely linked to identification procedures. Generally, a school district selects one conception of giftedness to serve as a foundation for all the gifted programming in the district and then creates related operational definitions for each service offered. Thus, definitions of giftedness link broad mission statements to specific program services through identification procedures.

## RATIONALE

Conceptions of giftedness have changed over time (Tannenbaum, 2000). Notions of giftedness are influenced by culture, politics, and research findings (Moon & Rosselli, 2000). Because giftedness is a somewhat controversial construct in school settings, it is important for school districts to examine different theories of giftedness and select a conceptual definition that is consistent with any existing state law defining giftedness, current theory and research, and the values of most of the stakeholders in the district.

Historically, the trend has been from narrow, intellectual conceptions of giftedness to broader, more inclusive definitions. Early scholars such as Lewis Terman and Lita Hollingworth defined giftedness as the ability to achieve a very high score on an individualized intelligence test (Hollingworth, 1926, 1942; Terman, 1925). These scholars defined giftedness primarily as an advanced ability to think and learn. Current scholars view giftedness more broadly. For example, Gardner speaks of multiple intelligences, only three of which are measured on traditional intelligence tests (Gardner, 1983, 1999). Sternberg conceptualizes giftedness as developing expertise, a more dynamic way of conceptualizing advanced abilities (Sternberg, 2000). Renzulli focuses on the development of gifted behaviors (Renzulli, 1978, 1986). He believes that gifted performances require above-average ability in combination with creativity and task commitment. Gagné combines many of these more current conceptions into a complex theory of giftedness that suggests that raw abilities (gifts) of many kinds are converted into demonstrated talents through a long-term process that involves intrapersonal and environmental catalysts (Gagné, 1985, 1999, 2000). Gagné has also presented a proposal for considering subcategories, or levels of giftedness, within any particular talent domain (Gagné, 1998).

The various types of conceptual definitions can be summarized in five categories:

1. Psychometric definitions are based on test scores. For example, Lewis Terman (1925) defined giftedness as a score over 140 on the Stanford-Binet IQ test, and Julian Stanley and his colleagues (Benbow & Stanley, 1983; Stanley, 1996) define giftedness as a high score on an off-grade-level test of mathematical or verbal reasoning ability. These definitions are very easy to operationalize; in fact, they are examples of situations where conceptual and operational definitions merge. Some states have adopted psychometric definitions of giftedness.

2. Neurobiological/cognitive definitions are based on findings from neuroscience and/or cognitive science. Gardner's multiple intelligences and Sternberg's analytical, creative, and practical intelligences are examples (Gardner, 1999; Sternberg, 1985; Sternberg & Clinkenbeard, 1995). These definitions are somewhat harder to operationalize through standardized tests than are psychometric tests and generally are operationalized with multiple measures, including both tests, when available, and performance-based assessments.

3. Creative-productive definitions are based on examining the life histories of creative-productive adults. Renzulli's three-ring conception of giftedness is an example (Renzulli, 1978). These definitions are usually operationalized with multiple measures, including standardized tests of intellectual ability and academic achievement in combination with authentic assessments; interviews; teacher, peer, and self-nominations; and other subjective measures of talent potential.

4. Psychosocial definitions emphasize the role of both the individual and his or her environment in the development of giftedness. Tannenbaum (1986) and Gagné (2000) are examples of scholars who have developed psychosocial conceptions of giftedness. Operationalization of these definitions is complex because the definitions are so broad. These definitions provide the broadest possible framework for giftedness and, as a result, provide the least guidance for creating operational definitions for specific programming options.

5. Composite definitions borrow from multiple theoretical perspectives. The 1972 Marland Report and the 1993 *National Excellence Report* promote composite definitions of giftedness for school settings (Marland, 1972; U.S. Department of Education, 1993). John Feldhusen (1995) has developed a composite definition, called TIDE, that focuses on talent identification and development in four domains in school settings. Legal definitions are often composite definitions modeled after the original Marland Report definition. The federal Jacob Javits Gifted and Talented Students Education Act includes a composite definition of giftedness, as do many state definitions. Composite definitions are generally operationalized with separate multiple assessment identification procedures for each of the talent areas addressed (e.g., intellectual, academic, creative, visual and performing arts, leadership).

## GUIDING PRINCIPLES

- Giftedness is a social construction that is influenced by culture, values, and politics.
- Definitions of giftedness should reflect current theory and research.

- Definitions of giftedness must reflect state or legal definitions.
- Definitions of giftedness must reflect the context in which they are implemented.
- Effective definitions of giftedness provide a foundation for identification and programming.

## TRAITS OR ATTRIBUTES THAT DEFINE HIGH QUALITY

### Legality

- To what extent does the definition reflect current legal definitions of giftedness?

### Soundness

- What are the research and theoretical bases for the definition?
- In which research and/or theory is the definition based?
- To what extent is the definition aligned with the research and/or theory?

### Feasibility

- What features of the definition are particularly appropriate for our students and our particular educational context (e.g., age of students, grade levels served)?

### Equity

- To what extent is the definition free of cultural, ethnic, and gender bias?

### Clarity

- To what extent will the definition be clear and understandable to all constituents?

### Utility

- To what extent does the definition provide guidance for the development of gifted education services?

## EXAMPLE IN NEED OF REVISION

Malcolmville School District A is a large, multicultural, urban school district in a state that defines giftedness as a score above 130 on an individualized intelligence test. The Malcolmville District defines giftedness as follows: Giftedness is exceptional ability to learn and to be creative.

## PROCEDURES FOR MAKEOVER

If your definition needs improvement in one or more of the listed traits of high quality, you should consider the steps listed here:

**Table 3.1**  Definition Rating

| Trait | 1 No Evidence | 2 Little Evidence | 3 Some Evidence | 4 Considerable Evidence | 5 Powerful |
|---|---|---|---|---|---|
| Legality | | | X | | |
| Soundness | X | | | | |
| Feasibility | X | | | | |
| Equity | | X | | | |
| Clarity | | X | | | |
| Utility | | X | | | |

- Legality: Review the legal definitions that apply to your district and create a new definition that reflects current existing legal definitions and the needs of your students.
- Soundness: Review current theories of giftedness and reports on gifted education and select one or more that is consistent with your district's values and context to serve as a theoretical framework for your definition.
- Feasibility: Review the definition in light of available resources and, if necessary, revise it so that it is more manageable and affordable.
- Equity: Eliminate any biased language and include a specific statement indicating that your program will serve students from all cultural and economic groups.
- Clarity: Ask a variety of stakeholders to read the draft and give you suggestions for improvement. Tell them you want to know if there are parts that are hard to understand. Revise based on their feedback and repeat.
- Utility: Ask a sample of the leadership (principals, superintendents, school board members, etc.) of your school district if they think the definition will provide guidance for the development of gifted programming.

## MAKEOVER EXAMPLE

After taking coursework in gifted education at a local university, two members of Malcolmville's broad-based planning committee decided that their current state and local definitions of giftedness were limited in scope and not serving their population well. They understood that their state defined gifted students as those who are able to score above 130 on a standardized test of intelligence and that this definition was a psychometric one with a focus on intellectually gifted students. The Malcolmville planning committee recommended that the board of education consider broadening the local definition to serve more students. The Malcolmville board of education agreed that intellectually gifted students are an important population to serve, but that the district could also serve academically, creatively, and artistically gifted students. Therefore, they approved the recommendation of the planning committee to create a new, composite definition that was adapted from the *National Excellence Report* (U.S. Department of Education, 1993) as follows:

Children and youth with outstanding talent perform or show the potential for performing at remarkably high levels of accomplishment when compared with others of their age, experience, or environment. These children and youth exhibit high performance capability in intellectual, creative, and/or artistic areas . . . or excel in specific academic fields. They require services or activities not ordinarily provided by the schools. Outstanding talents are present in children and youth from all cultural groups across all economic strata (p. 26).

The Malcolmville board of education stated that they believed this broader definition was consistent with their state definition, but more appropriate for an inner city, multicultural context.

## STRATEGIC PLAN TO DESIGN OR REVISE A DEFINITION OF GIFTEDNESS

*Objective:* To write a definition of giftedness that is consistent with state legislation, local policy, and our philosophy statement that can be used to guide talent identification and development in our school district

*Evidence:* Completed written definition with an accompanying bibliography of sources consulted in developing the definition.

*Task and Timeline:*

a. Select a writing team (preferably the same group that will be working on the mission statement). [summer]

b. Read and discuss current theories of giftedness and summarize each briefly. [fall]

c. Read and discuss statewide legislation and/or local policy on giftedness. [fall]

d. Discuss the needs, values, and culture of our school district community. [fall]

e. Reach consensus on a sound, feasible, conceptual definition. [winter]

f. Create a feedback rubric using the high-quality traits developed in the previous step. [winter]

g. Circulate the draft and feedback rubric to key stakeholders. [winter]

h. Revise the definition based on feedback. [spring]

i. Test the definition by translating it into one or two sample operational definitions (identification procedures) for projected program components at different developmental levels; revise again, as needed. [spring]

j. Seek adoption of the definition through all appropriate channels (e.g., administrators, central office staff, and board of education).

k. Incorporate the definition into your position statement. [spring]

## Questions to Guide Our Creation of a Definition of Giftedness

**Table 3.2**   Definition Quality Checklist

| Trait | Focusing Question | Our Thinking |
|---|---|---|
| Legality | What law and regulations govern gifted education in our state and/or nation? | |
| | Do the legal definitions of giftedness that govern our context provide sound and sufficient definitions of giftedness for our district? | |
| Soundness | How do current theorists in the field of gifted education define giftedness? | |
| | Which theories of giftedness are most in tune with our emerging philosophy and context? | |
| | Which theories of giftedness seem more supported by current research? | |
| | What type of definition do we want to adopt (psychometric, cognitive, creative-productive, psychosocial, composite)? Why? | |
| | What criteria should we use to select the theory of giftedness that we will use to craft our conceptual definition? | |
| Feasibility | Is the conceptual definition we have chosen feasible to implement in a school setting? | |
| | Will this conceptual definition work well for all developmental levels? | |
| | Can we implement our conceptual definition in our context with the resources we have available? If not, what are the odds that additional resources will be forthcoming to enable implementation? | |
| Equity | Will this conceptual definition help us develop, identify, and serve children from a wide variety of backgrounds and cultures? | |
| | Can this conceptual definition be operationalized in ways that are free of bias? | |
| Clarity | Will all of our stakeholders understand our conceptual definition? | |
| | Is our conceptual definition free of jargon? | |
| Utility | Will our conceptual definition provide useful guidance as we begin developing gifted education services? | |
| | Will our conceptual definition be operationalized into specific identification procedures? | |

## ADVICE FOR THE SOLE PRACTITIONER

The most important thing for a sole practitioner to do in developing a definition of giftedness is to develop his or her own knowledge about both *definitions* of giftedness and the *contexts* in which they are working. This knowledge will help the sole practitioner to promote and adopt a definition that is consistent with current research on giftedness, existing laws or policies that govern the district, the student population of the district, and the values of the community. The second most important thing for the sole practitioner to do is to make sure that s/he seeks broad input into the definition adoption process so that s/he will have support for the definition that is promoted. A good way to do this is to chair a task force, committee, or planning group charged by the superintendent or board of education to work on the task of adopting a definition that is consistent with current research and effective in the local context. (See Appendix A for procedures to establish an advisory committee.)

## MUST-READ RESOURCES

It is very difficult to select a handful of must-read resources to guide the development of a sound definition of giftedness. This is an area where extensive reading and/or the help of a consultant who is an expert in gifted education are needed. The references below provide only a starting point, a way to sensitize task force members to some of the issues involved. After reading these works, the task force might next read a summary chapter on definitions of giftedness in one or more introductory texts (Davis & Rimm, 2004). Then, each member of the group can become an "expert" in one or more of the conceptions of giftedness overviewed in the text by reading and summarizing that theorist's original work, using the references included here, as well as the references in the introductory text, as a starting point. There are no shortcuts to developing a sound definition of giftedness. The group charged with developing a definition for a school district will need to engage in considerable reading, discussion, and reflection.

Moon, S. M., & Rosselli, H. (2000). Developing gifted programs. In K. A. Heller, F. J. Monks, R. J. Sternberg, & R. F. Subotnik (Eds.). *International handbook of giftedness and talent* (pp. 499–522). Amsterdam: Elsevier. Provides an overview of contextual issues that affect definitions of giftedness from an international perspective.

Tannenbaum, A. J. (2000). A history of giftedness in school and society. In K. A. Heller, F. J. Monks, R. J. Sternberg, & R. F. Subotnik (Eds.), *International handbook of giftedness and talent* (pp. 23–54). Amsterdam: Elsevier. Provides an overview of the historical development of the concept of giftedness.

U.S. Department of Education. (1993). *National excellence: A case for developing America's talent.* Washington, DC: Author. Although it is somewhat dated at the time of printing, this document remains the best current national policy document on gifted education.

## REFERENCES

Bamberger, J. (1986). Cognitive issues in the development of musically gifted children. In R. J. Sternberg & J. E. Davidson (Eds.), *Conceptions of giftedness* (pp. 388–413). Cambridge, England: Cambridge University Press.

Benbow, C. P., & Stanley, J. C. (Eds.). (1983). *Academic precocity: Aspects of its development.* Baltimore: Johns Hopkins University Press.

Council of State Directors & the National Association for Gifted Children. (2002). *State of the states gifted and talented education report, 2001–2002.* Washington, DC: National Association for Gifted Children.

Davis, G. A., & Rimm, S. B. (2004). *Education of the gifted and talented* (5th ed.). Boston: Allyn & Bacon.

Feldhusen, J. F. (1995). *TIDE: Talent identification and development in education.* Sarasota, FL: Center for Creative Learning.

Gagné, F. (1985). Giftedness and talent: Reexamining a reexamination of the definitions. *Gifted Child Quarterly, 29*(3), 103–119.

Gagné, F. (1998). A proposal for subcategories within gifted or talented populations. *Gifted Child Quarterly, 42,* 87–95.

Gagné, F. (1999). My convictions about the nature of abilities, gifts, and talents. *Journal for the Education of the Gifted, 22*(2), 109–136.

Gagné, F. (2000). Understanding the complex choreography of talent development. In K. A. Heller, F. J. Monks, R. J. Sternberg, & R. F. Subotnik (Eds.), *International handbook of giftedness and talent* (pp. 67–79). Amsterdam: Elsevier.

Gardner, H. (1983). *Frames of mind: The theory of multiple intelligences.* New York: Basic Books.

Gardner, H. (1999). *Intelligence reframed: Multiple intelligences for the 21st century.* New York: Basic Books.

Hollingworth, L. S. (1926). *Gifted children.* New York: World Press.

Hollingworth, L. S. (1942). *Children above 180 IQ.* New York: World Book.

Marland, S. P., Jr. (1972). *Education of the gifted and talented: Report to the congress of the United States by the U.S. Commissioner of Education.* Washington, DC: U.S. Government Printing Office.

Moon, S. M., & Rosselli, H. C. (2000). Developing gifted programs. In K. A. Heller, F. J. Monks, R. J. Sternberg, & R. F. Subotnik (Eds.), *International handbook of research and development of giftedness and talent* (2nd ed., pp. 499–521). Amsterdam: Elsevier.

Renzulli, J. S. (1978). What makes giftedness? Re-examining a definition. *Phi Delta Kappan, 60,* 180–184, 261.

Renzulli, J. S. (1986). The three-ring conception of giftedness: A developmental model for creative productivity. In R. J. Sternberg & J. E. Davidson (Eds.), *Conceptions of giftedness* (pp. 53–92). Cambridge, England: Cambridge University Press.

Stanley, J. C. (1996). In the beginning: The study of mathematically precocious youth. In C. P. Benbow & D. Lubinski (Eds.), *Intellectual talent: Psychometric and social issues* (pp. 225–235). Baltimore: Johns Hopkins University Press.

Sternberg, R. J. (1985). *Beyond IQ: A triarchic theory of human intelligence.* Cambridge, England: Cambridge University Press.

Sternberg, R. J. (2000). Giftedness as developing expertise. In K. A. Heller, F. J. Monks, R. J. Sternberg, & R. F. Subotnik (Eds.), *International handbook of giftedness and talent* (pp. 55–66). Amsterdam: Elsevier.

Sternberg, R. J., & Clinkenbeard, P. R. (1995). The triarchic model applied to identifying, teaching, and assessing gifted children. *Roeper Review, 17,* 255–260.

Tannenbaum, A. J. (1986). Giftedness: A psychosocial approach. In R. J. Sternberg & J. E. Davidson (Eds.), *Conceptions of giftedness* (pp. 21–52). Cambridge, England: Cambridge University Press.

Tannenbaum, A. J. (2000). A history of giftedness in school and society. In K. A. Heller, F. J. Monks, R. J. Sternberg, & R. F. Subotnik (Eds.), *International handbook of giftedness and talent* (2nd ed., pp. 23–53). Amsterdam: Elsevier.

Terman, L. M. (1925). *Genetic studies of genius: Vol. 1. Mental and physical traits of a thousand gifted children.* Stanford, CA: Stanford University Press.

U.S. Department of Education. (1993). *National excellence: A case for developing America's talent.* Washington, DC: Author.

# 4

# Providing Programs for Special Populations of Gifted and Talented Students

*Christine J. Briggs, Sally M. Reis,
Rebecca D. Eckert, and Susan Baum*

It is not enough to prepare our children for the world; we must also prepare the world for our children.

—Luis J. Rodriguez

In 2002, the National Research Council published *Minority Students in Special and Gifted Education* (2002). The volume contains information about the striking overall pattern of underrepresentation of minority groups in programs and services for the gifted and talented. The Committee on Minority Representation in Special Education, the task force that authored the work, drew several conclusions and generalizations:

- The limited minority presence among top students is found using virtually all traditional measures of academic achievement, including school grades, standardized test scores, and class rank.
- Extensive under-representation is present at all levels of the educational system, beginning in kindergarten.

- The limited presence of several minority groups among high-achieving students cuts across class lines, that is, substantial minority-majority achievement gaps exist at all social class levels as measured by parent education and family income. (National Research Council, 2002, p. 81)

These conclusions are a call to arms for every practitioner in our field. If we are to provide equitable access to high-level services and programs, we must address the striking patterns of disproportion that exist in gifted programs and services in all parts of our country. This report must be viewed as a critical point of departure for our field, not a destination.

Christine Briggs, Sally Reis, Rebecca Eckert, and Susan Baum move us forward on our journey toward more equitable identification procedures and program and service options for all underrepresented populations, not just those among minority groups: second language learners, gay and bisexual students, students with multiple exceptionalities, gifted students with ADHD and Asperger's disorder, and those who have physical disabilities. In this chapter, they explore strategies, clustered in five different program areas that can contribute to the successful identification and retention of underrepresented populations. This chapter is most aligned with the following chapters: Developing a Definition of Giftedness, 3; Constructing Identification Procedures, 5; Articulating Gifted Education Program Goals, 6; Curriculum for Gifted Education Students, 8; and Developing a Plan for Evaluating a Program in Gifted Education, 15. It is also linked to the roles and responsibilities of gifted education advisory committees (Appendix A).

## DEFINITION

The underrepresentation of special populations of gifted and talented students in gifted programs has long been an area of concern in our field. Students with gifts and talents who are frequently overlooked in our programs include those with special needs (e.g., students with learning disabilities) as well as those who are culturally, linguistically, and ethnically diverse (CLED). As demographics in public schools across the nation continue to change, educators must learn how to better identify, serve, and sustain students whose gifts and talents have previously gone undiscovered. This chapter summarizes ways to identify and implement gifted education programs to improve the representation, participation, and performance of special populations in gifted and talented programs and services. We will consider the special populations within the community, the methods by which students are identified for services, the types of services that are currently offered, and the modifications that may need to be made in light of changing demographics or community expectations.

## RATIONALE

During the last two decades, researchers in the field of gifted education have turned their attention to special populations of gifted and talented students. They have explored two avenues of research: the nature of the special populations that comprise underrepresented students and the types of interventions that are required to ensure that these populations of students are identified and served in programs for the gifted and talented. Recent research clusters underrepresented populations of gifted students into two broad categories: CLED students and those with special needs, which are described, in turn, in the next sections.

## CLED Students With Gifts and Talents

The pervasive disparity in the proportion of CLED students identified and served in programs for the gifted is a major concern of many researchers and educators in gifted education (Maker, 1982; National Research Council, 2002; VanTassel-Baska, 1998). The primary reason cited for their underrepresentation is the absence of adequate assessment procedures and programming efforts (Ford, 2005; Frasier, Garcia, & Passow, 1995; Frasier & Passow, 1994; Kitano & Espinosa, 1995). The U.S. Department of Education report (1993), *National Excellence: A Case for Developing America's Talent*, states that "special efforts are required to overcome the barriers to achievement that many economically disadvantaged and minority students face" (p. 28). Various sections in this report also address the need to identify talents in youngsters from different socioeconomic and cultural backgrounds, as well as students with special needs.

In addition federal acknowledgment of the need for a more inclusive approach to gifted education was established with the passage of the Jacob K. Javits Gifted and Talented Students Education Act of 1988, which stated, "outstanding talents are present in children and youth from all cultural groups, across all economic strata, and in all areas of human endeavor" (U.S. Department of Education, 1993, p. 26). Although several efforts have been made in the last decade to identify and serve more CLED students, school districts and individuals still find themselves lacking equitable and inclusive identification systems and programming options. Although the accompanying CLED student resource table does not represent every possible population of CLED student, it provides guidance for those who want to locate more information about the unique learning needs of these students.

**Table 4.1**  CLED Student Resources

| | |
|---|---|
| **Second Language Learners** | Aguirre, 2003; de Wet, 2005; Diaz, 1998; Granada, 2002; Kitano & Espinosa, 1995 |
| **African American Students** | Dickson, 2003; Ford, 1996; Ford, Grantham, & Milner, 2004; Ford & Harris, 1991; Hébert, 2000 |
| **Latino Students** | Castellano, 2003, 2004; Castellano & Diaz, 2001; Diaz, 1998; Udall, 1989 |
| **Native American Students** | Callahan & McIntire, 1994; Foley & Skenandore, 2003; Klug, 2004 |
| **Asian American Students** | Plucker, 1996; Kitano & Chinn, 1986 |
| **Gay and Bisexual Students** | Cohn, 2003; Peterson & Rischar, 2000 |

## High-Potential and Gifted
## Students with Special Needs

The second broad category of underrepresented students includes high-potential or gifted students with special needs who require unique educational programs and services for both their academic and affective development. During the last 20 years, research has contributed to our understanding of the special needs of these exceptional young children; however, it is still clear that students with disabilities are more often recognized for their disability not their talents (Baum & Owen, 2004; Reis, Neu, & McGuire, 1997). These students are rarely identified as gifted and most attention is focused on their disabilities. The resources in the accompanying table highlight some of the limited knowledge we have about gifted students with disabilities.

**Table 4.2**    Special Needs Student Resources

| **High-Ability Students With Learning Disabilities** | Baum & Owen, 2004; Neu, 2003; Olenchak & Reis, 2002; Reis, McGuire, & Neu, 2000; Reis, Neu, & McGuire, 1997; Seeley, 1998 |
|---|---|
| **Gifted Students With ADHD** | Baum, Olenchak, & Owen, 1998; Baum & Owen, 2004; Moon, 2002; Mooney & Cole, 2000 |
| **Gifted Students With Asperger's Syndrome** | Atwood, 1998; Neihart, 2000 |
| **Hearing Disabled Gifted Students** | Yewchuk & Bibby, 1989 |

In spite of the research focus on the needs of underrepresented populations in programs and services for the gifted and talented, special populations continue to be over-identified for remedial classes and underrepresented in gifted and talented (G/T) programs and services (National Research Council, 2002). National surveys indicate that only 10% of students performing at the highest levels in academic settings are CLED students despite the fact that they represent 33% of the larger school population (Gallagher, 2002). A need exists, therefore, to improve access that enables special populations of students with gifts and talents to participate successfully in G/T programs and services. Research suggests the following critical areas can help to achieve this goal with CLED students and other special populations: understanding alternative behaviors that can indicate giftedness (Callahan & McIntire, 1994; Maker & Schiever, 1989; Reis, Neu, & McGuire, 1995); expanding identification and selection procedures for identification (Baum, 1990; Frasier & Passow, 1994; Frasier, Garcia, & Passow, 1995); understanding test bias (Ford & Harris, 1991); cultural awareness training and professional development focused on student needs (Reis et al. 1995; Rios & Montecinos, 1999); and providing appropriate programming that focuses on enhancing strengths, celebrating a diverse range of talents, and focusing on gifts, rather than perceived deficits (Baum & Owen, 2004; Renzulli & Reis, 1985, 1994; VanTassel-Baska, 1998).

# GUIDING PRINCIPLES FOR THE INCLUSION OF HIGH-POTENTIAL STUDENTS FROM SPECIAL POPULATIONS IN GIFTED AND TALENTED PROGRAMS

- A broad range (e.g., academic, artistic, creative, leadership) and level of talents (e.g., latent, emergent, novice) exists across all populations of students.
- Special populations of gifted students include those who (1) have multiple exceptionalities (e.g., learning disabled) and (2) are culturally, linguistically, and ethnically diverse (CLED).
- Most of the old rules and traditional methods for defining, identifying, and serving underrepresented gifted and talented students in special populations do not work.
- Adaptations must be made in local and state curriculum standards and gifted program guidelines and regulations to enable more flexible identification procedures.
- Gifted program curriculum, instruction, and services must be tailored and modified to meet the unique profile of students from special populations.
- Both affective (social and emotional) and academic needs of students should be considered when developing programming options.
- The way in which school districts identify and nurture student gifts and talents affects whether student potential is latent, emergent, or fully realized.
- Attempts must be made to develop a broad range of choices and services to enable the diverse group of special population students to develop their academic, artistic, creative, and leadership talents or potential talents during and after the school day as well as at other times of the year.
- Regular opportunities must exist to evaluate the identification of and provision of services for students with talents and gifts from special population groups.
- Parents of gifted students or high-potential children from special populations must be invited and encouraged to actively participate in the process of their children's talent development.
- Program evaluation practices should enable changes to occur that support successful program participation of CLED students and those with special needs.

# TRAITS OR ATTRIBUTES THAT DEFINE A HIGH-QUALITY PROGRAM

Recent research in schools throughout the United States (Briggs & Reis, 2003) suggested five areas that contribute to the successful identification and participation of both subsets of underrepresented populations: identification modifications, specific program support systems, selection of curriculum/instructional designs that enable success to emerge, community and parent/home connections, and program evaluation practices.

## Identification Modifications

The following practical strategies for increasing the numbers of CLED and special need students identified for gifted and talented programs and services are abstracted from three research studies (Briggs & Reis, 2003; Baum & Owen, 2004; Reis et al. 1995):

- Using talent pool and alternative identification pathways (Renzulli & Reis, 1985, 1997)
- Using early identification to enable the provision of targeted interventions services
- Using student performance information to identify high potential

The use of a talent pool and alternative pathways was characterized by the use of a variety of assessment tools (e.g., teacher recommendations, behavior checklists, portfolios, student interviews, performance assessments, peer nomination, self-nomination) and the elimination of formal identification procedures. The use of these procedures yielded larger numbers of students—including those with special needs—who, subsequently, received targeted enrichment services.

The second strategy is early identification. When high-potential students are identified early in their school careers, interventions can be implemented that enhance their strengths and compensate for experiences that may not have been provided but are prerequisite to later school success and talent development. Such experiences may include opportunities to become involved in more challenging curricular work at a very young age and earlier options for acceleration and enrichment.

The third strategy that has proven successful in identifying larger numbers of underrepresented gifted and talented students is student performance information. Student performance information includes student observations during enriched lessons to watch for signs of gifted behaviors, student work portfolios highlighting students' strengths and talents, and probationary placement in gifted services to provide opportunity for children to demonstrate their abilities within a new context. When emphasis on formal assessments (e.g., rigid "gatekeepers") is reduced and more weight and credibility are given to talent spotting opportunities, more traditionally underrepresented students surface for consideration for programs and services.

## Specific Program Support Systems

Research about exemplary programs (Briggs & Reis, 2003) suggests that if identification and services are going to be expanded to special populations, specific program supports must be provided to practitioners who are involved in the identification and service delivery processes. To achieve this goal, inservice and professional development was provided to gifted program teachers regarding learning characteristics and behaviors of underrepresented populations. Topics for these professional learning opportunities included cultural awareness training about the unique population(s) under consideration, information about the learning profiles of students with multiple exceptionalities, case studies, information about specific learning disabilities, test bias, district demographics, and any existing discrepancies between the district demographics and the students identified for gifted education programs and services. Sustained professional development, coupled with coaching and follow-up, resulted in increased student nominations and identification of underrepresented student populations.

Once students were identified, professional development was also provided to help faculty and staff work with students to develop a positive peer culture. This ongoing, inservice training was provided at the district and school level on topics such as nomination, identification, curriculum, and teaching for students from special population groups. This professional development also enabled the district coordinators to establish a network of counselors with the necessary experience to meet the social, emotional, and academic needs of students who were referred for gifted education services.

Baum (1990) and Reis et al. (1997) find that educators should encourage compensation strategies, develop an awareness of strengths and weaknesses, focus on developing the child's gift, and provide an environment that values individual differences. They also find that the social and emotional needs of gifted students with special needs must be addressed and that academic offerings must take into account interests in areas outside of traditional academic subjects in afterschool and summer offerings, as well as school-based opportunities.

## Selection of Curriculum/Program Designs

A program or curriculum design that is aligned with the unique learning needs of traditionally underserved populations is another attribute critical to the retention of special needs students in programs and services for the gifted and talented. The selection of an appropriate curriculum or program design enables these students to participate successfully. For example, program designs that use the front-loading of targeted services are key. The targeted services may include enrichment that is aligned with the regular classroom curriculum or include structured, rigorous interventions, such as Advancement via Individual Determination (AVID) and other such programs that are described in Chapter 8, on curriculum development. Whatever interventions are targeted for the learning needs of traditionally underserved students, the front-loading prepares students for participation in advanced-level content and thinking skills before the formal identification process or advanced program opportunities are offered. By preparing students ahead of time, front-loading helps to bridge the gap between the readiness level of promising students and the curriculum. Front-loading can take place in cluster groups as well as afterschool or summer programs.

The selection of an appropriate program or curriculum design must also take into account other unique needs of underrepresented gifted students. One way to consider the varied needs of these unique students is to use a program design that contains a continuum of services. (See Chapter 7.) In the case of underrepresented students, program personnel would select options from the continuum that build on students' existing strengths and abilities and develop skills or abilities that may not be fully realized. For example, providing instruction in higher-order problem solving and information processing enhances the development of academic coping strategies that can improve students' self-esteem as problem solvers as well as their academic performance (Hansford, 1987; Reis, McGuire, & Neu, 2000). Furthermore, because gifted/LD students tend to be more resourceful and strategic in approaching problems than are nongifted students who have learning disabilities, classroom activities that emphasize these skills may also improve self-esteem (Coleman, 1992).

Successful programs also provide programming for affective as well as cognitive growth of their diverse populations. This may involve modifying program curriculum to include practices directly aligned to the unique needs of diverse students and those with special needs, such as developing persistence or leadership skills, providing peer group support, organizing a mentorship experience, or providing college and financial aid counseling.

## Community and Parent/Home Connections

Research focusing on exemplary programs also suggests the need to provide increased support for high achievement and talent development through sustained interactions with families and the community (Briggs & Reis, 2003). This support is achieved in a variety of ways, such as using older students as role models and attempting to connect diverse students and those with special needs with other teachers and adults who can serve in support systems and as role models. In some successful programs, diverse students work with professionals in a high-interest field, address community problems, and are encouraged to give back to their communities. In programs that attempt to reduce the achievement gap, specific need areas are targeted. These need areas might pertain to language acquisition, culture, or access to content to bridge the disparity between school-valued knowledge and student strengths. Successful programs also foster parent/home connections by having family facilitators use the following strategies:

- Work with parent volunteers.
- Translate materials for meetings and print materials.
- Provide student homework that requires family participation.
- Encourage parents to be actively involved in their children's annual course selections.

## Program Evaluation Practices

District coordinators who are committed to increasing the number of underrepresented candidates for the program evaluate the program continually. They regularly review all gifted curriculum and program offerings to increase the alignment between the curriculum and the learning needs of students from underrepresented populations. They attempt to link program learning to real-world applications and address the achievement gaps they find between high-potential students and the various academic content areas. They work to assess carefully and thoroughly how they can increase the number of culturally diverse, academically talented students who participate in programs. Furthermore, they follow the progress and career paths of these students to learn if any program adjustments are needed. In some programs, teachers determine which students are eligible for admission and graduation from competitive colleges and universities and support their applications. In all program evaluation practices, they make special efforts to analyze the progress and success of CLED students and special populations by examining student achievement reports, increased enrollment of CLED and students with special needs in gifted programs, and the retention and graduation rates of these young people.

# EXAMPLE IN NEED OF REVISION

Anthony St. John was recently hired as the enrichment coordinator by the Coastal School District. As the person charged with providing a unified vision for gifted programming at all of the district's schools, Anthony was concerned that despite the presence in the community of a large population of poor farm laborers and a recent influx of immigrants from eastern Europe, most students identified for and served by the gifted and talented program at all levels (elementary and secondary) were from middle-class, professional families. In addition, it appeared that no pathways were in place to increase the representation of students from these special populations in the gifted program. Concerned about making the Coastal School District a place that promotes excellence in all high-potential students in the community, Anthony decided his highest priority was to ensure that the demographics in the district's gifted education programs and services matched those of the community at large.

# PROCEDURES FOR MAKEOVER

Anthony was aware of the five attributes that defined high-quality programs and services for diverse gifted education students. He considered each of the attributes, in turn, using the questions below. His goal was to use the answers to his questions to help him better align the programs and services of Coastal School District with the learning needs of its unique population of high-potential, yet underserved, students.

## Identification Modifications

1. Do our identification procedures comply with state and district standards?

2. Are there gatekeepers (e.g., standardized test scores, matrices with summed scores that "wash out" student strengths) in place that inhibit students from special populations from being identified for and participating in the gifted program?

3. Have we employed alternative identification instruments (e.g., interviews, classroom performance data, student portfolios, auditions) to better identify high-potential students from special populations?

4. Do alternate pathways exist (e.g., special nominations, peer nomination, self-nomination) for entrance into a talent pool of students?

5. Are students provided with advanced and enriched learning experiences before a formal identification process begins?

6. Have the faculty and staff received training on how to spot talent in students from special populations?

## Specific Program Support Systems

1. Have we provided professional development for faculty and staff regarding the learning characteristics and behaviors of special populations of students present in the school community?

2. Have we provided staff development about the nature of test bias and its implications for the identification of underserved populations of gifted and talented students?

3. Have we established peer support groups within each school to foster a positive peer culture?

4. Is there a network of counselors available who have experience in meeting the social, emotional, and academic needs of all students who are referred for gifted education services?

5. Have we assessed the need for community outreach programs like afterschool programs, summer enrichment opportunities, developmental preschool programs, and full-day kindergarten?

## Selection of Curriculum/Instructional Designs That Enable Success to Emerge

1. Do we offer a continuum of services designed to meet the various needs of gifted students at all grade levels?

2. Have we implemented procedures to ensure that CLED and high-potential students with disabilities are ready for participation in the talent development program?

3. Have we gathered learning profile information about our student population that includes their learning strengths and deficits?

4. Have we provided programming options that encourage students to gain information and communicate their ideas in creative ways based on individual talents and interests?

5. Have we enabled special needs students to use a metacognitive approach to their learning? That is, have we provided them with the training to understand their unique learning process and when and how to employ the compensation strategies that allow them to succeed in spite of their learning differences?

6. Is programming provided that supports the unique affective growth (as well as cognitive growth) in these diverse students, as well as others?

## Community and Parent/Home Connections

1. Have we included parents and community members from special populations in the planning and decision-making process of program design and implementation?

2. Have we considered the need for translating home and community communications into languages spoken in students' homes and communities?

3. Do we welcome all parents and community members into our school and provide them with information about the talent development program?

4. Do we encourage parent and community volunteers to serve as mentors and role models for our gifted and talented students?

5. Have we established reciprocal relationships with a range of community organizations?

6. Do we offer seminars for parents that address the needs of gifted students in special populations as well as the group at large (e.g., fostering gifts and talents, college planning)?

## Program Evaluation Practices

1. Have we collected and analyzed demographic data from the school, the gifted program, and the community at large to investigate potential inequities in our identification of gifted students?

2. Have we established procedures to regularly review student achievement reports, increased enrollment of CLED and students with special needs in gifted programs, and retention of students in gifted services?

3. Have we increased the number of culturally diverse gifted and talented students who are eligible for admission to and graduation from competitive colleges and universities?

4. Do we have longitudinal tracking systems in place that will help us assess not only the success of our special needs students, but also monitor and adjust, if necessary, the strategies we employ to meet their needs?

# MAKEOVER EXAMPLE

As a newcomer to the Coastal School District, Anthony St. John's first action was to collect data about the proportion of CLED students and learning disabled students in the Coastal School District and their proportion in the program for advanced learners. To obtain another perspective on the data, Anthony met with the district coordinator for special education services to discuss the issue. As they talked, she agreed with Anthony's concerns about the lack of CLED and special needs students in the gifted programs. In addition, she described her observation that the special education classes had a larger proportion of students for whom English was not a native language as well as students from low-income families. Together, they decided to convene a task force (see Appendix A) to modify the existing services and foster more inclusionary programming.

At least two faculty members and one parent from each school were enlisted as initial members of the task force. After identifying the underserved populations of students, additional community members with expertise and insight about special populations were recruited to aid in the planning and recommendations. After a few months of research and discussion, the task force provided the following recommendations to the superintendent and school board of the Coastal School District to address concerns about the limited participation of students from special populations.

Identification Modifications

Currently, the Coastal School District relies on one standardized assessment to identify students for participation in the talent development program. Consequently, the talent development program currently enrolls a homogeneous group of students. We recommend the use of multiple criteria to make the process of identification more inclusive, rather than exclusive. These multiple pathways for entrance into a talent pool of students should include an administrative review of achievement test scores and grades, a rating scale for parents and teachers, IQ tests, and a nonverbal cognitive assessment that has a demonstrated track record for identifying traditionally underrepresented populations. Additionally, all faculty and staff in the Coastal School District should receive professional development to increase their cultural awareness and the many ways in which giftedness can emerge and develop.

Specific Program Support Systems

We recommend that at least one school counselor at each school in the Coastal School District receive special training on providing support for gifted students and their families with an emphasis on the needs of students from special populations. This training will allow our counselors to facilitate peer support groups for gifted students and develop a series of culturally sensitive parent seminars on issues like planning for college and helping children cope with bullying. We also suggest that teachers continue to receive training and guidance on how to provide enrichment and acceleration within the regular classroom for all of our gifted students, including CLED and learning disabled students.

Curriculum and Instructional Designs to Enable Emergent Success

We recommend revising and expanding our continuum of services to reflect the changing needs of our growing talent pool of gifted and talented students. We are especially concerned with establishing enrichment opportunities that precede formal identification processes to enable emergent success. Therefore, we suggest establishing a summer enrichment academy that is designed to allow students to pursue areas of interest and passion, as well as to build academic skills. We also encourage the development of an enrichment seminar developed specifically for students receiving special education services. This seminar will allow enrichment and special education specialists to work together and share expertise and will also provide an environment in which school faculty and staff can spot emergent talents in an underserved segment of the school population.

Community and Parent/Home Connections

Our discussions with community leaders have indicated that there are no mechanisms in place for providing English instruction for the recent influx of immigrant families to our town. We recommend that all communications shared with families and community members be translated into students' home languages and that knowledgeable translators are present for parent meetings. In addition, English language instruction should be a featured component of our summer-school program and evening seminars with interested parents. Our fact-finding discussions with community leaders and parents have also provided us with an exciting partnership opportunity to develop an internship program for gifted high school students interested in scientific research. Local companies are particularly interested in recruiting students with knowledge about agriculture as well as students from diverse backgrounds. We hope that students who participate in this program will share their experiences and encourage younger students to pursue this opportunity in the future, thus sustaining the program.

Program Evaluation

To assess progress toward our goal of equitably identifying and serving gifted and talented students from all populations in our community, we will establish a biannual review panel. We recommend that the program be evaluated based on six data points: statistics, alignment with state and national standards, curriculum and assessment studies, services to program participants and community, satisfaction of stakeholders, and student success as indicated by test data and accomplishments. We also recommend that this review committee formulate a longitudinal plan that will analyze the success rate of our underrepresented students in their public school years, as well as later on in college, and the strategies that contributed most significantly to their success.

## STRATEGIC PLAN TO DESIGN OR REVISE THE EXAMPLE

*Objective:* To analyze and compare the proportion of students from special populations (both CLED and students with learning disabilities) present in the school's gifted and talented program with those in the larger school community to create a more inclusive and equitable talent development program.

*Evidence:* A committee will be established to collect demographic information about the school community. Based on this information and the current research in gifted education, the committee will make recommendations to the school board and superintendent about the following aspects of the talent development program: (a) identification modifications, (b) specific program support systems, (c) selection of curriculum/instructional designs that enable success to emerge, (d) community and parent/home connections, and (e) program evaluation practices.

## Tasks and Timeline

**Table 4.3**    G/T Programs for Special Populations Checklist

| September | Collect and evaluate school and community demographic data as well as information about the programming and services of the gifted education program.<br><br>Assemble a task force consisting of interested gifted specialists, teachers, parents, administrators, curriculum directors, and counselors. |
|---|---|
| October | Convene the task force and commence discussions related to the following questions:<br><br>• Who are the underserved members of our school population?<br>• What are the currently established elements of identification and programming for our talent development program? |
| November | Discuss the following in a task force meeting:<br><br>• What are the needs of our CLED students?<br>• What are the needs of our students with special needs? |
| November–December | Review current research in gifted education and recommendations for improving the participation and performance of underserved populations in gifted programs. |
| January–March | Reconvene the task force to form recommendations concerning the following practices:<br><br>• Identification modifications<br>• Specific program support systems<br>• Selection of curriculum/instructional designs<br>• Community and parent/home connections<br>• Program evaluation |
| April | Present findings and recommendations to the superintendent and school board. |

| May | Reconvene the task force to evaluate the success of the suggested modifications. The following information will be considered:<br><br>• Student achievement reports<br>• Increased enrollment of CLED students<br>• Increased enrollment of students with special needs<br>• Retention of students in gifted services<br>• Graduation and college acceptance rates<br>• Faculty and staff evaluations of staff development |
|---|---|

## TEMPLATE FOR PROVIDING G/T PROGRAMS FOR SPECIAL POPULATIONS

**Table 4.4**  Overview Checklist

| | *Elements Currently in Place* | *Identified Needs* | *Suggested Modifications* |
|---|---|---|---|
| Identification Modifications | | | |
| Program Support Systems | | | |
| Curriculum and Instructional Designs | | | |
| Community and Parent/Home Connections | | | |
| Program Evaluation | | | |

## ADVICE FOR THE SOLE PRACTITIONER

Building a more equitable and inclusive gifted program requires a solid foundation of information. As a sole practitioner, you will need to collect demographic information about the community, the school, and students who are served by your gifted program. You will also need to hone your knowledge about the needs and recommendations regarding students from the identified special populations within your school so that you can then share these resources with others and plan a course of action. As you begin to make modifications based on the five key features, remember that change (even change that is greatly needed) takes time and support, but your perseverance will be rewarded in the lives of many children. You may find it helpful to meet occasionally with someone who has a fresh view of the situation—someone who can applaud your positive progress, no matter how slight.

## MUST-READ RESOURCES

Baldwin, A. Y. (Vol. Ed.). (2004). Culturally diverse and underserved populations of gifted students. (Vol. 6). In S. M. Reis (Series Ed.), *Essential readings in gifted education*, Thousand Oaks, CA: Corwin.

Baum, S. (Ed). (2004). *Twice-exceptional and special populations of gifted students.* Thousand Oaks, CA: Corwin.

Baum, S. M., & Owen, S. V. (2004). *To be gifted and learning disabled: Strategies for helping bright students with LD, ADHD, and more.* Mansfield Center, CT: Creative Learning Press.

Boothe, D., & Stanley, J. C. (2004). *Critical issues for diversity in gifted education.* Waco, TX: Prufrock Press.

Castellano, J. A., & Diaz, E. (2001). *Reaching new horizons: Gifted and talented education for culturally and linguistically diverse students.* Boston: Allyn & Bacon.

National Research Council. (2002). *Minority students in special and gifted education.* Washington, DC: National Academy Press.

Neihart, M. (2000). Gifted children with Asperger's syndrome. *Gifted Child Quarterly, 44*(4), 222–230.

Reis, S. M., McGuire, J. M., & Neu, T. W. (2000). Compensation strategies used by high ability students with learning disabilities who succeed in college. *Gifted Child Quarterly, 44*(2), 123–134.

Reis, S. M., Neu, T. W., & McGuire, J. M. (1997). Case studies of high ability students with learning disabilities who have achieved. *Exceptional Children, 63*(4), 1–12.

Tomlinson, C. A., Ford, D. Y., Reis, S. M., Briggs, C. J., & Strickland, C. A. (2003). *In search of the dream: Designing schools and classrooms that work for high potential students from diverse cultural backgrounds.* Washington, DC: The National Association for Gifted Children and Storrs, CT: University of Connecticut, The National Research Center on the Gifted and Talented.

## REFERENCES

Aguirre, N. (2003). ESL students in gifted education. In J. A. Castellano (Ed.), *Special populations in gifted education: Working with diverse gifted learners* (pp. 17–28). Boston: Allyn & Bacon.

Atwood, T. (1998). *Asperger's syndrome: A guide for parents and professionals.* Philadelphia: Taylor & Francis.

Baum, S. (1990). *Gifted but learning disabled: A puzzling paradox.* Washington, DC: U.S. Department of Education (ERIC Document No. E479, downloaded March 3, 2005, from www.cectag.org).

Baum, S., Olenchak, F. R., & Owen, S. V. (1998). Gifted students with attention deficits: Fact and/or fiction? Or, can we see the forest for the trees? *Gifted Child Quarterly, 42*(2), 96–104.

Baum, S. M., & Owen, S. V. (2004). *To be gifted and learning disabled: Strategies for helping bright students with LD, ADHD, and more.* Mansfield Center, CT: Creative Learning Press.

Briggs, C. J., & Reis, S. M. (2003). An introduction to the topic of cultural diversity and giftedness. In C. A. Tomlinson, D. Y. Ford, S. M. Reis, C. J. Briggs, & C. A. Strickland (Eds.), *In search of the dream: Designing schools and classrooms that work for high potential students from diverse cultural backgrounds* (pp. 5–32). Washington, DC: The National Association for Gifted Children and Storrs, CT: University of Connecticut, The National Research Center on the Gifted and Talented.

Callahan, C. M., & McIntire, J. A. (1994). *Identifying outstanding talent in American Indian and Alaska Native students.* Washington, DC: Office of Educational Research and Improvement (ERIC Document Reproduction Service No. ED 367127)

Castellano, J. A. (2003). The "browning" of American schools: Identifying and educating Hispanic students. In J. A. Castellano (Ed.), *Special populations in gifted education: Working with diverse gifted learners* (pp. 29–44). Boston: Allyn & Bacon.

Castellano, J. A. (2004). Empowering and serving Hispanic students in gifted education. In D. Boothe & J. C. Stanley (Eds.), *In the eyes of the beholder: Critical issues for diversity in gifted education* (pp. 1–14). Waco, TX: Prufrock Press.

Castellano, J. A., & Diaz, E. (2001). *Reaching new horizons: Gifted and talented education for culturally and linguistically diverse students.* Boston: Allyn & Bacon.

Cohn, S. (2003). The gay gifted learner: Facing the challenge of homophobia and anti-homosexual bias in schools. In J. A. Castellano (Ed.), *Special populations in gifted education: Working with diverse gifted learners* (pp. 123–134). Boston: Allyn & Bacon.

Coleman, M. R. (1992). A comparison of how gifted/LD and average/LD boys cope with school frustration. *Journal for the Education of the Gifted, 15*(3), 239–265.

de Wet, C. F. (2005, Winter). The challenge of bilingual and limited English proficient students. *NRC/GT Newsletter,* 9–15.

Diaz, E. I. (1998). Perceived factors influencing the academic underachievement of talented students of Puerto Rican descent. *Gifted Child Quarterly, 42*(2), 105–122.

Dickson, K. (2003). Gifted education and African American learners: An equity perspective. In J. A. Castellano (Ed.), *Special populations in gifted education: Working with diverse gifted learners* (pp. 45–64). Boston: Allyn & Bacon.

Foley, K., & Skenandore, O. (2003). Gifted education for the Native American student. In J. A. Castellano (Ed.), *Special populations in gifted education: Working with diverse gifted learners* (pp. 113–122). Boston: Allyn & Bacon.

Ford, D. Y. (1996). *Reversing underachievement among gifted black students: Promising practices and programs.* New York: Teachers College Press.

Ford, D. Y. (2005, Winter). Intelligence testing and cultural diversity: Pitfalls and promises. *NRC/GT Newsletter,* 3–8.

Ford, D. Y., Grantham, T. C., & Milner, H. R. (2004). Underachievement among gifted African American Students: Cultural, social, and psychological considerations. In D. Boothe & J. C. Stanley (Eds.), *In the eyes of the beholder: Critical issues for diversity in gifted education* (pp. 15–32). Waco, TX: Prufrock Press.

Ford, D. Y., & Harris, J. J., III (1991). On discovering the hidden treasure of gifted and talented African-American children. *Roeper Review, 13*(1), 27–33.

Frasier, M. M., & Passow, A. H. (1994). *Toward a new paradigm for identifying gifted potential* (RM94112). Storrs, CT: University of Connecticut, The National Research Center on the Gifted and Talented.

Frasier, M. M., Garcia, J. H., & Passow, A. H. (1995). *A review of assessment issues ion gifted education and their implications for identifying gifted minority students* (RM95204). Storrs, CT: University of Connecticut, The National Research Center on the Gifted and Talented.

Gallagher, J. J. (2002). *Society's role in educating gifted students: The role of public policy* (RM0212). Storrs, CT: University of Connecticut, The National Research Center on the Gifted and Talented.

Granada, A. J. (2002). Addressing the curriculum, instruction, and assessment needs of the bilingual/bicultural student. In J. A. Castellano & E. I. Diaz (Eds.), *Reaching new horizons: Gifted and talented education for culturally and linguistically diverse students* (pp. 133–153). Boston: Allyn & Bacon.

Hansford, S. J. (1987). *Intellectually gifted learning disabled students: A special study.* Washington, DC: U.S. Department of Education, Educational Information Center (ERIC Document Reproduction Service No. ED287242)

Hébert, T. P. (2000). Defining belief in self: Intelligent young men in an urban high school. *Gifted Child Quarterly, 44*(2), 91–114.

Kitano, M. K., & Chinn, P.C. (1986). *Exceptional Asian children and youth.* Reston, VA: The Council for Exceptional Children (ERIC document No. ED276178)

Kitano, M. K., & Espinosa, R. (1995). Language diversity and giftedness: Working with gifted English language learners. *Journal for the Education of the Gifted, 18*(3), 234–254.

Klug, B. J. (2004). Children of the starry cope: Gifted and talented Native American students. In D. Boothe & J. C. Stanley (Eds.), *In the eyes of the beholder: Critical issues for diversity in gifted education* (pp. 49–72). Waco, TX: Prufrock Press.

Maker, C. J. (1982). *Curriculum development for the gifted.* Rockville, MD: Aspen.

Maker, C. J., & Schiever, S. W. (Eds.). (1989). *Critical issues in gifted education: Vol. 2. Defensible programs for cultural and ethnic minorities.* Austin, TX: Pro-Ed. (ERIC Document Reproduction Service No. ED329634)

Moon, S. M. (2002). Gifted children with attention-deficit/hyperactivity disorder. In M. Neihart, S. M. Reis, N. M. Robinson, & S. M. Moon (Eds.), *The social emotional development of gifted children* (pp. 193–201). Waco, TX: Prufrock Press.

Mooney, J., & Cole, D. (2000). *Learning outside the lines.* New York: Simon & Schuster.

National Research Council. (2002). *Minority students in special and gifted education.* Washington DC: National Academy Press.

Neihart, M. (2000). Gifted children with Asperger's syndrome. *Gifted Child Quarterly, 44*(4), 222–230.

Neu, T. (2003). When the gifts are camouflaged by disability: Identifying and developing the talent in gifted students with disabilities. In J. A. Castellano (Ed.), *Special populations in gifted education: Working with diverse gifted learners* (pp. 151–162). Boston: Allyn & Bacon.

Olenchak, F. R., & Reis, S. M. (2002). Gifted students with learning disabilities. In M. Neihart, S. M. Reis, N. M. Robinson, & S. M. Moon (Eds.), *The social emotional development of gifted children* (pp. 177–192). Waco, TX: Prufrock Press.

Peterson, J. S., & Rischar, H. (2000). Gifted and gay: A study of the adolescent experience. *Gifted Child Quarterly, 44*(4), 231–246.

Plucker, J. A. (1996). Gifted Asian-American students: Identification, curricular, and counseling concerns. *Journal for the Education of the Gifted, 19,* 315–343.

Reis, S. M., McGuire, J. M., & Neu, T. W. (2000). Compensation strategies used by high ability students with learning disabilities who succeed in college. *Gifted Child Quarterly, 44*(2), 123–134.

Reis, S. M., Neu, T. W., & McGuire, J. M. (1995). *Talents in two places: Case studies of high ability students with learning disabilities who have achieved* (RM 95113). Storrs, CT: University of Connecticut, National Research Center on the Gifted and Talented.

Reis, S. M., Neu, T. W., & McGuire, J. M. (1997). Case studies of high ability students with learning disabilities who have achieved. *Exceptional Children, 63*(4), 1–12.

Renzulli, J. S., & Reis, S. M. (1985). *The schoolwide enrichment model: A comprehensive plan for educational excellence.* Mansfield Center, CT: Creative Learning Press.

Renzulli, J. S., & Reis, S. M. (1994). *Schools for talent development.* Mansfield Center, CT: Creative Learning Press.

Renzulli, J. S., & Reis, S. R. (1997). *The schoolwide enrichment model: A how-to guide for educational excellence.* Mansfield Center, CT: Creative Learning Press.

Rios, F., & Montecinos, C. (1999). Advocating social justice and cultural affirmation: Ethnically diverse pre-service teacher's perspectives on multi-cultural education. *Equity and Excellence in Education, 32*(3), 66–75.

Seeley, K. (1998). Underachieving and talented learners with disabilities. In J. VanTassel-Baska (Ed.), *Excellence in educating gifted and talented learners* (pp. 83–93). Denver, CO: Love.

Udall, A. J. (1989). Curriculum for gifted Hispanic students. In C. J. Maker & S.W. Schiever (Eds.), *Critical issues in gifted education: Vol. 2. Defensible programs for cultural and ethnic minorities.* Austin, TX: Pro-Ed.

U.S. Department of Education. (1993). *National excellence: A case for developing America's talent.* Washington, DC: U.S. Government Printing Office.

VanTassel-Baska, J. (1998). Disadvantaged learners with talent. In J. VanTassel-Baska (Ed.), *Excellence in educating gifted and talented learners* (pp. 95–114). Denver, CO: Love.

Yewchuk, C. R., & Bibby, M. A. (1989). Identification of giftedness in severely and profoundly hearing impaired students. *Roeper Review 12*(1), 42–48.

# 5

# Constructing Identification Procedures

*E. Jean Gubbins*

It is amusing to discover, in the twentieth century, that the quarrels between two lovers, two mathematicians, two nations, two economic systems, usually assumed insoluble in a finite period should exhibit one mechanism, the semantic mechanism of identification—the discovery of which makes universal agreement possible, in mathematics and in life.

—Alfred Korzybski (American scientist and philosopher, 1879–1950)

There are many variations in the standards and guidelines that have been adopted by states regarding the procedures used to identify children who are gifted and talented. Passow and Rudnitski (1993) express the diversity well:

This analysis [of state policies] indicates considerable variability among states so that there is no single model that provides a pattern. . . . Some state policies are clearer, more positive and more directive than others. Some documents are stronger with respect to specific components (e.g., nature of mandate, identification, curriculum, or evaluation). (p. vii)

In spite of the variations that exist, the strongest procedures are enacted in places where there is a reliance on the long line of research about identification practices to guide the construction of a coherent identification system.

In this chapter, E. Jean Gubbins walks us through not only the research about identification practices but also the current best practices from the field. In addition, she provides us with a great deal of practical wisdom that she has gathered from her vast and varied experiences in gifted education.

It goes without saying that this chapter on identification procedures is linked inextricably to the chapter on the definition of giftedness. Constructing identification procedures also requires a look back and a look forward at other key chapters of this book. Most relevant to this topic are Developing a Mission Statement on the Educational Needs of Gifted and Talented Students, 2; Articulating Gifted Education Program Goals, 6; Comprehensive Program Design, 7; Curriculum for Gifted Education Students, 8; and Providing Programs for Special Populations of Gifted and Talented Students, 4. Local gifted education advisory committees (see Appendix A) are often involved in various facets of the identification process.

## DEFINITION

Identification procedures codify strategies to reflect local or state definitions of gifted and talented students. With input from key decision makers, a systematic approach to understanding, uncovering, and documenting the gifts and talents in young people is constructed. Teachers, administrators, school psychologists, curriculum directors, and parents with considerable understanding of assessment tools, data analysis, and documentation of identification procedures comprise the screening and selection team. This group of people is responsible for designing and implementing procedures that recognize gifts and talents in all stages of development (e.g., latent, emergent, manifest) in all segments of the school population (Gubbins, 2005). The screening and selection team describes the identification procedures in narrative or outline form to help persons responsible for the process to check the status of each procedure and ensure that it is responsive to students' needs.

## RATIONALE

Constructing identification procedures implies that actions will be designed and implemented to confirm or uncover students' talents and abilities that need to be addressed within the home and school learning environments (Gubbins, 2005). The inclusion of the term "constructing" implies that identification procedures cannot be adopted as-is without careful consideration of the needs of students and the available resources within each district. In addition, the construction of identification procedures must be sensitive to the diverse cultures and range of experiences within the school population (Ford, 2004, 2005).

Selected procedures are guides to identification and serve as checkpoints throughout the process as the final pool of identified students is determined. Well-articulated identification procedures answer the following questions:

- Who are the gifted and talented students?
- Why are we striving to identify them?
- How do we find them?

- What are the most appropriate tools for identifying students' gifts and talents?
- How are data from various tools analyzed and interpreted?
- Who is responsible for identifying students' gifts and talents?

# GUIDING PRINCIPLES

Guiding principles related to constructing identification procedures provide an opportunity for discussions about how to approach the design and development of strategies that will confirm and/or uncover students' latent talents and abilities. The following principles are based on prior research studies and practitioners' experiences. Many of the principles are reflected in the work by Borland (2004), Davis and Rimm (2004), Frasier and Passow (1994), Johnsen (2004), and Renzulli (2004).

- Identification procedures are logical, direct statements of how and where to start the process of screening and identifying gifted and talented students.
- Identification procedures are public information and presented in written form in the dominant language(s) of student and parent populations.
- Comprehensive identification procedures reflect characteristics of the student population and demographics of the district.
- Identification procedures incorporate multiple tools for observing, assessing, and documenting students' gifts and talents.
- Identification procedures are broad enough to include nominations of students with disabilities, students with dominant languages other than English, and students living in economically disadvantaged communities.
- Identification procedures reflect students' needs and the definition of giftedness selected by state or local educators.
- Identification procedures are defensible and inclusive, as opposed to exclusive.
- Techniques for checking potential bias in the identification procedures or assessment tools are explicit.
- Flexibility within the identification procedures occurs when students' educational profiles warrant alternative approaches.
- Identification procedures are communicated to persons who will be providing data through tests, rating scales, observation forms, interviews, portfolios, performances, and nominations (e.g., self, peer, teacher, parent, administrator).
- Identification procedures are assessed and updated at regular intervals to ensure that they reflect changes in the local demographics.

# ATTRIBUTES THAT DEFINE HIGH-QUALITY IDENTIFICATION PROCEDURES

Four attributes define high-quality identification procedures. Each attribute is followed by questions that need to be addressed by the screening and selection team. As work proceeds on the development and implementation of the identification procedures, the team should seek comments and reactions from representative groups of teachers and administrators and encourage suggestions for improvement.

## Comprehensive Approach

- To what extent are the identification procedures effective at all grade levels and sensitive to student age?
- Do the procedures confirm students' talents and abilities and uncover potential and emergent abilities?

## Student Characteristics

- Do parents, teachers, administrators, and students understand how gifts and talents are manifested in school and home environments?
- Are educators and parents knowledgeable about characteristics of gifted and talented students?
- Do the procedures include objective and subjective measures specific to different student characteristics (e.g., abilities, intelligence, artistic strengths, creativity, leadership)?
- Do the procedures reflect the diversity in primary languages, cultures, economics, and academics as the talents and abilities of students are assessed during the screening and selection processes?

## Objective and Subjective Tools

- Are objective tools administered under standardized conditions?
- Are selected tests appropriate for groups of students or individuals?
- Are selected instruments reliable and valid for screening and selection processes?
- Do the tools require the collection of data over time, as opposed to one data event such as a test?
- Do observation tools provide enough detail to distinguish the behavioral characteristics of gifted and talented students?
- Are data for portfolios and performance assessments collected by knowledgeable experts and analyzed in logical, sequential ways?

## Defensible and Inclusive Criteria

- Is there an obvious and defensible link between students' needs and the definitions and procedures related to identifying gifted and talented students?
- Do the identification procedures and respective tools (e.g., observation form, rating scale, test, interview protocol, portfolio, performance) match the type of skills and abilities that will be crucial for student success in programs and services?
- Do the identification procedures uncover the talents and abilities of students who may not perform consistently in all content areas?
- Are the technical qualities, such as reliability and validity, of identification tools well researched?
- Does the information from identification tools provide direction for programs and services?
- Does the final pool of identified students reflect the demographics of the district (e.g., language dominance, cultural diversity)?

- To what extent do the identification procedures conform to existing legal standards?
- Are the procedures internally consistent (i.e., connected to the definition of giftedness and the selected emphasis on the academics and/or the arts)?

## EXAMPLE IN NEED OF REVISION

The Chestnut Hill School District recognizes and supports the development of children's talents and abilities. Our mission statement reaffirms our commitment to helping students reach their potential. We believe it is important to identify gifted and talented children at an early age to ensure that our educational system is responsive to their needs throughout grades K–12.

We construct systematic and defensible procedures to screen and identify students' talents and abilities as a first step in understanding our talent base. We review each child's achievement and ability test scores on group-administered instruments. Students scoring at the 95th percentile (local norms) on the total achievement test or 135 or above on an intelligence test are designated as the screening pool. From this group of students, teachers complete two rating scales related to learning and motivation characteristics. Ratings on these scales are reviewed and added to the data from achievement and intelligence tests. Students who receive a minimal score of 300* (see following table of examples) across the four instruments are selected for the gifted and talented program. In the example table, Students 2 and 3 meet the qualifying score and are eligible for programs and services related to their talents and abilities in one or more academic areas.

| Screening Profile for Students Meeting High Academic Standards | | | | | |
|---|---|---|---|---|---|
| | Achievement Local Percentile 95+ | Intelligence Score of 135+ | Learning Rating 35+ | Motivation Rating 35+ | Total |
| Student 1 | 95 | 135 | 35 | 33 | 298 |
| Student 2 | 99 | 140 | 40 | 40 | 319* |
| Student 3 | 96 | 137 | 36 | 37 | 306* |

Formal identification procedures begin in Grade 2. Administrators, teachers, school psychologists, and curriculum directors suggest exposing students in grades K–2 to an enriched curriculum and involving parents and the community in the education of young students. Throughout these early grades, teachers and parents are encouraged to share anecdotes that describe behavioral characteristics well beyond grade-level expectations. These anecdotes are part of Chestnut Hill School District's Student Educational Profile, which is maintained through Grade 12.

To maximize the efficiency of the identification procedures, alternative objective and subjective tools are used in elementary, middle, and high schools. Alternative tools include nominations (e.g., self, peer, teacher, parent), grades, or writing sample. Teams of administrators, teachers, and school psychologists at their respective levels (elementary, middle, and high schools) determine the selection of alternative tools.

Students who meet the qualifying standards are invited to participate within the school day in a continuum of programs and services, such as ability grouping in math, writers' forum, debate club, and forensics society. They also meet with other identified students and teachers two hours a week as they conduct research projects related to their classroom studies in one or more subject areas.

## PROCEDURES FOR MAKEOVER

The previous section delineates attributes and related questions that define high quality for constructing identification procedures. Each attribute requires reflection and study of the extent to which identification procedures are effective at all grade levels. Members of the screening and selection team should seek informal data from teachers and administrators through focus groups, interviews, or surveys. The number of people participating in the data collection approaches might include 5% of the district teachers and administrators, as well as parent representatives, to provide general impressions across all schools about the quality and appropriateness of the procedures. Once data are collected and analyzed, identification procedures can be revisited to ensure the effectiveness in defining the population of students whose academic and artistic needs require programs and services beyond current academic offerings.

## MAKEOVER EXAMPLE

The Chestnut Hill School District recognizes and supports the development of children's talents and abilities. Our mission statement reaffirms our commitment to helping students reach their potential. We believe that it is important to identify gifted and talented children at an early age to ensure that our educational system is responsive to their needs throughout grades K–12.

We construct systematic and defensible procedures to screen and identify students' talents and abilities as a first step in understanding our academic talent base. We review each child's achievement and ability test scores on group-administered instruments. Students scoring at the 85th percentile (local norms) on the total achievement test score or 120 or above on an intelligence test are entered into the screening pool. From this group of students, teachers complete two rating scales related to learning and motivation characteristics. Ratings on these scales are reviewed and become part of the data profile of achievement and intelligence test results. The screening and identification team uses the data to complete a student educational profile and proceed with a case-study approach to selecting gifted and talented students whose academic needs exceed those of the general education program.

Formal identification procedures begin in Grade 2. Administrators, teachers, school psychologists, and curriculum directors suggest exposing students in grades K–2 to an enriched curriculum and involving parents and the community in the education of young students. Throughout these early grades, teachers and parents are encouraged to share anecdotes that describe behavioral characteristics well beyond grade-level expectations. These anecdotes are part of Chestnut Hill School District's student educational profile, which is maintained through Grade 12.

To maximize the efficiency and effectiveness of the identification procedures, alternative objective and subjective tools are used in the elementary, middle, and high schools. Alternative tools include nominations (e.g., self, peer, teacher, administrator, parent), grades, writing sample, portfolio, or performance. Teams of administrators, teachers, and school psychologists at their respective levels (elementary, middle, and high schools) determine the selection of alternative tools. Careful attention is given to selecting assessments that are sensitive to student age as well as grade level. Specifically, identification teams consider issues related to identification tools for students who are younger than their peers and/or who are accelerated. The full range of identification procedures is summarized in the accompanying table.

Students who meet the qualifying standards are invited to participate within the school day in a continuum of programs and services, such as ability grouping in math, writers' forum, debate club, drama club, and forensics society. Academically talented students also meet with other identified students and teachers four hours a week as they conduct research projects related to their classroom studies or personal research interests in one or more subject areas.

Student performance is the hallmark of identifying artistic talents. We encourage our art and music teachers to expose students to a wide variety of media and to document students' products. These products become part of students' portfolios that are presented to a panel of artists who review and critique the work and determine the level of artistic quality based on professional standards of the medium. Artists meet with the screening

| Identification Procedures | |
|---|---|
| *Academic Abilities* | *Artistic Talents & Abilities* |
| **Group Administered Tests**<br>**Spring of Grades 2–11 Talent Pool**<br><br>*85th percentile (local norms)—Achievement Test*<br>*120 or above—Intelligence Test* | **Nominations**<br><br>*Self, Peer, Teacher, Administrator, Parent* |
| **Teacher Ratings**<br><br>*Learning Scale*<br>*Motivation Scale* | **Teacher Ratings**<br><br>*Art, Music, Dance, Theater* |
| **Alternative Tools**<br>**Nominations**<br><br>*Self, Peer, Teacher, Administrator, Parent*<br><br>**Academic Grades**<br><br>**Writing Samples** | **Portfolios**<br><br>*Guided Collection Related to Artistic Talents and Abilities*<br><br>**Performances**<br><br>*Auditions, Presentations, Juried Shows, Recitals* |
| **Students' Educational Profiles**<br><br>*Academic Achievements and Accomplishments*<br>*Case Studies* | **Students' Educational Profiles**<br><br>*Ratings of Panel of Artists*<br>*Case Studies* |
| **Continuum of Programs & Services**<br><br>*Match Talents and Abilities to Goals* | **Continuum of Programs & Services**<br><br>*Match Talents and Abilities to Goals* |

and selection team to discuss each student's portfolio that receives an exemplary rating. Selected students are involved in opportunities with art and music teachers who have extensive training in their respective artistic fields.

Mentorships in academic and artistic fields of study are encouraged for students with well-defined goals that require interactions with persons who are experts in specific fields of study. Students interested in extended projects with a mentor prepare a brief proposal outlining their learning objectives. Proposals are then reviewed by a team of teachers in a related field who assume the responsibility of making connections between a mentor and the student.

Chestnut Hill School District is extremely proud of all the accomplishments of its students. Our teachers continually strive to nurture the talents and abilities of our young people.

# STRATEGIC PLAN FOR CREATING IDENTIFICATION PROCEDURES

*Objective:* To construct identification procedures that will confirm and uncover talents and abilities of young people who require access to programs and services responsive to their academic and/or artistic needs.

*Evidence:* Narrative and/or outline of identification procedures that codifies screening and selection approaches using objective and subjective tools that yield a group of gifted and talented students who need access to programs and services beyond those available to all students.

Identification procedures are reviewed by a committee of administrators, teachers, school psychologists, curriculum directors, and parents who are familiar with meeting the needs of gifted and talented students and are knowledgeable of various assessment tools and strategies.

*Timeline:* March—Seek nominations and recruit administrators, teachers, school psychologists, curriculum directors, and parents with prior knowledge and experience in developing procedures to identify a special population of students whose academic and/or artistic needs require programs and services beyond the general education curriculum.

April—Convene the committee and commence discussions related to three questions:

- What are the academic and/or artistic strengths of our student population that exceed developmental guidelines or milestones?
- What types of objective and subjective tools provide evidence of students' unique talents and abilities?
- What criteria will be used to determine the initial screening pool of students and the final identified group of gifted and talented students?

May—Screen and identify gifted and talented students based on the procedures and selected criteria.

June—For each student, develop an educational profile outlining access to special programs and services to meet academic and artistic needs.

November—Revisit the identification procedures used initially in the spring. Request progress reports from teachers and mentors involved in delivering programs and services to identified students. To what extent are students performing at high levels that distinguish them from other students who were not identified as gifted and talented? Are there other students who were not selected for special programs and services who should be considered for the screening pool? Submit nominations to the screening and selection team for their consideration.

January—Revise or clarify existing identification procedures.

## TEMPLATE TO HELP PRACTITIONERS JUMP-START THEIR THINKING

### Reflection

How do you define success in your school district? Think of the top five most successful students at the elementary, middle, and high schools. What characteristics do they have in common? How are they unique? Access their cumulative records and see if you can determine the predictors of future success. What did you learn about the predictability of student success?

As you think about constructing identification procedures, remember what you learned about predictors of success and make sure you include the strategy or technique as part of your identification procedures.

### Suggested Starting Points

It is critical to understand the importance of the first step in an identification procedure. The first step can limit or broaden personal and professional perspectives about manifestations of students' gifts and talents. If a strict cutoff score is chosen as the first step because of the availability of data from all students within specified grade levels, the initial pool of students resulting from this first step may be highly selective. Remember that constructing identification procedures is a process and the approaches may need to be changed to confirm and uncover the talents and abilities of academically and artistically diverse students.

The following suggestions should guide the construction of effective identification procedures:

- As you select the tools, reflect on the type of data each will provide and the extent to which it matches the behavioral characteristics of gifted and talented students who need special programs and services.
- Discuss approaches to analyzing resulting data from each tool. What is the best way to profile student data? How will the final selection of students be determined?
- Review the procedures again and discuss any plans for modifications or additions to screening and identification approaches.

## ADVICE FOR THE SOLE PRACTITIONER

Constructing identification procedures is a difficult task for one person. You will need the assistance of others who understand the complex issues involved. The process requires knowledge of program designs, service delivery models, assessment tools, and measurement issues. There is considerable decision making that starts with basic questions: Who are the students whose academic needs require further challenge and nurturing? What are the most appropriate methods for screening and identification? Answers to these questions affect all phases of program design and development, and they need to be studied carefully. It would be most advantageous to listen to several viewpoints from teachers, administrators, school psychologists, curriculum directors, and parents to construct effective and defensible identification procedures.

## RESOURCES FOR IDENTIFICATION TOOLS

The following is a list of possible objective and subjective tools that may be appropriate for screening and identifying gifted and talented students in academic areas.

### Norm-Referenced Achievement Tests

- Iowa Tests of Basic Skills assess students' academic skills in several content areas: reading, mathematics, social studies, science, and information sources (Grades K–9).

  Iowa Tests of Basic Skills
  Riverside Publishing Company
  Contact: www.riversidepublishing.com

- The Metropolitan Achievement Test focuses on reading, mathematics, language, writing, science, and social studies (Grades K–12).

  Metropolitan Achievement Test
  Harcourt Brace Educational Measurement
  Contact: www.harcourtassessment.com

- The Stanford Achievement Test assesses children in reading, mathematics, language, spelling, study skills, science, social studies, and listening (Grades K–12).

  Stanford Achievement Test
  Harcourt Brace Educational Measurement
  Contact: www.harcourtassessment.com

- The TerraNova assessment tools measure achievement in reading/language arts, mathematics, science, and social studies (Grades K–12).

  TerraNova
  CTB/McGraw-Hill
  Contact: www.ctb.com

## Group Intelligence/Ability Tests

- The Cornell Critical Thinking Tests measure students' ability to think critically when analyzing premises and conclusions, judge the reliability of information, and identify assumptions (Grades 5–14).

  Cornell Critical Thinking Tests
  Critical Thinking Books & Software
  Contact: www.criticalthinking.com

- Kuhlmann-Anderson Tests assess verbal and nonverbal abilities (Grades K–12).

  Kuhlmann-Anderson Tests
  Scholastic Testing Service
  Contact: www.ststesting.com

- The Cognitive Abilities Test Form 6 (CogAT) measures both general and specific reasoning abilities in three batteries: verbal, quantitative, and nonverbal (Grades K–12).

  The Cognitive Abilities Test Form 6 (CogAT)
  Riverside Publishing
  http://www.riverpub.com/

- The Naglieri Nonverbal Ability Test measures nonverbal reasoning and problem-solving abilities. Reading and math skills are not required to respond to each set of patterns (Grades K–12).

  Naglieri Nonverbal Ability Test
  Harcourt Brace Educational Measurement
  Contact: www.harcourtassessment.com

- The Otis-Lennon School Ability Test measures reasoning skills, including verbal comprehension, verbal reasoning, pictorial reasoning, figural reasoning, and quantitative reasoning (Grades K–12).

  Otis-Lennon School Ability Test
  Harcourt Brace Educational Measurement
  Contact: www.harcourtassessment.com

## Creative Thinking Skills

- The Group Inventory for Finding Creative Talent focuses on creativity via the following dimensions: imagination, independence, and multiple interests (Grades K–6).

  Group Inventory for Finding Creative Talent
  Educational Assessment Service
  Contact: www.sylviarimm.com

- The Torrance Tests of Creative Thinking (TCTT)—Figural TTCT (Grades K–adult) and Verbal TCTT (Grade 1–adult)—assess fluency, flexibility, and originality. The figural test also assesses elaboration.

  Torrance Tests of Creative Thinking
  Scholastic Testing
  Contact: www.ststesting.com

## Teacher Rating Scales

- The Gifted and Talented Evaluation Scales ask teachers to rate the following student characteristics: intellectual ability, academic skills, creativity, leadership, and artistic talent (Grades K–12).

  Gifted and Talented Evaluation Scales
  Pro-Ed
  Contact: www.proedinc.com

- The Scales for Rating the Behavioral Characteristics of Superior Students asks teachers to assess students on 10 dimensions: learning, motivation, creativity, leadership, art, music, dramatics, planning, communication (precision), and communication (expressiveness) (Grades 2–12).

  Scales for Rating the Behavioral Characteristics of Superior Students
  Creative Learning Press
  Contact: www.creativelearningpress.com

- Tracking Talents is used to screen and identify multiple talents: cognitive abilities, academic talents, social and physical abilities, and technological and artistic talents (Grades 4–7).

  Tracking Talents: Identifying Multiple Talents Through Peer, Teacher, and Self-Nomination
  Prufrock Press
  Contact: www.prufrock.com

## REFERENCES

Borland, J. H. (2004). *Issues and practices in the identification and education of gifted students from under-represented groups.* Storrs, CT: The National Research Center on the Gifted and Talented, University of Connecticut.

Davis, G. A., & Rimm, S. B. (2004). *Education of the gifted and talented* (5th ed.). Boston: Allyn & Bacon.

Ford, D. Y. (2004) *Intelligence testing and cultural diversity: Concerns, cautions and considerations.* Storrs, CT: The National Research Center on the Gifted and Talented, University of Connecticut.

Ford, D. Y. (2005, Winter). Intelligence testing and cultural diversity: Pitfalls and promises. *NRC/GT Newsletter,* 3–8.

Frasier, M. M., & Passow, A. H. (1994). *Toward a new paradigm for identifying talent potential.* Storrs, CT: The National Research Center on the Gifted and Talented, University of Connecticut.

Gubbins, E. J. (2005, Winter). NRC/GT offers a snapshot of intelligence. *NRC/GT Newsletter,* 1–2.

Johnsen, S. K. (2004). *Identifying gifted students: A practical guide.* Waco, TX: Prufrock Press.

Passow, A. H., & Rudnitski, R. A. (1993). *State policies regarding education of the gifted as reflected in legislation and regulation* (CRS93302). Storrs, CT: The National Research Center on the Gifted and Talented, University of Connecticut.

Renzulli, J. S. (Ed.). (2004). Identification of students for gifted and talented programs (Vol 2). In S. M. Reis (Series Ed.), *Essential readings in gifted education.* Thousand Oaks, CA: Corwin.

# 6

# Articulating Gifted Education Program Goals

*Cheryll M. Adams*

In the absence of clearly defined goals, we become strangely loyal to performing daily acts of trivia.

—Unknown

We have all lived long enough to appreciate the meaning that lies under this quotation. Without goals in our lives, we rarely focus on essential tasks or purposefully pursue meaningful activities. While we recognize the importance of clear goals in our daily lives, little has been written about what constitutes substantive, high-quality, and aligned goals for gifted education programs and services.

Cheryll Adams addresses the nature of these high-quality program goals and objectives in this chapter. She alerts us to the need to develop and articulate important goals that are aligned, valid, comprehensive, and clear. The development of program goals is only one piece of the program development and evaluation puzzle. Effective goals and objectives that specifically address the needs of gifted learners must be grounded in a clear definition of giftedness and a thoughtful mission statement, thereby ensuring that program goals remain neither static nor ignored in a high-quality program.

This chapter is a foundational one in this guidebook because many aspects of gifted programming depend on the goals we create: program design, curriculum, budgeting, learning resources, a professional development plan, and, of course, evaluation. It is, therefore, a chapter that requires much professional deliberation and reflection.

# DEFINITION

Program goals are a set of clear, explicit statements that delineates a school or district response to the learning and social and emotional needs of gifted students. In general, program goals outline what the school or district desires for its students. Program goals should be aligned with district goals to assure that gifted services are an integral part of the regular school program. Program goals also seek to define exactly what outcomes are expected from program services. Goals are broad statements that include our vision for students; yet goals may not ever be realized. Goals are very broad, such as, "To help students become life-long learners." This goal is virtually impossible to measure. An example of another broad programming goal specifically addressing the needs of talented learners is, "Gifted students will spend the majority of their time in school learning at an appropriately challenging level."

Objectives, on the other hand, are statements derived from goals that are more narrowly defined and measurable. An example of this is, "Ninety-five percent of all students in the program will score at or above the 95th percentile on the statewide mathematics assessment." Objectives add an additional layer of specificity, and a program goal may have several objectives listed under it to explain how the outcome of the goal will be attained.

Goals can be written in several forms. Some practitioners use a bulleted list, often beginning each goal with an infinitive phrase; others choose to write the goals in sentences. The choice is one of personal preference.

# RATIONALE

Program goals are important because they further clarify gifted program services and are derived from the mission statement and definition of giftedness used by the district. A set of clearly articulated program goals also provides a focus for evaluation and planning. Objectives that are derived from the program goals define the scope of the instruction and suggest the means by which student progress is monitored. According to Borland (1989),

> All programs for the gifted should have written, workable, clearly stated and validated goals that reflect the desired outcome of the program in response to demonstrated student needs. (p. 212)

Ornstein and Hunkins (1998) indicate program goals are necessary because they are used to provide the guidelines that point the direction towards a particular purpose. Callahan and Caldwell (1999) point out the need for goals quite succinctly: "It is not possible to evaluate that which you cannot describe" (p. 14). Goals are a critical aspect of program and service design. Both sets of researchers note that goals should be continually reviewed and revised as purposes evolve and change.

# GUIDING PRINCIPLES AND ASSUMPTIONS

- Goals for gifted program services should be based on a clearly articulated mission statement and a definition of giftedness, both of which are based on current theoretical models and best practices.

- Gifted program service goals should be derived from national, state, and local standards and legislation (Landrum, Callahan, & Shaklee, 2001).
- Goals should also reflect local needs and current research and should employ exemplary materials from the field of gifted education.
- Gifted program service goals should be delineated by a formal committee. (See Appendix A)
- The committee should be comprised of a cross section of stakeholders including administrators, teachers, gifted education coordinators, parents, board of education members, and students.
- The committee should reflect the socioeconomic and cultural demographics of the district.
- The committee should decide on three to six goals and prioritize them based on the cognitive and affective needs of the targeted students.
- Each gifted program service goal should be further delineated by objectives that address measurable learner outcomes.
- Gifted program services goals should be aligned with general education goals and should reflect the unique learning needs of high-potential students.
- The curriculum and instruction within the gifted program services should be aligned with the goals.
- Gifted program service goals should be communicated clearly to all stakeholders.
- Gifted program service goals should be contained in documents that are distributed to stakeholders and should be translated into other languages when necessary.
- Progress toward gifted program service goals must be regularly evaluated.
- Gifted program service goals should be reviewed for their alignment with students' changing cognitive and affective needs, as well as with changing district goals.

## TRAITS OF HIGH-QUALITY GOALS

To determine whether or not program goals are high quality, ask the following questions:

### Alignment

- Is this goal appropriate for the unique learning needs of high-potential children?
- Are the goals aligned with general education goals while reflecting the specific needs of high-potential students?
- Are the goals aligned with the program philosophy and with the definition of giftedness used by the school or district?
- Are the goals aligned with state and local policies and regulations?

### Validity

- Can progress towards our goals be evaluated?
- Is each goal further delineated by program objectives that clarify learner outcomes?
- Can curriculum and instruction be designed using the goals?
- Are the goals worthy of attainment?

- Do the goals reflect research-based, best practices in general education, and in the field of gifted education?

## Comprehensiveness

- Do the goals address the needs of all gifted students, including those traditionally underrepresented in gifted programs?
- Do the goals address the needs of gifted students in grades K–12?
- Do the goals address the learning needs of high-potential students, including academic, social, psychological, and career guidance?

## Clarity

- Are the goals easily understandable by all stakeholders (e.g., teachers, students, parents, administrators, board of education members)?
- Are the goals stated in terms of desired outcomes?
- Are the goals unambiguous and clear?

# EXAMPLES IN NEED OF REVISION

## Example # 1: Highland Community School District Goal

Students in the Highland Community School District will have a gifted curriculum and become lifelong learners.

| Trait | No Evidence | Little Evidence | Some Evidence | Considerable Evidence | Powerful |
|---|---|---|---|---|---|
| Alignment | | | | X | |
| Validity | | X | | | |
| Comprehensiveness | | X | | | |
| Clarity | X | | | | |

*Goal Evaluation:* One of the goals of the Highland School District is for all students to become lifelong learners. In that respect, the gifted program goal is aligned with the school goal. While the goal is certainly one worthy of attainment, it is virtually impossible to measure. Furthermore, gifted curriculum is not defined, and the statement implies that all students will be working with gifted curriculum rather than tailoring curriculum to the needs of readiness levels of a specific group of gifted learners. Because this is an ambiguous goal and its meaning is subject to interpretation, we cannot accurately determine if it is a goal that addresses the needs of gifted students.

### Example # 2: Bridgeport Schools Goal

To serve the top 5% of the student population in Bridgeport.

| Trait | No Evidence | Little Evidence | Some Evidence | Considerable Evidence | Powerful |
|---|---|---|---|---|---|
| Alignment | | X | | | |
| Validity | | X | | | |
| Comprehensiveness | X | | | | |
| Clarity | | | | X | |

*Goal Evaluation:* Bridgeport School District aims to meet the individual needs of all students. The definition of giftedness used by the district addresses general intellectual ability, specific academic ability, visual and performing arts ability, leadership, and psychomotor ability. This is a very broad definition. The goal, "To serve the top 5% of the student population" is a rather narrow interpretation of the definition. While inspection of district data can determine whether 5% are being served, the goal isn't particularly worthy of attainment and does not reflect best practices in the field. In addition, this goal reflects what the district will do, not a desired outcome for the students.

## PROCEDURE FOR REVISING OR ENHANCING A GOAL

If the goal lacks alignment:

Find your state standards documents, state gifted regulations, and corresponding school district documents. Be sure that the goals for gifted education services are an integral part of the education program, not add-ons.

1. In what ways do our gifted program goals reflect state and local law and regulations?

2. In what ways do our gifted program goals reflect school district documents and policies?

3. In what ways do our goals reflect the philosophy and definition of the gifted program?

4. To what extent do our goals reflect the unique learning profiles of our students (e.g., cultural backgrounds, socioeconomic levels, language(s) spoken, cognitive abilities and strengths, interests)?

5. Are there goals we have overlooked? How might we best incorporate them?

If the goal lacks validity:

For goals to be valid, they must be usable, practical, and effective. To revise goals that lack validity, the committee should make sure the goal is written in enough detail that it can be evaluated. In addition, the committee should explain the goal by including several objectives that further define the goal.

1. Have we listed several objectives that align with each goal?

2. To what extent can progress toward our goals be measured?

3. Are our goals worthy of attainment?

4. On what research have we based our goals?

If the goal lacks comprehensiveness:

To revise goals that lack comprehensiveness, the committee should research best practices in the field of gifted education, looking for topics that deal with instructional, social, and psychological needs of high-potential students, paying particular attention to the needs of traditionally underrepresented groups of gifted students.

1. Are our goals delineated and appropriate for all grade levels, K–12?

2. What needs of gifted students do our goals address?

3. In what ways can we incorporate issues of underrepresented groups of gifted students in our goals?

4. To what extent do our objectives incorporate a continuum of enrichment and acceleration options?

If the goal lacks clarity:

To revise goals that lack clarity, invite various groups of stakeholders to review the goals to be sure each group has the same understanding of the meaning of each goal. Have them examine the goals for ambiguity. Be sure the goals are stated in terms of outcomes.

1. Have we overlooked any stakeholders?

2. What are the outcomes implied by our goal?

3. Do we all agree on the meaning of the goal?

## MAKEOVER EXAMPLE

In the real world, programs for gifted and talented children will likely have two or three broad goals that address the cognitive and affective learning needs of targeted students. In the section that follows, only one goal from the previous section is revised to make it more valid, comprehensive, and clear. Readers can use the revision process illustrated in the strategic plan section of this chapter as one possible model to enhance the overall quality of their own goals and objectives.

### Revised Example: Highland Community School District

Program services for gifted students in the Highland Community Schools will address the specific learning needs of gifted students. To do so, it will

1. Provide a variety of appropriate types and levels of acceleration and enrichment in grades K–12 that are based on students' learning needs.

   (a) *Objective 1:* Conduct a needs assessment to determine: (1) the acceleration and enrichment options currently offered, and (2) the discrepancy between the current offerings and what needs to be offered, K–12, to address the learning needs of the targeted gifted and talented students.

   (b) *Objective 2:* Screen all students beginning at age 4 for early entrance into kindergarten.

   (c) *Objective 3:* In Grades 6–8, an accelerated mathematics curriculum will be offered to students based on their preassessment scores and interest.

2. Provide students with learning experiences at an appropriate level of challenge based on preassessment data.

   (a) *Objective 1:* Provide ongoing professional development and coaching related to preassessment, interpreting preassessment data, and differentiation options related to preassessment data.

   (b) *Objective 2:* Analyze the trends and patterns in gain score data for all students, including the data for gifted and talented students.

3. Design, develop, and implement high-quality curriculum that is supported by research-based models appropriate for gifted students.

   (a) *Objective 1:* Assess the overall curriculum quality for gifted and talented students using the NAGC Curriculum Division's rubric for assessing award-winning curriculum (Purcell, Burns, Tomlinson, Imbeau, & Martin, 2002).

4. Ensure that the curriculum for gifted students is aligned with and extends the regular classroom curriculum.

   (a) *Objective 1:* Gifted education specialists and administrators will evaluate the existing continuum of services to establish linkages with local, state, and national curriculum standards.

## STRATEGIC PLAN FOR CREATING GOALS

**Objective:**   To create or enhance gifted education program goals.

**Evidence:**   A completed set of goals that is aligned, valid, comprehensive, and clear.

**Tasks:**   For creating/enhancing goals

1. Gather together

   - State standards documents for general education and any state standards or regulations for gifted education
   - Local school district standards documents

- State and local achievement data
- Local demographics
- Resources that delineate best practices in gifted education, such as documents from NAGC, state gifted education associations, The National Research Center on the Gifted and Talented, university gifted centers, and works by leading scholars in the field to use in defining appropriate goals
- Research and best practices that address the learning and affective needs of underrepresented populations such as gifted students of color, learning disabled gifted students, and other twice-exceptional populations

2. Have available the gifted program mission statement, the definition of giftedness, and the identification procedures being used by the district/school.

- Analyze the school demographics for patterns and trends.
- Review learning profiles of gifted students to identify academic abilities and weaknesses, interests, students' goals (if available), etc.
- Synthesize a composite portrait of the students identified to receive gifted education services and programs.

3. Create a set of three to six goals based on the data and group deliberation that address students' academic, social, psychological, and career guidance needs.

4. Decide on a set of objectives to further define each goal.

5. Check to make sure that the objectives are written in such a way that they can be evaluated.

6. Distribute goals and objectives to all stakeholders for review.

7. Revise goals and objectives based on feedback from stakeholders.

8. Repeat Tasks 6 and 7 as often as necessary.

9. Submit goals and objectives to all administrators and board of education members for review and approval.

10. Integrate goals into the gifted program services document.

---

*Timeline:* September—Gather materials by contacting sources and/or by searching the Internet. Cull through the research; determine those that are essential readings for the committee; disseminate readings.

*October/November*—Convene the committee; develop goals and objectives.

*December*—Distribute goals and objectives to stakeholders.

*February*—Gather feedback from stakeholders and revise goals.

*March*—Distribute revised goals to stakeholders.

*April*—Revise goals if needed.

*May*—Integrate final goals into the gifted program services document.

# TEMPLATE FOR DESIGNING OR REVISING PROGRAM GOALS

| Trait | Ask Yourself | Report Card for Our Goals | | |
|---|---|---|---|---|
| | | Not Yet | Need Revision | Yes |
| **Alignment** | Are our goals appropriate for the unique learning needs of high-potential children? | | | |
| | Are our goals aligned with the general education goals while reflecting the specific needs of gifted students? | | | |
| | Are our goals aligned with our program mission statement and with the definition of giftedness used by the school or district? | | | |
| | Are the goals defensible in light of state law and policy? | | | |
| **Validity** | Can progress toward the goals be measured and/or documented? | | | |
| | Is each goal delineated by program objectives that further clarify learner outcomes? | | | |
| | Can curriculum and instruction be geared toward the goals? | | | |
| | Are our goals worthy of attainment? | | | |
| | Do our goals reflect research-based best practices in the field of gifted education? | | | |
| **Comprehensiveness** | Do our goals and objectives address the needs of all gifted students, including those traditionally underrepresented? | | | |
| | Do our goals and objectives address the learning needs of gifted students in Grades K–12? | | | |
| | Do our goals address the needs of gifted students, including academic, social, psychological, and career guidance? | | | |

| Trait | Ask Yourself | Report Card for Our Goals | | |
| --- | --- | --- | --- | --- |
| | | Not Yet | Need Revision | Yes |
| **Clarity** | Are our goals and objectives easily understandable by all stakeholders? | | | |
| | Are our goals and objectives stated in terms of outcomes? | | | |
| | Are our goals and objectives unambiguous and clear? | | | |
| | Can goal statements be readily translated into measurable objectives? | | | |

## ADVICE FOR THE SOLE PRACTITIONER

One of the most common errors made when writing program goals is to delineate goals that are good for all children, but not specifically for gifted and talented children. For the gifted education specialist who is trying to craft program goals alone, first look at the mission statement and definition used by the program. Derive three to six goals that are aligned with the mission and definition. To avoid the mistake referenced above, read each goal statement and ask yourself, "Is this goal good for *all* children?" If the answer is yes, revise the goal to address the unique cognitive and affective learning needs of gifted education students served in the community. Repeat the process as often as necessary.

## MUST-READ RESOURCES

There is little information dealing specifically with program goals. Most resources on program development mention the need for goals but give little guidance regarding how to create them. Below are some resources that you may find helpful.

Borland, J. H. (1989). *Planning and implementing programs for the gifted.* New York: Teachers College Press. Although this book is in need of revision, Chapter 3, A System Approach to Planning Programs for the Gifted, and Chapter 9, Evaluating Programs for the Gifted, address program goals.

Callahan, C. M., & Caldwell, M. S. (1999). *A practitioner's guide to evaluating programs for the gifted.* Washington, DC: National Association for Gifted Children. Chapter 4, Program Description and Its Importance in Evaluation, is particularly helpful.

Dick, W., Carey, L., & Carey, J. (2004). *The systematic design of instruction* (5th ed.). New York: Allyn & Bacon. This text provides a good discussion of goals and objectives, including examples.

McNamara, C. (1999). *Basic description of strategic planning.* Retrieved May 24, 2004, from http://www.managementhelp.org/plan_dec/str_plan/basics.htm. This source provides a good section on developing goals, using the SMARTER approach.

Smutny, J. F. (2003). *Designing and developing programs for gifted students.* Thousand Oaks, CA: Corwin. Chapter 1, From Needs and Goals to Program Organization: A Nuts-and-Bolts Guide, makes some mention of program goals.

VanTassel-Baska, J. (2003). *Curriculum planning and instructional design for gifted learners.* Denver, CO: Love. Chapter 6, Developing a Philosophy and Goals for a Gifted Program, is an excellent source of information.

# REFERENCES

Borland, J. H. (1989). *Planning and implementing programs for the gifted.* New York: Teachers College Press.

Callahan, C. M., & Caldwell, M. S. (1999). *A practitioner's guide to evaluating programs for the gifted.* Washington, DC: National Association for Gifted Children.

Landrum, M. S., Callahan, C. M., & Shaklee, B. D. (Eds.). (2001) *Aiming for excellence: Gifted program standards.* Waco, TX: Prufrock Press.

Ornstein, A. C., & Hunkins, F. P. (1998). *Curriculum: Foundations, principles, and issues* (3rd ed.). Boston: Allyn & Bacon.

Purcell, J. H., Burns, D. E., Tomlinson, C.A., Imbeau, M., & Martin, J. (2002). Bridging the gap: A tool and technique to analyze and evaluate gifted education curricular units. *Gifted Child Quarterly, 46*(4), 306–319.

# 7

# Comprehensive Program Design

*Sally M. Reis*

Always design a thing by considering it in its next larger context—a chair in a room, a room in a house, a house in an environment, an environment in a city plan.

—Eliel Saarinen, Finnish architect

In 1972, Commissioner of Education Sidney P. Marland's report to Congress noted that gifted education students "require differentiated educational programs and/or services beyond those normally provided by the regular school program to realize their contribution to self and society" (Marland, 1972, p. 2). More than 30 years have passed since the Marland Report; and hundreds of books have been written about how to develop the comprehensive program plans to which Marland referred.

Based on the mountain of information that has accrued since 1972, what should programs for the gifted and talented look like? There is no single answer to this question because a simple formula for appropriate programs does not exist. Each school's and district's population of highly able students is different from similar students down the road or across state lines. We do know that successful program designs must account for a common set of elements: the learning and social and emotional needs of the specific population of gifted education students, the mission statement of the program, program goals and objectives, personnel resources, budget appropriation, and potential linkages with other institutions and agencies, including schools and colleges.

Sally Reis, author of this chapter on program design, recasts the many topics related to program design into six easy-to-remember, overarching questions: *Who* will be served? *How* will students be identified? *What* program model will be used? *What* services will be offered?

*Where* and *when* will services be provided? By carefully following the procedures set forth in this chapter, we can learn to craft high-quality service delivery plans aligned with program goals and objectives to meet the needs of our students.

This chapter is most closely linked to three other chapters in this guidebook: Developing a Definition of Giftedness, 3; Articulating Gifted Education Program Goals, 6; and Developing a Plan for Evaluating a Program in Gifted Education, 15. Readers may also want to consult with Appendix A, on Establishing Gifted Education Advisory Committees.

## DEFINITION

A comprehensive program design (CPD) is a thoughtful, unified service delivery plan that has a singular purpose: to identify the many, varied ways that will be used to meet the needs of high-potential students. This plan is formulated by a variety of stakeholders, including faculty, administration, and parents. A high-quality program design takes into consideration (a) the unique learning profile of students who are identified for gifted education services within a school district, (b) the level of challenge in the regular curriculum for all students, (c) the ways in which high-potential students are already being served within and outside of the district, and (d) the areas in which high-potential students are lacking in services. A thoughtfully organized CPD also provides enrichment and exploratory opportunities for students with high potential who have not yet fully realized their abilities and talents. One of the most important functions of the CPD is that it incorporates educators' and community members' philosophical and theoretical beliefs as well as practical considerations into a comprehensive plan designed to meet the needs of a specific group of students. In addition, it is critical that educators who develop a CPD consider the importance of a rich and challenging curriculum for all students. A high-quality, regular classroom curriculum should always be the foundation for the learning activities provided in an effective gifted and talented program (Davis & Rimm, 2005; Renzulli, 1986).

The process of crafting a CPD is one of consensus building and decision making regarding a community's philosophy of giftedness and how best to meet the needs of its high-potential students. A CPD seeks to resolve the following six overarching questions: (1) *Who* will be served (defining the population)? (2) *How* will students be identified (developing a system to identify)? (3) *What* program model will be used? (4) *What* types of learning opportunities will be provided (based on philosophy and need)? and (5) and (6) *Where* and *When* will service options (e.g., pull-out, afterschool, summer services such as a Governor's School) be offered across grade and content levels both within the district and outside of the district? The answers to these questions depend on a number of factors, including funding, the availability of trained personnel, and the level of challenge and depth of the regular curriculum.

## RATIONALE

A cohesive, thoughtful, and comprehensive program design, sometimes called a service delivery model, serves a number of critical functions. First, it serves to communicate to teachers, administrators; and parents which student needs (academic, artistic, creative, leadership, instructional, and affective) will be met. Second, a clear program design provides teachers and administrators with an administrative design or plan for implementing and coordinating all aspects of a gifted program. For example, program goals and objectives are built on the foundation provided by the program design; a program evaluation is conducted to assess the effectiveness of the program plan to enhance student achievement, among other things. Finally, a comprehensive program design provides a rationale for the decision-making process. For example, a CPD can describe available acceleration options and the process by which students are identified for acceleration services at various grade levels.

## GUIDING PRINCIPLES OF A COMPREHENSIVE PROGRAM DESIGN (CPD)

- The CPD must demonstrate linkages between what is being provided in district and school classrooms with local and state curriculum standards and gifted program guidelines and regulations.
- A CPD must describe current program services as applied to the regular curriculum as well as to the gifted and talented curriculum.
- The CPD is a foundational, administrative design plan on which program goals and objectives are built (See Chapter 6, Articulating Gifted Education Program Goals).
- The CPD must provide opportunities for expansion of current services across all content areas and grade levels.
- A CPD should take into account a broad range of talents (e.g., academic, artistic, creative, and leadership) and the spectrum of talent development (e.g., latent, emerging, manifest, actualized).
- The CPD must consider affective (e.g., social and emotional) needs as well as academic needs.
- A CPD should describe curriculum philosophy and address grouping issues.
- A CPD must reflect a wide range of broad-based choices that will enable the talents or potential talents of a diverse group of students to be developed. These multifaceted educational opportunities can be provided during the school day, but also after school and in the summer, through the active participation of professional faculty and parents.

## TRAITS OF A HIGH-QUALITY COMPREHENSIVE PROGRAM DESIGN

There are at least seven traits of a high-quality comprehensive program design. Under each of the seven traits, a series of questions is provided to illuminate the varied facets of each trait.

### Derivation of the Services

- Was the CPD based on a needs assessment of the services already provided by the district in the regular classroom and gifted program?
- Has the level of existing curriculum in the district been assessed and considered?
- What are the beliefs of parents and professionals about the nature of gifts and talents and the types of services already provided in the district?

## Comprehensiveness

- Are academic and artistic talents and abilities considered in the CPD?
- In what ways have leadership, creativity, and students' social and emotional needs been addressed, either through programming options and a continuum of services or through targeted professional development for key constituents?
- Does the CPD broadly define the range of services across grade levels?
- What kind of plan has been developed for how, when, and where services will be offered?
- In what ways are plans for expansion and additions to the program outlined?
- Does the CPD include opportunities from within and outside of the district to enable the highest levels of talent to be developed (summer programs, community resources, online opportunities)?

## Practicality

- Does the CPD appear to be reasonable, given the resources and strengths of the district?
- Can district administrators and the board of education provide the budget necessary to deliver the services specified in the comprehensive program design?
- Are program services incorporated into district offerings over time?

## Consistency

- Does the CPD match both the definition of giftedness and the procedures for identification adopted by the district?
- Does the CPD align with the district's philosophy, mission statement, and program goals and objectives?
- Does the definition adhere to state regulations and/or policy?
- Is the CPD linked to students' learning profiles (e. g., interests, academic strengths and weaknesses, cognitive skills strengths and weaknesses, learning style preferences)?

## Clarity

- Is the CPD written in language that is easy to understand by teachers, administrators, and parents who have not participated in the program planning and design committee?
- If a diagram is used, is the diagram or description clear and easily understood?

## Availability

- Is the CPD readily available to principals, teachers, and parents?
- Has training been provided to teachers, specialists, and parents about their responsibilities in the process of talent development?

## Continuation, Extension, and Evaluation

- Who is in charge of ensuring that the program plan is implemented?
- What type of annual report or program evaluation will provide feedback on the success of the CPD, and what types of data will be collected and analyzed?

- Will the CPD be updated and extended as the program is implemented? Will additional resources be sought and additional program services provided over time?
- Has an advisory board been formed to monitor the progress of the CPD?
- How will new members from all constituency groups be continuously recruited for the advisory board?

## EXAMPLE IN NEED OF REVISION

Plainville School District provides its gifted and talented students with a pull-out program in which advanced curriculum units in science and social studies are covered. The program is provided to academically gifted students in Grades 4 and 5 for one hour each week on Wednesday afternoon from 1:00 to 2:00.

## PROCEDURES FOR
## IMPROVING AND ENHANCING
## THE COMPREHENSIVE PROGRAM DESIGN

Two years ago, a group of Plainville faculty and administrators formed a planning committee to create a new strategic plan for the school district. It took a full year for committee members to gather the requisite materials and craft a new, revised strategic plan.

Beth Bergeron, enrichment specialist for Plainville Schools, contacted former members of the Plainville Strategic Planning Committee. She asked them to help review the gifted program design and make recommendations about how to increase its alignment with the district's strategic plan, as well as to students' learning needs. To review systematically all aspects of program design, they used the six questions contained in Table 7.1 to guide their analysis.

The information contained in the table provides readers with a guide for assessing the overall quality of any comprehensive program design and making subsequent refinements. On the left-hand side of the table are listed the six overarching questions discussed at the beginning of this chapter. The next column, Existing Practices, provides readers with a place to identify current plans and policies. The third column, Menu of Possible Options, lists a variety of choices that might be considered as answers to the guiding question and is designed to jump-start readers' thinking about how to increase the alignment and/or comprehensiveness of existing services. The menus are derived from national standards (Landrum, Callahan, & Shaklee, 2001). The last column provides space for readers to make notes about how to revise existing practices to better meet the needs of the targeted population.

For the sake of this example, the Existing Practices column contains a description of the practices used by the Plainville School District. As you read through each question, think through what you would have done had you been Beth Bergeron, enrichment specialist in Plainville Schools. What revisions would you have made to increase the comprehensiveness and alignment between the students' learning needs and the services?

**Table 7.1** Assessing a Comprehensive Program Design

| Guiding Question | Existing Practices | Menu of Possible Options | Revisions Based on the Options Selected |
|---|---|---|---|
| *Who* will be served? | Students scoring in the top 3% on indicators of scholastic aptitude | • Academically gifted<br>• Specific academic aptitude<br>• Creatively gifted<br>• Talented in the visual and performing arts<br>• Leadership<br>• Latent or emergent talents | Students scoring in the upper 10% of the population using local norms |
| *How* will students be identified? | • Measure of scholastic achievement administered in Grade 3<br>• Teacher recommendation | • Performances<br>• Work samples<br>• Conferences<br>• Interviews<br>• Portfolios<br>• Teacher recommendations<br>• Behavior checklists<br>• Self-nomination<br>• Peer nomination<br>• Teacher nomination<br>• Parent nomination<br>• Achievement tests | Multiple criteria approach using:<br><br>• Work samples<br>• Portfolios<br>• Teacher recommendations<br>• Parent nominations<br>• Self-nominations<br>• Peer nominations |
| *What* program model(s) will be used? | No model was specified | • SMPY<br>• Autonomous Learner<br>• Purdue<br>• SEM<br>• The Grid<br>• Talents Unlimited | • SEM<br>• SMPY |
| *What* types of services? | • Field trips<br>• History Day<br>• Science Fair<br>• AP courses: English literature and biology | **Enrichment and Differentiation Options**<br><br>• Preassessment in the regular classroom<br>• Open-ended learning activities<br>• Choices in learning activities and products<br>• Tiered lessons<br>• Curriculum compacting<br>• Purposefully selected field trips<br>• Guest speakers<br>• Purposefully selected contests and competitions (e.g., History Day) | **Enrichment and Differentiation Options**<br><br>• Preassessment<br>• Curriculum compacting<br>• Purposefully selected field trips that align with the regular curriculum<br>• Purposefully selected contests and competitions that align with the regular curriculum<br>• Afterschool enrichment |

| Guiding Question | Existing Practices | Menu of Possible Options | Revisions Based on the Options Selected |
|---|---|---|---|
| | | • Supplementary enrichment programs (e.g., Junior Great Books) <br> • Mentorships <br> • After-school enrichment programs <br> • Saturday programs <br> • Individual and small group investigations <br> • Governor's Schools | |
| | | **Acceleration Options** <br> • Early entrance to kindergarten <br> • Multiage grouping <br> • Single subject acceleration <br> • Grade skipping <br> • Advanced content in cluster groups <br> • Concurrent enrollment <br> • AP courses | **Acceleration Options** <br> • Early entrance to kindergarten <br> • Single subject acceleration <br> • Pre-AP and AP courses |
| | | **Guidance and Counseling Services** <br> • Bibliotherapy <br> • Small-group sessions on selected topics (e.g., effective communication, listening skills, conflict resolution, perfectionism, gender issues, stress management) <br> • Career counseling | **Guidance and Counseling Services** <br> • Small-group sessions on selected topics <br> • Career counseling |
| *Where* will services be provided? | • Resource room <br> • Regular classroom | • Resource room <br> • Regular classroom <br> • Community <br> • Local museums and centers <br> • College or university | • Resource room <br> • Regular classroom |
| *When* will services be provided? | • During school | • Before school <br> • During school <br> • Afterschool <br> • Summer <br> • Saturday | • During school <br> • Afterschool |

# MAKEOVER EXAMPLE

Having gathered all of the pertinent information and taken the time to organize and review the data, Beth Bergeron and the other committee members were ready to begin the decision-making process.

## Who?

At their first meeting, the group realized that the demographics of the public school population had changed since the gifted education program was designed eight years earlier. The district had an increasing number of families from India and Sudan and, most recently, had seen an influx of Asian families who were employed at two, large, well-known resorts located in an adjacent town. The demographics of the students in the gifted program no longer matched the demographics of the town.

To increase the match between the town demographics and the demographics of the program, committee members decided to expand the number of students identified for services. They agreed to identify up to 10% of the student population using local norms.

Committee members also decided to identify academically talented students in Grades K–5 in their first year of the revised program. In the second year, they agreed to expand the identification process to address students in Grades 6–12. They also expressed a desire to identify talented children, K–12, in the third year of the plan.

## How?

To ensure more equitable access to the program, committee members agreed to change the procedures used to identify students. Instead of using only two measures—a standardized measure of student aptitude and a teacher recommendation—they decided that they would use a multiple-criteria approach. Equally important, all measures would have an equal weight. No longer would students need to score at least 130 on a measure of scholastic aptitude before other measures would be considered.

Committee members looked carefully at their student population and decided on several important indicators. Most important, they included student work samples and portfolios. These pieces of evidence would surely demonstrate some of the abilities and talents of their underrepresented populations. In addition, they included teacher recommendations and peer nominations. Many of the teachers were struck by how easily students identified the leaders and artists in their midst, and this validated their decision to expand the range of talents in their comprehensive program design.

## What Program Model(s)?

Committee members considered several program models before deciding on a blend of two: the Schoolwide Enrichment Model (SEM) (Renzulli & Reis, 1985, 1997) and Study for Mathematically Precocious Youth (SMPY) (Assouline & Lupkowski-Shoplik, 2003; Benbow & Stanley, 1986). They chose the SEM because it included a behavioral definition of giftedness (i.e., above-average ability, task commitment, and creativity) that would provide a more inclusive approach to gifted education service, and it addressed the learning needs of all students—including those with demonstrated and potential gifts and talents—through a continuum of enrichment services. They also chose the SMPY model because it focused on the unique learning needs of mathematically gifted young people. The emerging learning profile of students in Plainville illuminated a population with very high potential in mathematical reasoning. Both models linked closely with students' learning needs.

## What Types of Services Will Be Offered?

Beth and her colleagues carefully reviewed the services that were currently offered and made two important observations. First, the number of services—three, to be exact— was very limited. Second, they concluded that current services were not aligned with students' cognitive and affective needs. They agreed to add a variety of services from all three areas: enrichment and differentiation, acceleration, and guidance and counseling. With respect to enrichment and differentiation, they recommended that each teacher be trained in and use preassessment in the regular classroom to provide appropriate, ongoing levels of challenge for all students, not only those with unique gifts and talents. In addition, curriculum compacting would help teachers eliminate course material for students who had already mastered large portions of curriculum content. They also decided to expand field trips and competitions so that they spanned the content areas: social studies, science, mathematics, the arts, and language arts. At the same time, they also made a clear recommendation that each field trip and competition be linked closely to and enhance the regular curriculum. Guest speakers, who had made small and large accomplishments in the community, were added to the assembly program for all students to encourage and support emerging, young leaders.

Committee members made a commitment to an afterschool program, called Power-Hour, one day a week that was open to all students, Grades 1–5. In the first quarter of the year, the focus of the activities was science, and in the second quarter, the focus was history, and so forth through the last quarter so that four content areas were covered throughout the course of the school year. During each Power-Hour, three teachers—from regular education classrooms and the gifted program—monitored highly motivating games and activities related to the targeted content area. Often, students were invited to select their activities. At other times, classroom teachers recommended particular activities for small groups of children based on students' interests, learning strengths, or need for review. These enrichment and differentiation activities provided for a much closer link to the academic needs of their changing population of gifted education students. In addition, the activities served as fun and engaging ways for underserved students to demonstrate and refine their not-yet-developed talents and abilities.

Finally, the committee recommended that pull-out services be reconfigured to encourage and address students' desire to complete individual and small-group independent investigations. These direct services to students had proven powerful in the past because they increased student motivation and provided ongoing levels of challenge for interested students.

Beth and her colleagues also recommended adding three acceleration options: early entrance to kindergarten, single-subject acceleration, and pre-AP and AP (Advanced Placement) courses. The addition of early entrance to kindergarten was considered the most effective way to deal with very young children with advanced abilities (Colangelo,

Assouline, & Gross, 2004; Rogers, 2002). By allowing them to advance early in their school career, the committee was convinced they would better meet the cognitive and affective needs of their students and, concurrently, reduce the number of parents who requested grade skipping in subsequent grades. They decided to use the Iowa Acceleration Scale (Assouline, Colangelo, Lupkowski-Shoplik, Lipsomb, & Forstadt, 2003) to help them make important decisions about which students would be good candidates for whole-grade acceleration, K–8. Single-subject acceleration was added to serve the needs of students who demonstrated advanced abilities in one or two content areas.

Furthermore, Beth and her colleagues reviewed the current AP course offerings at the high school. Only two courses were offered. The committee agreed that at least five core AP courses should be offered as soon as possible: English literature, biology, U.S. history, calculus, and statistics. The decision to emphasize mathematics was based on the learning profile of their student population. These additions not only increased advanced-level options at the secondary level, but also had relatively low impact on the school district budget.

In addition, the committee made two other recommendations with respect to the AP program, a cornerstone of the SMPY program model. They asked Beth to explore the pre-AP courses, especially those that could be offered via Vertical Teaming in mathematics, science, and English; that could be offered in the middle grades; and that might be especially appropriate for students who had potential but who had not yet demonstrated strong abilities. The committee asked Beth to come back with a proposal regarding which pre-AP courses might be especially appropriate for Plainville students. The second request of Beth was to research the providers and fee structures of AP distance learning programs, such as Virtual High Schools (VHS) and Apex Learning. They asked Beth to provide the group with recommendations regarding the feasibility and budget implications for expanding their AP course offerings through technology.

Finally, Beth and her colleagues added two guidance and counseling services. The first consisted of small-group discussions around students' affective needs (e.g., perfectionism, stress reduction, multipotentiality, and gender issues). Beth felt strongly that these discussions should be held in the resource room for cross-grade groups of interested students. The second counseling service was college counseling. These services would be offered in the resource room, begin in middle school, and culminate in a wide array of services in high school.

## Where?

Plainville's reconfigured services for high-achieving students were distributed across the regular classroom and the resource room. Beth and her colleagues agreed that small-group and independent investigations, as well as the small-group discussions focused on affective and counseling issues, should be held in the resource room. They also concluded that many of the enrichment and differentiation activities would take place in the regular classroom. This made a great deal of sense to them because many of these activities were good for all children, not just those with potential or manifest abilities.

## When?

As much as possible, Beth and her colleagues tried to keep their activities within the school day. This was important for Plainville students whose parents often worked on the weekends. For the Power-Hour, which took place after regular school hours, they made sure that they had school buses available to drop students close to their homes. They discovered that parents often worked second and third shifts in the local resorts and were not always available to transport their children after the regular school day ended.

Beth and her colleagues reviewed the principles that guided the program design process, which were included earlier in this chapter. After reviewing, they determined that they had made considerable progress. Plainville's revised program design:

- Demonstrated much stronger linkages between Plainville classrooms and the NAGC standards related to program design
- Delineated services that would be delivered in the regular curriculum and the gifted education curriculum
- Targeted several areas for program expansion as it relates to identification (i.e., incorporating more grade levels and additional talent areas) and program services (i.e., distance learning)
- Targeted both academic and artistic and creative talents
- Included interventions to deal with students' cognitive and affective learning needs
- Provided for multifaceted educational opportunities within the school day and afterone word school

They realized that their new program design was a beginning and that it would change over time. There were many areas where they could—even now—tweak it to make it more comprehensive and/or aligned with students' learning needs. For the time being, however, the revised plan did a far better job of reflecting student needs and the school district philosophy than what had previously been in place.

## STRATEGIC PLAN FOR CREATING THE PROGRAM DESIGN

Beth and her colleagues reflected on the process they had used to create a comprehensive strategic plan for Plainville. They had met regularly for about a year and had been involved in a wide variety of tasks. Their tasks clustered into the following stages:

### Stage 1 (3 to 6 months): Learning and Starting to Plan

The committee read selected chapters from seminal works (Renzulli, 1986, Chapter 1; Davis & Rimm, 2005, Chapter 3), reviewed other program design plans, visited programs, and conducted a needs assessment. The committee carefully reviewed options currently available for talented students across a broad spectrum of areas (e.g., academics, arts, guidance, social-emotional). They considered ways to involve staff in ownership and planning. They also reviewed state and national standards such as the NAGC program standards (Landrum et al., 2001)

### Stage 2 (6 to 9 months): Planning, Seeking Consensus, and Input

The districtwide committee prepared a preliminary program design and presented findings from the needs assessment and background research to focus groups of faculty, parents, and board of education members. They also gathered input and addressed budget considerations.

To build the optimal conditions for consensus among diverse members, they adopted the "80% rule." When 80% of the committee agreed on components of the CPD, a decision would be made to move ahead with the planning. Use of this rule would prevent them from getting bogged down in the process.

### Stage 3 (9 to 12 months): Developing an Initial Plan for Comprehensive Program Design

The committee developed an initial CPD plan. They included what would be done over a preliminary period to ensure that all key constituent groups were aware of their roles and responsibilities.

### Stage 4 (1 to 3 years): Revising and Modifying the CPD Based on Evaluation, Feedback, and Students Needs

The plan was implemented and progress was evaluated regularly to make decisions about what would be effective for gifted students' continuous progress. A program leader or administrator was identified to monitor what would be done over the two- to three-year period to ensure that all key constituent groups understood that program design was an ongoing, continuing approach with increasing levels of staff support and input. The committee continued to evaluate and assess faculty involvement and professional development to analyze progress toward program goals.

During the process of CPD development, the following program components were remodeled and/or developed:

1. A needs assessment was completed to gather information about the needs of gifted and talented students and what the school district was already providing.

2. A district definition of talented and gifted students was adopted that reflected state regulations.

3. Consistency was considered, as the definition of giftedness needed to match the identification system and the programming model or services provided.

4. To that end, an identification system was developed that matched the definition and state regulations.

5. Program goals matching the definition and the needs assessment were developed and included clearly defined services that would be provided to students.

6. A comprehensive program design (including curriculum, program services for students across grade levels, grouping options, and teaching responsibilities) was based on the program needs assessments, definition, goals, and desired outcomes.

7. Curriculum development (for students in a separate program) and curriculum differentiation (within both heterogeneous and homogeneous classrooms) were implemented based on the needs assessment, program goals, and design discussed above.

8. Professional development was provided to classroom teachers, counselors, and specialists. Gifted education specialists with higher levels of background and training in gifted education were selected and trained for teaching more advanced student offerings.

9. Program evaluation guided the continued development and expansion of program services for identified students.

**Figure 7.1** A Flowchart for Designing a Comprehensive Program

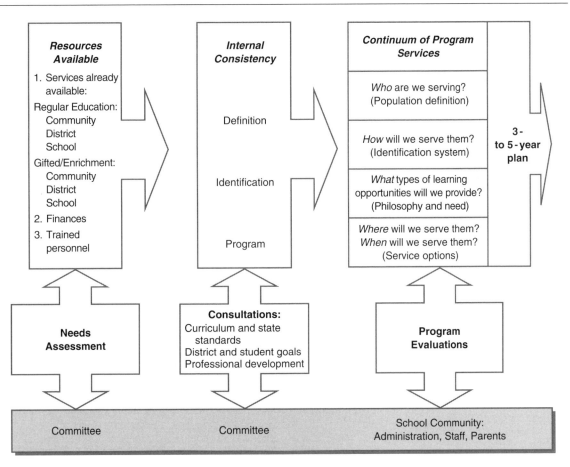

## ADVICE FOR THE SOLE PRACTITIONER

Because a CPD is designed to be an all-encompassing roadmap for the development of programs and services tailored to the needs of gifted students in your district, the process of developing and implementing a CPD can seem like an overwhelming task for an individual. A sole practitioner who is interested or charged with the responsibility for designing a comprehensive continuum of program services should consider assembling a small committee of interested faculty, staff, administrators, and parents to provide critical insight and support (see Appendix A). The goals of this group are to arrive at a consensus about how to meet the needs of gifted and talented students and about what a comprehensive program for gifted and talented students should provide. The series of questions raised in the chapter are critical to this process and can serve to guide group discussions and decisions: *Who* needs special services (defining the population)? *How* will they be identified and selected? *What* types of learning opportunities will be provided (based on philosophy and need)? *Where* and *When* the services will be provided?

## REFERENCES

Assouline, S. G., Colangelo, N., Lupkowski-Shoplik, A. E., Lipscomb, J., & Forstadt, L. (2003). *The Iowa Acceleration Scale* (2nd ed.). Scottsdale, AZ: Great Potential Press.

Assouline, S. G., & Lupkowski-Shoplik, A. E. (2003). *Developing mathematical talent: A guide to challenging and educating gifted students in math.* Waco, TX: Prufrock Press.

Benbow, C. P., & Stanley, J. (1986). SMPY's model; for teaching mathematically precocious students. In J. S. Renzulli (Ed.), *Systems and models for developing programs for the gifted and talented* (pp. 1–25). Mansfield Center, CT: Creative Learning Press.

Colangelo, N., Assouline, S. G., & Gross, M. U. M. (2004). *A nation deceived: How schools hold back America's brightest students.* Iowa City: IA: University of Iowa.

Davis, G. A., & Rimm, S. B. (2005). *Education of the gifted and talented* (5th ed.). Boston: Pearson.

Landrum, M. S., Callahan, C. M., & Shaklee, B. D. (Eds.). (2001). *Aiming for excellence: Gifted program standards.* Waco, TX: Prufrock Press.

Marland, S. P., Jr. (1972). *Education of the gifted and talented: Vol. 1, Report to the Congress of the United States.* Washington, DC: U.S. Government Printing Office.

Renzulli, J. S. (Ed.) (1986). *Systems and models for developing programs for the gifted and talented.* Mansfield Center, CT: Creative Learning Press.

Renzulli, J. S., & Reis, S. M. (1985). *The schoolwide enrichment model: A comprehensive plan for educational excellence.* Mansfield Center, CT: Creative Learning Press.

Renzulli, J. S., & Reis, S. M. (1997). *The schoolwide enrichment model: A how-to guide for educational excellence.* Mansfield Center, CT: Creative Learning Press.

Rogers, K. B. (2002). *Reforming gifted education: Matching the program to the child.* Scottsdale, AZ: Great Potential Press.

# 8

# Curriculum for Gifted Education Students

*Deborah E. Burns, Jeanne H. Purcell, and Holly L. Hertberg*

What we want is to see the child in pursuit of knowledge, and not knowledge in pursuit of the child.

—George Bernard Shaw

Do you remember the phrase, coined by political consultant James Carville, "It's the economy, stupid"? It is the phrase Carville invented to keep everyone *on message* in the presidential campaign of 1992. The phrase caught on with the American public and helped to guide William Jefferson Clinton to the presidency in the same year. William Schmidt, research coordinator for the Third International Mathematics and Science Study (TIMSS), capitalized on the popularity of Carville's political slogan. He talked about the relationship between what students study and how deeply they learn and concluded with a message for educators: "It's the curriculum, stupid" (Viadaro, 1997).

Since Schmidt's clever use of Carville's political slogan, much research has been conducted about the nature and characteristics of effective schools. Research has begun to confirm the connection between curriculum and student achievement (Levine & Lezotte, 1990; Marzano, 2000, 2003; Scheerens & Bosker, 1997).

With this powerful research about student achievement as a backdrop, Deborah Burns, Jeanne Purcell, and Holly Hertberg turn our attention to another key feature of gifted education: curriculum. It is at the heart of all programs and services for these students and is one of the seven critical criteria in the National Association for Gifted Children's *Pre-K–Grade 12 Gifted Program Standards* (Landrum & Shaklee, 1998; Landrum, Callahan, & Shaklee, 2001 [see Appendix B]). While there are connections between curriculum and all the other sections in the guidebook, it is most naturally aligned with the following chapters: Articulating Gifted Education Program Goals, 6; Comprehensive Program Design, 7; Selecting

Learning Resources 11; and Aligning Gifted in the Education of the Gifted Education Services With General Education, 17.

## DEFINITION

Many definitions of curriculum exist, and they range from specific to general. Some believe that curriculum includes all the experiences children have in school; this view may be rooted in Dewey's (1938) definition of experience and education.

For the purposes of this chapter, we define curriculum specifically. Curriculum is a design plan that fosters the purposeful, proactive organization, sequencing, and management of interactions among the teacher, the learners, and the content knowledge, understandings, and skills we want students to acquire. This specific definition is aligned with the work of Taba (1962) and Bruner (1966).

As a plan for learning, a basic curriculum document can describe the content that students are to learn, the teaching and learning activities that support student achievement, and the methods for assessing student attainment. A more comprehensive curriculum document also describes the resources that students and teachers use to support learning, the assignments and products students create to practice or demonstrate their learning; the extension activities that help students transfer and apply learned content to relevant; new, and/or more complex situations; and the time allocations recommended for the lessons and learning activities.

Another component described in many curriculum documents suggests the grouping strategies recommended for teaching and learning. Students may work alone, in pairs, in small groups, or in large groups as they engage in varied activities. One of the most frequently cited purposes for varied grouping strategies in gifted education is to address the unique characteristics of advanced-level learners.

Curriculum differentiation, another component of many curriculum plans, is a process teachers use to enhance student learning by matching various curriculum components to characteristics shared by subgroups of learners (e.g., cognitive ability, prior knowledge, learning style preferences, interests, habits of mind, or learning rate). The most effective and efficient differentiation practices involve proactive changes in the depth or breadth of student learning.

These curriculum components—content, assessment, introduction, grouping practices, teaching strategies, learning activities, resources, products, extensions, and modifications—are the building blocks for any curriculum material. Curriculum developers modify these components, singly or in combination, to address the goals and purposes of their models. Practitioners use the components in a similar way. They modify them, singly or in combination, to address the learning needs of their students, including those with high abilities.

## RATIONALE

The most powerful reason for an intense focus on high-quality curriculum is student achievement. The literature is replete with citations about the central role that a viable curriculum contributes to increased student achievement (Lipsey & Wilson, 1993; Marzano, 2000, 2003; National Education Commission on Time and Learning, 1994; Schmidt, McKnight, & Raizen, 1996). Most recently, Marzano (2003) completed a meta-analysis of school-level factors associated with student achievement. His meta-analysis suggests that there are five school-level factors associated with student achievement: guaranteed and viable curriculum, challenging goals and feedback, parent and community involvement, safe and orderly environment, and collegiality and professionalism. He then rank ordered the factors according to their statistical strength to impact student achievement. His research suggests that a guaranteed and viable curriculum holds the greatest power to affect student achievement.

While all students benefit from a high-quality curriculum, two subsets of students will benefit especially from a viable, rich curriculum that contains escalating levels of challenge. The first subset includes gifted and talented children. For over half a century, leaders in the field of gifted education have advanced our understanding of the many varied ways curriculum and curriculum models can address the needs of these learners (Betts, 1985; Feldhusen & Kolloff, 1986; Gallagher, 1975; Gallagher, et al., 1982; Guilford, 1967; Kaplan, 1974, 1986; Maker, 1982; Marland, 1972; Meeker & Meeker, 1986; Renzulli, 1977, 1988; Renzulli, Leppien, & Hays, 2000; Stepien, Gallagher, & Workman, 1993; Taba, 1962; Tomlinson, 1998; Tomlinson et al., 2002; Treffinger, 1986; VanTassel-Baska & Little, 2003; Ward, 1961).

The second subset of children who stand to benefit from rich, high-quality curriculum includes promising students who have been traditionally underrepresented in programs for the gifted (National Research Council, 2002). Increasingly, information is available about a small number of structured, rigorous preparation programs that are designed to increase the likelihood of these students' academic success in high school and beyond. See the section on special programs for underserved populations later in this chapter.

## GUIDING PRINCIPLES AND BEST PRACTICES

Curriculum is a proactive plan that fosters the purposeful sequencing of interactions among teachers, students, and content knowledge. It is based on a number of important principles that apply to the pre-K–12 curriculum.

- A comprehensive curriculum plan or model includes essential components, including, but not limited to, content, assessments, grouping strategies, an introduction, teaching strategies, learning activities, products, resources, and modifications for learner characteristics.
- The use of a comprehensive and aligned set of curriculum components makes curriculum more effective and increases the extent to which it can enhance student achievement.
- Curriculum components can be modified, singly or in combination, to address the learning needs and strengths of diverse learners.
- A curriculum for high-potential students should be aligned with state and national standards and the district-level scope and sequence; it should supplement and extend the regular classroom curriculum.
- The mission statement of the gifted education program should describe the kind of learning the program intends to enhance.
- The curriculum for gifted and talented students should be inclusive of many theories to meet the diverse learning needs of these young people.

- District curriculum and curriculum model(s) for the gifted education program should be strongly aligned with the program's mission statement.
- The exemplary characteristics of the various curriculum components can be used as criteria with which to evaluate its effectiveness.
- An implemented curriculum should be evaluated to measure its impact on student achievement.

# TRAITS OF A HIGH-QUALITY CURRICULUM FOR ALL STUDENTS, INCLUDING THOSE WITH HIGH ABILITIES

The following 10 traits are components of a high-quality, comprehensive curriculum. Focusing questions are provided for each trait to clarify its meaning.

1. **Content:** Broad statements about what we want students to know, understand, and be able to do

   - Do the content goals for the curriculum unit address the concepts, principles, generalizations, skills, and dispositions that are core to the discipline?
   - Do the concepts, principles, and generalizations align with local, state, and/or national standards?
   - Are the content goals clearly stated?
   - Are the content goals developmentally appropriate, and do they align with the grade-level expectations, K–12?
   - Do the content goals align with the other curriculum components?

2. **Assessments:** The varied tools and techniques teachers use to measure students' acquisition of content knowledge

   - Are the assessments aligned with the content goals?
   - Does the unit contain preassessments, ongoing assessments, and a postassessment?
   - Are the assessments efficient (i.e., respectful of students' and teachers' time), reliable, valid, and motivating?
   - Do the assessments contain rubrics with a high enough ceiling and low enough baseline to pinpoint the current levels of the full range of learners and track their progress throughout the course of the unit?

3. **Introduction:** A forward or transition to the curriculum unit

   - Is the introduction explicitly stated?
   - Does it align with the other components?
   - Does it heighten student attention, enjoyment, or interest?

4. **Grouping strategies:** The varied approaches for arranging students for effective teaching and learning in the classroom

   - Do the grouping strategies reflect students' learning strengths and needs?
   - Are the grouping strategies aligned with the content goals, teaching methods, and learning activities?

5. **Teaching Activities:** Activities designed and/or conducted by the teacher to provide students with the information, challenge, support, and ongoing experiences they need to process knowledge and improve performance related to the lesson's learning goal(s)

   - Are the teaching strategies aligned with the content? With students' learning profiles?
   - Are teaching strategies varied?
   - Do they promote students' cognitive engagement?
   - Do the selected teaching methods provide support for students' thinking and their active involvement with the content and skills to be learned?

6. **Learning Activities:** Cognitive tasks for students that are designed to develop the knowledge, understanding, and skills specified in the content and learning goals

   - Are the learning activities aligned with the content goals, teaching methods, and students' learning profiles?
   - Are the learning activities motivating?
   - Do they promote student thinking and transfer?
   - Do the learning activities provide for appropriate levels of challenge for various groups of students?

7. **Products:** Performances, assignments, or work samples created by students that provide evidence of student learning

   - Are the products and assignments aligned with the content goals, teaching methods, and students' learning profiles?
   - Are they authentic to the discipline?
   - Are they varied and motivating?
   - Are the products efficient?
   - Can the products be used to assess student learning?

8. **Resources:** Materials that support the learning and teaching process

   - Are the resources aligned with the content goals, teaching methods, and students' learning profiles?
   - Are they authentic and varied across the unit?
   - Are they motivating?
   - Are the resources appropriate for varying students' language, reading, and cognitive proficiencies?

9. **Extensions:** Preplanned or serendipitous experiences that emerge from the learning objectives, activities, teacher or student reflection, and students' interests or needs

   - Are the extension experiences linked to the content goals?
   - Are they authentic and open ended?
   - Are they aligned with students' interests and strengths?
   - Are extension activities practical and efficient?
   - Do the learning experiences enrich or enhance student learning?

10. **Differentiation:** Curriculum modifications made by the teacher to accommodate students' varied levels of prior knowledge, cognitive skills, habits of mind, learning styles, or interests

- Is the differentiation strategy developed proactively?
- Are the differentiation experiences aligned with the content goals and students' differences?
- Are the differentiation strategies respectful, relevant, and motivating for learners at all places on the learning continuum?
- Are the strategies effective in promoting increased achievement?

## EXAMPLES IN NEED OF REVISION

### A Taste of Greece—Interdisciplinary Greek Festival, Grade 6

This interdisciplinary, ancient civilizations unit outline was developed by sixth-grade, middle-school teachers. Designed for four classes, it culminated in a well-attended parents' night during which students demonstrated what they had learned about Greece. The curriculum components for this unit are listed down the left side of the accompanying chart, and a description of each component is included in the right-hand column. Compare each component in the chart with the attributes of the corresponding high-quality curriculum components explained in the previous section. Recognizing that it is impossible to remodel the whole unit, prioritize the two to three components that are most in need of revision. Then, compare your thinking with the revisions that are listed in the section on Revising the Example.

Two additional examples follow this Grade 6 interdisciplinary outline. The two additional examples use the same format, but they target different grade levels and disciplines. The first revision is a Grade 1 outline dealing with astronomy, and the other is a Grade 11 American literature lesson outline.

| Component | Original Unit Outline |
| --- | --- |
| **Content** | • Social Studies: Students will increase their knowledge of Greek culture.<br>• Math: Students will convert U.S. money to Greek equivalents.<br>• Math: Students will make Greek foods and use appropriate fractions when measuring ingredients.<br>• English: Students will learn vocabulary from Greece, make acrostic poem, and learn to say and sing the Greek national anthem.<br>• Science: Students will learn about Greek medicine and scientists.<br>• Art: Students will make Greek masks. |
| **Assessment** | • Survey from parents who attended Parents' Night |
| **Introduction** | • Students will read about ancient Greece in their textbooks. |
| **Grouping strategies** | • Mostly large-group instruction will take place.<br>• Students will work in small groups of their choosing to create the Greek festival for parents. Group choices include mask making, preparing and making Greek food, and singing and acting the Greek national anthem, in Greek. |

| Component | Original Unit Outline |
|---|---|
| **Teaching activities** | • Have students copy vocabulary words into their notebooks.<br>• Show students pictures and recipes of Greek foods.<br>• Provide students with ditto with Greek and American coin and dollar equivalents and then provide practice problems. |
| **Learning activities** | • Have students read their chapter about Greece.<br>• Ask them to do the questions at the end of the chapter.<br>• Give students time to do their group work. |
| **Products** | • Greek festival for parents<br>• Acrostic poems<br>• Practice problems involving U.S. and Greek money conversions |
| **Resources** | • History textbook<br>• Greek myths |

## An Example in Need of Revision: Groundhog Day, Grade K–Grade 1

The accompanying outline reflects one or two lessons developed originally by kindergarten teachers. They expressed the belief that the legend of Groundhog Day was an opportunity to teach students about science and social studies.

| Component | Original Unit Outline |
|---|---|
| **Content** | • Hard to tell; nothing was written down |
|  | • Appeared to be an attempt to create linkages between science and social studies through the annual event of Groundhog Day |
| **Assessment** | None |
| **Introduction** | The teacher read a children's story about Punxsutawney Phil, *Punxsutawney Phil and His Weather Wisdom*, by Julia Spencer Mourtran. |
| **Grouping strategies** | Whole group activity completed during morning meeting time. |
| **Teaching activities** | The teacher explained Groundhog Day: "Punxsutawney Phil is a famous groundhog. If he sees his shadow on February 2, he goes back into his winter home. There, he will sleep through six more weeks of cold, winter weather. If Punxsutawney Phil does not see his shadow, he thinks of it as a sign of spring. He stays above ground." |
| **Learning activities** | The teacher created a T chart with "yes" and "no" written under either side of the chart. She gave each student a small cutout of a groundhog and asked each student to guess whether Punxsutawney Phil would see his shadow. Students who predicted "yes" placed their groundhog in the "Yes" column on the chart. Those that predicted "no" put their groundhog on the other side of the chart. |
| **Products** | T chart |
| **Resources** | • Book about Punxsutawney Phil<br>• Tape<br>• 28 cutout pictures of little groundhogs |

### An Example in Need of Revision: Robert Frost

Two teachers in the English department of a medium-sized, suburban high school used the following lesson outline to guide their instruction with 11th graders over four days. It deals with an important literary genre: lyric poetry. The representative author is Robert Frost, an important American writer whose work has widely influenced poetry in the 20th and 21st centuries.

| Component | Original Unit Outline |
|---|---|
| **Content** | • Language Arts: Students will learn about the American lyric poet Robert Frost by engaging in conversations about the themes of the selected poems: life's choices and obligations. |
| **Assessment** | • Answers to questions at the end of the poetry selections: "The Road Not Taken" and "Stopping by Woods on a Snowy Evening" by Robert Frost |
| **Introduction** | • Whole-class silent reading about the biographical information provided about Frost in their anthology<br>• Lecture about Robert Frost's life |
| **Grouping strategies** | • Whole-group discussion about the "correct" answers to the questions at the end of the selected poems in their anthology |
| **Teaching activities** | • Teacher-led, whole-class discussion about the content of the two lyric poems; 3–4 students do most of the talking |
| **Learning activities** | • Listening, taking notes, sometimes doodling |
| **Products** | • Students' answers to the questions in their anthology that follow each poem |
| **Resources** | • Anthology |

## PROCEDURES FOR ENHANCING OR IMPROVING A CURRICULUM UNIT

- If the content is superficial, fact-oriented, or a list of activities, consult high school and college textbooks, national council standards, and/or state standards for the concepts and principles that guide this area and revise accordingly.
- If the assessments are missing or not aligned, review the content and develop an aligned set of rubrics, pre- and postassessments, and ongoing assessments.
- If the introduction is missing key features or lacking quality, determine which key feature(s) is missing and/or lacking quality and revise to improve the comprehensiveness or overall quality. For example, if there is no rationale, make a plan to show students what experts in the discipline do, question, develop, or investigate.
- If grouping strategies are missing or lacking, ensure a variety of formats that will help students acquire the content objectives.

- If teaching strategies emphasize one type of teaching or if they are missing, ensure a variety of teaching formats that (1) are aligned with the content, (2) address students' learning profiles, and (3) require students to derive their own understanding of the content.
- If the learning activities require little mental processing from students, provide varied constructivist learning opportunities that require students to infer and induce their own understanding about the essential concepts and principles.
- If products are singular in nature and/or not aligned with the content, ensure alignment, vary the format to accommodate students' expression styles, and/or offer choice with respect to format.
- If resources are of only one or two types, seek out and include a variety of engaging primary and secondary resources to provide appropriate challenge for students at different reading and cognitive levels. The Internet is invaluable.
- If extensions are missing or unrelated to the learning objective, ensure alignment, seek real-world problems/issues and subjects related to the representative topic, or ask content area specialists to help brainstorm authentic extensions.
- If differentiation is missing or not aligned with the content or students' learning needs, a wide variety of adjustments may be made based on the nature of the content and learner needs, including (1) inviting learners to transfer their skills and thinking to a related, more complex or less complex problem, (2) providing students with additional raw data to examine and question, (3) using more or less scaffolding to support concept attainment, and (4) using Socratic questions that require more or less inference to scaffold students' understanding of the central principles.

## MAKEOVER EXAMPLES

### Ancient Civilizations— A Study of Similarities and Contrasts

| Component | Comment About Original Component | Examples of Makeover Options |
|---|---|---|
| **Content** | Original objectives are activities. | • Understand that geography, resources, and climate shaped early Greek and Incan cultures.<br>• Understand that all cultures share common elements that shape people's lives: social organization, language, customs and traditions, art and literature, religion, economic systems, and forms of government. |
| **Assessment** | • Original assessments were not aligned with the content. | • Preassessment: Ask students to complete a Venn diagram in which they list the commonalities and differences between two early cultures: Greek and Incan.<br>• Postassessment: Meeting of the Minds: Students are invited to create a dialogue between two famous archeologists who studied ancient Greece and the |

*(Continued)*

(Continued)

| Component | Comment About Original Component | Examples of Makeover Options |
|---|---|---|
| | | Incan culture, respectively. In the dialogue, the characters will compare and contrast the two ancient civilizations across selected cultural universals. The dialogue can be written, audiotaped, or dramatized. |
| **Introduction** | Introduction is not motivating. | • Show pictures of Greek and Incan architecture, art, stories; use of primary source material from Hiram Bingham's diary.<br>• Provide a Venn diagram as an advance organizer to help students see the similarities and differences among cultures. |
| **Grouping strategies** | Strategies lack variety. | • Provide large-group instruction for unit introductions and debriefings.<br>• Assign small-group work comparing the cultures, organized around the elements of culture; group assignment based on student interest. |
| **Teaching activities** | Activities are not varied and do not require mental processing. | • Teach inductively; provide information and resources, and ask students to derive information about each culture, as well as principles about the relationships between geography, resources, climate, and culture.<br>• Use Socratic questioning to guide students' thinking. |
| **Learning activities** | Learning activities are not constructivist in nature. | • Have students examine high school texts to identify the major elements of culture; have students explain why the cultural elements are not always the same in each book. |
| | | • Ask students to examine old *National Geographic* articles that chronicle Bingham's discovery of the lost city of Machu Picchu and his theories about the rise, evolution, and disappearance of the Inca culture.<br>• In small groups, invite students to compare the geography, resources, and climate of Peru and Greece. Ask students to suggest theories about why religion, ceremonies, art and architecture, trade, and family life evolved the way they did. |
| **Products** | Products are not aligned with the content, and they lack variety. | • Venn diagrams<br>• Students' derived principles about the factors that influence culture<br>• Meeting of the Minds essays, audiotapes, or performances |

| Component | Comment About Original Component | Examples of Makeover Options |
|---|---|---|
| **Resources** | Resources lack variety. | • History textbook<br>• Selected literature, pictures of art work and architecture from the two cultures<br>• Maps and globes<br>• Selected high school anthropology textbooks<br>• *National Geographic* magazines or CDs |
| **Extensions** | There were no extensions. | • Research the recent controversy regarding the ownership of artifacts taken by Bingham from Machu Picchu.<br>• View a video that explains how archeological digs are completed. |
| **Differentiation** | No differentiation was included. | • Using the Inca and/or Greek civilization as a base, invite students to compare/contrast a contemporary civilization.<br>• Interview a local explorer in any field to determine how people in their discipline think and work.<br>• Invite interested students to think about the fit between themselves and archeologists, historians, or journalists. |

## Makeover Example: Astronomy—Looking Into the Sky, Kindergarten and Grade 1

The revised earth science unit outline was developed by the same teachers who taught Groundhog Day. They revised this outline after they participated in a daylong workshop that helped them "unpack" their state standards. They realized that the original Groundhog Day unit missed the mark. It did not address any of the science and social studies standards they originally believed it addressed.

Initially, the teachers thought that the revised content in the next box was too advanced for their first graders. Their most important realization about the unit, on reviewing the pre- and postassessment data, was that they underestimated the abilities of all their students, including those with high abilities.

| Component | Comment About Original Component | Examples of Makeover Options |
|---|---|---|
| **Content** | Hard to tell. | • Understands that we live on earth<br>• Understands that the sun appears to move across the sky in the daytime, but in reality the earth is moving<br>• Understands that we need the sun for life<br>• Understands that the shape of the moon changes a bit each day, but looks the same again in about a month |

*(Continued)*

(Continued)

| Component | Comment About Original Component | Examples of Makeover Options |
|---|---|---|
| **Assessment** | No assessments were included. | Pre- and postassessment were designed and completed with young students in an interview format. Student answers are scripted because many students at this age do not have fluency with writing.<br>• What is astronomy?<br>• What do you think astronomers study?<br>• What do you see in the sky during the daytime?<br>• What do you see in the night sky? |
| **Introduction** | Original introduction is not aligned with authentic science or social studies content. | • Show students pictures of astronauts.<br>• Engage students in a discussion in which they wonder what the astronomers were viewing. |
| **Grouping strategies** | Original grouping strategies lack variety. | Groupings vary depending upon the nature of the learning activities:<br>• Small groups for making observations about phenomenon and conducting related experiments<br>• Individual and pairs at centers and stations<br>• Whole-class grouping for introductions, directions, and debriefings |
| **Teaching activities** | Teaching activities do not require mental processing by students. | • Questioning and feedback to bridge between students' current level of understanding and the new knowledge they need to acquire<br>• Modeling<br>• Providing examples<br>• Tactile-kinesthetic teaching |
| **Products** | Original product, e.g., the T chart, was not varied. | Student:<br>• Pre- and postassessments<br>• Journals of observations<br>• Moon drawings<br>• Moon models<br>• Constellation designs |
| **Extensions** | There were no extensions. | • Letter home to parents requesting their hel conducting activities at home related to the night sky<br>• A visit to a nearby planetarium<br>• Books from the school and public library |

| Component | Comment About Original Component | Examples of Makeover Options |
|---|---|---|
| **Differentiation** | No differentiation was included. | A variety of modification's was offered for advanced-level learners who displayed a great deal of information on the preassessment:<br>• The study of shadows was eliminated for all students because it was too abstract for young children. It was, however, included as an extension activity for advanced-level students.<br>• Making a solar oven and using a thermometer to determine the temperature inside the oven.<br>• Creative writing assignments that extend the lesson.<br>• Researching related topics including, for example: constellations, Stonehenge, and ocean tides. |

## Makeover Example: Robert Frost—An American Icon: Only Seemingly Simple, Grade 11

This revised lesson outline illustrates changes in almost all the curriculum components. Of particular significance are the changes in content, assessment, resources, and teaching strategies. Perhaps most important, the developer made changes to the introduction to enhance the attention and interest of adolescents, who typically find poetry hard to understand and distant from their own lives. This outline requires a minimum of six to eight lessons.

| Component | Comment About Original Component | Examples of Makeover Options |
|---|---|---|
| **Content** | • Original objective is too topical; it describes how students will learn. As written, it does not explain what students will understand as a result of their exposure to the two poems by Frost. | • Understands the defining characteristics of American lyric poetry<br>• Understands the effects of complex literary devices and techniques (i.e., symbolism) on the overall quality of a work<br>• Understands that literature can evoke multiple responses<br>• Writes in response to literature and suggests an interpretation<br>• Writes a reflective composition that uses personal experience as a basis for reflection on some aspect of life and moves from specific examples to generalizations about life |
| **Assessment** | Original assessments are not aligned with the content; are not | • Small group oral presentations that illuminate multiple interpretations of lines/stanzas of selected poems |

*(Continued)*

| Component | Comment About Original Component | Examples of Makeover Options |
|---|---|---|
| | compelling for adolescents. | • Reflective essay (See Differentiation row in this table)<br>• Teacher-made trait rubric |
| **Introduction** | The original introduction is not engaging. | • Pictures of Frost at various points in his life: alone, with family members, friends<br>• If readily available, video clips of Frost reading his poem, "The Gift Outright," at the lectern during the inauguration of President John F. Kennedy in 1961. The poem addresses our allegiances as a nation. Prior to the Revolutionary War, we were possessed by and paid allegiance to England. Subsequently we found ourselves as a nation and chose to turn our allegiances to the land and our own history.<br>• Posing engaging question for small-group discussion: What choices do we face in life? What choices do we make alone? As a small group? As a nation? What choices, related to allegiance, did the Kennedy administration make?<br>• Short, purposefully selected, provoking quotations by Frost about poetry coupled with opportunities for students to "think-pair-share" about the meaning of the quotations (e.g., "Poetry is a way of taking life by the throat." (*Vogue*, March 15, 1963) |
| **Teaching strategies** | Original strategies lack variety; do not address critical learning differences among students; were not motivating to adolescents; did not promote higher levels of thinking and reflection. | • Give short lecture about the characteristics of lyric poetry and the use of symbolism.<br>• Provide small-group instruction about the characteristics of lyric poetry and symbolism using Frost's poems; more/less feedback is provided, depending upon the learning needs of students.<br>• Use Socratic questioning while roving from group to group; purposefully pose questions that require more or less inference to fit the learning needs of students. |
| **Learning activities** | Original learning activities lack variety; did not respond to students' prior knowledge. | • Invite students to work with primary source documents (e.g., original manuscripts, notes by Frost); audio clips of him reading his poetry, available on the Web).<br>• Provide students with literary critiques about "Stopping by Woods" and "The Road Not Taken" that have been purposefully selected to present conflicting interpretations about the poems. At the same time, provide Frost's own reflections about the poems. Invite students to explain why there can be so many different interpretations. |

| Component | Comment About Original Component | Examples of Makeover Options |
|---|---|---|
| **Grouping strategies** | Strategies lack variety. | • Whole-group instruction for introduction, minilectures, and debriefing activities<br>• Small groups for (1) considering the characteristics of lyric poetry, (2) looking at Frost's use of symbols, (3) interpreting lines or stanzas of poetry, and (4) considering the various perspectives contained in the critiques<br>• Small group mini-lessons related to the technical aspects of writing, as necessary<br>• Pairs for peer editing<br>• One-on-one conferences with students about their writing, if needed |
| **Products** | Original products are not aligned with the content; lack variety. | • Small-group oral presentations in which poems, stanzas of poems, or critiques are discussed<br>• Posters that display symbols used in the adolescent culture<br>• Student essays. Topics are differentiated (see below).<br>• Student drafts<br>• Students' final essays |
| **Resources** | Resources lack variety; are not engaging. | • Primary source material (e.g., copies of Frost's manuscripts, letters, audiotapes of him reading his work)<br>• Biographical information about Frost<br>• Literary reviews of Frost's poems<br>• Frost's personal reflections about his poems, "Stopping by Woods" and "The Road Not Taken"<br>• Frost's reflections on poetry as an art form |
| **Extensions** | There were no extensions. | • Read additional poems by Frost such as "Mending Wall" and "Spring." Explain orally or in writing which are your favorites/least favorites and why.<br>• Read selections from other American poets who wrote lyric poetry, such as Carl Sandberg, Marianne Moore, Lucille Clifts, Richard Wilbur, and others. Share your reflections in a medium of your choice. |

*(Continued)*

(Continued)

| Component | Comment About Original Component | Examples of Makeover Options |
|---|---|---|
| | | • Consider the sacrifices that poets make throughout their lifetime. Would you be willing to make those kinds of sacrifices? Why or why not? |
| **Differentiation** | No differentiation was included. | The teacher differentiated the writing assignment to address critical differences in students' ability to think abstractly and reflectively about poetry. Some students struggled with symbolism and an author's use of this literary device; other students were quick to grasp the author's intentional and complex use of it. He developed three essay topics that provided ongoing challenge to all learners in the classroom, including those with advanced abilities, and assigned students to groups based upon his knowledge of them: |
| | | • Group 1: The teacher provided students with a list of symbols ("Stopping by Woods": the owner of the land, the horse, the woods, promises, sleep; "The Road Not Taken": two roads, yellow wood, traveler, difference), some possible interpretations for each, and asked them to interpret one of the poems from their point of view in a two-page essay (for struggling learners). |
| | | • Group 2: For this group of students, the teacher provided the poems only. He asked them to identify the symbols in one of the poems, think about how they interact within the poem, and generate a two-page reflective essay about its meaning/lack of meaning to their lives (for grade-level learners). |
| | | • Group 3: The teacher provided these students with a copy of the two poems and a quotation by Frost: "Metaphor . . . saying one thing and meaning another, saying one thing in terms of another; poetry is simply made of metaphor." The teacher asked these students to consider how the symbols worked interdependently to create a metaphor about life. He asked students to choose one of the poems and present their reflections in a two-page essay (for advanced-level learners). |

# A STRATEGIC PLAN TO ADDRESS THE CREATION OR REVISION OF A CURRICULUM UNIT

*Objective:* To create an effective, or remodel an inefficient, curriculum unit. (The members of each grade-level team or department will be working concurrently on a curriculum unit that they have selected.)

*Evidence:* A revised or new six-week curriculum unit that contains powerful, standards-based content, aligned preassessment, and postassessments to measure student achievement, grouping strategies, as well as aligned teaching and learning activities, diverse resources and products, and extension activities.

*Tasks:* Create a new curriculum unit or revise an existing unit that lacks power and cohesiveness.

*Timeline:* Some time during the school year. (Curriculum revision is an ongoing process that may be completed by discipline. In fact, more than one curriculum area may be revised concurrently. The timeline explained here may need to be modified by practitioners to align with district initiatives)

- As a grade-level team or department, identify a curriculum unit(s) in need of revision.
- Integrate the curriculum unit revision process within the district plan for reviewing curriculum content, K–12, in general and special education.
- Communicate with central office staff regarding the intended work on the targeted unit and representative topics to ensure a coordinated approach to the curriculum revision process.

Throughout the remainder of the school year

- Gather standards and related material about the representative topic(s) (e.g., standards, high school and college level textbooks, existing curricular materials).
- Review selected readings about curricular approaches for gifted and talented students including, *Problem-Based Learning* (Stepien et al., 1993), the *Schoolwide Enrichment Model* (Renzulli & Reis, 1985), the *Integrated Curriculum Model* (VanTassel-Baska & Little, 2003), and the *Parallel Curriculum Model* (Tomlinson et al., 2002).
- Decide which approach or approaches to curriculum revision are best aligned with the learning needs of all students, including those who are gifted and talented students.

## Summer

- Conduct successive meetings with the grade-level team/department to revise content and then modify/create all related curriculum components.
- Using vertical teams, ensure the fit of the unit within the larger K–12 sequence of instruction.

### Subsequent school year

- Field-test revised curriculum unit.
- Collect and analyze the pre- and postassessment data.
- Assess the strengths and weaknesses of the unit(s) as they apply to all learners, as well as the learning needs of gifted and talented learners (if taught in a heterogeneous setting).
- Make necessary revisions to the unit.
- Share the new unit with teachers for additional feedback, field-testing, and revisions.

## TEMPLATE FOR THINKING ABOUT THE CURRICULUM REVISION PROCESS

Content Area: _____ Unit: _____ Grade Level: _____

Regular Classroom: _____ Gifted Education Program: _____

| Component | Comment | Needed Revision(s) |
|---|---|---|
| **Content** | | |
| **Assessment** | | |
| **Introduction/Debriefing** | | |
| **Grouping strategies** | | |
| **Teaching strategies** | | |
| **Learning activities** | | |
| **Products** | | |
| **Resources** | | |
| **Extensions** | | |
| **Differentiation** | | |

# SPECIAL PROGRAMS FOR UNDERSERVED POPULATIONS

Historically, research has been sparse on effective curriculum and programming for gifted high school learners (Sytsma, 2000), and research on effective curriculum and programming for gifted high school learners from traditionally underserved populations almost nonexistent. However, with the recent national push for expanded participation of minority students and students from low socioeconomic status (SES) backgrounds in rigorous high school courses such as Advanced Placement (AP) classes (e.g., Thomas, 2004), educators are looking for ways to appropriately prepare talented high school learners from all populations to meet the challenge of these courses.

Recent research studies indicate that participation in rigorous courses such as AP courses involves expanded challenges for minority students and students from low SES backgrounds (Picucci & Sobel, 2003; Hertberg et al., in press). These challenges vary according to context but often include being the first in their families to take advanced coursework; experiencing peer pressure to remain in remedial classes; battling low expectations that they may hold for themselves and that some school staff hold for them (Picucci & Sobel, 2003); facing the already-established and often alienating social environment of advanced courses; entering advanced courses without the requisite skill packages expected of advanced students; and being unfamiliar with the "unspoken secrets" of academic success such as asking for help, knowing how to talk to teachers, and relying on other students for advice about which teachers and courses to take and avoid (Hertberg, et al., in press).

As educators seek to expand the numbers of students from traditionally underrepresented populations taking advanced high school courses, it is becoming increasingly clear that merely trying to recruit a greater number of diverse students into AP courses is not enough. In order for these students to succeed in advanced courses, it is also necessary to prepare them for the rigors of these courses and to provide them with support before and while they take on these challenges. Research indicates that the following characteristics describe necessary components of programs designed to increase the participation of students from traditionally underserved populations in advanced high school coursework. These programs

- are context-driven, created in response to the assessed needs of the target population with regard to the resources available;
- entail shared vision, commitment, and involvement among students, faculty, building and district-level administrators, parents, and members of the community;
- involve a culture of high expectations for all students;
- involve vertical training of all K–12 teachers in recognizing diverse manifestations of talent in, and providing appropriate curricular challenge for, a broad range of gifted learners;
- include curriculum within and outside of advanced courses that is responsive to the needs of a wide variety of students;
- entail systematic, planned support to students to develop the skills necessary for success in advanced coursework (e.g., writing skills, analytical thinking skills, time management skills, future orientation, study skills);
- involve an organized peer support network for students so that they do not feel alone in their pursuit of advanced coursework;
- involve relentless and individualized recruitment methods;

- involve committed adults who provide students with both academic and social/emotional support; and
- focus on skills acquisition and taking on challenges rather than on test scores. (Hertberg, et al., in press; Picucci & Sobel, 2003)

Several programs across the country are engaged in the endeavor of preparing students early for the rigors of AP, other advanced courses, and college, as well as providing students with the support they need as they tackle these challenges. Brief descriptions of three of these programs are given in the following sections, along with information about Web sites and articles that can be accessed for further, more detailed information. A large, national program and a smaller, single-district program are included to provide a sense of the spectrum of programs proving effective in increasing the number of traditionally underserved students participating and succeeding in advanced high school courses.

## Advancement via Individual Determination (AVID)

Founded in 1980, Advancement via Individual Determination (AVID) is an academic support program for students in Grades 5 through 12 that focuses on preparing students for college eligibility and success. The AVID program is currently in place in more than 1,900 schools throughout the world.

The AVID program targets motivated, academically average students and places them in advanced courses. Often, AVID's target students come from low-income or minority families, and frequently these students will be the first in their families to attend college. The AVID program is grounded in the philosophy that these students are capable of a high level of academic achievement if challenged by rigorous curriculum and provided with appropriate support.

In line with this philosophy, the AVID program consists of several components that nurture AVID students' academic potential: advanced curriculum, the AVID elective, and professional development of AVID school teachers. The AVID curriculum is centered around WIC-R (writing, inquiry, collaboration, and reading), an active-learning approach in which students focus on developing their reading and writing skills. Furthermore, students are encouraged to learn through their own questions rather than through teacher lecture, be collaborators with their teachers and fellow students in the learning process, and be critical readers and consumers of information. This WIC-R curriculum is used in AVID elective courses as well as in content-area courses in AVID schools.

Students attend the AVID elective course once per school day. In the elective course, students gain the skills they need to be successful students in advanced courses (such as organizational, study, and critical thinking and questioning skills), receive academic tutoring, and build the confidence necessary to believe that college is attainable. All teachers teaching the AVID elective are trained for this program, as are all teachers and administrators in AVID schools.

Research data support the effectiveness of the AVID approach (Alkan, Cossio, Huerta, & Watt, 2003; Cunningham, Redmond, & Merisotis, 2003; Guthrie & Guthrie, 2000, 2002; Mehan, Villanueva, Hubbard, & Lintz, 1996; U.S. Department of Education, 1998; Watt, Yanez, & Cossio, 2002). AVID students attend four-year colleges at a significantly higher rate (3:2) than do other U.S. high school students (Guthrie & Guthrie, 2000, 2002; Watt et al., 2002). In addition, the proportion of Latinos taking AP exams is seven times higher among AVID students than among U.S. students overall

(63% as compared to 9%), and the proportion of Blacks is nearly twice as high (9% as opposed to 5%).

Promising research is only now becoming available about the effectiveness of the program when it is implemented with middle school students. In a sample of 26 AVID middle and high schools, researchers reported that

- Teachers and counselors were instrumental in placing students in rigorous courses.
- AVID students, in all grade levels, outperformed all other students on end-of-course grades, state assessments, and attendance (Watt, Huerta, & Cossio, 2002).

Further information about the AVID program is available at www.avidonline.org

## The Advanced Placement Network

Wakefield High School in Arlington, Virginia, has received a great deal of attention from the media recently because of its demonstrated commitment to encouraging its diverse population of students to tackle the challenges of AP courses (e.g., Clark & Natale, 2004; Mathews, 2004). Wakefield has nearly doubled the number of students taking AP tests in the past five years, and scores have climbed. In 2003, 18% earned the top score of 5—triple the number from 1999 (Clark & Natale, 2004).

Wakefield has created a program called The AP Network, a schoolwide initiative to prepare more of its students for the rigors of college through taking AP courses. The program consists of several components designed to build important skills prior to entering AP courses and to support students while they are taking these courses. The six components include the Foundations Pre-AP Program, the Pre-AP Summer Bridge Program, the AP Summer Bridge Program, the Double Math Initiative, the Cohort Program, and Spanish Immersion. The Foundations Pre-AP Program prepares students for the rigors of AP courses by offering students advanced and intensified levels of English, math, biology, and world history in classes with low student–teacher ratios. In these courses, students can develop the skills and knowledge necessary for successful performance in AP courses.

Two Summer Bridge programs are offered. The Pre-AP Summer Bridge is given over three days during the summer to ninth-grade students taking advanced, intensified, or AP courses. During the course of this program, students meet their teachers; learn about the content of the courses they will be taking; learn coping, organization, time-management, and study skills; and begin a four-year college plan. The AP Summer Bridge Program, offered to both new and returning AP students, provides supports similar to those of the Pre-AP Summer Bridge and meets for a week during the summer.

The Double Math Initiative is designed to allow students who are not on pace for taking AP Calculus to catch up. Students are encouraged to take both Geometry and Algebra II their sophomore year, with afterschool tutoring provided to help students tackle this challenge.

The Cohort Program is open to any Hispanic or Black male with a GPA of 2.0 or above, and it is designed to provide the social and academic support needed to prepare these students to enroll and succeed in AP courses. Students enter the Cohort Program in ninth grade, attending weekly lunch meetings with their peers to discuss both academic and social/emotional issues. One of the primary benefits of the Cohort Program is the development of a supportive peer group of students engaged in a unified endeavor of seeking academic challenge.

Finally, the Spanish Immersion program prepares ninth-grade students to take the AP Spanish Language and AP Spanish Literature exams. Coursework experiences are supplemented through travel and study abroad.

Several articles (Beitler, 2004; Clark & Natale, 2004; Mathews, 2004) provide further information on the AP Network and its effectiveness with encouraging expanded participation of minority students in AP courses.

## Posse

The Posse Foundation is an organization that identifies public high school students with high levels of academic and leadership potential who might have been overlooked by the traditional college selection process. Since 1989, the foundation has been identifying candidates from diverse cultural and economic backgrounds who form multicultural teams called *posses*. Posses are small groups of friends who look out for one another and back each other up to ensure college success and graduation. These small teams composed of 10 students, are prepared—while still in high school—through an eight-month training program to enroll and support each other at top universities across the country. The program was developed in response to a large number of students from New York City who enrolled in college but then dropped out six months later.

Posse has three goals that are critically important to public high schools and institutions of higher learning: (1) to enhance the recruitment and selection process at universities and colleges, (2) to improve the retention and graduation rate of students from culturally and socially diverse backgrounds, and (3) to help build and maintain integrated communities on college campuses across the country. The Posse Foundation has developed an alternative way to identify candidates who have the potential to succeed in college called the Dynamic Assessment Process (DAP). Initially, Posse's network of public high schools and community-based organizations nominate potential candidates. Then, nominated students are invited to participate in a unique evaluation protocol that has three parts, which include both group and individual interviews. Students are asked to work in teams to demonstrate their intrinsic leadership abilities; their skills at working in a team setting, such as public speaking, listening, and negotiation and communication skills; and their motivation and desire to succeed. Approximately 60% of first-round students are invited back for the second phase of the process, the individual interview. The last stage of recruitment is the finalist workshop. Potential candidates are invited to participate in activities that allow further evaluation of group behavior and individual potential. Together, the Posse Foundation and the university partner evaluate the participation of candidates and agree on 10 Posse Scholars for the next entering class. Selected candidates are awarded four-year leadership scholarships by the university.

From January to August of the selected students' senior year, Posse Scholars meet weekly for two-hour workshops that address four areas: team building, cross-cultural communication, leadership, and academic excellence. The goal of this precollegiate program is to prepare the scholars for leadership roles on campus and high levels of academic excellence. The alternative identification process has shown promise for identifying high-potential leaders.

The second goal of the program is to improve the retention and graduation of Posse Scholars. The Posse on-campus program was developed to address these twin goals. Posse staff members visit partner universities twice each semester. There are Posse team meetings every two weeks. Each year a Posse retreat is held for all Posse Scholars, as well as other members from the student body. The goal of these retreats is to discuss important campus issues that are identified by the Posse Scholars.

The final goal of the Posse Foundation is to help build integrated communities on university and college campuses. Because traditional college admission processes have not been effective in increasing the number of culturally and economically diverse students on campuses, the demographics of undergraduate programs in colleges and universities continue to reflect high percentages of nonminority students. It is the hope of the foundation that each Posse will act as a model of cultural diversity in student life and act as an agent for social change on campus.

The Posse program has witnessed success since its inception in 1989. It has placed into top colleges and universities more than 1,200 students antecedent have been awarded more than $112 million in scholarships from Posse partner universities. Posse Scholars are persisting and graduating at a rate close to 90%. Only 50% of all American students attend college; of that number, only half graduate. Posse currently has sites in five major cities in the country: New York, Boston, Chicago, Los Angeles, and Washington, DC.

Information about the program is available at www.possefoundation.org

## ADVICE FOR THE SOLE PRACTITIONER

The sole practitioner faces a daunting task to familiarize him- or herself with all of the key features of gifted education programs and services. Each one of the components requires considerable background knowledge, especially curriculum. Perhaps the first thing to realize about this key feature is that there are many practitioners within the school and school system who have expertise in the disciplines and who would be eager to collaborate. Identify the one or two people who are experts in each content area and who are willing to collaborate in an ongoing fashion.

The next task for the sole practitioner is to make a crazy sounding request: Ask to be placed on district-level curriculum revision committees. There are three important reasons for requesting the addition of so many meetings into one's already full schedule! First, as a committee member, you will deepen collegial relationships with teachers who have expertise and a willingness to engage in critical dialogues about curriculum issues. Second, you will learn about the strength of the district curriculum in each content area, as well as the places where it might need more challenge. You can offer your expertise to committee members related to the latter condition. Finally, you will gain a thorough understanding of the regular curriculum and develop an understanding of the natural intersection points where the gifted education curriculum and the regular education program can be aligned to benefit student learning.

## MUST-READ RESOURCES

Landrum, M. S., Callahan, C. M., & Shaklee, B. D. (Eds.). (1998). *Pre-K–Grade 12 gifted program standards.* Washington, DC: National Association for Gifted Children.

Purcell, J. H., Burns, D. E., Tomlinson, C. A., Imbeau, M. B., & Martin, J. L. (2002). Bridging the gap: A tool and technique to analyze and evaluate gifted education curricular units. *Gifted Child Quarterly, 46*(4), 306–321.

Tomlinson, C. A., Kaplan, S. N., Renzulli, J. S., Purcell, J., Leppien, J., & Burns, D. (2002). *The parallel curriculum model: A design to develop high potential and challenge high-ability students.* Thousand Oaks, CA: Corwin.

VanTassel-Baska, J., & Little, C. (2003). *Content-based curriculum for high-ability learners.* Waco, TX: Prufrock Press.

# REFERENCES

Alkan, E., Cossio, G., Huerta, J., & Watt, K. (2003). *2001–2002 Texas AVID data: State report.* Austin, TX: Center for Applied Research in Education.

Beitler, A. (2004, December). *Making this team. Principal leadership* (pp. 16–21). Reston, VA: National Association of Secondary School Principals.

Betts, G. (1985). *The Autonomous Learner Model for gifted and talented.* Greeley: CO: Autonomous Learning.

Bruner, J. S. (1966). *Toward a theory of instruction.* Cambridge, MA: Harvard University Press.

Clark, C. S., & Natale, J. (2004, October). Toward a more perfect school: Teachers and students are throwing out tradition to pursue excellence. *Washingtonian*, p. 104.

Cunningham E., Redmond, C., & Merisotis, J. (2003, February). *Investing early: Intervention programs in selected U.S. states.* Washington, DC: Institute for Higher Education Policy.

Dewey, J. (1938). *Experience and education.* New York: Macmillan.

Feldhusen, J. F., & Kolloff, P. B. (1986). The Purdue three-stage enrichment model for gifted education at the elementary level. In J. S. Renzulli (Ed.), *Systems and models for developing programs for the gifted and talented* (pp. 126–152). Mansfield Center, CT: Creative Learning Press.

Gallagher, J., Kaplan, S. K., Passow, A. H., Renzulli, J. S., Sato, I. S., Sisk, D., & Wickless, J. (1982). *Principles of differentiated instruction.* Unpublished report, National/State Leadership Training Institute on the Gifted and Talented. Ventura, CA.

Gallagher, J. J. (1975). *Teaching the gifted child* (2nd ed.). Boston: Allyn & Bacon.

Guilford, J. P. (1967). *The nature of human intelligence.* New York: McGraw-Hill.

Guthrie, L., & Guthrie, G. (2000). *Longitudinal research on AVID 1999–2000: Final report.* Burlingame, CA: Center for Research, Evaluation, and Training in Education.

Guthrie, L., & Guthrie, G. (2002). *The magnificent eight: AVID best practices study.* Burlingame, CA: Center for Research, Evaluation, and Training in Education.

Hertberg, H. L., Callahan, C. M., Kyburg, R. M., Brighton, C. M., Hench, E. P., & Yoo, H. (in press). *Advanced placement and International Baccalaureate programs: A good fit for gifted learners?* (research monograph). Charlottesville, VA: University of Virginia, National Research Center on the Gifted and Talented.

Kaplan, S. N. (1974). *Providing programs for the gifted and talented: A handbook.* Ventura, CA: Office of the Ventura County Superintendent of Schools.

Kaplan, S. N. (1986). The Grid: A model to construct differentiated curriculum for the gifted. In J. S. Renzulli (Ed.), *Systems and models for developing programs for the gifted and talented* (pp. 180–194). Mansfield Center, CT: Creative Learning Press.

Landrum, M. S., & Shaklee, B. (Eds.). (1998). *Pre-K–Grade 12 gifted program standards.* Washington, DC: National Association for Gifted Children.

Landrum, M. S., Callahan, C. M., & Shaklee, B. D. (Eds.). (2001). *Aiming for excellence: Annotations to the NAGC Pre-K–grade 12 gifted program standards.* Waco, TX: Prufrock Press.

Levine, D. U., & Lezotte, L. W. (1990). *Unusually effective schools: A review and analysis of research and practice.* Madison, WI: National Center for Effective Schools Research and Development.

Lipsey, M. W., & Wilson, D. B. (1993). The efficacy of psychological, educational, and behavioral treatment: Confirmation of meta-analysis. *American Psychologist, 48*(12), 1181–1209.

Maker, J. C. (1982). *Curriculum development for the gifted.* Rockville, MD: Aspen.

Marland, S. P., Jr. (1972). *Education of the gifted and talented.* Vol. I, *Report to the Congress of the United States by the U.S. Commissioner of Education.* Washington, DC: U.S. Government Printing Office.

Marzano, R. J. (2000). *A new era of school reform: Going where the research takes us.* Aurora, CO: Mid-continent Research for Education and Learning. (ERIC Document Reproduction Service No. ED454255).

Marzano R. J. (2003). *What works in schools: Translating research into practice.* Alexandria, VA: Association for Supervision and Curriculum Development.

Mathews, J. (2004, February 17). Arlington school pushing AP courses. *The Washington Post.* Retrieved April 1, 2005, from http://www.washingtonpost.com/ac2/wp-dyn?pagename=article&contentId=A46511-2004Feb16&notFound=true

Meeker, M., & Meeker, R. (1986). The SOI system for gifted education. In J. S. Renzulli (Ed.), *Systems and models for developing programs for the gifted and talented* (pp. 194–215). Mansfield Center, CT: Creative Learning Press.

Mehan, H., Villanueva, I., Hubbard, L., & Lintz, A. (1996). *Constructing school success: The consequences of untracking low-achieving students.* Cambridge, UK: Cambridge University Press.

National Education Commission on Time and Learning. (1994). *Prisoners of time.* Washington, DC: U.S. Department of Education.

National Research Council. (2002). *Minority students in special and gifted education.* Washington, DC: National Academy Press.

Picucci, A., & Sobel, A. (2003). *Executive summary: Collaboration, innovation, and tenacity: Exemplary high-enrollment AP Calculus programs for traditionally underserved students.* Austin, TX: Charles A. Dana Center. Retrieved August 23, 2005, from http://www.ccsso.org/content/pdfs/APF03 High EnrollmentAPCalculus.pdf

Renzulli, J. S. (1977). *The enrichment triad model: A guide for developing defensible programs for the gifted and talented.* Wethersfield, CT: Creative Learning Press.

Renzulli, J. S. (1988). *The multiple menu model for developing differentiated curriculum for the gifted and talented.* Unpublished manuscript, Bureau of Educational Research, University of Connecticut, Storrs, CT.

Renzulli, J. S., & Reis, S. M. (1985). *The schoolwide enrichment model: A comprehensive plan for educational excellence.* Mansfield Center, CT: Creative Learning Press.

Renzulli, J. S., Leppien, J. H., & Hays, T. S. (2000). *The multiple menu model: A practical guide for developing differentiated curriculum.* Mansfield Center, CT: Creative Learning Press.

Scheerens, J., & Bosker, R. (1997). *The foundations of educational effectiveness.* New York: Elsevier.

Schmidt, W. H., McKnight, C. C., & Raizen, S. A. (1996). A *splintered vision: An investigation of U.S. science and mathematics education: Executive summary.* Lansing, MI: Michigan State University, U.S. National Research Center for the Third International Math and Science Study.

Stepien, W. J., Gallagher, S. A., & Workman, D. (1993). Problem-based learning for traditional and interdisciplinary classrooms. *Journal for the Education of the Gifted, 16,* 5–17.

Sytsma, R. (2000). *Gifted and talented programs in America's high schools: A preliminary survey report.* The National Research Center on the Gifted and Talented Newsletter. Retrieved March 1, 2005, from http://www.gifted.uconn.edu/nrcgt/newsletter/ spring00/sprng004.html

Taba, H. (1962). *Curriculum development: Theory and practice.* New York: Harcourt, Brace and World.

Thomas, D. (2004). *Little Rock Students to benefit from education grant: Advanced Placement Incentives Program helps students achieve in advanced courses.* U.S. Department of Education. Retrieved March 12, 2005, from http://www.ed.gov/news/pressreleases/2004/04/04122004.html

Tomlinson, C. A. (1998). *The differentiated classroom: Responding to the needs of all learners.* Alexandria, VA: Association for Supervision and Curriculum Development.

Tomlinson, C. A., Kaplan, S. N., Renzulli, J. S., Purcell, J., Leppien, J., & Burns, D. (2002). *The parallel curriculum model: A design to develop high potential and challenge high-ability students.* Thousand Oaks, CA: Corwin.

Treffinger, D. (1986). Fostering effective, independent learning through individualized programming. In J. S. Renzulli (Ed.), *Systems and models for developing programs for the gifted and talented* (pp. 429–460). Mansfield Center, CT: Creative Learning Press.

U.S. Department of Education. (1998). *Tools for schools: School reform models supported by the National Institute on Education of At-Risk Students.* Washington, DC: Office of Education Research and Improvement.

VanTassel-Baska, J., & Little, C. A. (2003). *Content-based curriculum for high ability learners.* Waco, TX: Prufrock Press.

Viadaro, D. (1997, April 2). Surprise! Analysis link curriculum, TIMSS test scores. *Education Week,* p. 6.

Ward, V. S. (1961). *Educating the gifted: An axiomatic approach.* Columbus, OH: Charles Merrill.

Watt, K., Huerta, L., & Cossio, G. (2002). Leadership and comprehensive school reform: Implementation of AVID in four South Texas schools. *Catalyst for Change, 33*(2), 10–14.

Watt, K., Yanez, D., & Cossio, G. (2002). AVID: A comprehensive school reform model for Texas. *National FORUM Journal of Educational Administration and Supervision, 19*(3), 43–59.

# 9

# Services That Meet Social and Emotional Needs of Gifted Children

*Maureen Neihart*

The most common counseling need of this [gifted] population is assistance in coping with stressors related to growing up as a gifted child in a society that does not always recognize, understand, or welcome giftedness.

—Sidney M. Moon

The social and emotional needs of gifted education students, while long recognized, have only recently begun to receive an emphasis in the literature. In the first half of the 20th century, Leta Hollingworth, a pioneer in this area, documented that gifted education students do have social and emotional needs that merit attention (1926, 1942). She was one of the first to discuss the effect that schools had on some highly able children, and she anticipated difficulties that some able children would have with their peers. Finally, she was one of the first to notice what we, today, call asynchronous development. In 1942, she noted this gap and foresaw the impact it might have on children, "To have the intellect of an adult and the emotions of a child combined in a childish body is to encounter certain difficulties" (Hollingworth, 1942, p. 282).

Our understanding about the social and emotional needs of gifted children has come a long way since Leta Hollingworth's work. However, we still know more about the affective characteristics of gifted students than the methods for fostering socio-emotional growth. A recent literature review prepared for the National Association for Gifted Children (NAGC) Counseling and Guidance Division indicated that in the past seven years, 82 publications representing 35 studies had been released on the topics of giftedness and guidance and counseling issues, practices, and techniques. Experts in NAGC agree that affective services for gifted students should be purposefully included in gifted education planning as a proactive support mechanism for students. In this chapter, Maureen Neihart shares with readers how the research about the affective needs of gifted students can be practically applied in schools. This chapter is most aligned with those on curriculum development, 8; professional qualifications, 13; and comprehensive program design, 7.

# DEFINITION

Social and emotional needs are conditions that must be met for positive adjustment. They are requirements associated with inter- and intrapersonal well-being and high achievement. They have to do with understanding of self and others, social functioning, and expression and regulation of arousal and emotion. A recent review of the research conducted by a national task force for NAGC concluded that all gifted children require at least three academic provisions to meet their social and emotional needs. These include the opportunity to learn with others of similar interest, ability, and drive; an appropriate level of challenge in the regular classroom; and flexible pacing through the curriculum (Neihart, Reis, Robinson, & Moon, 2002).

Studies also indicate that some gifted children will need assistance coping with their heightened sensitivity, perfectionism, asynchronous development, peer relationships situational stressors, and college and career planning (Neihart et al., 2002). Like other children, some gifted children have emotional or behavioral difficulties related to learning disabilities, depression, underachievement, or ADHD, for example, and require extra support or intervention to manage them.

It is important to note at the outset that gifted children with dual exceptionalities are different from other children with dual exceptionalities. Research supports greater frustration for gifted students because of the larger discrepancies between their abilities and disabilities (Baum, Cooper, & Neu, 2001; Moon, Zentall, Grskovic, Hall, & Stormont, 2001; Zentall, Moon, Hall, & Grskovic, 200). As a result, they may be more at risk for social and emotional adjustment problems. Research also supports that they demonstrate greater coping skills when they are provided with appropriate interventions (Baum & Owen, 1988; Moon, 2001; Olenchak & Reis, 2001).

# RATIONALE

Social and emotional needs of gifted students must be addressed in a systematic way to develop talent, maximize learning, and promote positive adjustment. There is clear evidence that failure to address some of the affective needs of gifted children contributes to academic underachievement, peer relationship difficulties, and other problems with adjustment (Baker, 1996; Ford, 1992; Gross, 1993; Janos, Robinson, & Lunneborg, 1989; Neihart et al., 2002).

# GUIDING PRINCIPLES

Three research-based principles guide the development of affective services in gifted programs and services. The first and most important principle is that gifted education students have a variety of social and emotional learning needs that must be met to increase their social and emotional adjustment and to help them maximize their potential. Sustained, systematic, and differentiated guidance and counseling activities must be coupled with access to true peers (i.e., people with similar abilities, interests, and drive), appropriate levels of academic challenge in the classroom, and flexible pacing options in the school curriculum. These three provisions are minimally necessary to meet the social and emotional needs of gifted children.

The second guiding principle is that a variety of approaches is required to address the social and emotional needs of high-potential students. Accommodations must be differentiated along a continuum of supports to address need variations related to culture, socio-economic status, and gender. The continuum ranges from in-classroom guidance activities and parent meetings to focus groups and individual and family counseling.

The third principle is that school-based plans to meet the social and emotional needs of gifted students must be designed purposefully and grounded in best-evidence decision making. Teachers, guidance counselors, and other related professionals must collaborate, using the best available research, to create plans that classroom teachers and guidance counselors can use to meet the unique affective needs of gifted and talented students. See Chapter 20, regarding scientifically based research practices.

# ATTRIBUTES THAT DEFINE HIGH QUALITY

These three basic, but critical, principles set the backdrop for our thinking about the nature of guidance and counseling services for highly able young people. The next step for practitioners is to think about a vision for high-quality guidance and counseling services in both the classroom and the larger school community. Exemplary guidance and counseling services for highly able young people exhibit the following characteristics:

- They have a schoolwide emphasis. All school personnel who work with gifted students acknowledge the unique social and emotional needs of this population and are prepared to address them.
- Services address diversity. Most every school district is facing an increase in the diversity of its students. They come from more cultural backgrounds, speak an increasing variety of languages, come from all economic strata, and represent more cultures than ever before. Increasingly, practitioners are designing interventions to address a host of counseling issues, such as those required to counteract the conflicts that some high-potential students encounter when their achievement values are not shared by the mainstream culture. Other interventions might include the delivery of long-term programs that are required to reverse patterns of academic underachievement.
- Classroom teachers can address diversity issues by using flexible grouping practices, for example, and assessing classroom curriculum materials to ensure that they are culturally sensitive.

- Services provide access to intellectual peers. Truly exemplary services provide opportunities for gifted education students to work with others of similar interests, abilities, and drive for at least a portion of their time in public school. Classroom teachers can help to ensure this access to intellectual peers though flexible grouping practices within their classroom, as well as across grade-level classrooms when opportunities arise.

- Services include differentiated guidance services. Differentiated guidance and counseling includes targeted supports and interventions for common concerns that specific groups of gifted education students share, such as gender-related services and college or career counseling. As part of the differentiated program of counseling services, guidance personnel work collaboratively with teachers and administrators to support students' optimal learning and adjustment. Teams of committed professionals work proactively to prevent behavior patterns that lead to concerns that are more serious.

- Exemplary guidance and counseling services promote acceleration options. At a minimum, acceleration options include grade skipping, subject acceleration, early entrance to kindergarten, and concurrent enrollment. There are written policies and procedures for accelerating qualified students. See, for example, the acceleration policy adopted by NAGC (National Association for Gifted Children, 2004).

- Classroom teachers have a special role to play in the acceleration of a student. They provide the evidence to shape the decision-making process and can ease the transition of the student if the decision is made to accelerate.

- Services support a variety of enrichment options. Exemplary services include a written, systematic plan for enrichment for all students, including those who are gifted and talented. These activities can help bring to the forefront students whose talents may be hidden due to cultural, economic, or personal circumstances. Enrichment options include opportunities to explore personal interests and new topics, to pursue advanced and rigorous subjects, and to master cognitive and affective skills needed for high achievement.

- Classroom teachers are often the first to see evidence of an emerging interest and talent. As first-line "talent spotters," teachers can encourage a student's talent by encouraging follow-up activities such as reading a related article, watching a video, or talking to a local expert.

- Exemplary services require a needs assessment. They are matched purposefully to students' guidance and counseling needs. Periodic surveys or assessments of students, parents, and teachers are key to pinpointing students' most pressing social and emotional needs.

- Services include input and require support from parents and community members. Parents need information about the nature of the social and emotional needs of their children. With information, they can provide support to the counseling work of professionals in the schools.

- Exemplary services include a scope and sequence for the affective curriculum. In addition, the curriculum contains expected social and emotional outcomes and provides content and processes that

  - Help students understand what it means to be gifted/talented

  - Develop students' self-advocacy skills

- Strengthen students' self-regulatory abilities

- Teach students strategies for coping with challenges and stressors common to gifted students

- Provide differentiated college and career guidance

- Increase parents' effectiveness in guiding their gifted children

## EXAMPLE IN NEED OF REVISION

As you read the example that follows about Loving School District, think about your own district and school. Compare your guidance and counseling services to those described here. To what extent are the services in your school similar to or different from those offered in Loving?

Loving School District strongly believes in the value of inclusion and mixed-ability classrooms. The district offers its gifted education students a weekly pull-out program at the elementary and middle school levels and a wide range of accelerated courses at the high school. At the elementary and middle schools, a counselor is available who is familiar with the needs of high-potential students and who has experience with focus groups and short-term individual and family counseling with gifted children. There are no differentiated guidance services offered for gifted students at the high school. College and career counseling is available at the high school for anyone who requests it and is offered primarily to juniors and seniors.

Schoolwide inservice training on the social and emotional needs of gifted students was provided three years ago. Since then, no formal staff development on teaching high-ability students has been provided. However, there have been many opportunities for informal updates for interested personnel. Teachers attend the annual state conference and are provided with updates through short presentations at faculty meetings, optional early morning or afterschool meetings, and their collaboration with other personnel. Also, a district newsletter about the gifted program is distributed to all school personnel and parents of gifted students.

Within the weekly pull-out programs, teachers conduct guidance activities about twice a month during which they address the most common student concerns, such as managing stress or anxiety, coping with perfectionism, and understanding giftedness. The school counselor occasionally helps with these classes but does not offer any focus groups for students. Subject acceleration is available when parents push for it, but the administration discourages grade skipping. Guidance regarding college and other postsecondary options is not offered at the middle school.

## PROCEDURES FOR REVISION

How did your school's services compare to Loving's guidance and counseling services? Loving's services are fairly typical. There are several changes that Loving could make to improve guidance and counseling services for its high-achieving students.

First, there is an obvious need to provide information about acceleration to classroom teachers and administrators. The research is very clear that acceleration options such as grade skipping, subject acceleration, early entrance, and concurrent enrollment are effective means for increasing achievement and promoting healthy adjustment for qualified students (Colangelo, Assouline, & Gross, 2004; Rogers, 2002; Southern & Jones, 1991). The school district should develop a brief written policy that describes the procedures parents and teachers are to follow when they wish to recommend a student for acceleration options. For example, the Iowa Acceleration Scale (IAS) (Assouline, Colangelo, Lupkowski-Shoplik, Lipscomb, & Forstadt, 2003) is a tool to assist in the decision making concerning a student's trajectory in school. All teachers should be aware of the IAS and its usefulness to families and members of child-study teams in making decisions about acceleration.

In addition, teachers, administrators, and parents need to be provided with information about other acceleration options such as pre-AP courses, AP courses, and distance learning options. All students, especially those with unique gifts and talents, should have opportunities to take advantage of these high-level learning options.

Second, there needs to be a provision for districtwide enrichment that provides all students with opportunities to demonstrate abilities that may be hidden due to cultural, economic, or personal circumstances. These enrichment options include preassessment, individual and small-group investigations, afterschool enrichment opportunities, and Saturday programs.

Third, the district should evaluate whether gifted students have adequate access to their intellectual peers. High-ability students should be grouped in ways that provide ongoing access to other students with similar motivation, interests, and abilities.

Fourth, there is an apparent need for differentiated guidance services at all levels, but particularly at the high school level where there are few specialized services. Interested counselors who have training in the social and emotional development of gifted children must be encouraged to provide brief seminars, meetings, or counseling groups on topics relevant to the needs of gifted students. The district may want to invite student, parent, and teacher input regarding topics or skills that should be a priority. The lack of college and career guidance opportunities for gifted students at the secondary level is an obvious omission. Some college/career counseling should be offered at the middle school for all high-achieving students, and pinpointed college counseling should be available for all gifted education students through their senior year (Arnold, Noble, & Subotnik, 1999; Berger, 1989; Colangelo & Assouline, 2000; Greene, 2002; Rysiew, Shore, & Leeb, 1998).

Finally, it is not clear whether the district's efforts to meet the social and emotional needs of gifted students are grounded in a broad scope and sequence of affective goals and objectives, or that there is knowledge about and agreement regarding the desired outcomes. Practitioners need to collaborate to develop a reasonable scope and sequence and agree on expected outcomes. They will also need to discuss these outcomes to ensure they address the cultural and economic makeup of the student body.

To summarize, personnel in Loving should follow these steps to improve their guidance and counseling services for high-achieving students:

- Use the characteristics of exemplary services listed previously to assess current provisions at all levels. Note strengths as well as areas that need revision.
- Prioritize areas for improvement (e.g., differentiated guidance services).
- Determine desired affective outcomes at each level and write broad goals for students.
- Identify yearly objectives for each goal.
- Select curriculum materials, resources, and activities to support the objectives.
- Arrange professional learning opportunities for counselors, teachers, administrators, and parents.

# MAKEOVER EXAMPLE

With the help of the gifted education specialist, the district formed a task force to assess current provisions and to conduct a needs assessment among staff, parents, and students regarding the social and emotional needs of gifted students. Based on data that were gathered, the task force prioritized needs and proposed an action plan to address them. The plan was approved by the administration, sanctioned by the board of education, and implemented over three years.

A team of Loving practitioners met to examine the policies and provisions related to acceleration. They crafted a written policy to guide parents and teachers in making effective decisions about grade skipping, early enrollment in kindergarten, concurrent enrollment, and subject acceleration. The procedure includes use of the Iowa Acceleration Scale (Assouline et al., 2003).

In an effort to improve its identification of students with hidden talents, the district expanded enrichment opportunities for all students by instituting minicourses and enrichment clusters at the elementary and middle school level and by providing ongoing training in a wide variety of classroom enrichment strategies for all teachers (Betts & Kercher, 1999; Gubbins, 1995; Tomlinson, 2001; Winebrenner, 1992). It later added specialized training in enrichment strategies for disadvantaged children (Sarouphim, 1999).

In light of the recent Templeton Report (Colangelo, Assouline, & Gross, 2004), a small group of interested staff members decided to review the research on acceleration practices. They plan to make a presentation to the whole faculty at the end of the school year and to propose recommendations about offering accelerated courses of study in the middle school in subsequent years.

One counselor at the high school was identified as a specialist in guidance services for high-potential students and provided with additional training. She offers one seminar or workshop for one group of interested students each quarter. In addition, a middle school counselor collaborates with teachers to provide exploratory college and career activities. He also offers a focus group on college/career planning each semester for interested students. At all levels, there is increased collaboration between the school counselor and those teachers who work with high-ability students. The counselors provide miniworkshops on topics such as stress and time management, effective goal setting, and healthy competition.

The following broad, affective goals were agreed on for the district's gifted students:

1. Students will be able to describe in their own words the common characteristics of gifted people and identify ways that these individuals are similar to and different from others.

2. All secondary gifted students will be able to advocate for their learning needs with classroom teachers.

3. Beginning in the middle school, gifted girls, gifted students of color, and disadvantaged gifted students will evaluate potential conflicts that may arise for them and that stem from mixed messages about achievement and affiliation.

4. Students will explore afterschool and summer enrichment opportunities.

5. All gifted students will develop self-regulatory skills and coping skills to enhance their adjustment and achievement. Skills might include strategies for self-calming, anxiety reduction, improving flexibility, managing perfectionism, and discriminating between faulty and valid feedback.

6. Students will explore postsecondary options relevant to their interests, goals, and values.

7. Parents of gifted students will be able to explain the ways that the development and education of gifted children differ from those of other children.

8. Parents will encourage and support their children in appropriate self-advocacy at school.

At least three objectives for each goal were determined for elementary, middle, and high school gifted students. The district now has more of a scope and sequence for affective curriculum within services for gifted students. For example, here are objectives for Goal 5 at the middle school level:

- Students will compare and contrast three strategies for managing stress and determine which one is most effective for their individual use.
- Students will understand and practice five different strategies for coping with anxiety or other kinds of intensity. They will be able to document which strategy works best in different kinds of situations.
- Students will evaluate the ways in which they are perfectionistic and the conditions under which their perfectionism is adaptive or maladaptive for them.

The district designed a method for assessing the impact of these changes every three years. A stratified sample of students, teachers, and parents is asked to complete annually a short questionnaire about student achievement and social and emotional progress. A small number of randomly selected students and their parents are also invited every two years to be interviewed about the program's impact on the students' social and emotional needs and achievement.

## A STRATEGIC PLAN TO DEVELOP AN EFFECTIVE APPROACH FOR MEETING THE SOCIAL AND EMOTIONAL NEEDS OF GIFTED STUDENTS

*Objective:* To develop or improve school services that address the social and emotional needs of gifted education students.

*Evidence:* A menu of documented supports, interventions, and policies that support the social and emotional needs of gifted students in Loving School District.

*Tasks:* Conduct a survey of current provisions, identify priorities for improvement, and develop an action plan for making improvements.

| Date | Action | Person Responsible | Evidence |
|------|--------|--------------------|----------|
| Month 1 | Meet with guidance personnel to identify services provided for gifted students | G/T coordinator | List of services by school |
| Month 1 | Create survey for teachers | Advisory committee chair | Copies of survey |
| Month 2 | Distribute and collect survey to all teachers to identify provisions and priorities | Building administrator | Completed surveys |
| Month 2 | Summarize survey results | Advisory committee chair | Short, narrative summary of key findings with list of priorities |
| Month 3 | Formulate parent questionnaire | Parent and G/T teacher | Questionnaire |
| Month 3 | Ask parents to complete questionnaire at fall parent workshop | Chair of parent advisory group | Completed questionnaires |
| Month 4 | Summarize questionnaire results | Chair of parent advisory group | List of key findings and priorities |
| Month 4 | Create student questionnaire | Advisory committee chair | Finished questionnaire |
| Month 4 | Select stratified sample of students | Director of technology | List of student names with their homeroom teacher |
| Month 5 | Students complete questionnaire during homeroom | Building administrator | Completed questionnaires sent to G/T coordinator |
| Month 6 | Summarize student questionnaires | Advisory committee chair | List of key findings and priorities; selected examples of student comments |
| Month 6 | Identify top three priorities for services and staff development | Advisory committee chair | List of priorities |
| Months 7–8 | Develop action plan to address priorities | G/T coordinator | Written action plan |

## TEMPLATE FOR ASSESSING GUIDANCE AND COUNSELING SERVICES

The assessment scale in Table 9.1 is offered as a tool to begin assessment of services to meet the social and emotional needs of gifted students in a district. The higher the rating, the more likely it is that the district has exemplary guidance and counseling services for gifted education students. Very low and very high ratings on individual items illuminate weaknesses and strengths, respectively. The key: 1—not at all; 2—to a limited extent; 3—satisfactory; 4—exemplary.

**Table 9.1**    Assessing Services to Meet the Social and Emotional Needs of G/T Students

| | | | | |
|---|---|---|---|---|
| 1. All personnel have had training in the social and emotional needs of gifted students. | 1 | 2 | 3 | 4 |
| 2. All gifted students have regular access to others with similar interests, ability, and drive. | 1 | 2 | 3 | 4 |
| 3. All gifted students receive an appropriate level of academic challenge in the regular classroom. | 1 | 2 | 3 | 4 |
| 4. A range of acceleration options is available. | 1 | 2 | 3 | 4 |
| 5. There is a written policy for acceleration. | 1 | 2 | 3 | 4 |
| 6. The differentiated needs of culturally diverse gifted students are recognized. | 1 | 2 | 3 | 4 |
| 7. Guidance personnel work collaboratively with teachers of high-ability students to address social and emotional needs. | 1 | 2 | 3 | 4 |
| 8. Differentiated guidance services are offered for gifted students at the elementary level. | 1 | 2 | 3 | 4 |
| 9. Differentiated guidance services are offered for gifted students at the middle school level. | 1 | 2 | 3 | 4 |
| 10. Differentiated guidance services are offered for gifted students at the high school level. | 1 | 2 | 3 | 4 |
| 11. Parents are regularly offered information related to the social and emotional needs of their gifted children. | 1 | 2 | 3 | 4 |
| 12. There is districtwide agreement concerning desired affective outcomes for gifted students. | 1 | 2 | 3 | 4 |
| 13. Broad goals for meeting social and emotional needs of gifted students have been identified at the elementary level. | 1 | 2 | 3 | 4 |
| 14. Broad goals for meeting social and emotional needs of gifted students have been identified at the middle level. | 1 | 2 | 3 | 4 |
| 15. Broad goals for meeting social and emotional needs of gifted students have been identified at the high school level. | 1 | 2 | 3 | 4 |
| 16. There is an identified affective curriculum for gifted students with a scope and sequence across grade levels. | 1 | 2 | 3 | 4 |

## ADVICE FOR THE SOLE PRACTITIONER

Sole practitioners should be encouraged. Studies from our field suggest that small things can have a big impact on children's overall adjustment. Indeed, the single best predictor of long-term positive outcomes for children living with chronic stress or adversity is a long-term relationship with a caring adult. Therefore, anything and everything that sole practitioners can do to support and strengthen the relationships gifted children have with adults will be helpful. Providing interested teachers and school counselors with succinct, practical information about strategies to address the social and emotional needs of gifted students in the classroom will increase the number of adults who can effectively respond to these children.

In addition, we know that educating parents about the social and emotional characteristics and needs of their children will help them to be better advocates. Several Web sites have information about the social and emotional needs of gifted education children that parents will find helpful. Two gateway sites are mentioned here:

- *Supporting the Emotional Needs of the Gifted (SENG):* SENG is dedicated to fostering environments in which gifted adults and children, in all their diversity, understand and accept themselves and are supported, nurtured, and valued by their families, schools, workplaces, and communities. SENG is online at www.sengifted.org
- *Understanding Our Gifted:* This publication is a bimonthly newsletter that addresses the intellectual, social and emotional needs of gifted youth. It includes practical advice, social and emotional concerns, strategies for parents to use at home and school, and educational options. The URL is www.openspacecomm.com

If sole practitioners have time to conduct guidance activities themselves, they will find many useful resources (e.g., Betts & Kercher, 1999; Betts & Neihart, 1985; Delisle & Galbraith; 2003; Galbraith, Delisle, & Espeland, 1996; Hipp, 1985; Peterson, 1995; Seligman, 1995).

Finally, there will be times when sole practitioners find that they are the only ones available to provide direct guidance to gifted students or their families. At those times, practitioners need to be prepared with referral information regarding local specialists, national information centers, and reliable Web sites where they and parents can find the information and support that they need. Taking a small amount of time up-front to prepare a list of locally accessible specialists and centers will enable single practitioners to dispense high-quality referrals and recommendations efficiently. A list of Web sites and organizations will prove equally valuable.

## MUST-READ RESOURCES

Moon, S. (Vol. Ed). (2004). Social/Emotional issues, underachievement, and counseling of gifted and talented students. (Vol. 8). In S. M. Reis (Series Ed.), *Essential readings in gifted education.* Thousand Oaks, CA: Corwin.

Neihart, M., Reis, S., Robinson, N., & Moon, S. (Eds.). (2002). *The social and emotional development of gifted children: What do we know?* (Vol. 8). Waco, TX: Prufrock Press.

## REFERENCES

Arnold, K., Noble, K., & Subotnik, R. (1999). To thine own self be true: A new model of female talent development. *Gifted Child Quarterly, 43,* 140–147.

Assouline, S. G., Colangelo, N., Lupkowski-Shoplik, A., Lipscomb, J., & Forstadt, L. (2003). *The Iowa Acceleration Scale* (2nd ed.). Scottsdale, AZ: Great Potential Press.

Baker, J. (1996). Everyday stressors of academically gifted adolescents. *Journal of Secondary Gifted Education, 7,* 356–368.

Baum, S., & Owen, S. (1988). High ability/learning disabled students: How are they different? *Gifted Child Quarterly, 32,* 321–326.

Baum, S. M., Cooper, C. R., & Neu, T. W. (2001). Dual differentiation: An approach for meeting the curricular needs of gifted students with learning disabilities. *Psychology in the Schools, 38*(5), 477–490.

Berger, S. (1989). *College planning for gifted students.* Reston, VA: The Council for Exceptional Children.

Betts, G. T., & Kercher, J. (1999). *Autonomous learner model: Optimizing ability.* Greeley, CO: ALPS.

Betts, G. T., & Neihart, M. (1985). Eight effective activities to enhance the social and emotional development of the gifted and talented. *Roeper Review, 8,* 18–23.

Colangelo, N., & Assouline, S. G. (2000). Counseling gifted students. In K. A. Heller, F. J. Monks, R. J. Sternberg, & R. F. Subotnik (Eds.), *International handbook of giftedness and talent* (2nd ed., pp. 595–607) Amsterdam: Elsevier.

Colangelo, N., Assouline, S. G., & Gross, M. U. W. (2004). *A nation deceived: How schools hold back America's brightest students.* Iowa City, IA: University of Iowa.

Delisle, J., & Galbraith, J. (2003). *When gifted kids don't have all the answers: How to meet their social and emotional needs.* Minneapolis, MN: Free Spirit Publishing.

Ford, D. Y. (1992). Determinants of underachievement as perceived by gifted, above-average, and average Black students. *Roeper Review, 14,* 130–136.

Galbraith, J., Delisle, J., & Espeland, P. (1996). *The gifted kids' survival guide.* Minneapolis, MN: Free Spirit.

Greene. M. J. (2002). Career counseling for gifted and talented students. In M. Neihart, S. M. Reis, N. M. Robinson, & S. M. Moon (Eds.), *The social and emotional development of gifted children: What do we know?* (pp. 223–236). Waco, TX: Prufrock Press.

Gross, M. U. M. (1993). *Exceptionally gifted children.* London: Routledge.

Gubbins, E. J. (Ed.). (1995). *Research related to the enrichment triad model* (RM95212). Storrs, CT: University of Connecticut, The National Research Center on the Gifted and Talented.

Hipp, E. (1985). *Fighting invisible tigers: A stress management guide for teens.* Minneapolis, MN: Free Spirit.

Hollingworth, L. S. (1926). *Gifted children: Their nature and nurture.* New York: Macmillan.

Hollingworth, L. S. (1942). *Children above 180 IQ.* New York: World Book.

Janos, P. M., Robinson, N. M., & Lunneborg, C. E. (1989). Markedly early entrance to college: A multi-year comparative study of academic performance and psychosocial adjustment. *Journal of Higher Education, 60,* 496–518.

Moon, S. M. (2001). Gifted children with attention-deficit/hyperactivity disorder. In M. Neihart, S. M. Reis, N. M. Robinson, & S. M Moon (Eds.). *The social and emotional development of gifted children: What do we know?* (pp. 193–201). Waco, TX: Prufrock Press.

Moon, S. M., Zentall, S. S., Grskovic, J. A., Hall, A. & Stormont, M. (2001). Emotional and social characteristics of boys with AD/HD and/or giftedness: A comparative case study. *Journal for the Education of the Gifted, 24*(3), 207–247.

National Association for Gifted Children. (2004) *Acceleration.* [position paper]. Washington, DC: Author.

National Association for Gifted Children Counseling and Guidance Division (n.d.). Recent research on guidance, counseling and therapy for the gifted. Retrieved March 8, 2005, from http://www.nagc.org/divisions/CounGuide/guide.html

Neihart, M., Reis, S. M., Robinson, N. M., & Moon, S. M. (Eds.). (2002). *The social and emotional development of gifted children: What do we know?* Waco, TX: Prufrock Press.

Olenchak, F. R., & Reis, S. M. (2001). Gifted students with learning disabilities. In M. Neihart, S. M. Reis, N. M. Robinson, & S. M Moon (Eds.), *The social and emotional development of gifted children: What do we know?* (pp. 267–289). Waco, TX: Prufrock Press.

Peterson, J. S. (1995) *Talk with teens about feelings, family, relationships, and the future: 50 guided discussions for school and counseling groups.* Minneapolis, MN: Free Spirit.

Reis, S., & McCoach, B. (2000). The underachievement of gifted students: What do we know and where do we go? *Gifted Child Quarterly, 44,* 152–170.

Rogers, K. (2002). Effects of acceleration on gifted learners. In M. Neihart, S. Reis, N. M. Robinson, & S. M. Moon (Eds.), *The social and emotional development of gifted children: What do we know?* (pp. 3–12). Waco, TX: Prufrock Press.

Rysiew, K. J., Shore, B. M., & Leeb, R. T. (1998). Multipotentiality, giftedness, and career choices: A review. *Journal of Counseling & Development, 77,* 423–430.

Sarouphim, K. M. (1999). DISCOVER: A promising alternative assessment for the identification of gifted minorities. *Gifted Child Quarterly, 43,* 244–251.

Seligman, M. (1995). *The optimistic child.* New York: HarperPerennial.

Southern, W. T., & Jones, E. D. (1991). *The academic acceleration of gifted children.* New York: Teachers College Press.

Tomlinson, C. A. (2001). *How to differentiate instruction in mixed-ability classrooms.* Alexandria, VA: Association for Supervision and Curriculum Development.

Winebrenner, S. (1992). Teaching gifted kids in the regular classroom: Strategies and techniques every teacher can use to meet the academic needs of the gifted and talented. Minneapolis, MN: Free Spirit.

Zentall, S. S., Moon, S. M., Hall, A. M., & Grskovic, J. A. (2001). Learning and motivational characteristics of boys with AD/HD and/or giftedness: A multiple case study. *Exceptional Children, 67,* 499–519.

# 10

# Creating a Comprehensive and Defensible Budget for Gifted Programs and Services

*Carolyn R. Cooper*

Money is a terrible master but an excellent servant.

—Phineas Taylor Barnum,
U.S. circus showman (1810–1891)

Except for administrators, few educators are as sensitive to the state of the school budget as are practitioners in the field of gifted education. The reason for this sensitivity is well-known. In many states, the health of gifted education programs and the practitioners who work in them fluctuates with the health of the local and state economy. A little more than half (58%) of the states in the United States allocate money for gifted education (Council of State Directors and National Association for Gifted Children, 2003). In the remaining states, gifted education programs are funded at the local level because the educational community and the citizens who reside in them value the services.

It follows, then, that creating a budget and being accountable for resource allocation are of paramount importance. To maintain the current level of services, it is critical that teachers and coordinators of gifted programs understand and participate in the entire budgeting process. The budgeting process includes creating a budget and being accountable for program expenditures. When practitioners can demonstrate that tax dollars have been spent wisely and have yielded student growth, they are in a much stronger position to advocate on behalf of the gifted education program and the students they serve. In many ways, the budget and budgeting process can be our servant, just as circus showman Phineas Barnum wisely said over a century ago. Instead of ruling our lives, we can use money and the budgeting process to provide accountability and support for our programs and services.

Understandably, this chapter is closely linked to many others in this guidebook: Articulating Gifted Education Program Goals, 6; Comprehensive Program Design, 7; Curriculum for Gifted Education Students, 8; Selecting Learning Resources in the Education of the Gifted, 11; Roles, Responsibilities, and Professional Qualifications of Key Personnel for Gifted Education Services, 13; Designing a Professional Development Plan, 14; and Developing a Plan for Evaluating a Program in Gifted Education, 15. In many ways, the linkages here parallel those in our homes. We know that budgets are linked inextricable to all of the activities our families undertake.

Carolyn Cooper, a longtime coordinator of programs for the gifted in large school districts, as well as a former state director in Maryland, has had many years of experiences with budgets and advocating for programs. In this chapter, she shares with us many practical strategies that practitioners can use to make the budgeting process transparent and defensible.

## DEFINITION

Among the nuts and bolts of a program's organization and operation are several components, without which the program cannot function. One of these components is the program's budget.

The budget of a gifted and talented education program is a structure that supports the program's expenses. The program budget need not be huge, but it must contain funds for specific expenditures required to achieve the stated program goals and student performance outcomes. It connects closely with the program's goals and objectives, activities, timeline, evaluation scheme, and the personnel needed to implement these components. In short, the budget is a key management tool for achieving the program's intended results; and at the same time, it can be used to demonstrate fiscal responsibility.

## RATIONALE

The gifted education budget is one of the most critical components of the program. It assigns a dollar value to each goal and describes the objectives and activities to achieve the goal. Its primary role is twofold: (1) to organize all elements of the program for logical accounting and (2) to assist in program planning. As a communication tool, the budget also conveys to stakeholders how efficiently, effectively, and economically funds are both encumbered and, ultimately, expended to accomplish each program goal.

Requisite resources and materials must be provided to support the efforts of gifted education programming, as explained in the Program Standards published by the National

Association for Gifted Children (Landrum, Cox, & Evans, 2001). Just as a checkbook or online accounting system helps an individual manage his or her personal funds, so, too, the budget informs financial decisions the program director must make with respect to implementing program components (Pan, Rudo, Schneider, & Smith-Hansen, 2003). The purpose of both the personal and program budgeting systems is the same: decision making for future planning.

In effect, the budget is a program evaluation tool. It must be considered at the time the program administrator is planning student identification strategies, instructional services, and needed evaluation data (Davis & Rimm, 1989). As an evaluation tool, it reflects the program's priorities, the degree to which those priorities are addressed throughout the budget period, extenuating circumstances that interrupt the flow of priority achievement, and program decisions made to modify original plans. As a measure of program effectiveness, the gifted education budget provides ongoing direction for program decision making, the purpose of any evaluation instrument.

## GUIDING PRINCIPLES

- Budgets are prepared by gifted education (G/T) coordinators and/or administrators to provide essential services to students in gifted education.
- The budget and budgeting process will differ from district to district and state to state.
- Depending on state and district expectations, G/T coordinators and administrators have different levels of involvement and responsibility with regard to budgets and budgeting.
- All G/T coordinators must be knowledgeable about all aspects of the budget process to enable them to advocate accordingly.
- All budget expenditures are made to accomplish the program's goals and objectives.
- Gifted education budgets that are a part of the governing agency's budget build administrative ownership for the program (Cooper, 1995).
- School budget line items designated for gifted education programming reflect the program's integration with the total school curriculum, which helps with public relations, staff ownership, and administrative efforts to support the program (Cooper, 2000).
- Budget integrity leads to fiscal accountability, which must be maintained continuously.

## TRAITS OF A HIGH-QUALITY BUDGET

### Comprehensiveness

- A budget includes every type of expenditure needed to accomplish the program's stated goals.
- No expenditure is too small for inclusion in the budget. Every cent allocated by the district or state must be accounted for in the program budget.

### Consistency

- The budget aligns completely with the program's stated goals, objectives, and services.
- Every line item belongs to a category with a corresponding line on the agency's master budget form for the program.

## Alignment

- All line items in the budget must be realistic and reflect federal, state, and local figures as well as vendors' current prices.

## Clarity

- All line items and attendant cost designations must be easily understood.
- Only items linked directly to the program's goals are included in the budget.
- Every line item is a function of program planning, implementation, or management.

## Accuracy

- A budget must be accurate from its conceptualization to its daily management.
- Any in-kind expenses must be calculated accurately and accounted for as a critical component of the total program budget.
- Fixed charges must be current and included correctly on the agency's required forms.
- Items substituted for others listed in the budget must be justified and costs modified throughout the entire budget to maintain the original budget total.
- Budget categories that carry limitations with regard to transferring funds to/from other categories must be respected and monitored regularly for accuracy.
- Budget accuracy makes for a cleaner, trouble-free audit.

# EXAMPLE IN NEED OF REVISION

The following example illustrates budget construction flaws within each of the five quality markers: comprehensiveness, internal consistency, alignment, clarity, and accuracy.

**Table 10.1** Budget in Need of Revision

| Line Item | Calculation | Program Cost | In-Kind | Total Item Cost |
|---|---|---|---|---|
| **Salaries & Wages** | | | | |
| Program director | $35,000 | | | $35,000 |
| Secretary | $4.10/hr. | 40 hrs. | | $8,200 |
| Evaluator | $70,000 | 7 months | Supplies | $70,000 |
| **Contracted Services** | | | | |
| Consultant on differentiation | $1,500/day | $4,500 | Travel | $4,500 |
| Conference: *The Slow Learner* | 10 teachers @ $2,500 | $23,800 | $1,200 | $25,000 |

**Table 10.1** (Continued)

| Supplies & Materials | | | | |
|---|---|---|---|---|
| Books for teachers | 300 | $10,000 | $5,000 | $16,000 |
| Buses for field trip | $125/hour | $1,500 | $1,500 | $1,500 |
| Evaluator's supplies | estimated cost | $250 | | $250 |
| Office supplies (stationery, computer disks, printer paper, electric pencil sharpener, notepads, Rolodex, planner, clips, etc.) | estimated cost | $250 | $100 | $350 |
| **Other Charges** | | | | |
| Social Security | 5 people | 20% | | $50,000 |
| **Equipment** | | | | |
| New printer | $400 | $400 | | $400 |
| Desk & chair | $1,400 | $1,000 | $400 | $1,400 |
| **TOTAL** | | | | $179,410 |

# PROCEDURES FOR REVISING THE EXAMPLE

The corrective actions suggested here can help remove the flaws and substantially strengthen the gifted education program budget.

**Table 10.2**    Budget Flaws and Suggested Corrections

| Quality Marker | Budget Flaw | Corrective Action Suggested |
|---|---|---|
| Comprehensiveness | Incomplete listing of expenditures | Add enrichment specialist(s), evaluator's supplies, and the required unemployment insurance and worker's compensation |
| Consistency | *Slow Learner* conference not consistent with program goals | Substitute NAGC annual convention |
| | Program goals, objectives, and activities not articulated as the introduction to the budget; alignment of budget and program goals, etc., not apparent | Specify program goals, objectives, and activities with which to align gifted education program budget |

*(Continued)*

**Table 10.2** (Continued)

| Quality Marker | Budget Flaw | Corrective Action Suggested |
|---|---|---|
| Alignment | Cost of some items not current<br>• Secretary's salary too low<br>• Evaluator's salary inflated<br>• Social Security not aligned w/current federal rate<br>• Unemployment Insurance and Worker's Compensation not listed | Update secretary's hourly wage to $14.10/hr.<br><br>Adjust evaluator's salary to $35,000 for 7 months or increase length of contract<br><br>Rework Social Security and Unemployment Insurance to reflect percent of total personnel cost:<br>• Soc. Sec.: 7.41%<br>• Unempl. Ins.: 0.0023%<br><br>Rework Worker's Comp. at rate determined by employer's plan |
| Clarity | Program Cost too vague a column label<br><br>Some item descriptions vague (e.g., "books for teacher")<br><br>Secretary's salary calculation incomplete<br><br>Length of consultant's contract not clear<br><br>Total amounts are listed only for entire budget | Change to Budgeted Amount<br><br>Specify: 300 books on differentiation @ $50/ea.<br><br>Specify work period: $14.10/hr. × 40 hrs./wk × 50 wks<br><br>Specify terms: 3 days @ $1,500/day<br><br>Each major category should be calculated with separate subtotals in each column. |
| Accuracy | Line items in incorrect categories and/or columns<br><br>• Evaluator listed in Salaries and Wages<br>• Buses for field trips listed in Supplies and Materials<br>• Evaluator's supplies listed in In-Kind column under Salaries and Wages *and* in Supplies and Materials<br>• Money and other information listed in In-Kind column<br>• Total Item Cost column contains several errors of format and addition | Reposition incorrectly categorized line items:<br><br>• A private contractor, evaluator is listed in Contracted Services.<br>• Buses are contracted for; they should be listed in Contracted Services.<br>• A line item can be entered only once in a budget. List all supplies in Supplies and Materials category.<br>• List only the dollar value of an item contributed by the district, school, and/or others in the In-Kind column.<br>• Line up figures for more accurate addition; record subtotal of each category; double-check by adding total of Budgeted Amount and In-Kind columns. This total must equal the Total Item Cost column. |

# MAKEOVER EXAMPLE

**Table 10. 3**  Revised Budget

| Line Item | Calculation | Budgeted Amount | In-Kind | Total Item Cost |
|---|---|---|---|---|
| **Salaries & Wages** | | | | |
| Program director | $35,000/12 mo. | $ 35,000 | | $35,000 |
| Secretary | $14.10/hr.× 40 hrs./wk. × 50 wks. | $ 28,200 | | $28,200 |
| Enrichment Specialist | 2@ $45,000/ 10 mo. | $ 90,000 | | $90,000 |
| **Subtotal** | | **$153,200** | | **$153,200** |
| **Contracted Services** | | | | |
| Evaluator | $70,000/10 mo. | $50,000 | $20,000 | $70,000 |
| Consultant on differentiation | $1,500/day × 3 days | $3,000 | $1,500 | $4,500 |
| Buses for field trip | 2 @ $125/hour × 6 hrs. | $750 | $750 | $1,500 |
| **Subtotal** | | **$53,750** | **$22,250** | **$76,000** |
| **Supplies & Materials** | | | | |
| Teacher books on differentiation | 300 @ $50 | $10,000 | $5,000 | $15,000 |
| Office supplies | $1000/12 mo. | $600 | $400 | $1,000 |
| Evaluator's supplies | $250/10 mo. | $250 | | $250 |
| **Subtotal** | | **$10,850** | **$5,400** | **$16,250** |
| **Other Charges** | | | | |
| Social Security | 7.41% × total personnel cost | $11,436 | | $11, 436 |
| Unemployment Insurance Worker's | .0023% × total personnel cost | $355 | | $355 |
| Compensation | 4 @ $441 | $1,764 | | $1,764 |
| **Subtotal** | | **$13,555** | | **$13,555** |
| **Equipment** | | | | |
| New printer | 1 @ $400 | $400 | | $400 |
| Desk and chair | Desk (1) @ $1,000; chair (1) @ $400 | $1,000 | $400 | $1,400 |
| **Subtotal** | | **$1,400** | **$400** | **$1,800** |
| **TOTALS** | | **$232,755** | **$28,050** | **$260,805** |

# STRATEGIC PLAN FOR DESIGNING AN EXEMPLARY GIFTED EDUCATION PROGRAM BUDGET

| | |
|---|---|
| *Objective:* | To create a gifted education program budget that is effective, efficient, and economical. |
| *Format:* | The table format used in the makeover just described contains categories of program expenditures that are standard for most educational agencies' budgets and can be used successfully in developing a new budget or remodeling an ineffective one. As decisions are made about how the program's goals will be met, important line items can be added to the budget categories to achieve the program's goals. |
| *Evidence that objective has been met:* | A budget that is comprehensive, aligned with the program and building goals, clear, and accurate. |
| *Major considerations in budget development:* | Developing an effective budget for a gifted education program requires three major considerations: (1) time to construct it, (2) data to feed into it, and (3) a logical plan for organizing the data for ease in managing the budget on a daily basis. The person constructing the program budget must focus on each category of the budget: how it aligns with the program's goals, objectives, and activities; the components in each category that will help achieve these goals; cost of these components; and the probability of receiving in-kind contributions from the school district, individual schools, and/or other sources to help offset the overall expense of operating the gifted education program. |

## Step 1: Preparation

Before placing figures on the budget worksheet, the person constructing the budget must

- Gather all data needed for each budget category. These data include descriptive program documents, enrollment projections, previous program budgets, and pay scales/benefits package costs for district's professional and classified personnel.
- Collect all forms—including the budget process calendar—that the school and/or district requires for recording the completed budget. Have accurately spelled names and locations of personnel to whom copies of the budget must be sent.
- Understand that each line item of the gifted education program budget must be defensible to supervisors and/or the school board during the district's budget process.
- Become thoroughly familiar with the final program budget so as to be helpful in the event of a program or fiscal audit.

Methodical preparation for constructing the budget pays substantial dividends for the duration of the program. Nothing substitutes for being prepared!

## Step 2: Timeline Development

With the school calendar in hand, the person constructing the program budget develops a simple timeline that lists all budget construction tasks and the projected date of completion. The accompanying chart is a recommended prototype for the first months of budget preparation.

Once the gifted education program's budget proposal is submitted to the appropriate administrators, there is often a brief hiatus for budget developers before the central office finalizes the district's overall budget proposal for review by the board of education and, finally, the public. Thus, the steps identified in the timeline are only the beginning of the long process, which continues until the board authorizes publication of the accepted budget for the following academic year.

**Table 10.4**  Budget Creation Timeline

| Date | Task |
|---|---|
| Early October | • See Step 1: Preparation (above).<br>• Gather necessary data on cost of consultants included in program plan (per diem, travel, etc.); prices of equipment desired; current prices of instructional and professional materials; and informational materials for parents and community members (e.g., *Parenting for High Potential* magazine). |
| Mid October | • Request meeting with building administrators to discuss upcoming budget process, changes from last year's process, and issues that may impact budget construction (e.g., total amount district has allocated to gifted education budget for the coming year).<br>• Discuss budget priorities with small group of staff representatives, i.e., what is desired and possible within fiscal constraints.<br>• Create a file for each budget category, and place in it every piece of information, question, or issue pertinent to that category.<br>• Draft a worksheet form for each budget category. Use the template below to guide you. |
| Early December | • Prepare a draft of each budget category on that category's worksheet.<br>• Total all categories' worksheets to get a general idea of the grand total of the gifted education program's draft budget to date. |
| Mid January | • Refine draft of program budget in preparation for discussing it with supervisor for suggestions.<br>• Review draft with supervisor for modifications, if needed. |
| Late January/ Early February | • Modify program budget draft. Send modified draft to supervisor and attach the original draft he/she reviewed earlier. (This saves his/her time, and the thoughtful gesture is appreciated.)<br>• Make further modifications, as requested by supervisor. Deliver—in person—the latest version of program budget proposal to supervisor for final approval and obtain his/her initials signifying permission to submit final budget proposal at this time. (This step makes his/her approval official and can be valuable later.) |

# TEMPLATE FOR PLANNING

This template reflects widely accepted categories of expenditures presented in a systematic manner. It is intended to jog readers' minds about the many and varied categories of budget development so that no budget item is inadvertently overlooked. This template has been designed with an eye for the practitioner in all 50 states with recognition that not all categories are applicable in all contexts due to available resources and legislation.

**Table 10.5** Template

| **1.0 Salaries and Wages** |
|---|
| 1.1  Program Director |
| 1.2  Clerical Assistant (secretary) |
| 1.3  G/T Education Specialists (teachers, if not included in agency's personnel budget) |
| 1.4  G/T Education Specialists (central office, if not included in agency's personnel budget) |
| **2.0 Fringe Benefits** (fixed charges) |
| 2.1  Social Security (7.41% of personnel cost) |
| 2.2  Unemployment Insurance (.0023% of personnel cost) |
| 2.3  Worker's Compensation ($441 \times N$ of employees) |
| 2.4  Health Insurance (generally, in agency's master budget) |
| **3.0 Contracted Services** |
| 3.1  Program Evaluator |
| 3.2  National Consultants (individuals or teams) |
| 3.3  Other Consultants |
| 3.4  College Board (for Advanced Placement [AP] and pre-AP teacher training) |
| 3.5  College Board (for student data reports) |
| 3.6  Online Courses |
| 3.7  Regional Education Service Center (for curriculum resources—human, print, nonprint) |
| **4.0 Supplies and Materials**<br>(includes shipping/handling charges) |
| 4.1  Office (start-up): General operation supplies (paper goods, software, agency stationery, etc.) |
| 4.2  Office (ongoing): May include duplicating costs, phone, A-V rental, postage. (Check with agency's financial officer for specifics.) |
| 4.3  Professional Resources (library supplies)<br>    4.3.1  National Research Center on the Gifted and Talented (NRC/GT) research report<br>    4.3.2  National Association for Gifted Children (NAGC) for membership and *Gifted Child Quarterly*<br>    4.3.3  *State of the States* Report<br>    4.3.4  Journal/Magazine subscriptions (e.g., *Education Leadership, Gifted Child Today, Journal of the Education of the Gifted, Journal of Secondary Gifted Education, Roeper Review, Teaching Exceptional Children, Understanding Our Gifted*)<br>    4.3.5  Essential books for the professional library and nonprint materials including evaluation, curriculum, program models and theoretical frameworks, and information on special populations of G/T students (see chapters throughout this book for must-read resources) |

**Table 10.5** (Continued)

| |
|---|
| 4.4 Data collection materials for student identification, including instruments and training manuals |
| 4.5 Specialized teacher training materials (e.g., technical manuals, videos, etc.) |
| 4.6 Parent and community resources (e.g., *Parenting for High Potential*, college planning guides, etc.) |
| 4.7 Student resources (instructional supplies including but not limited to online advanced-level courses, how-to books, college planning guides, national/state/local competition or contest fees, admission fees for museums, science centers, and artistic performances, and miscellaneous specialized supplies for student products) |
| 4.8 Evaluator's supplies and materials |
| **5.0 Travel** |
| 5.1 In-state: local mileage and tolls; routine operations; employee drives personal vehicle |
| 5.2 In-state conferences, seminars, training; employee drives personal vehicle |
| 5.3 Out-of-state meetings, conferences, seminars, training; employee uses plane, train, rental car, airport shuttle bus to/from hotel, taxi, or personal vehicle (if reasonable) |
| **6.0 Equipment** |
| 6.1 New: first-time purchase of this specific item using current FY's budget |
| 6.1.1 Computers for program director, clerical assistant, office staff, evaluator |
| 6.1.2 Printer |
| 6.1.3 Technology hook-ups with external agency |
| 6.1.4 Overhead or LCD projector |
| 6.1.5 Office files, furniture (desks, chairs, table, etc.) |
| 6.2 Replacement: purchased with current FY's budget to substitute for outdated or disabled equipment item |
| 6.3 Rental |
| 6.4 Hand-held tools for student products (digital camera, camcorder, lab equipment, etc.) |
| **7.0 Other Charges** |
| 7.1 Honoraria (for noncontracted speakers, etc.) |
| 7.2 Short-term clerical/secretarial support (additional or substitute) |
| 7.3 Facility rental (for meetings, training, etc.) |
| 7.4 Awards (plaques, gifts to speakers, certificates, etc.) |
| 7.5 Car phone (cost of work-related calls; check with agency financial director for policy) |
| 7.6 Duplicating/Printing (for special jobs done outside agency) |
| 7.7 Postage (may be for private parcel service only if agency covers general postage costs) |
| 7.8 Food for meetings (may be disallowed; check with agency financial officer for policy) |

## ADVICE FOR THE SOLE PRACTITIONER

Creating a budget for the first time can be a daunting task—especially if you are working on your own. The sole practitioner must first recognize that budgeting is a local issue and decisions are dependent on the context in which he or she is working. Therefore, it is important to meet with the school or district budget officer to have a conversation about administrative expectations and the interface between the G/T budget and the whole school budget. You should view the construction of a budget proposal similarly to building a puzzle. One budget category after the next gives the budget its distinct character, and, like a puzzle, it comes together in a remarkable creation. As you build *your puzzle*, think about meeting your students' needs first and, if you are able, reserve some money for professional development and meeting with other practitioners in adjacent school districts with an eye toward building more support for yourself and your program.

## REFERENCES

Cooper, C. R. (1995). Integrating gifted education into the total school curriculum. *The School Administrator, 52*(4), 8–9, 12–15.

Cooper, C. R. (2000). Gifted and talented education. In S. Tonnsen (Ed.), *What principals should know about . . .* (pp. 27–50). Springfield, IL: Charles C Thomas.

Council of State Directors and the National Association for Gifted Children. (2003). *State of the states: Gifted and Talented Education Report, 2001–2002.* Washington, DC: National Association for Gifted Children.

Davis, G. A., & Rimm, S. B. (1989). *Education of the gifted and talented* (2nd ed.). Englewood Cliffs: NJ: Prentice Hall.

Landrum, M. S., Cox, G. L., & Evans, M. (2001). Program administration and management. In M. S. Landrum, C. M. Callahan, & B. D. Shaklee (Eds.), *Aiming for excellence: Gifted program standards* (pp. 15–26). Washington, DC: National Association for Gifted Children.

Pan, D., Rudo, Z. H., Schneider, C. L., & Smith-Hanen, L. (2003). *Examination of resource allocation in education: Connecting spending to student performance* (Southwest Educational Development Laboratory Research Report). Retrieved on September 14, 2004, from http://sedl.org/rel/policydocs/Examination.pdf

# 11

# Selecting Learning Resources in the Education of the Gifted

*Ugur Sak and C. June Maker*

The art of teaching is the art of assisting discovery.

—Mark Van Doren

Selecting curriculum materials for any population of students is a daunting charge. The first indicator of the difficulties associated with this task is the sheer number of glossy advertisements that flood teachers' mailboxes. The reason for the enormous volume of ads is simple. Spending on curriculum materials is increasing at a rate of 7.7% each year. Some market analysts project that educators, across all sectors of the field, will spend $47.5 billion on curriculum resources in 2004. A recent Google search that requested information on education publishing companies yielded over 1.9 million hits, each advertising their company's educational materials.

How does one begin the task of locating appropriate curriculum resources for any group of students, including those who are gifted and talented? What are the indicators of high quality that one might use to narrow curriculum resource choices into a short list? How does one know if the materials are aligned with state, local, and/or national curriculum standards? In this chapter, Ugur Sak and June Maker provide us with practical answers to these multifaceted questions.

This chapter is most aligned with three other chapters. For understandable reasons, it is tied to the chapter on budget, 10, as well as the chapter on curriculum, 8. For less apparent reasons, it is also linked to the chapter that addresses the alignment between general and gifted education, 17. In this era of accountability, all practitioners must answer calls for increased student achievement, including the achievement of gifted education students. To impact the achievement of our gifted education students, much of our gifted education curriculum—and the resources used to support the curriculum— must link to our national, state, and local standards that are being implemented in classrooms across the country.

# DEFINITION

Resource, as a concept, means source of information, expertise, supply, or support. With respect to education, resources are sources of knowledge for students and teachers. Teachers use resources to enhance their content knowledge and instructional and assessment practices. Students use curriculum materials to scaffold their learning and assist in product development.

Resources can be classified into two basic categories: human and nonhuman resources. Human resources comprise content-area specialists, older students, and business personnel. Nonhuman resources include print and nonprint resources. Print resources include Web articles, manuals, maps, and the like. Nonprint resources may be, among many other things, antiques, tools, videotapes, musical instruments, and paintings. Any of these resources can be used to facilitate curriculum content, instruction, and/or assessment.

Resources—whether they are used in teaching, learning, or assessment—promote thinking and clarity about content goals. Furthermore, exemplary resources foster student engagement when they are varied and closely linked to students' reading levels, cognitive strengths, and interests.

# RATIONALE

Why are resources important? Since the late 1990s, researchers have been working to establish the link that many practitioners intuitively acknowledge between what students study and their academic achievement (Bransford, Brown, & Cocking, 1999; National Research Council, 2004; Marzano, Pickering, & Polluck, 2001; Viadaro, 1997). Many experts and practitioners believe that there is a correlation between what students study and their ongoing achievement. Specifically, curriculum resources play a vital role in this linkage because they determine what is being taught.

Practitioners face many dilemmas as they select curriculum resources. First, few curriculum materials have been evaluated to determine their effectiveness to enhance student learning. As a result, local practitioners—who make decisions about which curriculum materials will be used—do not always have valid, informative, and credible data to assist them in their decisions. The second dilemma is the sheer number and variety of resources that are available for use. The exploding bodies of knowledge in every discipline, the access to this knowledge that is readily available on the Web, as well as the countless glossy advertisements that proclaim the resource as "the expert's choice," "tested extensively," or "groundbreaking," make decisions about resources more complicated, yet more critical, than ever before.

Until such time as the field has a large body of evidence about the effectiveness of curriculum materials for enhancing the achievement of all students, including those who are gifted and talented, practitioners will need to base their decisions on a detailed content analysis and, of course, logic. As they consider resource materials, they must answer the following questions:

- What are my content goals?
- What are the learning profiles of my students (e.g., prior knowledge, learning rate, readiness to learn, learning style preferences, interests)?
- Which resources are most appropriate for students' learning profiles?
- Which resources will be most effective for my students as they construct their own understanding of the targeted content goals?
- Which resources might be appropriate for assessments that could be constructed to assess students' understanding about the content goals?
- Which resources are most appropriate for my learning needs as the teacher?

## GUIDING PRINCIPLES

The most effective curriculum resources are those with a research base that demonstrates their ability to impact student achievement for the range of learners. Resources for learning should be aligned with curricular, instructional, and assessment standards. The curricular standards include those from the district, state, and national subject councils (e.g., National Council of Teachers of Mathematics, National Council for the Social Studies).

The most effective curriculum resources contain depth and allow learners to make inferences about the content goals, within and across disciplines, across era and cultures, about methodological skills, and about themselves as learners, both now and in the future. Here follows some additional guiding principles:

- Effective curriculum resources must be authentic to the discipline.
- The most effective curriculum materials should provide students with multiple opportunities to construct their own understanding of the content goals (e.g., solve open-ended mathematics problems and share problem-solving strategies with peers; create and analyze data sets about local weather to determine patterns and trends; compare, contrast, and make inferences about different eyewitness accounts of historical events; and determine the fit among selected poems, biographical information about the poet's life, and their own lives).
- The most effective curriculum materials must be varied and accommodate critical differences among students including, for example; reading level, learning style, prior knowledge, learning rate, and readiness to learn.
- Teaching and learning resources should respect all cultures, ethnic backgrounds, and socioeconomic groups and contain no gender bias.
- Resources for learning must be accurate and contain no misleading information.
- The most effective curriculum materials should be accessible (e.g., reading level) and developmentally appropriate for students.
- Curriculum materials should promote student curiosity and interest.
- Resources for teachers must contain clear and easy-to-use directions.
- Curriculum resources should be affordable.
- The most effective curriculum materials are durable and will withstand several years of student use.

# CHARACTERISTICS OF HIGH-QUALITY RESOURCES

Another way to think about curriculum resources is the function for which they are used: content, process, and product (Maker, 1982; Kaplan, 1974). Whether resources are for teachers or students, they can be used to enhance content knowledge, process knowledge, or student products. The dimensions of high-quality resources are listed below.

## Content

*Alignment.* The resources are purposefully selected to link with and/or extend the local, state, and/or national content standards and objectives and will assist learners to clarify their thinking about these objectives. In some instances, students' learning needs may exceed the standards, in which case the resource selections should adhere to the remaining criteria.

*Depth.* Depth refers to the level(s) of knowledge contained in learning materials. High-quality curriculum materials focus on concepts and principles (Maker, 1982; Taba, 1962; VanTassel-Baska & Little, 2003). Facts are used to support learning about the guiding concepts and principles.

*Research Base.* The materials have been researched and have demonstrated the capacity to increase student achievement for the range of learners, including those who are gifted and talented.

*Authenticity.* Materials reflect the content of the discipline, the skills or methodology of the practicing professional, and the attitudes and dispositions of those who work in the discipline.

*Accuracy.* The content in the materials is correct and precise.

*Accessibility.* The materials are appropriate for the reading level and background experiences of the students. In addition, the content is sequenced in such a way as to enhance learning.

*Engaging.* The curriculum materials are interesting to students, promote student thinking and motivation, and invite reflection.

## Process

*Promote high-level thinking.* The materials promote analytical, critical, and creative thinking (Burns, 1993; Maker, 1982).

## Product (for teachers and students)

*Alignment.* The products are aligned with the targeted curriculum objectives.

*Variety.* The resources support a variety of product formats, including self-selected responses, to accommodate students' expression style preferences.

*Assessment criteria.* The curriculum materials contain assessment criteria and/or rubrics for all assessment tasks. The criteria and rubrics contain high ceilings and low baselines to accommodate the wide range of learners in the classroom.

## Other

*Variety.* The curriculum materials include a variety of human and nonhuman resources that appeal to the diversity of teachers' and students' readiness levels and learning styles.

*Ease of Use.* The resources are clear and contain high quality, easy-to-use directions and/or instructions.

*Durability.* The materials are sturdy and will hold up over several years of reasonable student use.

*Cost.* The cost is the price of the curriculum resource, per unit.

# EXAMPLE IN NEED OF REVISION: MR. MAHONEY'S QUEST

Mr. Mahoney teaches science to sixth-grade gifted students in a pull-out program. He believes that teaching the content of eighth-grade science to sixth-grade gifted students will meet their intellectual needs because students will be exposed to more advanced scientific content. He examines several eighth-grade science books. He reviews the tables of content, scans each unit, and checks to see what major topics are covered. He sees that there is some alignment between what is covered in the book and what sixth-grade students will learn when they reach eighth grade. Equally important, he sees that there are topics in the book that are not traditionally covered by students in the eighth-grade sequence. He decides to focus and teach his gifted education students these nontraditional topics because they will be new to students.

Then, he examines sample experiments, looks through end-of-unit questions, and reads the publisher's complimentary outtakes in the glossy promotional literature. He checks the publication date to make sure the book is current. Finally, he calls a science teacher in the neighboring district and gets her opinion.

Mr. Mahoney spends a whole school year using only this book to teach his gifted education students. In the end-of-year assessment, students demonstrate knowledge from every topic covered during the year, and have completed the end-of-unit questions. However, they have difficulty connecting their learning across broad concepts such as system and change, inferring cause-and-effect relationships, and preparing products that are aligned with the content goals.

Mr. Mahoney's single-resource approach to providing for his gifted sixth-graders is rated in the accompanying chart.

**Table 11.1**   Resource Rating

| Characteristic | Inappropriate | Needs more | Appropriate |
|---|---|---|---|
| Content | | X | |
| Process | X | | |
| Product | X | | |
| Other | Not available | | |

# PROCEDURES FOR REVISING RESOURCE ACQUISITION

The following framework features the dimensions or attributes of high-quality curriculum resources described earlier. Listed under each dimension is this section are questions designed to address the multiple facets of each attribute. Practitioners can use the questions to analyze systematically the utility of the resource and the likelihood that it will deliver the intended impact for all students, including those who are gifted and talented.

## Content

*Alignment*

- What is the content (e.g., facts, concepts, principles, skills, dispositions) that is explicitly taught in the resource?
- To what extent does the content in the resource align and/or extend the stated content objective(s) within the resource?
- To what extent is the content in the resource aligned with local, state, and/or national standards and objective(s)?
- In what ways will the materials help students clarify and deepen their thinking about the objective(s)?

*Depth*

- What concepts and principles are taught explicitly?
- What facts support the teaching of the concepts and principles?
- To what extent will students be able to make inferences about the content to more sophisticated core content; across fields, disciplines, and cultures; to more sophisticated methods, skills, and products; to themselves as future practitioners in the field?

*Research Base*

- What evidence is provided about the effectiveness of the materials with the broad range of learners, including those who are on grade level, below grade level, or beyond grade level?

*Authenticity*

- To what extent does the content mirror the content that is at the heart of the discipline?
- To what extent do the skills and dispositions reflect those used by practicing professionals?
- To what extent do the products/assessments reflect those produced by practitioners in the field?

*Accuracy*

- To what extent is the material correct and precise?
- To what extent does it contain inaccuracies and/or ideas that are not true to the discipline?

*Accessibility*

- Will students be able to read and understand this material?
- Is the subject matter developmentally appropriate?
- To what extent are the materials respectful of all cultures and groups?
- To what extent does the sequencing of the content support the principles of learning and cognition?

*Engagement*

- Would my students find this material interesting?
- Are there varied, real-world connections between the content and my students' lives?
- To what extent will this material motivate my students?

## Process

*Use of Thinking Skills*

- To what extent do the materials require students to construct their own meaning or "think their way through" the concepts, principles, skills, and dispositions?
- To what extent are there opportunities for students to use analytical thinking? Critical thinking? Creative thinking?

## Products

*Assessments*

- To what extent do the preassessments, ongoing assessments, and postassessments align with the content?
- To what extent are the assessments aligned with each other?
- Are there rubrics, criteria, or rating scales included that have a high ceiling and low baseline to capture the range of learners in the classroom?
- Are there answer keys and accompanying notes for the teacher?

*Products*

- What are my students' expression style preferences?
- To what extent are the products/performances varied to accommodate the expression styles of my students?
- Are there rubrics or rating scales included that have a high ceiling and low baseline to capture the range of learners in the classroom?

## Other

*Variety*

- What are the learning profiles of my students?
- What other curriculum materials might I use to support this resource and accommodate my students' learning style preferences?
- What human resources might I tap?
- What other print resources are available to supplement the resource currently under consideration?
- What nonprint resources might support the current resource?

### Ease of Use

- Are the directions clear for students?
- Does the layout (i.e., text, print, white space) support learning?
- Do the headings reflect the organization of the content and help to scaffold learning?
- Do the pictures and graphics elaborate on the main ideas and invite reflection?
- To what extent are the time allocations realistic?
- What is the quality and fidelity of the notes to the teacher regarding implementation of the resource?

### Durability

- Is the binder or cover made of sturdy materials?
- What proportion of the materials are consumables?

### Cost

- What is the price per unit?
- Is the price reasonable in light of the durability of the resource?

## MAKEOVER EXAMPLE

### Mr. Mahoney's Quest

Mr. Mahoney first consults with the science department chairwoman at the high school and the assistant superintendent for curriculum. He asks them to verify his understanding of the grade-level objectives in science for sixth-grade students. He discovers that all sixth-grade students learn one unit in each of the three branches of science: life, earth, and physical. They are the Human Body, Weather and Elements, and Mixtures and Compounds, respectively.

He looks closely at the content for each of the units to see the concepts, principles, skills, and dispositions that they feature. The earth science unit about weather intrigues him because it is a highly complex topic that he can build upon in many different ways. He can easily extend the traditional sixth-grade unit by (1) covering in more depth the current technologies that meteorologists use, (2) helping students use the Internet to track and record data about national and worldwide weather and make their own predictions (versus the tracking done by students in the standard sixth-grade unit on local and regional weather), and (3) helping students explore and gather the current research and information about the effect of ocean currents on world weather.

Equally important, he has a conversation with the department chairwoman and assistant superintendent about the overarching macroconcepts that guide the weather unit: systems, patterns, and cause and effect. Together, they agree that there are many valid intradisciplinary connections (e.g., the human body, geology, ecology) and interdisciplinary connections (e.g., government systems, number systems) that he can capitalize on and build into his teaching for advanced-level students. Mr. Mahoney is particularly pleased with the connections he can build into this unit for gifted education students because many of them are abstract thinkers. He knows that he can build in a wide variety of honest connections, should his students need them.

With his ideas about the content of his unit in place, Mr. Mahoney first consults the Internet for resources on meteorology. He finds four books that look like a match. He calls several area bookstores and discovers that these merchants carry three of the four titles he is seeking. Using the checklist above to select his resources, he decides that two of the books are suitable. They focus on the idea of weather as a system. In addition, they are readable, cover ocean currents and their effect on weather, and contain many colored pictures and charts explaining the currents and their movement around the globe. Although he cannot locate any research about the effectiveness of the books on student achievement, he notes that they are written by scientists for novice meteorologists. Unlike textbooks, these resources do not contain any assessments. Mr. Mahoney does not worry about this because he already knows what he wants his students to do to demonstrate their understanding of the content. He wants them to create a weather log in order to track weather at different locations around the globe and then, using the data, make predictions that they will compare to the actual weather data. This project, among others, will require students to think their way through the cause-and-effect relationships that are an integral part of our weather system.

He makes the decision that these two books will be good resources for his students, and that they will share copies. The remaining book, a college text, is too technical for his students. He asks the school to purchase all the books, however. He decides to use the college text as a resource for himself.

Mr. Mahoney next goes to the Internet. He discovers that many resources are available for his students at no cost: worldwide weather maps, temperature and precipitation data, jet stream data, as well as maps of ocean currents and temperatures that are updated daily. There is even one site that has actual real-time pictures that show the temperatures of ocean currents. In addition, he looks at the newspaper to which the school library subscribes. He is delighted to find that the weather information is very detailed. He decides that he has more than enough resources for his gifted education unit. If he has time, he will try to locate one or two meteorologists from neighboring state universities to ask if they will visit with students and/or host his students on a field trip to their weather stations.

## A STRATEGIC PLAN FOR SELECTING RESOURCES

*Objective:*  To select learning resources for a unit designed for gifted education students.

*Evidence:*  A list of varied and aligned resources that are appropriate for (1) a unit of study and (2) targeted students.

*Tasks:*  Steps for selecting learning resources:

1. Identify the facts, concepts, principles, skills, and dispositions in the classroom unit that will be extended for gifted education students.

2. Check the local, state, and national standards related to the topic to discover (1) what has already been covered and (2) what has yet to be covered.

3. With the standards in mind, consider the many and varied ways the regular classroom unit can be modified or extended to address the learning needs of gifted education students. The new unit might include more sophisticated core content, focus on more advanced-level methodological skills, connect the learning to other fields and/or disciplines, and/or focus on the personal connection between the content and students' current interests and goals.

4. Consider the learning profiles of students.

5. With the curriculum objectives and students' learning profiles in mind, develop an initial pool of resources. The initial list will emerge from books in one's individual collection, the book room, visits to vendors' booths at conferences, the school and public library, and the Internet, among others.

6. Using the framework above, narrow the initial list down to a small set of varied resources that addresses the concepts and principles in the unit, as well as students' learning needs.

7. Use the resources with students. Gather feedback from them about the quality and effectiveness of each. Revise accordingly.

## ADVICE FOR THE SOLE PRACTITIONER

It is impossible for the sole practitioner to ensure that the learning needs of gifted and talented learners are considered in content-area objectives and the acquisition of curriculum

**Table 11.2**   A Framework for Selecting High-Quality, Appropriate Resources

| Resource Name:<br><br>Publisher:<br><br>Year:<br><br>Price per Unit: | | | Noteworthy characteristics of the target population of students (e.g., age, reading level, academic strengths, prior knowledge, interests, learning style preferences, expression style preferences, areas in need of remediation) |
|---|---|---|---|
| Characteristics of High Quality Curriculum Resources | Content | Alignment | Notes: |
| | | Depth | |
| | | Research Base | |
| | | Authenticity | |
| | | Accuracy | |
| | | Accessibility | |
| | | Engagement | |
| | Process | Use of High-Level Thinking Skills | |
| | Products | Assessments | |
| | | Products | |
| | Other | Variety | |
| | | Ease of Use | |
| | | Durability | |
| | | Cost | |

materials, K–12, in a relatively short period of time. To make the job more manageable, an alternative would be for the sole practitioner to volunteer to sit on district-level textbook adoption and curriculum review committees. In many school districts, each content area is subject to review every five years or so. For example, the science curriculum—and related science curriculum materials—are reviewed in 2004. The social studies, and accompanying curriculum materials, are reviewed in 2005, and so forth until all the content areas have been examined.

By sitting on these committees, the sole practitioner gains in three important ways. First, he or she becomes acquainted with his or her colleagues throughout the system. Second, he or she can provide expertise about the learning needs of gifted education students to the group's consideration of the content-area learning goals and curriculum materials, thereby ensuring that these students' needs are considered in the regular classroom. Equally important, participation in the committees spreads the efforts of the gifted education teacher across several years and makes the workload manageable.

Another strategy for the sole practitioner is to work collaboratively with district and public librarians to assess the adequacy of school and public resources to extend the curriculum for gifted and talented students. Collaboration will help to ensure a variety of challenging resources in topics frequently taught by regular and gifted education teachers.

## MUST-READ RESOURCES

Purcell, J. H., Burns, D. E, Tomlinson, C. A., Imbeau, M. B., & Martin, J. L. (2002). Bridging the gap: A tool and technique to analyze and evaluate gifted education curricular units. *Gifted Child Quarterly, 46*(4), 306–321.

Renzulli, J. S. (1994). *Schools for talent development: A practical guide to total school improvement.* Mansfield, CT: Creative Learning Press.

VanTassel-Baska, J., & Little, C. A. (2003). *Content-based curriculum.* Waco, TX: Prufrock Press.

## REFERENCES

Bransford, J. D., Brown, A. L., & Cocking, R. R. (1999). *How people learn: Brain, mind, experience, and school.* Washington, DC: National Academy Press.

Burns, D. E. (1993). *A six-phase model for the explicit teaching of thinking skills.* Storrs, CT: The National Research Center on the Gifted and Talented, University of Connecticut.

Kaplan, S. N. (1974). *Providing programs for the gifted and talented: A handbook.* Ventura, CA: Office of the Ventura County Superintendent of Schools.

Maker, C. J. (1982). *Curriculum development for the gifted.* Rockville, MD: Aspen.

Marzano, R. J., Pickering, D. J., & Polluck, J. E. (2001). *Classroom instruction that works: Research-based strategies for increasing students' achievement.* Alexandria, VA: ASCD.

National Research Council. (2004). *On evaluating curricular effectiveness: Judging the quality of K–12 mathematics evaluations.* Retrieved June 2, 2004, from http://www.nap.edu/books/0309092426/html

Taba, H. (1962). *Curriculum development: Theory and practice.* New York: Harcourt, Brace and World.

VanTassel-Baska, J., & Little, C. A. (Eds.). (2003). *Content-based curriculum for high-ability learners.* Waco, TX: Prufrock Press.

Viadaro, D. (1997, April 2). Surprise! Analyses link curriculum, TIMSS scores. *Education Week,* p. 6.

# 12

# Managing a Communication Initiative in Gifted Education

*Kelly A. Hedrick*

Seek first to understand, then to be understood.

—Stephen Covey (1990)

Stephen Covey's powerful quotation and his book *The Seven Habits of Highly Effective People* (Covey, 1990) serve to remind us about the very powerful role that communication plays in our media-dominated world. Many would argue that teachers, including those who are involved in gifted education programs, are engaged in one form of communication or another more than 70% of their waking moments. It is not surprising, then, that the vast majority of competencies designed to measure teacher effectiveness contain criteria by which to measure a teacher's ability to communicate with a wide variety of constituencies (Danielson, 1996).

This chapter considers a critical aspect of gifted education programming: communication and its role in the educational enterprise. In this time of accountability and collaboration, the nature and clarity of our communication is one key to the quality and longevity of programs and services to our students. With clear information about program goals, achievements, and needs, as well as students' activities, constituents have the information they need to advocate on behalf of gifted education services and the students they serve.

This chapter contains information about various stakeholders in the field and explores a variety of communication vehicles that can be used to meet their needs efficiently and effectively. It is most aligned with Articulating Gifted Education Program Goals, 6; Creating a Comprehensive and Defensible Budget for Gifted Programs and Services, 10; and Developing a Plan for Evaluating a Program in Gifted Education, 15. All of these chapters are concerned with aspects of programs and services that must be communicated clearly with stakeholders. Because advocacy is built upon effective communication, there is also a natural link between this chapter and Chapter 18, Planning for Advocacy, as well as to Appendix A, Establishing Gifted Education Advisory Committees.

# DEFINITION

Communication is the means by which information is transmitted from one person to another. A communication initiative in gifted education is a plan to share information about all aspects of programs and services among the groups of constituents, including students, parents, regular classroom teachers, building administrators, central office personnel, board of education members, and state department of education personnel. A variety of vehicles is required to communicate effectively and meet the unique needs of each constituent group.

# RATIONALE

Effective communication is essential to the success of gifted education teachers, programs, and services. The growing research base related to communication skills and processes is testimony to the increasing importance of communication as a factor in effective and productive organizations. The inclusion of performance assessments for teaching certification and licensure validate the importance of communication in the teaching profession. Quite simply, teachers cannot be effective unless they are able to communicate clearly to their students, colleagues, and other stakeholders. It is not surprising that recent literature on teacher effectiveness posits communication as a critical skill of successful teachers (Danielson, 1996; Stronge, 2002).

An effective communication initiative about gifted education services:

- Establishes the need for and benefit of services to high-ability students
- Plans proactively
- Aligns with program goals and long-range plans
- Ensures clarity about all aspects of gifted education programming
- Attracts attention in a world inundated with information
- Prevents misconceptions
- Establishes trust and openness
- Invites and supports collaboration
- Establishes mechanisms for giving and receiving input from all stakeholders
- Promotes program ownership
- Provides a base of understanding and acceptance for program additions/changes

- Ensures equity and fairness
- Promotes advocacy

# GUIDING PRINCIPLES OR ASSUMPTIONS

There are many groups of people who have a vested interest in understanding gifted education and whose knowledge and understanding of program initiatives are critical for program advocacy (e.g., students, classroom teachers, building administrators, central office personnel, board of education members, and parents of gifted education students, citizens, and state department of education personnel).

A variety of communication vehicles must be used to communicate effectively with the different constituency groups in gifted education. Continuous revision of the repertoire of communication formats adds to the effectiveness of the process in response to changes, such as technology.

- All communication is influenced by the political climate. It is critical to understand the political leadership and culture of a school division and its community to communicate effectively with constituency groups.
- When appropriate, alignment of gifted education and other district communication vehicles can facilitate efficient communication with constituents.
- Effective communication is responsive and based on a careful analysis of the needs of each constituency group.
- Effective communication carefully aligns the vehicle and content with the specific needs of the constituency group.
- Effective communication encourages dialogue among constituency groups.
- Effective communication anticipates misconceptions and must include necessary and sufficient information to avoid confusion and misunderstandings.
- Effective communication is sensitive and respectful, meaningful, and relevant.
- Effective communication is clear, precise, and timely.
- Effective communication reflects correct usage and grammatical conventions.

# COMMONLY USED COMMUNICATION VEHICLES IN GIFTED EDUCATION

## With Students

- Program introduction, which serves as a bridge from regular education setting and expectations to those of the gifted program
- Teacher narratives detailing student performance(s)
- Portfolios developed with students
- Individual and/or small-group advocacy sessions before and after school and during lunch

## Report Card Narratives

- Student schedules planned and updated on a regular basis to provide an opportunity for goal setting and exposure to new opportunities

- Learning profiles and interest inventories updated regularly with students
- Program brochure highlighting opportunities for students and contact information
- Student evaluations on program effectiveness, curriculum units, and specific program offerings through surveys, interviews, focus groups, and exit interviews
- Assessment results designed to provide feedback for student growth
- Web sites at the district and school levels
- Newsletters at the district and school levels

## With Parents

- Flyers at the beginning of each school year sent to all homes in the school division describing the gifted program and identification procedures and providing contact information
- Direct mailings sent to homes announcing program initiatives, parent meetings, and advocacy meetings
- Parent shelf of gifted education resources in each school site
- Parent orientation packet designed to assist parents in understanding the division's gifted services and in advocating for their child
- Parent program brochures developed to include an overview of program initiatives and services as well as brochures on specific program areas (e.g., identification procedures, enrichment offerings, and gifted curriculum)
- Identification procedures including processes for referral, screening, placement, and appeal in a variety of formats
- Program evaluation through interviews, surveys, exit interviews, and/or focus groups
- Student-led conferences and portfolio reviews
- Newsletters at the division and school levels
- Parent meetings on specific areas of interest (e.g., social and emotional issues, planning for college, transition from elementary to middle and from middle to high school, and summer camps) at the division and school levels
- Videos on a variety of topics relevant to parents (e.g., social and emotional issues, underachievement, gifted girls, twice-exceptional learners, differentiation)
- Web sites at the division level and the school level
- Flyers announcing gifted education conferences with opportunities for parents, parent resources such as books and articles, and parent workshops
- E-mail communication

## With Classroom Teachers

- Program overview through a handbook, workshops, brochures, videos, and newsletters
- Program brochures describing program areas such as screening and identification procedures, program goals, program initiatives, and ways for teachers to become involved
- Brief (12- to 15-minute) presentations at faculty meetings on one program area or initiative

- Handbook of identification procedures including specific information on teacher referral and teacher recommendations
- Student learning profiles in a variety of formats
- Curriculum units and lessons that include specific suggestions for differentiating for gifted learners (units are designed as teaching tools demonstrating how curriculum goals and objectives are put into practice)
- Teacher newsletter detailing program areas in action, highlighting classroom teachers in the newsletter
- Flyers announcing coursework in gifted education and conferences that include a focus on gifted education
- Pictures of students, parents, and teachers engaged in program areas that are shared through videos, slideshows, teacher workshops, newsletters, and brochures
- Collaborative sessions and training workshops with gifted education specialists
- Surveys to gather teacher input on program areas
- Workshop feedback asking for teacher input on the effectiveness and usefulness of the training
- E-mail communication

## With Administrators

- Handbook that includes program overview, curriculum goals and objectives, identification procedures including pertinent eligibility dates, description of the administrator's role in gifted program implementation, and central office personnel contact information
- Program evaluation through interviews, surveys, and/or focus groups
- E-mail communication
- Program budget documents
- Board of education reports, including budget documents
- Presentations at administrator meetings to include updates on program goals, status of existing and pending program initiatives, program strengths, and areas for improvement
- Multimedia presentations and videos on program areas made available for administrator use in their schools

## With Board of Education Members

- Program updates through memoranda and e-mail
- Program overview in brochure format
- Program evaluation reports
- Program budget annual reports
- Board of education reports
- Handbook describing critical areas (e.g., program model, identification procedures, short- and long-range program plans, curriculum model(s) utilized, curriculum goals and objectives, inventory of program resources, certification requirements for teachers of the gifted, list of gifted staff and related contact information, contact information and meeting dates for District Task Force on Gifted Education if applicable)
- Web site

## With Media

- Program overview in succinct written form
- Written outline of important events including contact person for each event
- Program brochure with a paragraph summary of all program areas and current initiatives
- Interviews
- Brief speech prepared on all program areas
- Figures and charts that contain relevant data
- Contact on a regular basis with education reporters in print media and producers in radio and television stations to build rapport and open communication
- Press releases
- News articles including updates on program areas that have changed

# CHARACTERISTICS OF HIGH-QUALITY COMMUNICATION INITIATIVES IN GIFTED EDUCATION

Education leaders should examine six factors to ensure effective communication between the gifted education program and key stakeholders. Guiding questions are offered for each key area.

## Stakeholder Analysis

- Have all constituent groups (e.g., students, parents, classroom teachers, building administrators, central office personnel, board of education members, and state department of education officials) been identified?
- Have the information needs of each group been analyzed and identified?
- Have misconceptions held by each group been uncovered and identified?

## Communication Vehicles

- Have the most effective and efficient communication vehicles for each group been identified (e.g., PowerPoint presentation, program brochure, workshop, handbook, flyer, newsletter, Web site, student schedules, and e-mails)?
- Have vehicles been aligned with the purpose and content of the communication?
- Do the vehicles include a mechanism for constituent feedback and input?

## Communication Content

- Has the content been organized effectively for each group?
- Has the content (i.e., program or initiative proposal, program evaluation, program budget, curriculum plan, curriculum goals and objectives, identification guidelines) been organized with efficiency in mind?

## Meaningfulness

- To what extent is the information provided relevant to the audience?
- Is the amount of information provided to constituents at any one time reasonable (i.e., neither insufficient nor overwhelming)?

### Timeliness

- Is the frequency of communication reasonable for each constituency group?
- To what extent is the timing of communication sensible for each constituent group in light of the needs and responsibilities that each has?

### Clarity

- Is written communication precise, clear, and accurate?
- Does written communication reflect correct usage and the proper grammatical conventions?
- Is audible communication clear and accurate?
- Is all communication neutral (i.e., nonjudgmental)?

## AN EXAMPLE IN NEED OF REVISION

Sally Moran, a gifted and talented education teacher, is responsible for overseeing gifted education services to students in Grades 6–8 in Harrison Middle School. She communicates regularly with her students through e-mail and notices in the daily bulletin. Twice a year, she sends out a newsletter to teachers and parents. When her program and services are evaluated every other year, she sends copies of the evaluation to school administrators and the board of education members.

## RATING THE EXAMPLE

This example is weak in a number of areas. It does not use a variety of communication vehicles. Daily announcements may not be the vehicle to generate interest for and attendance in student activities. This example is also weak because the newsletters to parents may not be frequent enough to provide them with timely information about their children's educational services. Finally, this example is weak because little assessment was done to determine the information needs of three key constituent groups: regular education teachers, administrators, and board of education members (stakeholder analysis). These groups need more and different types of information than what is provided in newsletters and biannual program evaluations.

## MAKEOVER EXAMPLE

Sally Moran realized that she needed to communicate regularly with each of her constituent groups. At the same time, she also realized that her work with students took up the largest percentage of her time. To maintain sufficient time with her students, she would have to redesign her communication efforts.

To increase the effectiveness and efficiency of her communication initiative, she met with small groups of students, parents, teachers, and administrators to discover what information they wanted to know, the most effective communication vehicle, and the frequency with which they wanted information. While she was talking with different groups, she tried to make inferences about the background knowledge each group had about giftedness in general and the variety of gifted education programs and services available to Harrison students.

When she compiled her notes from the meetings, she decided to use the chart in Table 12.1 to help her organize and visualize the communication needs of her stakeholders. She placed an X under the most effective communication vehicle(s) for each constituent group. Then, she moved across the top of the chart to the right-hand columns that contain the names of the months. For each constituent group, she placed an X in the months they required some form of communication.

When she saw her information displayed in the chart, she decided to capitalize on the district's Web site to increase the accessibility of her information. With the help of the district Web coordinator, she created a Web page. Creating a link for each constituency group, she placed appropriate newsletters, video clips, program overviews, brochures, reports, and the like. She also included a link to her e-mail account so constituents could e-mail her. Sally told her students about the Web page, sent a flyer home via regular mail, and announced it on both the school's marquee and the morning announcements. Parents and students were encouraged to sign up for the Web page Listserv for monthly alerts when the page was updated.

By capitalizing on state-of-the-art technology, Sally provided more effective and timely communication to a broad array of constituents. Furthermore, the efficiency of her new communication methods provided her with time to have important face-to-face meetings to discuss more complicated or sensitive matters with students, parents, teachers, administrators, and board of education members.

## A STRATEGIC PLAN FOR DEVELOPING OR ENHANCING COMMUNICATION INITIATIVES IN GIFTED EDUCATION

*Objective:* To create or enhance a communication initiative to support gifted education programming.

*Evidence:* A portfolio that contains a variety of communication vehicles that have been created for the full range of gifted education constituents.

*Tasks:* For creating or modifying a communication initiative:

- Identify which constituent groups are currently served and which need to be included in the communication process.
- Analyze the current information needs of each group; determine which information needs are already being met and which have yet to be met.
- Gather the information to meet the needs of each stakeholder group.
- Target the communication vehicles most appropriate and effective for each constituent group. Identify vehicles to add or eliminate.

- Develop a short-term and long-term schedule for delivering enhanced communication to each constituency group.
- Create and implement a plan to evaluate the effectiveness of the communication initiative.

---

*Timeline:*

September

- Convene a meeting of the District Task Force on Gifted Education (see Appendix A on establishing an advisory Committee) ensure that representatives from each constituency group are present, if possible (e.g., gifted education teacher, classroom teacher, building administrator, central office personnel, board of education member, parent, student, citizen). In a large school division, more than one District Task Force on Gifted Education meeting should be held in several different locations throughout the district to allow parents, students, teachers, building administrators, and citizens to provide input.
- With input from task force member (a) compile the information needs of each constituency group, (b) target the most effective communication vehicle(s) for each group, (c) identify where the information they need is located or accessed, and (d) estimate the frequency with which communication should occur. In a large school district, task force recommendations should be reviewed by district leadership to ensure support from the various administrative departments including building administration.
- Ask all task force members to share the information with their respective peers to solicit feedback and suggestions. In a large district, it may be necessary to post the information on a division-wide Web site, have gifted specialists hold meetings in their schools, and develop a survey to share the information and gather input.

October

- Review the feedback and suggestions from each constituency group.
- Revise accordingly.
- Develop a short-term and long-term plan to phase in the communication initiative with each constituency group.
- Sequence an action plan.

November

- Share the revised plan with all constituents.
- Begin implementation.
- Design a survey with three to four short-answer questions to assess the effectiveness of the communication with each constituency group.

December–April

- Monitor the flow of information to and from constituent groups to constantly assess whom you are reaching and whom you are missing with existing communication vehicles.
- Meet with the task force for feedback shared with them by constituency groups.

May

- Distribute the surveys to constituents.
- Reconvene the task force to review the collected data and assess the effectiveness of the initiative.
- Use the feedback to make revisions.

This one-page chart (Table 12.1) has been designed to help teachers and coordinators of gifted education programs assess, design, or revise their communication initiative. Down the left column are the names of various stakeholders. Across the top of the chart are three categories of information: content, vehicles, and the months of a year. The content column contains a listing of some of the most common types of information needed by all stakeholders. The vehicle column contains some of the most often-used communication vehicles. The right-hand side of the chart contains columns marked with letters—to stand for months in a year. Because of the space limitations of a single-page graphic organizer, not all types of content are listed, nor are all the communication vehicles. The chart should be modified to address the unique needs of one's (or "the stakeholders") school or district.

To visualize existing communication practices, for example, place an X in the appropriate boxes to describe the content, vehicles, and frequency with which each constituency group receives information. The Board of Education (BOE) row has been completed here as an example. Based on the data in that row, one sees very quickly that BOE members need other types of information that will best be communicated in a variety of vehicles beyond the current PowerPoint about the program budget.

## TEMPLATE FOR ASSESSING THE STRENGTHS OF A DISTRICT'S COMMUNICATION INITIATIVE

The following checklist can be used to assess the quality of an existing communication initiative. Read each statement and rate how successfully this aspect of your communication plan has been addressed. A score of 1 indicates that the characteristic has not been addressed; 2 indicates that some attention has been given to it; and 3 indicates that the characteristics has been addressed and is functioning well in your district.

The higher the total score, the more likely it is that your district has a high-quality communication initiative. Low scores on any item illuminate aspects of the plan that may be in need of revision.

| Characteristic | 1 (not addressed) | 2 (some attention) | 3 (works well) |
| --- | --- | --- | --- |
| We have a communication initiative for gifted education programs and services. | | | |
| All constituency groups have been identified. | | | |
| A variety of effective communication vehicles is used for each constituent group. | | | |
| Communication for each group is meaningful. | | | |
| Communication for each group is timely. | | | |
| Communication for each group is clear and precise. | | | |
| Communication vehicles allow constituents to provide information and input to educators of the gifted as well as receive information from them. | | | |

# ADVICE FOR THE SOLE PRACTITIONER

Technology is the most important tool for the sole practitioner because its potential for enhancing communication is limitless. At the outset, the gifted education teacher should explore the technology options that are available at the district and school level. Most school districts—especially the most remote—have e-mail. The next step is to create distribution lists of parents, teaches, administrators, and students. Distribution lists will be the medium for a wide variety of critical communication messages between the gifted education specialist and key stakeholder groups. A Web site, either at the school or district level, is also an important step because it provides instant access to essential information about gifted education for any stakeholder.

**Table 12.1** Graphic Organizer for Designing or Revising a Communication Initiative for Gifted Education Programs and Services

| Constituent Group | Content | | | | | | | | Vehicles | | | | | | | | Months | | | | | | | | | | | |
|---|---|---|---|---|---|---|---|---|---|---|---|---|---|---|---|---|---|---|---|---|---|---|---|---|---|---|---|---|
| | Program Proposal | Orientation | Program Evaluation | Program Budget | Curriculum Plan | Curriculum goals and Objectives | ID Guidelines | Other: | Press releases | Newsletter | Web site | E-mails | PowerPoint Presentations | Program Brochure | Surveys | Other: | January | February | March | April | May | June | July | August | September | October | November | December |
| Students | | | | | | | | | | | | | | | | | | | | | | | | | | | | |
| Classroom Teachers | | | | | | | | | | | | | | | | | | | | | | | | | | | | |
| Building Administrators | | | | | | | | | | | | | | | | | | | | | | | | | | | | |
| Central Office Personnel | | | | | | | | | | | | | | | | | | | | | | | | | | | | |
| BOE members | | | | X | | | | | | | | | X | | | | | | | | | | | | | | | X |
| Parents | | | | | | | | | | | | | | | | | | | | | | | | | | | | |
| Citizens | | | | | | | | | | | | | | | | | | | | | | | | | | | | |
| SDE personnel | | | | | | | | | | | | | | | | | | | | | | | | | | | | |
| Other: | | | | | | | | | | | | | | | | | | | | | | | | | | | | |

## MUST-READ RESOURCES

Friend. M., & Cook, L. (1992). *Interactions: Collaboration skills for school professionals.* New York: Longman.

## REFERENCES

Covey, S. R. (1990). *The seven habits of highly effective people.* New York: Simon & Schuster.

Danielson, C. (1996). *Enhancing professional practice: A framework for teaching.* Alexandria: VA: ASCD.

Stronge, J. H. (2002). *Qualities of effective teachers.* Alexandria, VA: ASCD.

# 13

# Roles, Responsibilities, and Professional Qualifications of Key Personnel for Gifted Education Services

*Jann H. Leppien and Karen L. Westberg*

If you want to build a ship, don't drum up people together to collect wood and don't assign them tasks and work, but rather teach them to long for the sea.

—Antoine de Saint-Exupery

When we think about the No Child Left Behind Act of 2001 (NCLB), it is likely that many will think about the controversies this important federal law has generated. At the same time, however, specific parts of the legislation address important and vital issues in education. For example, the federal legislation reminds us of the critical need for qualified teachers in core academic areas: English, reading and language arts, mathematics, science, foreign language, civics and government, economics, history, geography, and the arts. By the end of the 2005–2006 school year, each district that receives funds under Title I must have a plan to ensure that all the public elementary and secondary school teachers they employ fulfill the definition of being "highly qualified."

Although not specifically included in NCLB, gifted educators should be no exception to this rule. To best serve gifted education students, practitioners in our field must have the knowledge, competencies, and dispositions required to carry out their roles and responsibilities. But what are the prerequisite knowledge and skills that practitioners in our field need so that they may address the cognitive and affective learning needs of our students? What are the competencies that are required of those who sit in administrative positions in gifted education?

In this chapter, Jann Leppien and Karen Westberg describe the foundational knowledge that is a prerequisite for teachers and administrators in gifted education. In addition, they share a comprehensive description of the varied roles and responsibilities of those charged with educating gifted education students. This chapter is most closely aligned with the chapter on professional development, 14, and it addresses the following guiding principle contained in the professional development standard of the National Association for Gifted Children (NAGC) *Pre-K–Grade 12 Gifted Program Standards* (Landrum & Shaklee, 1998): "Only qualified personnel should be involved in the education of gifted learners." In addition, the competencies, skills, and knowledge included in this chapter align with the National Council for Accreditation of Teacher Education (NCATE) initial standards for teacher preparation programs in gifted and talented education (NAGC & CEC 2006).

# DEFINITION

Professional qualifications are the knowledge, competencies, and dispositions required by district personnel to effectively carry out their roles and responsibilities for providing a comprehensive and continuous set of services for gifted learners. Gifted children deserve to learn from highly qualified professionals who are aware of and able to respond to the unique qualities and characteristics of the students they instruct (NAGC, 1994). These professional qualifications will vary according to job responsibility as well as according to accreditation standards established by individual states.

# RATIONALE

The finest service plan for the education of children who are gifted is of little use without effective instructional personnel. Any educator who spends a substantial amount of time with gifted and talented students in an academic setting, whether homogeneous or heterogeneous, must possess the requisite knowledge, competencies, and traits to implement the goals of differentiated education that are responsive to the students' academic and psychosocial needs. To provide appropriate learning experiences for gifted and talented students, key personnel need to possess knowledge and understanding of

- The nature of individual differences, especially as applied to exceptional abilities
- The origins and nature of various manifestations of giftedness
- The cognitive, social, emotional, and environmental factors that enhance or inhibit the development of giftedness in all populations
- A variety of methods for identifying and assessing students with extraordinary potential
- The historical and theoretical foundations of the field of gifted education, current trends and issues, and potential future directions of the field
- A research-based rationale for differentiated programs and services for gifted students
- Theoretical models, program prototypes, and educational principles that offer appropriate foundations for the development of differentiated curriculum for gifted students

- The unique potentials of gifted students from underserved populations, including but not limited to, gifted females, students who have disabilities, or students who are racially or ethnically diverse, economically disadvantaged, or underachieving
- Curriculum and instruction that is appropriate for meeting the needs of gifted learners
- State mandates that guide district program design, identification procedures, delivery of services, and evaluation guidelines
- Program evaluation as a systematic study of the value and impact of services provided
- Current educational issues, policies, and practices including their relationships to the field of gifted education

## GUIDING PRINCIPLES OR ASSUMPTIONS

Several research studies suggest that persons with training in gifted education are more effective in meeting the particular educational needs of gifted learners. Therefore, schools that successfully address these needs view gifted education programming as a collaborative effort integrated into the general education program. The following principles and assumptions that guide this chapter are based on these perspectives (Delcourt & Evans, 1994; Hansen & Feldhusen, 1994; Kirschenbaum, Armstrong, & Landrum, 1999; Landrum & Shaklee, 1998; Neihart, Reis, Robinson, & Moon, 2002; Purcell & Leppien, 1998; Renzulli & Reis, 1991; Shore, Cornell, Robinson, & Ward, 1991; Shore & Delcourt, 1996; Tomlinson, Coleman, Allan, Udall, & Landrum, 1996; Tomlinson et al., 1994).

- Those with special training in gifted education content and pedagogy are more effective than those without such training in delivering services for advanced learners.
- Key personnel are required to implement a comprehensive program for gifted learners.
- The roles and responsibilities of key personnel must be articulated to effectively implement a continuum of services to pre-K–Grade 12 gifted learners.
- Key personnel require specific knowledge, competencies, and dispositions to provide for the educational needs of gifted learners.
- Ongoing professional development is required to assist key personnel in acquiring the knowledge and competencies to address the needs of gifted students.
- Professional qualifications should guide the hiring practices of personnel responsible for providing services for advanced learners.

## ROLES, RESPONSIBILITIES, AND COMPETENCIES OF KEY PERSONNEL WORKING WITH GIFTED STUDENTS

Those who create comprehensive gifted programs must consider how and by whom the program will be implemented. To effectively serve gifted learners, a school district should identify highly qualified personnel whose responsibility it is to provide services to gifted and talented students. Table 13.1 identifies the roles of key personnel, their responsibilities, and the knowledge and competencies required to deliver services to gifted learners. While these roles and responsibilities may vary according to school district and state programming guidelines, the competencies articulate a range of qualifications needed by professionals to ensure that gifted learners receive services commensurate with their academic and social needs. Knowledge of these competencies should help districts recognize the types of professional qualifications and commitment necessary. States and school districts should refer to the policy statements that address these competencies (see, Landrum, Callahan, & Shaklee, 2001; NAGC, 1994, 1995; NAGC & CEC, 2006; and VanTassel-Baska, 1994). In districts where only one person has been assigned the responsibility for delivering services to gifted and talented learners, it is recommended that the list be used to target the most essential duties from among the listed responsibilities to provide a minimum of services.

## AN EXAMPLE IN NEED OF REVISION

The Gray School District hired a new gifted education (G/T) coordinator who had recently received an Ed.S. degree in special education from a neighboring state university that included one course in gifted education. The newly hired teacher had experience as a special education teacher and coordinator. The Superintendent explained that the individual holding the position would be expected to (1) increase the number of Advanced Placement (AP) courses offered at the high school, (2) work with elementary principals to make a few changes in the services provided for students, (3) complete reports about G/T services required by the state and the district, and (4) ensure that the district was in compliance with the new regulations required by the state. The superintendent explained that he wanted the new coordinator to "respond to parents when they raised concerns about G/T issues and services." In addition, he stated that he didn't really have time to be involved in the program and wanted someone who could assume the role without causing undue attention to gifted education services in the district.

### Consequences of Not Identifying the Appropriate Roles and Responsibilities of Key Personnel

When school districts hire individuals who do not have the skills and competencies necessary to carry out the responsibilities for implementing effective gifted education services, the results, unfortunately, are often predictable. Personnel without proper qualifications and training cannot develop appropriate identification procedures, develop and promote high-quality differentiated learning opportunities for gifted learners, facilitate a robust program evaluation that supports refinements to programs and services over time, or communicate knowledgeably with program stakeholders. Over time, the program loses support from parents, administrators, board of education members, and teachers. Eventually, the program budget is reduced or eliminated, which has tragic consequences for bright students.

## MAKEOVER EXAMPLE

The superintendent of the Gray School District formed a broad-based committee that wrote a job description for the gifted education coordinator position in their district. The job description outlined specific qualifications and responsibilities, such as providing ongoing professional development to teachers at all levels, responding to the changing demographic characteristics of the student population, and establishing a continuum of services within

*(Text continues on page 176)*

**Table 13.1** Competencies Required by Administrators (This category combines building level and central office personnel. Responsibilities will vary according to the number of people who have responsibilities for administering programs for the gifted and talented.)

| Responsibilities | Knowledge | Competencies |
|---|---|---|
| Planning and implementing districtwide programs and services for pre-K–12 gifted learners | Understand that a continuum of programming services must be available for gifted learners including cluster group options, special pull-out classes, homogeneous classes, special or magnet schools, mentorships, dual enrollment, special counseling services, etc., to address students' academic and psychosocial needs. | Establish programming services for pre-K–12 that are specifically designed for the identified needs of the population.<br><br>Develop services that address all types of giftedness including general academic, specific academic, creativity, leadership, and visual and performing arts.<br><br>Develop policies for early entrance, grade skipping, ability grouping, dual enrollment, and curriculum modification. |
| | Understand that variations exist in educational settings (e.g., philosophy, values, size, organizational, cultural conditions), which may affect the gifted program in unique ways. | Assess the current level of services provided to gifted students within the district to develop a comprehensive pre-K–12 program. |
| | Understand that gifted education programs and services must be (1) designed from both a theoretical and empirical perspective (i.e., research that supports particular designs or practices with gifted learners) and a practical perspective (i.e., resources available) and (2) planned in collaboration with those who are knowledgeable in the field. | Design programs in consultation with informed experts and within the parameters of established and "best" practices in the field.<br><br>Develop and disseminate programming documents describing the gifted education programming mission statements, goals, and objectives. |
| Establishing and maintaining financial resources for personnel and materials for programs for the gifted | Understand that gifted education funding should be part of the continuous budget planning process and should receive support comparable to similar efforts within the district. | Establish and sustain funding specific to the continuum of gifted education services provided by the school and district. |

(Continued)

**Table 13.1** (Continued)

| Responsibilities | Knowledge | Competencies |
|---|---|---|
| Guiding the identification and placement of selected students for special services | Understand that a comprehensive, cohesive, and coordinated process for student nomination results in more accurate and equitable identification of students. The use of multiple sources of information provides information about students' abilities that can be overlooked when using objective data. A comprehensive nomination process provides opportunities for the referral of students from special education teachers, parent recommendations, psychologists, curriculum specialists, etc. | Develop an identification plan that assures the individual assessment of potentially gifted students' knowledge and abilities as specified by state regulations or district policy. Select assessments that go beyond a narrow conception of giftedness and include multiple sources of information about students. |
| Selecting key personnel to work with gifted education students | Understand that gifted learners are entitled to be served by professionals who have (1) specialized preparation in gifted education, (2) expertise in developing appropriately differentiated content and instructional methods, (3) ongoing professional development, and (4) exemplary professional/personal traits. | Develop a procedure for selecting teachers with specific responsibility for the identification and provision of services for gifted and talented students. Hire specialist teachers in gifted education that possess a certification/specialization or degree in gifted education. Develop a comprehensive ongoing professional development plan for all key personnel who work with gifted learners. Articulate the roles and responsibilities of all persons working with advanced learners. Teachers with primary responsibility for teaching gifted learners should be evaluated to assure their competency in delivering differentiated curricula and instruction. Create orientation programs to inform parents of the services available to their children. |

| Responsibilities | Knowledge | Competencies |
|---|---|---|
| Developing and maintaining education programs and services for parents of gifted students | Understand the importance of informing parents of the services that are available to their children and that parents of gifted learners should have regular opportunities to provide input and make recommendations about program services. | Disseminate information regarding policies and practices in gifted education (e.g., student referral and screening, appeals, informed consent, student progress, curricular options, etc.). |
| | | Provide workshops to assist parents in understanding the psychosocial and academic needs of gifted learners. |
| | | Establish an advisory committee that reflects the cultural and socioeconomic diversity of the school or school district's total student population, which includes parents, community members, students, and school staff members. |
| | | Implement an appropriate curriculum that assures mastery of basic skill requirements of the general curriculum and allows for modification, extension, and integration of this general curriculum into any specialized curriculum for the gifted. |
| Facilitating a decision-making process among all district personnel to establish a comprehensive curriculum for pre-K–12 gifted learners. | Understand that gifted services must be designed to supplement or extend the academic skills and knowledge learned in regular classrooms at all grade levels to ensure continuity as students progress through the program. | Articulate the curriculum for the gifted program within the context of the general curriculum, state and national standards, and the differences required for a specialized curriculum. |
| | Understand curriculum models and demonstrate strong skills related to the implementation and evaluation of such models. | Develop and implement a comprehensive staff development program for teachers of the gifted, regular classroom teachers, and support staff that delivers and improves the curriculum and instruction of gifted learners. |

*(Continued)*

**Table 13.1** (Continued)

| Responsibilities | Knowledge | Competencies |
|---|---|---|
| | Understand that a comprehensive gifted education program must establish a plan to recognize and nurture the unique socioemotional development of gifted learners. | Support a well-defined affective curriculum that addresses personal/social awareness and adjustment, academic planning, and vocational/career awareness for gifted learners. |
| Implementing effective data management systems and accountability requirements for gifted students and district personnel | Understand that program evaluation provides a systematic study of the value and impact of services and provides a means by which programs can be improved. | Develop formative and summative evaluation of the gifted program that focuses on both quantitative and qualitative outcomes and leads to ongoing revision of the curriculum and instructional approaches.

Allocate adequate time, financial support, and personnel to conduct systematic program evaluation. |

**Table 13.2** Competencies Required by A Coordinator of Gifted Services

| Responsibilities | Knowledge | Competencies |
|---|---|---|
| Implementing a comprehensive gifted education program based on standards | Knowledge of state and national standards | Develop comprehensive services for pre-K–12 gifted learners based on state and national standards. |
| Implementing the district or state identification process and procedures | Knowledge of the identification procedures for intellectually, academically, creatively, culturally diverse, and twice-exceptional gifted learners. Understand the relevance of cultural, ethnic, and socioeconomic factors in relation to assessment and achievement for individual students. | Implement the district and state gifted identification procedures, and interpret assessments to identify the unique needs of gifted students. Collaborate with classroom teachers to nominate students for gifted education programming services on an ongoing basis. Conduct meetings to inform parents and teachers of students' eligibility and district procedures for program placement and services. |
| Planning the organization and implementation of curricular offerings for gifted students | Knowledge of educational and psychological needs of the gifted and talented and application of a variety of instructional models and/or educational strategies appropriate for use with gifted and talented learners. | Develop a differentiated curriculum scope and sequence plan for pre-K–12 appropriate to meeting the unique intellectual and emotional needs and interests of gifted and talented students. Implement a range of recommended strategies for differentiating the core curriculum, such as acceleration/pacing, depth, complexity and novelty, and grouping for appropriate instruction, as well as individualized planning to assist gifted students in realizing their unique potentials. |

(Continued)

**Table 13.2** (Continued)

| Responsibilities | Knowledge | Competencies |
|---|---|---|
| Integrating gifted programming services into the general education program | Understand the principles of collaboration to ensure the integration of gifted education into the general education program. | Create environments in which giftedness can emerge and gifted students feel challenged and safe to explore and express their uniqueness. |
| | | Develop effective ways to communicate with school personnel and to disseminate information regarding major policies and practices in gifted education. |
| | | Articulate and support the roles and responsibilities of those involved in the delivery of services to gifted learners. |
| | | Provide consultation, collaboration, and staff development services in gifted education for teachers, administrators, and counselors in the general education program. |
| | Knowledge of the principles of differentiated curriculum and instruction to match the distinct characteristics of gifted learners | Assist teachers in using the principles of differentiated curriculum and instruction designed to match the distinct characteristics of gifted learners, including those who have been traditionally underrepresented in programs and services. |
| | | Incorporate instructional strategies for the gifted into the regular curriculum to ensure academic rigor through the development of high-level proficiency in all core academic areas. |
| | | Locate appropriate materials and resources to facilitate programming services for gifted learners. |

| Responsibilities | Knowledge | Competencies |
|---|---|---|
| | Understand the guidance and counseling needs of gifted learners. | Collaborate with counselors to increase their understanding of the socio-emotional needs of gifted learners and develop a comprehensive guidance and counseling program that addresses personal/social awareness and adjustment, academic planning, and vocational and career awareness. |
| Providing advocacy for the continued support of gifted education services | Understand how to communicate and work in partnerships with colleagues, administrators, school boards, students, families, business, and industry on behalf of gifted learners. | Network with community members and businesses to provide support and resources. |
| | | Recruit business and community members to serve as facilitators of mentorships and apprenticeships. |
| | | Create communication vehicles that explain the programming services available to gifted and talented students. |
| | | Locate a variety of resources to share with parents to support their gifted children at home. |
| | | Develop activities to encourage parental and community involvement in the education of the gifted, including the establishment and maintenance of an effective advisory committee. |
| | | Participate professional organizations related to gifted and talented education to inform the school district of best practices. |

*(Continued)*

**Table 13.2** (Continued)

| Responsibilities | Knowledge | Competencies |
|---|---|---|
| Organizing the evaluation of the gifted and talented program using formal and informal evaluation techniques. | Understand how systematic gathering, analyzing, and reporting of formative and summative data can be used to improve the existing program. | Organize and implement district and state evaluation procedures.<br><br>Gather information, using reliable and valid instruments and procedures, to address pertinent questions raised by all constituency groups and to respond to the needs of all stakeholders. |
| Planning ongoing professional development in the field of gifted education. | Knowledge and implementation of the current practices and "best practices" defined in the field to provide services to gifted learners | Engage in continuous professional development regarding the characteristics of gifted learners and their related social and emotional development. |

**Table 13.3**  Competencies Required by Teachers of the Gifted

| Responsibilities | Knowledge | Competencies |
|---|---|---|
| Implementing the district and state identification process and procedures | Knowledge of the characteristics of and identification procedures for intellectually, academically, creatively, culturally diverse, and twice-exceptional gifted learners. Understand the relevance of cultural, ethnic, and socioeconomic factors in relation to assessment and achievement for individual students. | Implement district and state gifted identification procedures, and interpret assessments to identify the unique needs of gifted students. Collaborate with classroom teachers on an ongoing basis in nominating students for gifted education programming services. Conduct meetings to inform parents and teachers of students' eligibility for program placement and services. Communicate with school personnel about the characteristics and needs of individuals with gifts and talents. Use assessment information in making eligibility, program, and placement decisions for individuals with gifts and talents, including those from culturally and/or linguistically diverse backgrounds. Interpret assessment data to plan appropriate curricular offerings based on individual profiles of the students. |
| Planning and implementing curricular offerings for gifted students. | Knowledge of educational and psychological needs of the gifted and talented and application of a variety of instructional models and/or educational strategies appropriate for use with gifted and talented learners. | Develop a differentiated curriculum appropriate to meeting the unique intellectual and emotion needs and interests of gifted and talented students. |

(Continued)

**Table 13.3** (Continued)

| Responsibilities | Knowledge | Competencies |
|---|---|---|
| | Knowledge of educational and psychological needs of the gifted and talented and application of a variety of instructional models and/or educational strategies appropriate for use with gifted and talented learners | Integrate instruction in a variety of fields to encourage interdisciplinary thought and studies in gifted students. |
| | | Assess students' strengths, interests, and learning preferences to plan curricular experiences for gifted learners. |
| | Knowledge of the principles of differentiated curriculum and instruction to match the distinct characteristics of gifted learners | Use current, research-based methods for assessing and reporting on the progress of gifted students for purpose of making differentiated educational decisions. |
| Collaborating with other key personnel in delivering gifted education programming services | Understand the importance of collaboration in delivering quality services for gifted learners in a variety of settings. | Use performance data and information from all stakeholders to make or suggest modifications in learning environments. |
| | | Collaborate with other key personnel who provide services to gifted learners, including classroom teachers, counselors, gifted education coordinator, content area specialists, special education teachers, and curriculum directors to support and advocate for continuous programming services for gifted learners. |
| | | Model techniques and coach others in the use of instructional methods and accommodations. |
| | | Foster respectful and beneficial relationships between families and professionals. |

**Table 13.3** (Continued)

| Responsibilities | Knowledge | Competencies |
|---|---|---|
| | | Disseminate and communicate information regarding the program activities. |
| | | Network with curriculum committee teams to advocate for the acquisition of advanced materials and resources. |
| Networking with families about their children's academic and social progress. | Understand how to communicate and work in partnerships with colleagues, administrators, school boards, students, families, business and industry, and the pubic in advocating appropriate programming for gifted students. | Collaborate with guidance personnel in implementing intervention strategies for at-risk gifted students.<br><br>Inform parents of their children's academic and social development and progress through a variety of communication vehicles.<br><br>Foster partnerships with the families of gifted students to facilitate a total learning environment. |
| Participating in appropriate professional development about giftedness and gifted education. | Knowledge and implementation of the current practices and "best practices" defined in the field to provide services to gifted learners. | Engage in ongoing professional development regarding the characteristics of gifted learners and their related social and emotional development. |

the district. After a national search and extensive interviews, the district hired someone who had an M.A. degree in gifted education as well as experience as a gifted education coordinator and specialist. More important, at her previous district she had been successful in providing vision and leadership that resulted in a strong program of services for gifted learners. Shortly after being hired, she formulated a gifted advisory committee representing all levels. With the coordinator's leadership, the advisory committee worked on a needs-assessment plan that resulted in a mission statement, an action plan for the upcoming year, and a three-year plan. The goals on the action plan included tasks such as examining the services being provided to students at the middle school level, reexamining the identification plan to ensure its fairness in representing the demographics of the district, increasing professional development opportunities for classroom teachers, examining the alignment of the curriculum in the gifted program services with the curriculum in the regular program, providing more communication to the school board and administrators, and developing a series of sessions on key issues for parents. After three years, the coordinator requested and received increased financial support from the superintendent and the school board. As a result of this careful planning, the Gray district has a reputation as a system that provides support for all of its learners, including its most capable students.

# PLANNING CHART FOR ARTICULATING THE ROLES, RESPONSIBILITIES, AND PROFESSIONAL QUALIFICATIONS OF KEY PERSONNEL

The planning guide above can be used by districts to evaluate the degree to which they have articulated the roles and responsibilities and the knowledge and competencies of key personnel who will be involved in delivering services to gifted learners. After reviewing the competencies tables shown earlier in this chapter, make revisions or clarifications to your district's gifted program by identifying the practices you desire.

## ADVICE FOR THE SOLE PRACTITIONER

Creating ownership for a gifted education program is one of the most successful ways to ensure its success. When one gifted education specialist has the sole responsibility for implementing a gifted and talented program in a district, our best advice would be to develop strategies for ensuring program ownership. The first thing that can be done to promote ownership is to establish a gifted education advisory group (see Appendix A). An advisory group serves as a working group of faculty members, administrators, and parents who have responsibilities for developing a comprehensive gifted program for learners in pre-K–12 levels. At the elementary level, this team would include parents, community resource persons, administrators, and faculty representatives from each grade level, as well as art, music, physical education, or media specialists. At the middle school and secondary levels, this team would include faculty members from each department. This team would assume some of the responsibilities of the administrative role, such as conducting a districtwide needs assessment, developing an identification plan, making decisions about how services will be delivered, and establishing a schoolwide

*(Text continues on page 181)*

**Table 13.4**  Competencies Required by Classroom Teachers

| Responsibilities | Knowledge | Competencies |
|---|---|---|
| Implementing the district and state identification process and procedures | Understand how gifted students are identified for programming services using district and state identification procedures. | Collaborate with the gifted education teacher(s) and coordinator in nominating students for gifted education programming services on an ongoing basis. |
| Planning and implementing curricular offerings for gifted students | Knowledge of the characteristics of giftedness, the educational and psychological needs of the gifted and talented, application of a variety of instructional models and/or educational strategies appropriate for use with the gifted, as well as the ability to modify, adapt, and design appropriate curricular experiences for gifted learners | Develop differentiated curriculum using instructional strategies that support inquiry, self-directed learning, discussion, metacognition, debate, and other appropriate modes of learning. |
| | Knowledge of the principles of differentiated curriculum and instruction, including preassessment, to match the distinct characteristics of gifted learners | Implement differentiation strategies for modifying existing curriculum to meet the academic needs of gifted learners. |
| | | Apply curricular and instructional modifications and adaptation to the core curriculum to develop rigorous and challenging curriculum for advanced learners. |
| | | Compact the core curriculum for gifted students so that learning experiences are developmentally appropriate for their needs, interests, and abilities. |
| | | Use a variety of teaching and learning patterns: flexible grouping, large- and small-group instruction, homogeneous and heterogeneous grouping, teacher and student-directed learning, and opportunities for independent study. |

(Continued)

**Table 13.4** (Continued)

| Responsibilities | Knowledge | Competencies |
|---|---|---|
| Collaborating with other key personnel in delivering gifted education programming services. | Understand the importance of collaboration in delivering quality services for gifted learners in the classroom. | Network with teacher of the gifted or coordinator of services to locate resources and materials to augment differentiated curriculum and to supplement independent study opportunities for individual students. |
| | | Collaborate with guidance personnel in implementing intervention strategies for at-risk gifted students. |
| | | Participate in the gathering of information that can be used to evaluate the gifted education program. |
| Communicating with families about their children's academic and social progress | Understand that developing partnerships with the families of gifted students helps provide an effective learning environment for gifted learners. | Inform parents of their children's academic and social development and progress through a variety of communication vehicles. |
| Participating in ongoing professional development in the field of gifted education | Knowledge and implementation of the current practices and best practices defined in the field to provide services to gifted learners | Engage in ongoing professional development regarding the characteristics of gifted learners and their related social and emotional development. |

**Table 13.5** Competencies Required by Guidance and Counseling Personnel

| Responsibilities | Knowledge | Competencies |
|---|---|---|
| Implementing the guidance and counseling services for gifted learners | Understand, nurture, and provide services to address the unique socio-emotional development of gifted learners. | Develop and implement counseling and guidance services specifically designed to address the unique needs of gifted students. |
| | | Collaborate with key personnel in providing intervention strategies for at-risk gifted students that can take place in school, at home, or in the community. |
| | | Establish referral procedures to provide intervention strategies for at-risk gifted students. |
| | | Provide information and support to parents regarding at-risk gifted students. |
| Participating in ongoing professional development in the field of gifted education | Knowledge and implementation of the current practices and best practices defined in the field to provide services to gifted learners | Engage in ongoing professional development regarding the characteristics of gifted learners and their related social and emotional development. |

**Table 13.6** Planning Chart for Redesigning Roles and Responsibilities

| Role (e.g., administrator, coordinator) | Current responsibility, competency, or knowledge | Desired responsibility, competency, or knowledge | Opposing forces (Barriers) | Supporting forces (Opportunities) | Action ideas |
|---|---|---|---|---|---|
|  |  |  |  |  |  |
|  |  |  |  |  |  |
|  |  |  |  |  |  |
|  |  |  |  |  |  |
|  |  |  |  |  |  |
|  |  |  |  |  |  |

professional development program for the staff. This team can then assist the gifted education specialist in creating ways to bring about the necessary changes that may need to occur to implement comprehensive programs and services.

Depending on the size of the district, the overall structure of the district, as well as the diverse academic and social and emotional needs of gifted learners, different decisions must be made to implement an effective program. For example, a small district may determine that they can best meet the needs of students by clustering students in classrooms, while the role of the gifted education specialist serves as a collaborative consultant to those classroom teachers who will work directly with these students. At the secondary level, a district may decide to have honor classes, and the gifted education specialist may play the role of establishing mentorships for students who want to be engaged in independent studies. At both levels, an advisory team can assist the gifted education specialist in figuring out a plan to best meet the needs of advanced learners. The gifted education specialist can use the planning chart provided in this chapter to brainstorm possible implementation plans with the advisory team to ease the daunting challenge of creating a comprehensive program.

## REFERENCES

Delcourt, M. A. B., & Evans, K. (1994). *Qualitative extension of the learning outcomes study.* Storrs, CT: National Research Center on the Gifted and Talented, University of Connecticut.

Hansen, J. B., & Feldhusen, J. F. (1994). Comparison of trained and untrained teachers of gifted students. *Gifted Child Quarterly, 38,* 115–123.

Kirschenbaum, R. J., Armstrong, D. C., & Landrum, M. S. (1999). Resource consultation model in gifted education to support talent development in today's inclusive schools. *Gifted Child Quarterly, 43,* 39–47.

Landrum, M. S., & Shaklee, B. (Eds.). (1998). *Pre-K–Grade 12 gifted program standards.* Washington, DC: National Association for Gifted Children.

Landrum, M. S., Callahan, C. M., & Shaklee, B. D. (Eds.). (2001). *Aiming for excellence: Annotations to the NAGC pre-K–Grade 12 gifted program standards.* Washington, DC: National Association for Gifted Children.

National Association for Gifted Children. (1994). *Competencies needed by teachers of gifted and talented students* [position statement]. Washington, DC: Author.

National Association for Gifted Children. (1995). *Standards for graduate programs in gifted education* [position statement]. Washington, DC: Author.

National Association for Gifted Children & Council for Exceptional Children (2006). *Initial NCATE standards for teacher preparation programs in gifted education.* Washington, DC: Author.

Neihart, M., Reis, S. M., Robinson, N. M., & Moon, S. M. (Eds.). (2002). *The social and emotional development of gifted children: What do we know?* Waco, TX: Prufrock Press.

Purcell, J. H., & Leppien, J. H. (1998). Building bridges between general practitioners and educators of the gifted: A study of collaboration. *Gifted Child Quarterly, 42,* 172–180.

Renzulli, J. S., & Reis, S. (1991). The reform movement and the quiet crisis in gifted education. *Gifted Child Quarterly, 35,* 26–35.

Shore, B. M., & Delcourt, M. A. B. (1996). Effective curricular and program practices in gifted education and the interface with general education. *Journal for the Education of the Gifted, 20,* 138–154.

Shore, B. M., Cornell, B. G., Robinson, A., & Ward, V. S. (1991). *Recommended practices in gifted education.* New York: Teachers College Press.

Tomlinson, C. A., Coleman, M. R., Allan, S. D., Udall, A., & Landrum, M. S. (1996). Interface between gifted education and general education: Toward communication, cooperation, and collaboration. *Gifted Child Quarterly, 40,* 165–171.

Tomlinson, C. A., Tomchin, E. M., Callahan, C. M., Adams, C. M., Pizzat-Tinnin, P., Cunningham, et al. (1994). Practices of preservice teachers related to gifted and other academically diverse learners. *Gifted Child Quarterly, 38,* 106–114.

VanTassel-Baska, J. (1994). *Comprehensive curriculum for gifted learners* (2nd ed.). Needham Heights, MA: Allyn & Bacon.

# 14

# Designing a Professional Development Plan

*Marcia B. Imbeau*

Schools have little trouble setting goals for themselves. And, with the current emphasis on standardized tests, few schools lack access to critical information about student progress and achievement. If student achievement is not what teachers and administrators hope for, what then might be some possible next steps?

Although there are several answers to this question, one of the most likely answers includes the nature, quality, and frequency of professional learning opportunities. What is it that teachers need to know to ensure ongoing levels of learning for all students, including those who have high abilities?

All practitioners need high-quality professional learning opportunities that are tied to or nested inside school improvement plans. One might liken professional development to one of the small, Russian Matryoshka nesting dolls, the popular Russian folk art. Inside the largest doll are identical dolls in incrementally smaller sizes. Continuous improvement for gifted and talented students is nested inside continuous improvement for all students, which, in turn, is nested inside the professional development plan. All finally reside inside the school improvement plan.

This chapter is about professional development. Marcia Imbeau walks us through a plan to help articulate meaningful staff development experiences that relate to the learning needs of gifted and talented students. This chapter is closely linked to those on Articulating Gifted Education Program Goals, 6; Developing a Definition of Giftedness, 3; Constructing Identification Procedures, 5; Roles, Responsibilities and Professional Qualifications of Key Personnel for Gifted Education Services, 13; and Strategic Planning and Gifted Program, 21. It is also a natural link to chapter 17, Aligning Gifted Education with General Education.

## DEFINITION

A professional development plan is a set of activities designed to increase the effectiveness of teachers and administrators in meeting the needs of all students, including those of high-ability learners, in their charge. These experiences must consist of relevant knowledge, effective strategies or skills, and necessary dispositions that allow a teacher to enhance and continuously refine his or her practice. The plan must use a variety of formats and include input from a broad range of stakeholders.

Landrum, Callahan, and Shaklee (2001) suggest that "professional development is an ongoing, systemic process" (p. 68). They further state that "school staff members enter and exit the enduring cycle of professional development activity based on previous knowledge and experience and the need for information as it relates to their professional role in the education of gifted learners" (Landrum et al., 2001, p. 68).

## RATIONALE

The National Staff Development Council created a set of standards for professional development in 1994 that were revised in 2000 as a reaction to the frequent abuses of staff development in all educational fields (NSDC, 2000). These standards provide professionals guidance in planning staff development, from concept to implementation (Roy & Hord, 2003).

Tomlinson and Allan (2000) remind professionals that "the power of staff development to support educators in making change is likely greater than we have acknowledged. For example, studies tell us that teachers who know a great deal about teaching and learning and who work in environments that allow them to know students well are a very powerful factor in determining student achievement—a far more powerful determinant than class size" (p. 78). These studies provide leaders with a rationale for high-quality, powerful professional development because they have the potential to shape our thinking and influence our actions as they pertain to teaching gifted and talented individuals.

The National Foundation for the Improvement of Education (1996) further provides support for professional development:

> Changing times require that schools become learning enterprises for teachers and for students. The way teachers currently learn on the job was designed for teachers of an earlier time before the public grew concerned with higher standards and improved performance for all students. . . . Today's teachers must take on new roles within the school and be able to teach young people from diverse backgrounds by drawing on a large repertoire of subject matter and teaching skills. (Preface; http://www.neafoundation.org/publications/charge/preface.htm)

Finally, Marzano (2003) discusses the need for teachers to engage in meaningful staff development experiences. However, he cautions that "although many schools have regularly scheduled staff development sessions, much of what is done in these sessions is not necessarily meaningful or useful in terms of impacting student achievement" (Marzano, 2003, p. 65). Therefore providing staff development or having a plan for doing so is insufficient for influencing teacher effectiveness. Quality components must also be considered in developing a comprehensive plan.

## GUIDING PRINCIPLES

The professional development plan that addresses the needs of gifted and talented learners should

- be aligned with other district staff development efforts "that make(s) systematic change possible and manageable" (Zmuda, Kuklis, & Kline, 2004, p. 19);
- be an "integral part of a deliberately developed continuous improvement effort" (Zmuda et al., 2004, p. 5);
- be designed and implemented collaboratively by classroom teachers, specialists in gifted education, and administrators;
- include long-term goals for the school or district program and outline a process for determining appropriate interim steps that would be necessary to achieve the goals;
- contain content that is viewed by participants "as a necessary means to achieve the desired end" (Zmuda et al., 2004, p. 19);
- be consistent with recommended strategies of experts in gifted education and staff development;
- differentiate staff development to address critical differences among participants; and
- include a plan for assessing the effectiveness of the staff development goals.

## TRAITS OF A HIGH-QUALITY PROFESSIONAL DEVELOPMENT PLAN

Every teacher has participated in professional development efforts that were less than satisfying and made little difference in their thinking and/or practice. Occasionally, teachers have also attended powerful staff development initiatives that resulted in lasting learning. Little (1993) explains why some activities do not result in the change.

> Much staff development or inservice communicates a relatively impoverished view of teachers, teaching, and teacher development. Compared with the complexity, subtlety, and uncertainty of the classroom, professional development is often a remarkably low-intensity enterprise. It requires little in the way of intellectual struggle or emotional engagement and takes only superficial account of teachers' histories or circumstances. Compared with the complexity and ambiguity of the most ambitious reforms, professional development is too often substantively weak and politically marginal. . . . Professional development must be constructed in ways that deepen the discussion, open up the debates, and enrich the array of possibilities for action. (p. 14)

Therefore, a quality plan for professional development should respond to the following probing questions in eight key areas:

### 1. Alignment

- To what extent do the professional learning experiences align with the district mission statement and the professional development for general education?

- To what extent does the professional development align with the basic competencies of gifted education teachers and administrators?
- To what extent does the professional development address the learning needs of the teachers and administrators involved with the gifted education program?
- To what extent are the professional development sessions purposefully aligned and sequenced with each other to deepen professional learning?
- To what extent are professional learning experiences linked with professional responsibility?

## 2. Content

- To what extent are the desired learning outcomes based on a sound diagnosis of participants' prior knowledge and experience (National Staff Development Council)?
- To what extent does the content reflect current research or best practice?
- Is the content grounded in theory?
- Does the content have meaning and/or relevance for the participants?

## 3. Comprehensiveness

- Do professional learning opportunities span the needs of gifted education students, pre-K–Grade 12?
- To what extent do professional learning opportunities attend not only to cognitive, but also to the social and emotional learning and counseling needs of gifted and talented students?

## 4. Nature of Professional Learning Opportunities

- To what extent do the professional learning experiences provide practitioners with opportunities to construct meaning about their new learning (e.g., focused conversations, small-group conversations for reflection or summarizing, guided practice)?
- Is the professional development differentiated to attend critical differences among practitioners?
- To what extent are different formats used to deliver the professional development activities and attend to critical differences among the learners? (See Figure 14.1.)
- To what extent do teachers have a choice in the ways in which they acquire new information, deepen understanding, and practice new skills in supportive environments?
- To what degree is there an alignment of individual educator's professional development goals with the program goals?

## 5. Follow-Up Opportunities

- To what extent are there structured opportunities for reflection?
- What is the nature and extent of follow-up learning (e.g., critical friends groups, planning time for collaborative lesson planning, analyses of student work samples)?
- To what degree do opportunities exist for coaching and scaffolding teachers' practice?
- Are there procedures to refine skills, share successes, address concerns, and problem-solve new issues?
- Are there opportunities for educators to share their expertise either as presenters, coaches, critical friends, and so forth?

## 6. Resources

- To what extent are resources made available to support the professional development?
- Are multiple ways of learning incorporated into the professional development plan (e.g., multimedia, print articles, supplementary readings, videos)?

## 7. Scheduling

- Are learning opportunities scheduled in such a way throughout the year so that they maximize professional learning?
- To what extent are teachers released during the school day to attend professional development activities?

## 8. Evaluation

- Are evaluations conducted about the quality of professional learning experiences?
- To what extent are the data from the evaluations used to inform professional development practices?

**Figure 14.1** Formats for Professional Development

Professional development planners need to consider a variety of formats when designing staff development options for educators. The following models are offered as possible ideas and should be shared with teachers so as to allow choice and buy-in to the improvement efforts that are the focus of school and district. Planners may wish to survey staff members to determine their preferences for particular formats and use the data to build or refine their professional development efforts.

| _____Whole-Group Workshop | _____Study Groups |
|---|---|
| _____Conference Attendance | _____Conference Presentation |
| _____Staff Share Sessions | _____Online courses |
| _____Retreats | _____Technology |
| _____Brown-Bag Lunch | _____Community Expert |
| _____Demonstration Classrooms | _____Cross-Grade Cadres |
| _____Peer Review | _____Friday Forums |
| _____Resource Team | _____Grade-Level Leaders |
| _____Multiyear Model | _____Action Research |
| _____Coaching | _____Analyze Student Work |
| _____Independent Study | _____School or Classroom Visits |
| _____Graduate Coursework | _____Institutes or Academies |

## EXAMPLE IN NEED OF REVISION

**Memorandum**

**To:**       All Ellen B. Smith School Faculty/Staff
**From:**    Building Principal
**Subject:** Upcoming Inservice
**Date:**    March 1, 2004

To meet state and district requirements, our school's annual inservice for gifted and talented education will be held on March 11 from 3:30 to 5:00 p.m. All faculty and support staff are required to attend. The inservice presenter will be our enrichment specialist, Mr. Baker.

## PROCEDURES FOR REVISING

Quality staff development is not achieved in one-shot, afterschool inservice sessions on random topics. These kinds of professional learning opportunities would certainly not be sufficient to address the needs of gifted and talented students. The quality components outlined in the section on Traits of a High-Quality Professional Development Plan and the additional features suggested by Garet and his colleagues are critical for professional development planners. Garet, Porter, Desimone, Birman, and Yoon (2001) surveyed more than 1,000 teachers and found that the following staff development principles, if adhered to, increased the likelihood that practitioners will change their teaching behaviors. Professional development is effective when it

- is a reform rather than traditional type;
- is sustained over time;
- involves groups of teachers from the same school;
- provides opportunities for active learning;
- is coherent with other reforms and teachers' activities; and
- is focused on specific content and teaching strategies.

How can one improve on a professional development plan? Compare your district professional development opportunities to each of the markers of exemplary professional learning contained in the section on Traits of a High-Quality Professional Development Plan. For example, to what extent is your professional development based on current research and best practices? Or, to what extent does your plan provide for multiple ways of learning, such as through print, videotapes, and/or electronic forms of learning? On one hand, if your assessment reveals that your staff development rates highly on each of the markers, you need to maintain the quality of your professional development for gifted education. On the other hand, if you find that your staff development does not measure up on one or more of the quality markers, identify all areas in need of improvement and then prioritize where you need to concentrate your efforts. Work systematically to increase the quality of each of the elements until you are satisfied that you have an effective staff development program for gifted education teachers and administrators.

## MAKEOVER EXAMPLE

The following is a professional development plan that has been revised to incorporate the characteristics of high-quality staff development plans. To check your understanding of these characteristics, highlight elements of this plan that have been revised and reflect these characteristics.

### Memorandum*

**To:**      All Ellen B. Smith Faculty/Staff
**From:**    School Improvement/Professional Development Committee
**Subject:** Continuing Our Learning
**Date:**    January 25

*sent via e-mail and hard copy in faculty/staff mailboxes

This year we will continue our professional learning about techniques for improving student learning and achievement. To respond to the feedback received from teachers about their preferred professional development topics, we will focus on the diversity of students in our classrooms. Our professional work will include careful examination of the characteristics of not only those learners who are experiencing difficulty in our classrooms, but also those who have advanced learning needs. We have created a series of carefully planned professional development experiences that are based on the most recent and research based instructional practices. Many sessions are based on the work of Dr. Carol Ann Tomlinson. Each month we will have a presentation for the entire faculty that focuses on one type of learner. We have in-house and district specialists who can assist us with planning and delivering ideas. Subsequent to the presentation for the entire staff, each grade-level team or department meeting will include time to share teachers' successes and struggles related to meeting these students' needs. By doing so, we hope that practitioners will benefit from each others' practices. As always, your comments and reflections are important. We will be conducting evaluations at the end of each session and seeking your input regarding how we can increase antecedent effectiveness. The following schedule is proposed for this semester's monthly inservice meetings. As in the past, these sessions are scheduled during the school day and substitutes will be provided:

January – Advanced Learners
February – Students With Learning Disabilities
March – Students With Moderate/Severe Disabilities
April – Student Work Samples Reviewed
May – Planning Our Next Steps for Follow-up

As each monthly session approaches, you will receive a packet of information about each topic. The selections, which may be print, electronic, or video, have been carefully selected as noteworthy resources.

# STRATEGIC PLAN FOR DESIGNING A PROFESSIONAL DEVELOPMENT PLAN

This strategic plan is based on the assumption that no professional development plan exists for gifted education practitioners. Readers in districts that already have a plan in place are invited to pinpoint, within the following plan, where they need to address their efforts.

*Objective:* To develop a plan for professional development for gifted education (G/T) practitioners.

*Evidence:* A comprehensive plan for professional development that is aligned with the mission statement of the school, the professional development plan for general education, and the learning needs of the gifted education teachers and administrators. It will address the competencies expected of all educators of the gifted and talented.

*Tasks:*

### December

Convene a committee that is charged with designing, implementing, and evaluating an effective professional development plan for gifted education practitioners. Invited members should include (1) classroom teachers from general education, (2) gifted education teachers, (3) a building administrator, and (4) central office personnel.

### January–February

Meet with the committee members over time to review the following:

- The existing school mission statement.
- The existing plan for professional development for general education.
- The gifted education position statement.
- The goals for the gifted education program.

### March

Develop, administer, and analyze a simple needs assessment to assess the competencies. A list of competencies is contained in Figure 14.2.

### April

Keeping the results, G/T program goals, mission statement, and schoolwide professional development plan in mind, generate one to two long-range goals for professional development (e.g., practitioners will be able to provide standards-based curriculum differentiation options for G/T students both in the regular and the G/T program).

**Figure 14.2** Competencies for Gifted Education Specialists

What follows is a basic list of competencies for gifted education specialists. It is not intended to be comprehensive, nor does it attend to the variations that exist among states' certification and endorsement regulations. It can be used, however, to help educational leaders who are charged with developing professional development plans for gifted education practitioners. (See generally Landrum, Callahan, & Shaklee, 2001; National Association for Gifted Children, 1994; NAGC & CEC, 2006. See also Chapter 13)

**Identification**

1. Understand the most commonly used assessment instruments for the identification of G/T students, including those instruments that are likely to identify underserved populations. Common assessments for all populations of students include: disaggregated state assessment data, IQ assessments, ability tests (verbal and nonverbal), norm-referenced assessments, achievement tests, primary grade assessments, teacher recommendations, behavior rating scales, portfolios, and peer nominations.
2. Select those assessments most appropriate for the demographics of the community.
3. Create and implement the procedures for the identification of gifted and talented students, pre-K–12.
4. Understand and communicate to any constituency the state policies that regulate the identification and servicing of gifted education students.
5. Explain the alignment between the state definition and the district-level definition, should there be a variation.
6. Based on the identification process, develop a general learning profile of the students who have been identified that includes a composite picture of students' interests, academic strengths and weaknesses, learning style preferences, expression style preferences, and social and emotional needs.

**Program Planning**

7. Understand broadly the district-level curriculum in all content areas: language arts, science, social studies, mathematics, foreign language, and the visual and performing arts.
8. Identify the most appropriate theoretical and administrative model(s) for service delivery.
9. Create program goals and objectives (See Chapter 6) that take into consideration gifted education students' learning needs and that are aligned with the district-level curriculum.
10. Create, implement, and assess an aligned and comprehensive set of curriculum units for gifted education students who are serviced in a pull-out administrative model. (See Chapter 8.)
11. Create and implement a continuum of acceleration and enrichment options that is aligned with the learning needs of gifted education students, pre-K–12, and the district curriculum.
12. If one is required, prepare an Individual Education Program (IEP) in concert with parents.
13. Prepare and maintain a program budget Creating a Comprehensive and Defensible Budget for Gifted Program and Services (See Chapter 10.)
14. Identify and purchase high-quality resources in the Education of the Gifted. (See Chapter 11.)
15. Plan and implement ongoing activities for student related to college planning. (See the references listed at the end of Chapter 9, Developing Services That Meet the Social and Emotional Needs of Gifted Children.)

**Program Evaluation**

16. Plan and implement a program evaluation and disseminate the results of the evaluation to all stakeholders. (See Chapter 15.)

**Advocacy**

17. Manage an ongoing communication initiative. (See Chapter 12.)
18. Develop and sustain advocacy at the local and state level that is aligned with the district plan. (See Chapter 18.)

**Professional Development**

19. Design and implement a professional development plan for gifted education teachers that is aligned with the district professional development plan.
20. Develop and implement professional development for regular classroom teachers about the learning needs of gifted education students.
21. Work collaboratively with regular classroom teachers to support curriculum differentiation for students.

*May*

For each long-term goal, generate two to three short measurable objectives (e.g., G/T teachers will be able to develop differentiated lessons in social studies, Grades 4–8, that attend to students' learning needs, or G/T teachers will be able to develop differentiated lessons in mathematics in grades K–3 to attend to students' unique learning needs).

*June–August*

Create an ongoing series of learning opportunities that will support the acquisition of the target knowledge and methodologies. Identify who will provide the training, when and where it will be held, and the duration of the training. Ensure a variety of learning formats and differentiated learning options, based on the prior knowledge of the practitioners involved. (See Figure 14.1.)

Secure any resources that will be needed to support the training (e.g., books, articles, audiovisual materials).

Develop and implement an assessment of the professional learning opportunities that is tied to the teachers' work resulting from the professional learning: (1) checklists of various types (e.g., the number of requests of differentiated lesson plans from regular classroom teachers), (2) teacher reflections, (3) student work, (4) teacher lesson plans, and (5) sample assignments.

*September–May*

Implement and coordinate the professional development activities.

*June*

Analyze, compile, and share the assessment data with all stakeholders. Make recommendations and adjust the professional development plan as required.

## TEMPLATE FOR PROFESSIONAL DEVELOPMENT PLANNING

Table 14.1 has been designed to help practitioners begin to think about their planning for professional development. Down the left-hand side of the chart are the tasks that are required to complete a comprehensive, long-lasting, and effective professional development plan. Across the top of the Table 14.1 are columns that can be used to: (1) add details to the tasks, (2) indicate who is responsible, and (3) provide a timeline for task completion.

## ADVICE FOR THE SOLE PRACTITIONER

Designing a quality professional development program is the responsibility of several persons within a school system, and a person who has sole responsibility for a program would find collaborating with others a benefit. Researching who may be of assistance in

**Table 14.1**  Planning for Professional Development

| Tasks | Outline of tasks to be completed | Person responsible | Timeline |
|---|---|---|---|
| Convene a committee. | | | |
| Review all related documents. | | | |
| Develop and administer a needs assessment. | | | |
| Generate two to three long-term professional development goals and related objectives. | | | |
| Create an ongoing series of professionally related opportunities. | | | |
| Secure resources. | | | |
| Develop and implement an evaluation of the professional development plan. | | | |
| Modify the professional development plan. | | | |

designing and implementing professional development opportunities would be helpful to enhance the success of such efforts. This collaboration would also increase the likelihood that such efforts were a part of a total school professional develop plan and perhaps solicit help in carrying out the work.

## MUST-READ RESOURCES

Landrum, M. S., Callahan, C. M., & Shaklee, B. D. (Eds.). (2001). *Aiming for excellence: Gifted program standards.* Washington, DC: National Association for Gifted Children.

Tomlinson, C. A., & Allan, S. D. (2000). *Leadership for differentiating schools and classrooms.* Alexandria, VA: Association for Supervision and Curriculum Development.

Zmuda, A., Kuklis, R., & Kline, E. (2004). *Transforming schools: Creating a culture of continuous improvement.* Alexandria, VA: Association for Supervision and Curriculum Development.

## WEB RESOURCES

Schlechty Center for Leadership in School Reform: www.schlechtycenter.org/

National Staff Development Council. Retrieved August 12, 2005, from www.nsdc.org/standards/strategies.cfm

## REFERENCES

Garet, M., Porter, A. C., Desimone, L., Birman, B. F., & Yoon, K. S. (2001). What makes professional development effective? Results from a national sample of teachers. *American Education Research Association Journal, 38*(4), 115–145.

Landrum, M. S., Callahan, C. M., & Shaklee, B. D. (Eds.). (2001). *Aiming for excellence: Gifted program standards.* Washington, DC: National Association for Gifted Children.

Little, J. W. (1993). Teachers' professional development in a climate of educational reform. *Education Evaluation and Policy Analysis, 15*(2), 129–151.

Marzano, R. J. (2003). *What works in schools: Translating research into action.* Alexandria, VA: Association for Supervision and Curriculum Development.

National Association for Gifted Children (1994). *Competencies needed by teachers of gifted and talented students* [position paper]. Washington, DC: Author.

National Association for Gifted Children & Council for Exceptional Children (2006). *Initial NCATE standards for teacher preparation programs in gifted education.* Washington, DC: Author.

National Foundation for the Improvement of Education. (1996). *Teachers take charge of their learning: Transforming professional development for student success.* Washington, DC: Author.

NSDC. (2000). National Staff Development Council standards: Designs and strategies. Retrieved August 12, 2005, from National Staff Development Council Web site: http://www.nsdc.org/standards/strategies.cfm

Roy, P., & Hord, S. (2003). *Moving NSDC's staff development standards into practice: Innovation configurations.* Oxford, OH: National Staff Development Council.

Tomlinson, C. A., & Allan, S. D. (2000). *Leadership for differentiating schools and classrooms.* Alexandria, VA: Association for Supervision and Curriculum Development.

Zmuda, A., Kuklis, R., & Kline, E. (2004). *Transforming schools: Creating a culture of continuous improvement.* Alexandria, VA: Association for Supervision and Curriculum Development.

# 15

# Developing a Plan for Evaluating a Program in Gifted Education

*Carolyn M. Callahan*

He who asks a question is a fool for a minute; He who does not, remains a fool forever.

—Chinese Proverb

In 1988, James Gallagher (1988) made an important observation: "We risk losing fair documentation of the genuine contribution that such [gifted] programs make if we cannot come forth with a general strategy of how to design appropriate evaluation programs and assessment procedures for these special groups" (p. 112). The call for improved evaluation procedures for gifted education programs and services is not new. It was recognized as a critical need as early as the Marland Report (Marland, 1972) and has been considered an important topic by those interested in scholarly and thoughtful discussions of national-level educational matters (Passow, 1979). In the 1970s, Joseph Renzulli authored one of the first guidebooks on program evaluation (Renzulli, 1975). In 1986, June Maker devoted a chapter to program evaluation in her book, *Critical Issues in Gifted Education* (Maker, 1986).

Since the mid 1980s, much has been written about program evaluation and assessment procedures. The National Research Center on the Gifted and Talented has published several monographs on the topic (Callahan, Tomlinson, Hunsaker, Bland, & Moon, 1995; Fetterman, 1993). Carolyn Callahan (2004) provides a historical overview of evaluation in our field; Joyce VanTassel-Baska and Annie Feng (2004) provide an overview of evaluation models in the field and offer information about widely used evaluation tools: surveys, structured observation forms, focus groups, and student data. The characteristics of high-quality program evaluations are contained in the National Association for Gifted Children's *Pre-K–Grade 12 Gifted Program Standards* (Landrum, Callahan, & Shaklee, 2001).

In spite of publication efforts, however, many programs and services continue without adequate evaluation procedures to document their effectiveness. In this chapter, Carolyn Callahan provides us with the principles that guide program evaluation, shares her insights on how to improve the evaluations of gifted education programs and services, and offers a possible action plan for developing a rigorous and defensible evaluation plan that can document the effectiveness of gifted education services.

Evaluation and assessment are tied to every other key feature addressed in this guidebook: mission statement, definition of gifted and talented, procedures for identifying students, program goals, program design, curriculum, curriculum resources, budget, personnel, and professional development. If we consider this guidebook a rich tapestry, this chapter is one of the *warp*, or support threads that shape this multicolored cloth. One cannot possibly pull on the support thread without affecting the quality and dimension of the overall piece. This chapter is, therefore, an important one that deserves the serious consideration of practitioners who are concerned about the delivery of high-quality and long-lasting services to gifted education students.

## DEFINITION

Evaluation of a gifted program is a systematic process of collecting data from multiple sources to help decision makers at all levels make informed judgments about the effectiveness of the various components of services offered to gifted students. In the field of evaluation, we seek to collect both formative and summative evaluation data. Formative evaluation is the process of gathering data about a program during its evolution and as part of an effort to make a program better as it develops. Formative evaluation seeks to guide in the determination of the strengths and weaknesses of a program that contribute to the overall program effectiveness and factors that may hinder or contribute to the achievement of the program goals. Summative evaluation is designed to make judgments about the merit or worth of the program or specific components of a program and to make judgments about whether it should be modified, retained, or eliminated. In the summative evaluation stage of evaluation, data are presented to inform stakeholders about the success of the program in achieving its goals and possibly about other unanticipated effects of the program. In formative evaluation, the evaluator may discover that the teachers have not been trained to use appropriate instructional strategies with gifted students and suggests that, therefore, it is unlikely the students will achieve the expected educational outcomes. At that point, it would be appropriate for the evaluator to suggest specific staff development or coaching interventions. Summative data may document that the expected goal of increased numbers of students enrolling in and achieving a score of 3 on Advanced Placement tests had not been achieved.

## RATIONALE

Evaluation is critical to the success of gifted education programs (Joint Committee on Standards for Educational Evaluation, 1994; Reineke, 1991; Tomlinson, Bland, & Moon, 1993; Tomlinson, Bland, Moon, & Callahan, 1994). Equally important, gifted education programs, like all educational programs, are accountable to their constituencies to document that resources committed to the program are effectively and efficiently expended.

Funding agents have the right and responsibility to ensure that the resources are well used; parents have the expectation that the educational program offered to their children is of high quality; teachers and administrators should be eager to know that their efforts are in line with best practices in the field; and gifted students have the right to expect us to provide a challenging and engaging program of studies addressing their educational and social and emotional needs.

An effective evaluation plan and its implementation

- Should be specifically and purposefully planned.
- Must be supported with an adequate budget.
- Involve key stakeholders from the very beginning of the process through the stage of planning for implementation of the recommendations. (See Appendix A, on Gifted Education Advisory Committees.)
- Are both formative and summative in design and implementation.
- Must match data collection strategies to the evaluation questions asked.
- Should use multiple data collection methods and sources.
- Must use reliable and valid assessment tools.
- Present findings in oral and written forms that are directed toward the specific interests and needs of the stakeholders in program.
- Take into account the unique issues involved in programming for gifted students.
- Are an open, public, and interactive process.

## GUIDING PRINCIPLES OR ASSUMPTIONS

Evaluation of a gifted program is an integral part of the program development cycle. There are many groups of people who have a vested interest in the services offered to gifted students in any school division (e.g., students, classroom teachers, building administrators, central office personnel, members of the board of education, parents of gifted education students, citizens, state department of education personnel). These stakeholders are critical sources of guidance in the formulation of a quality evaluation plan and should be represented on a steering committee that is consulted in the formulation of the plan and in its subsequent implementation.

- The evaluation of a gifted program can be a very threatening activity, especially if stakeholders are not given the opportunity to participate in the planning of the evaluation.
- Traditional indicators of success in educational programs such as standardized achievement tests are not likely to be valid or reliable in measuring the goals and objectives of gifted programs.
- Effective evaluations cannot rely on only process or survey data; outcomes or goals must be carefully and operationally defined and assessed.
- While outcomes must be assessed, a quality evaluation will also provide data to help understand the reasons why outcomes are achieved or why those goals have not been achieved.
- Effective evaluations are sensitive and respectful of the persons involved in delivering services to gifted students.
- Effective evaluations communicate findings in meaningful, relevant, clear, and precise summaries that reflect local context and take into account state and local policies and regulations.

- Effective evaluations are conducted by persons who are knowledgeable about both the field of gifted education and the field of evaluation.
- Effective evaluations communicate their findings in a timely fashion.

## ATTRIBUTES THAT DEFINE HIGH-QUALITY PROGRAM EVALUATION

### Responsiveness

- Does the evaluation take into consideration the concerns of those individuals who have a stake in the implementation and outcomes of the services offered to gifted students?

### Importance

- Does the evaluation design address important evaluation questions, not just those easy to answer?

### Alignment

- Does the evaluation give appropriate attention to defining and taking into account the goals, objectives, and intended outcomes of the program?

### Fairness and Impartiality

- Is the evaluation designed to give equal voice to all constituencies and examine all issues, no matter how sensitive, with appropriate weight to all voices, not just those with power and influence?
- Are assessment tools selected or created with careful attention to reliability and validity in measuring the component under consideration?

### Respect for All Involved

- Has care been taken to design an evaluation that is considerate of the context and the situational factors impacting schools and the personnel in those schools?
- Have all instruments and data-gathering procedures been examined to ensure they will not offend constituencies involved?
- Will data actually be used? Has care been taken not to waste students', teachers', or other stakeholders' time in evaluation activity that does not contribute to good decision making?

### Adequate Funding

- Has sufficient funding been allocated to complete the evaluation as designed?

### Timeliness and Relevance

- Have data been collected, analyzed, and reported in time for consideration in the decision-making process?
- Have results and recommendations been presented to relevant audiences in formats that make the information clearly understood?

# EXAMPLE IN NEED OF REVISION

When asked to provide an evaluation of the gifted program, the program coordinator called together the gifted facilitator staff members and asked them to generate questions for a questionnaire to be sent out to parents. The coordinator and the staff generated a survey that addressed parent satisfaction with the identification process, the curriculum, and communication. In addition, the questionnaire addressed parent perceptions of the students' satisfaction with instruction they were provided. However, key stakeholders were omitted from the process.

### Task 1: Identification of Key Stakeholder Groups

The members of the committee first identified all those groups that have a vested interest in the way gifted services are delivered, the quality of administration of the program, the curriculum and its effectiveness, and the like. The persons on the committee were asked to be as broad as possible in identifying these groups. The groups they identified were

- Parents of gifted students
- Gifted students
- Superintendent and other central office administrators
- School board members
- Gifted facilitators
- Classroom teachers
- The coordinator of the program
- Building principals
- Parents of students not identified as gifted and talented

### Task 2: Development of Strategies for Gathering Information on Areas of Concern of Each of These Stakeholder Groups

Once the stakeholder groups were identified, the committee identified a small group of key persons (five to six) in each group who were likely to be able to articulate the areas that should be considered in creating an evaluation plan. A survey was constructed and mailed to the designated parents, students, classroom teachers, building principals, and the parents of students not identified as gifted. This open-ended survey asked the respondents to identify areas of concern they had about the gifted program and to write down the questions they would ask if they were conducting an evaluation of the program. Interviews were scheduled and held with the chair of the school board, the superintendent, and the assistant superintendent of curriculum.

### Task 3: Review of Data

The members of the committee reviewed all the data resulting from Task 2 and created an extensive list of evaluation concerns. They then rank ordered this list based on the frequency of mention, the level of intensity, and their judgment of the importance of the concern to gathering data that would improve the services to gifted students.

# DESIGNING OR REVISING AN EVALUATION PLAN OR CREATING A STRATEGIC PLAN FOR EVALUATION

In the section that follows, the steps for revising the inadequate evaluation plan are enumerated. However, the sequential nature of these steps would also provide a good guideline for program administrators who are in the process of developing a strategic plan. For each step, there is an accompanying question(s) to guide the actions you take.

## Step 1: Preparing for the Evaluation

| Action | Questions to Ask |
|---|---|
| a. Identify or develop a clearly articulated list of goals and objectives for all components of the services for gifted students. | What is the projected outcome of the identification process? The curriculum development process? The staff development for teachers? For administrators? What is the projected outcome of the instruction given to gifted students? How do the *NAGC Pre K– Grade 12 Gifted Program Standards* inform us about which components of our program we should evaluate and what standards we should apply? |
| b. Assure commitment to meaningful evaluation. | Have adequate time, resources, and money been provided to carry out and disseminate the results of the evaluation? |
| c. Identify varied internal and external interest groups or stakeholders to serve as an active evaluation steering committee. | Have all stakeholders been invited? Do they represent the varied perspectives and points of view? Can they work effectively as a guiding force to ensure the evaluation will be used? |
| d. Gather evaluation concerns from identified stakeholder groups. | Has sufficient input been gathered from all groups that have a vested interest in the quality of services for gifted students? |
| e. Develop a written evaluation plan based on priorities of concern. | Does the plan reflect the most important concerns raised by stakeholders? Does it have clearly delineated steps and procedures for implementing the evaluation? Are there appropriate guidelines for data gathering, analysis, and dissemination? |
| f. Select individuals to conduct the evaluation who are knowledgeable about evaluation and gifted education. | Is there someone from the school system who has the appropriate level of expertise to conduct an evaluation or is there a need for an outside consultant? Who might provide the expertise or names of reputable evaluators? |
| g. Consider the political implications of evaluation. | Have persons been identified who are key decision makers? Has someone contacted them? Are networks in place to support the evaluation process and its findings, both inside and outside the school district? |
| h. Establish provisions for confidentiality and sensitivity in handling data and evaluation results. | Has permission to conduct a program evaluation been granted from the school's governing body? Will information be kept confidential? |
| g. Consider the political implications of evaluation. | Have persons been identified who are key decision makers? Has someone contacted them? Are networks in place to support the evaluation process and its findings, both inside and outside the school district? |
| h. Establish provisions for confidentiality and sensitivity in handling data and evaluation results. | Has permission to conduct a program evaluation been granted from the school's governing body? Will information be kept confidential? |

## Step 2: Designing Data Collection

| Action | Questions to Ask |
|---|---|
| a. Develop clearly stated evaluation questions. | Do the evaluation questions address program goals, structures, functions, and activities? Can they be answered? If they are answered, will the answers affect decisions? Are findings likely to yield information that will be useful in improving services to gifted students? |
| b. Develop plans to use multiple data sources. | Does the plan include collecting data from parents of students identified as gifted, parents whose children have not been identified, teachers, students identified as gifted, administrators, and so forth, so that various perspectives will be considered? |
| c. Plan to employ varied data collection strategies. | Are there plans to include such strategies as face-to-face interviews, focus groups, surveys, telephone interviews, classroom observations, and objective and subjective measures of student outcomes, and the like? |
| d. Collect process data. | Are there ways to collect process data that can show whether the program is functioning as desired? For example, attendance records, documents from staff development sessions, newsletters or other communications to parents or classroom teachers, observation data from classrooms where gifted students are served, teacher or student journals, lesson plans or other curriculum documents, identification procedures and documents, and/or values data (interviews, surveys, etc.). |
| e. Collect outcome data. | Are there ways to collect outcome data that can show whether student cognitive and affective growth have occurred as a result of program participation (comparison of varied achievement measure outcomes of eligible participants and eligible nonparticipants, use of out-of-level assessments, use of comparison groups, portfolio/product ratings, use of valid and reliable self-concept or self-efficacy measures)? |
| f. Select valid and reliable measures. | Which sources of information on test quality have been consulted, such as the *Mental Measurements Yearbook*? |
| g. Specify ways data will be analyzed and reported. | What techniques will be used to analyze quantitative and qualitative data? What is the best way to communicate what was learned about gifted education programming? |

## Step 3: Conducting the Evaluation

| Action | Questions to Ask |
| --- | --- |
| a. Involve multiple stakeholders consistently and in meaningful ways. | Do all stakeholders have the opportunity to review data collection and analysis plans? |
| b. Ensure that understanding of process by all sources of information. | Are there multiple opportunities and multiple vehicles for explaining how and why data are being collected? |
| c. Monitor and review evaluation process to ensure that samples are representative and not biased. | Have all data collection plans been reviewed to ensure that everyone has had an opportunity to have a voice in the process? For example, is there an open forum time when those who might not have been preselected for interview can share their perspectives? |
| d. Ensure timely data analysis and feedback. | Does the data management plan include clear timelines and contingencies for ensuring data are collected and analyzed in time for the decision-making deadlines (budget, hiring, assignments, etc.)? |
| e. Develop a plan for use of the findings—aimed at turning findings into action. | Is there a plan that identifies the roles that evaluators, program personnel, and stakeholders play in using the evaluation findings? |

## Step 4: Reporting Findings and Follow-Up

| Action | Questions to Ask |
| --- | --- |
| a. Assess the impact of evaluation findings. | Have stakeholder groups been involved in the interpretation of the findings? |
| b. Prepare reports according to interests and needs of stakeholders. | Has jargon been avoided in the reports? Have reports been tailored to the needs of decision makers? |
| c. Include specific recommendations in the report that guide decision makers to follow through. | Can decision makers see the context in which recommendations are made? Do recommendations take into account the philosophy, the politics, and the financial circumstances? |
| d. Present the report in a timely fashion. | When are key decisions made? |

# MAKEOVER EXAMPLE

When asked to provide an evaluation of the gifted program, the program coordinator met with the assistant superintendent for curriculum to identify individuals to serve on an advisory committee for the evaluation process. This committee was carefully constructed to represent the teachers who served as gifted facilitators, parents of gifted students, teachers of classrooms that contained identified gifted students, principals, and identified gifted students (see Appendix A). In a series of meetings, the coordinator asked these groups to carry out three tasks.

# TEMPLATE FOR ASSESSING THE STRENGTHS OF A DISTRICT'S EVALUATION PLAN

The following checklist is a tool that can be used to assess the quality of a design for and implementation of evaluation procedures. Consider each statement and rate how successfully this step or component of your evaluation plan has been addressed: 1 indicates that the characteristic has not been addressed at all; 2 indicates that some attention has been given to it; and 3 indicates that the characteristics has been fully addressed and is clearly a part of the evaluation process in the school district.

The higher the total score, the more likely it is that your district has a high-quality evaluation initiative. Low scores on any item draw attention to aspects of the plan that may be in need of revision.

| *Characteristic* | 1 | 2 | 3 |
|---|---|---|---|
| 1. We have involved key stakeholders in creating our evaluation plan. They have been involved in ensuring we have identified the critical issues and concerns in the evaluation process and in identifying the kinds of data that will be considered in decision making. | | | |
| 2. Key stakeholder groups are kept informed of the implementation steps throughout the evaluation process. | | | |
| 3. We have adequate funds for the evaluation. | | | |
| 4. We have a written plan for evaluation that is approved by the key stakeholder groups. | | | |
| 5. We have the expertise to conduct the evaluation or have sought outside expertise. | | | |
| 6. A variety of effective communication vehicles is used for each constituent group. | | | |

*(Continued)*

(Continued)

| Characteristic | 1 | 2 | 3 |
|---|---|---|---|
| 7. We have identified important evaluation questions that include assessment of the effects of services on gifted students. | | | |
| 8. All goals of our program are evaluated—both process and product goals. | | | |
| 9. We have considered gathering data through a variety of means to answer each evaluation question and have chosen the most direct means of gathering data. | | | |
| 10. We have selected reliable and valid instruments for our data collection. | | | |
| 11. We have gathered data from a variety of sources. | | | |
| 12. We have gathered data in ways that allow us to attribute outcomes to our services to gifted students, not other programs, the students' natural development, or other factors. | | | |
| 13. We have made sure to adequately sample our sources to reduce potential bias in data. | | | |
| 14. We have selected appropriate procedures for analyzing quantitative and qualitative data. | | | |
| 15. We have a clear plan to communicate and distribute the results of the evaluation to decision makers. | | | |

## ADVICE FOR THE SOLE PRACTITIONER

A program evaluation is a complex and demanding undertaking for even a team of well-trained researchers. It is considerably more daunting for the sole practitioner. The single practitioner can consider the following three suggestions to assist in the program evaluation process. First, he or she might reach out to colleagues in neighboring towns. Colleagues can work collaboratively to assist each other in the many of the tasks related to program evaluation.

Sole practitioners who do not have the expertise, either by themselves or collectively as a regional duo or team, can consider a second option. Collectively they can hire an outside expert to either conduct the respective program evaluations or to act as an advisor as program coordinators undertake the program evaluation tasks.

A final option is to contact the state consultant on the gifted and talented. On occasion, these individuals are available to assist in the evaluation process. If they are unable to assist in conducting the evaluation themselves, they will surely have available a list of well-qualified, locally accessible consultants.

## MUST-READ RESOURCES

Callahan, C. M. (Vol. Ed.). (2004). Program evaluation in gifted education (Vol. 11). In S. M. Reis (Series Ed.), *Essential readings in gifted education.* Thousand Oaks, CA: Corwin.

Callahan, C. M., & Caldwell, M. S. (1995). *A practitioner's guide to evaluating programs for the gifted.* Washington, DC: National Association for Gifted Children.

Callahan, C. M., Tomlinson, C. A., Hunsaker, S. L., Bland, L. C., & Moon, T. (1995). *Instruments and evaluation designs used in gifted programs.* Charlottesville, VA: University of Virginia, The National Research Center on the Gifted and Talented.

Gallagher, J. J. (1988). National agenda for educating gifted students: Statement of priorities. *Exceptional Children, 55,* 107–114.

Fetterman, D. M. (1993). *Evaluate yourself.* Storrs, CT: The National Research Center on the Gifted and Talented, University of Connecticut.

Joint Committee on Standards for Educational Evaluation. (1994). *The program evaluation standards* (2nd ed.). Thousand Oaks, CA: Sage.

Landrum, M. S., Callahan, C. M., & Shaklee, B. D. (Eds.). (2001). *Aiming for excellence: Gifted program standards.* Waco, TX: Prufrock Press.

Maker, J. C. (Ed.). (1986). *Critical issues in gifted education: Defensible programs for the gifted.* Rockville, MD: Aspen.

Marland, S. P., Jr. (1972). *Education of the gifted and talented. Report to the Congress of the United States by the U.S. Commissioner of Education.* Washington, DC: U. S. Government Printing Office.

Passow, A. H. (Ed.). (1979). *The gifted and talented: Their education and development. The seventy-eighth yearbook of the national society for the study of education.* Chicago: University of Chicago Press.

Reineke, R. A. (1991). Stakeholder involvement in evaluation: Suggestions for practice. *Evaluation Practice, 12,* 39–44.

Renzulli, J. S. (1975). *A guidebook for evaluating programs for the gifted and talented.* Ventura, CA: Office of the Ventura County Superintendent of Schools.

Tomlinson, C. A., Bland, L., & Moon, T. R. (1993). Evaluation utilization: A review of the literature with implications for gifted education. *Journal for the Education of the Gifted, 16,* 171–189.

Tomlinson, C. A., Bland, L., Moon, T. R., & Callahan, C. M. (1994). Case studies of evaluation utilization in gifted education. *Evaluation Practice, 15,* 153–168.

Tomlinson, C. A., & Callahan, C. M. (1994). Planning effective evaluations of programs for the gifted. *Roeper Review, 17,* 46–51.

VanTassel-Baska, J., & Feng, A. X. (Eds.). (2004). *Designing and utilizing evaluation in gifted program improvement.* Waco, TX: Prufrock Press.

## REFERENCES

Callahan, C. M. (Vol. Ed.). (2004). Program evaluation in gifted education (Vol. 11). In S. M. Reis (Series Ed.), *Essential readings in gifted education.* Thousand Oaks, CA: Corwin.

Callahan, C. M., Tomlinson, C. A., Hunsaker, S. L., Bland, L. C., & Moon, T. (1995). *Instruments and evaluation designs used in gifted programs.* Charlottesville, VA: University of Virginia, The National Research Center on the Gifted and Talented.

Gallagher, J. J. (1988). National agenda for educating gifted students: Statement of priorities. *Exceptional Children, 55,* 107–114.

Fetterman, D. M. (1993). *Evaluate yourself.* Storrs, CT: The National Research Center on the Gifted and Talented, University of Connecticut.

Joint Committee on Standards for Educational Evaluation. (1994). *The program evaluation standards* (2nd ed.). Thousand Oaks, CA: Sage.

Landrum, M. S., Callahan, C. M., & Shaklee, B. D. (Eds.). (2001). *Aiming for excellence: Gifted program standards.* Waco, TX: Prufrock Press.

Maker, J. C. (Ed.). (1986). *Critical issues in gifted education: Defensible programs for the gifted.* Rockville, MD: Aspen.

Marland, S. P., Jr. (1972). *Education of the gifted and talented. Report to the Congress of the United States by the U.S. Commissioner of Education.* Washington, DC: U.S. Government Printing Office.

Passow, A. H. (Ed.). (1979). *The gifted and talented: Their education and development. The seventy-eighth yearbook of the national society for the study of education.* Chicago: University of Chicago Press.

Reineke, R. A. (1991). Stakeholder involvement in evaluation: Suggestions for practice. *Evaluation Practice, 12,* 39–44.

Renzulli, J. S. (1975). *A guidebook for evaluating programs for the gifted and talented.* Ventura, CA: Office of the Ventura County Superintendent of Schools.

Tomlinson, C. A., Bland, L., & Moon, T. R. (1993). Evaluation utilization: A review of the literature with implications for gifted education. *Journal for the Education of the Gifted, 16,* 171–189.

Tomlinson, C. A., Bland, L., Moon, T. R., & Callahan, C. M. (1994). Case studies of evaluation utilization in gifted education. *Evaluation Practice, 15,* 153–168.

VanTassel-Baska, J., & Feng, A. X. (Eds.). (2004). *Designing and utilizing evaluation in gifted program improvement.* Waco, TX: Prufrock Press.

# 16

# Connecting Program Design and District Policies

*Karen B. Rogers*

Success comes before work only in the dictionary.

—Anonymous

All school districts have policies to help ensure high-quality learning experiences for children. There are policies related to professional development, curriculum, homework, special education, communication with parents, and the purchase of curriculum materials, just to name a few. The two things that all effective school policies have in common is that they clearly connect with and elaborate on the school district's goals or mission and they are also based on current educational research and theory.

Karen Rogers has written this chapter to help ensure the existence of district-level policies that address the learning needs of gifted and talented students. She provides us with a unique and overarching framework for organizing the many and varied learning options appropriate for these learners. In addition, she describes guidelines for developing local policies that will facilitate the use of learning options that best fit the needs of highly able learners. The learning strategies provided in this chapter have a sound research base behind them, which makes this chapter especially important for those charged with developing, supporting, and maintaining services and policies for gifted and talented students.

Because this chapter seeks to provide guidance on translating a comprehensive program design into district policies, it is most closely related to Chapter 7, Comprehensive Program Design. However, it is also aligned closely with several other chapters, including

Developing a Mission Statement, 2; Developing a Definition of Giftedness on the Educational Needs of Gifted and Talented Students, 3; Articulating Gifted Education Program Goals, 6; Curriculum, 8; Designing a Professional Development Plan, 14; and State Policies in Gifted Education, 19, as well as to Appendix for Gifted Education Students, which addresses the creation of a local gifted education advisory committee.

## DEFINITIONS

Related district policies include statements about what a district will offer as instructional management, instructional delivery, and curriculum differentiation options for an individual, a small group, or a whole population of learners with gifts and/or talents. These administrative policies will most often elaborate on the articulated state or government policies, perhaps providing more scope or more breadth to possible options (Gallagher, 2002). In some cases, a district may decide to offer options not articulated in a state policy document as a consequence of the unusual nature of its gifted and talented population or setting. These district policies will correspond closely with the district position statement, in many cases operationalizing the belief statements contained in that document. Another perspective on a district's policy statement is that it can serve as an "insurance policy" that guarantees the educational rights or needs of this unique group of students (Passow & Rudnitski, 1993).

District policies for gifted education students may center on three overarching clusters of options: instructional management, instructional delivery, and curriculum differentiation (Rogers, 1991, 1998, in press). Instructional management is defined as how gifted learners may be organized for their instruction and has nothing directly to do with what or how they are taught. There are at least seven individualization strategies as one category of instructional management, each either producing a unique plan for an individual learner or allowing the learner to progress flexibly through the K–12 curriculum. Among the grouping strategies of instructional management are those strategies that group by ability and those that group by performance. The third category of instructional management strategies includes seven forms of either grade-based acceleration (allowing a gifted learner to shorten the number of years in the K–12 system) or subject-based acceleration (providing advanced exposure to knowledge and skills beyond the learner's age or grade level).

Instructional delivery refers to the ways in which gifted learners need to be taught. The research on this is much sparser than for instructional management and centers around teaching to gifted learners' preferences as well as teaching to the qualitative differences in how they learn. For curriculum differentiation, there is a variety of research-based strategies, not necessarily connected with a specific curriculum model, that teachers use to adapt, modify, extend, or differentiate what the gifted learner will be taught. There are many more strategies in Table 16.1 than any district could possibly include in its array of services, but this listing can serve admirably as a menu from which any district, no matter how large or small, can select the options it can provide. Each option listed has a strong research base to support it (Rogers, 1991, 1998, in press).

---

Editor's Note: See *Re-forming gifted education: Helping parents and teachers to match the option to the child* (Rogers, 2002) for fuller definitions of these options and for specific information about which options are most beneficial at each building level.

**Table 16.1**   Gifted Education Policy Options

| **Instructional Management Options** |
| --- |
| *Individualization Options* |
| Compacting the Curriculum |
| Preassessment of student's mastery of regular curriculum with subsequent design of appropriately differentiated replacement experiences with the time "bought" through demonstration of mastery. |
| Mentorship/One-on-One Tutoring |
| Placement of gifted learner with an expert or professional for exploring or advancing a specific interest or proficiency that cannot be provided in the regular setting. |
| Independent Study |
| Structured projects agreed on by learner and supervising teacher that allow student to individually investigate an area of high interest or to advance knowledge. |
| Nongraded/Multiage Classes |
| Placing learners in a classroom without regard to age or grade and allowing them to work through the materials at a pace and level appropriate to their individual ability and motivational levels. |
| Multigrade/Combination Classes |
| Placing learners in a two-grade classroom (e.g., Grades 1–2) and allowing them to work through the materials at a pace and level appropriate to their individual ability and motivational levels. |
| Credit for Prior Learning |
| Allowing students to demonstrate mastery of previously learned material through some form of assessment or evaluation of their previous learning experience. |
| Testing Out |
| Provision of testing programs whereby the learner, after successful completion of a test, will be offered a specified number of course credits or be placed in a more advanced course level. |
| *Grouping by Ability or Performance Options* |
| Cluster Grouping |
| Identify and place top five to eight high-ability learners in the same grade level in one class with a teacher who likes them, is trained to work with them, and devotes proportional class time to differentiating for them. |
| Special Full-Time Schools, Classes/Magnet Schools |
| Gifted learners spend all academic learning time with other gifted learners. |
| Send-Out Programs |
| Removal of gifted learners from a regular classroom for a specified period of time each day or week to work with trained specialist on differentiated curriculum. |
| Like Ability/Performance Cooperative Learning |
| Organizing of learners in three- or four-member teams of like ability and adjusting the group task accordingly. |

*(Continued)*

**Table 16.1** (Continued)

| |
|---|
| **Regrouped Advanced/Honors/Accelerated Classes for Specific Subjects** |
| Sorting students by their current performance level in a specific subject area for a curriculum that is appropriately differentiated. |
| **Within-Class Performance Grouping** |
| Sorting of students topic by topic or subject by subject within one classroom for the provision of differentiated learning for each group. |
| **Cross-Graded Classes** |
| Grouping children by their achievement level in a subject area rather than by grade or age level. |
| *Acceleration Options* |
| **Grade Skipping** |
| Double promoting a student such that he or she bypasses one or more grade levels. |
| **Grade Telescoping** |
| Shortening the time to progress through a school level, such as junior or senior high, by one year while still covering all the curriculum. |
| **Early Admission to College** |
| Permitting a gifted learner to enter college as a full-time student without completion of a high school diploma. |
| **Early Entrance to School** |
| Allowing selected gifted children showing readiness to perform schoolwork to enter kindergarten or first grade one to two years earlier than the usual beginning age. |
| **Concurrent/Dual Enrollment** |
| Allowing students to attend classes in more than one building level during the same school year. |
| **Advanced Placement/International Baccalaureate Programs** |
| Provision of course with college-level content at the secondary school level, affording student the opportunity to "test out" of or be given college credit for its completion. |
| **Subject Acceleration** |
| Allowing a gifted learner to bypass, skip, or move more rapidly through the usual progression of skills and content mastery in a single subject area. |
| **Instructional Delivery Options** |
| *Teaching to G/T Learner Preferences* |
| **Independent Projects Individually or With One Like-Ability Peer** |
| Opportunity for student(s) to pursue a topic of interest with more depth and complexity than provided in the regular classroom. |
| **Self-Instructional Materials/ Programmed Instruction** |
| Developed learning package that teaches a subject, with periodic diagnostic testing to ensure apprehension; learner works at own pace through the package. |

*(Continued)*

**Table 16.1** (Continued)

| |
|---|
| ### Conceptual Closure Discussions |
| High-level discussions of themes, concepts, issues, generalizations, and problems, rather than review of facts, terms, or details. |
| ### Simulations and Games With Embedded Individual Benchmarks |
| Using the game or simulation as a means for evaluating learner's current performance levels and to set performance outcomes for the student's next product or performance. |
| ### Hands-On Learning for New Learning Acquisition (only) |
| Learner engages in experiential task in which something new will be discovered or learned, not to review what was previously mastered. |
| ### Multimodal Lecture |
| Presenting a "burst" of concentrated information through visual and auditory modalities simultaneously. |
| *Teaching to Qualitative Learning Differences* |
| ### Pacing |
| Providing flexible presentation "speeds" according to depth and complexity of content presented. Often this means going more rapidly than the normal class pace. |
| ### Elimination of Excess Drill and Review |
| Once concept or skill is mastered, gifted learner reviews it no more than two to three times at spaced intervals. |
| ### Whole-to-Part Conceptual Teaching |
| Presenting a new concept or generalization in its entirety upfront, followed by time for analysis of its parts and reconstruction of its whole. |
| ### Depth of Content |
| Full elaboration of knowledge, concept, or skill as a whole for apprehension of its meaning and scope. |
| ### Opportunity for Reflection/Analysis |
| Structuring experiences so that gifted learner can understand the underlying significance of what has been presented or learned. |
| ### Daily Challenge in Specific Talent Area(s) |
| Gifted student is provided daily opportunity to learn something new and more advanced in specific subject area of talent. |
| ### Trained G/T Teachers |
| Teachers who have engaged in preservice, inservice, continuing education, or graduate coursework on nature and needs of gifted, curricular and instructional differentiation, and psychology of giftedness. |
| **Curriculum Differentiation Options** |
| *Content Modifications* |
| ### Abstract Content |
| Content that goes beyond surface detail and facts to underlying concepts, generalizations, and symbolism. |

*(Continued)*

**Table 16.1** (Continued)

| |
|---|
| **Complex Content** |
| Providing multiple-step or detailed projects or tasks for advanced knowledge and skill acquisition. |
| **Multidisciplinary Content** |
| Providing theme-related content across more than one subject area simultaneously. |
| **Study of People** |
| Relating a topic of study to the famous people and human issues and social problems within that field. |
| **Methods of Inquiry** |
| Relating a topic of study to the methods and practices of people who work in that field. |
| *Process Modifications* |
| **Higher-Order Thinking Skills—Training and Practice** |
| Questioning in discussions or providing activities based on processing that requires analysis, synthesis, evaluation, or other critical-thinking skills. |
| **Open-Ended Thinking, Training, and Practice** |
| Providing learners with tasks and work that do not have single right answers or outcomes. Timelines, sequence of activities to be accomplished, and outcomes may also vary depending on student needs. |
| **Proof and Reasoning** |
| Requiring students to cite their evidence to support ideas or concepts they generate. |
| **Guided Discovery Learning/Problem-Based Learning/Shared Inquiry** |
| Providing learners with a problem or question that they must explore, solve, or answer for themselves. |
| **Value of Group Production** |
| Structuring experiences so that gifted learner discovers the product or performance of the group is inherently better than what could have been done individually. |
| *Product Modifications* |
| **Systematic, Corrective Feedback** |
| Consistent, regular evaluations of student's products, performance, and knowledge acquisition for both corrective and reinforcement purposes. |
| **Individual Benchmark Setting** |
| Working with an individual student to set performance outcomes for the student's next product or performance. |

# RATIONALE

An articulated policy is the most powerful form of communication a school district can provide its community. It states explicitly what the schools in that district can or cannot, by omission, provide for individual students with gifts or talents (Gallagher, 2002;

Rogers, 2002; Zirkel, 2003). The process of developing such a policy requires program planners to think carefully about the school setting, students' attributes, and teacher and administrator attributes and then identify options that will correspond to these potentially different sets of school variables. The absence of a policy leaves a district with its hands tied when individual exceptions occur. With its policy "on the books," a district has solid reference points for making decisions and taking actions regarding individual or groups of gifted learners.

# GUIDING PRINCIPLES OR ASSUMPTIONS

- Local policies should define the mechanism(s) by which advanced learning opportunities are extended to gifted learners.
- Local policies should align with all pertinent state policies.
- All options targeted by a school and/or district must be written into a policy that is adopted by all constituencies and shared with parents and other community members.
- A district should carefully define and develop procedures for carrying out those management, instructional delivery, and modification options it includes in its policy.
- A district must develop a system for optimally matching gifted or talented learners with the instructional management, instructional delivery, and curriculum modification options it can offer.
- A district should identify two to three individualization options that take into account the variety of settings, students, teachers, and administrators present in the district.
- A district must identify two to three grouping options that take into consideration the variety of school settings, students, teachers, and administrators present in the district.
- A district should identify two to three accelerative options that address the needs of the school, students, teachers, administrators, and curriculum present in the district.
- A district must use the instructional management options to ensure that the variety of appropriate instructional delivery options can be implemented.
- A district should provide curriculum and instructional units differentiated for learners with gifts or talents that incorporate at least two to three content and process modifications and one product modification per unit.
- Professional accountability systems should reflect the nature and intent of local policies.

# TRAITS OF A HIGH-QUALITY ARTICULATED DISTRICT POLICY

## Comprehensiveness

- Does the policy offer viable individualization, grouping, and acceleration management options that are aligned with the needs of each school in the district?
- Does it offer every pre-K-Grade 12 gifted learner, regardless of domain of ability or level of performance, a variety of learning options that will meet his or her educational needs satisfactorily?

- To what extent will each gifted education student receive daily challenge in his or her specific area or areas of talent?

### Rationale

- To what extent does the policy include research-based practices that will optimize student learning?
- To what extent will the policies ensure that gifted learners have the opportunity to learn as much as they are capable of learning rather than remaining in an age/ grade arbitrary placement?

### Internal Consistency and Articulation

- Does the policy align with the district position statement and the articulated state policy?
- Does the policy provide checks and balances that ensure implementation is congruent (e.g., the plan accompanying the policy identifies who will be responsible for carrying out the services, by when these will be in place, and how implementation will be assessed as successful)?
- Do the options provided in the policy build on each other as students progress from building level to the next higher level (e.g., if a child has been subject accelerated in math in elementary and has already mastered the middle school math curriculum, the child will not repeat this curriculum when at middle school)?
- Is there a cumulative record of student engagement and performance outcomes based on policy placements, K–12 (e.g., the student records list and assess student's performance in gifted services offered by the district)?
- Does the articulated policy align with staff development provisions for practitioners, including teachers, administrators, and guidance counselors?

### Clarity

- Is the policy written clearly so that all users (e.g., community members, school board members, administrators, teachers, and students) will understand its intent?
- Is the policy written clearly so that all users understand how each district option is to be offered to gifted students (e.g., via grouped activity, independent learning, special school, etc.)?

### Feasibility

- To what extent can the policy be implemented under most sets of circumstances (budget shortfalls, teacher strikes, increasing or declining school population, new building construction, climatic conditions, hiring of new personnel, etc.)?

## EXAMPLES IN NEED OF REVISION

All classroom teachers in Jonesville Schools will compact the curriculum for their gifted and talented learners. They are also responsible for providing replacement activities that are appropriately differentiated.

*Commentary:* Although the service is explained to the extent that it can be carried out, no reference is made to (1) the research, (2) how teachers will be trained and monitored, (3) how building-level differences will be accommodated, or (4) which content areas will be targeted, both now and in the future.

*Rating:*

| Trait | 1<br>No<br>Evidence | 2<br>Little<br>Evidence | 3<br>Some<br>Evidence | 4<br>Considerable<br>Evidence | 5<br>Powerful |
|---|---|---|---|---|---|
| Comprehensiveness | X | | | | |
| Rationale | | X | | | |
| Internal Consistency and Articulation | X | | | | |
| Clarity | | X | | | |
| Feasibility | X | | | | |

### Intermediate Exemplar: Good but Not Perfect!

Each school within the Smithsville District must identify at least one individualization, grouping, and acceleration strategy for managing the instruction of its gifted learners. Teachers in each school must be trained to implement these management options as well as in how to implement the instructional delivery options and curriculum modification options selected by the school. Strategies include compacting, multiage grouping, combination classes, a send-out program, regrouped classes, concurrent enrollment, subject acceleration, grade skipping, and early entrance to school. All teachers with gifted students in their classrooms will also be responsible for using flexible pacing, breadth and depth of content, independent study projects, and like-ability-grouped projects in their classes whenever possible.

*Commentary:* Each school has been given a choice of management, delivery, and curriculum modification options. The following dimensions of the policy have not been articulated: (1) how to match the option choices with building level and school differences, (2) in which content areas various delivery and modification options will be emphasized, and (3) how teachers will be monitored.

## PROCEDURES FOR ENHANCING OR IMPROVING THE STATUS OF AN ARTICULATED POLICY

If a policy document is rated low in *comprehensiveness,* add or elaborate on the following: (1) whether the option is for an individual or group of gifted learner(s), (2) which domains of gift or talent the option will address, (3) which building level(s) would benefit most from use of the option, and (4) how the option can be operationalized on a daily—or consistent—basis.

If a policy document is rated low in *rationale*, then (1) specify the research support for the options selected at the district level, citing the reported effect sizes, if at all possible, and (2) provide data about the unique profile of teachers and/or students to demonstrate the need for the service options.

If a policy is rated low in *internal consistency* and articulation, add or elaborate on the following: (1) how the options align with the district position statement and articulated state policy, (2) purpose(s) of the options chosen, (3) how the options used at different grade levels build on or reinforce what has been used at a prior level, (4) where documentation of individual student participation in options can be found, and (5) how the targeted option(s) address students' learning needs.

If a policy is rated low in *clarity*, elaborate or specify (1) the intent or purposes of the options chosen and (2) operational definitions of each option.

If a policy is rated low in *feasibility*, add or elaborate on the resources needed (materials, personnel, training, attitudes) to fully implement each selected option.

## REVISING THE EXAMPLE

Each school within the Smithsville District must identify at least one individualization, grouping, and acceleration strategy for managing the instruction of its gifted and talented learners and a qualitative learning difference teaching strategy. The options available at each building level are listed in Table 16.2. (See Table 16.1 for definitions of each option.) Guidelines for identifying the options a school will adopt should take into consideration the nature of the school's student population, background of the teachers in the school, community attitudes about gifted programming, and the specific gifts and talents in evidence in the school. Once options are selected, it is important to provide the training, support, and materials that school personnel will require to implement these options consistently. An ongoing annual plan to assess the effectiveness of each option is recommended. Likewise, documentation about the effects of an option on student achievement will help each school determine whether or not their option selections are most appropriate for their learners. This documentation should be studied annually.

## MAKEOVER EXAMPLE

Each school within the central school district will receive professional development on the potential individualization, grouping, and acceleration strategies for managing the instruction of its gifted learners, from which school administrators will identify at least one to two individualization, grouping, and acceleration strategies most appropriate to the school setting. Teachers in each school must be trained to implement these management options as well as in how to implement the instructional delivery options and curriculum modification options selected by the school. Mathematics and science content will be delivered at a pace two to three times faster than the "normal" class pace, and drill and review will be limited to two to three iterations (at spaced intervals) after mastery. Individual research will be an option for differentiated study in every unit of science, social studies, and literature taught. The content of these disciplines will be structured by the big ideas and concepts or generalizations, presented in a whole-to-part fashion, that are the foundation of each subject domain. Compacting the curriculum will be the first step of instructional delivery in every subject area to ensure that gifted learners repeat do not what has already been mastered. Design of the replacement activities in mathematics will incorporate exposure to advanced concepts, skills, and procedures unlimited by grade or building level. Design of the replacement activities in science, social studies, and literature or humanities will provide a balance of content modified by abstraction, complexity, study of people, and methods of inquiry integrated with higher-order thinking skills, open-ended thinking, proof and reasoning, freedom of choice, and discovery learning wherever possible. Products will incorporate solutions to real-world problems and transformational uses of what has been learned. Teachers responsible for these strategies, whether gifted and talented (G/T) resource teachers or regular classroom teachers, will be monitored by school and district administration as to the fidelity of implementation. The students will be assessed biannually through achievement measures, attitudinal scales, or product assessments for expected academic gains associated with the strategies. It is expected that approximately one and a half years' curriculum will be covered on average for every year the gifted learner is in school.

*Commentary:* Each school has been given a choice of management, delivery, and curriculum modification strategies. Policy has articulated (1) in which content areas various delivery and modification options will be developed, (2) how teachers will be monitored, and (3) how student progress will be monitored. There also will be training of administrative staff in how to make the best matches of services and strategies for individual differences in each setting, which helps to ensure appropriate matches of services to settings.

# A STRATEGIC PLAN TO ADDRESS THE CREATION OR REVISION OF AN ARTICULATED DISTRICT POLICY ON THE EDUCATION OF GIFTED AND TALENTED STUDENTS

*Objective:* To create a district policy that contains appropriate service options for instructional management, instructional delivery, and curriculum modification for learners with gifts and talents.

*Evidence:* A completed district policy document on G/T service options offered in the district for each domain of giftedness and for each building level.

*Tasks:* Create a policy document or revise an existing one.

**Step 1:** Brainstorm the names of personnel who might sit on the G/T Task Force (e.g., classroom teachers, parents of G/T students, parents of students who have not been identified, administrators, and board of education members).

**Step 2:** Create a well-balanced task force. (See Appendix A)

**Step 3:** Gather essential documents prior to convening the task force (e.g., a synthesis of the learner profiles of G/T students, district demographics, a listing, K–12, of the current learning options offered to G/T students, the research base for options that may prove noteworthy for district students).

**Table 16.2** Building-Level Instructional Options, Curriculum Areas, and Attributes for Success

| Option Choices | Student Attributes for Success in Option | Building Level | Curriculum Area |
|---|---|---|---|
| Early Entrance to School | Two standard deviations (SDs) ahead on ability test OR first-grade achievement level in reading or math; one year of successful preschool experience can expect a half year's jump in achievement at time of implementation. | Elementary/ Primary | All academic areas, but focus is on advanced reading or math skills and performance |
| Grade Skipping | Two SDs ahead on ability test OR two grade levels ahead in all academic achievement areas; successful score on Iowa Acceleration Scale; can expect one year's growth in achievement and equivalent achievement when compared to older aged, gifted peers. | All building levels | All academic areas. Child should show no weak curriculum area in performance |
| Concurrent Enrollment | Two grade levels ahead in specific academic area; no teachers in current building able to subject-accelerate individual child; can expect one-third year's additional growth in specific area for which advanced class is taken. | All building levels | Any academic area, but probably shouldn't be offered in more than two areas for any individual child |
| Subject Acceleration | Two grade levels ahead in specific academic area: need teacher to supervise continued appropriateness of the advanced curriculum; can expect three-fifths year's additional growth in the specific area of acceleration. | All building levels | Any academic area for which the grade-level curriculum is too basic or limited in scope, especially math, world language, science |
| Compacting | Child or children frustrated with repetition and willing to learn new content, high degree of self-direction and preference for learning more independently, indication that child already knows much about topic or subject area; can expect four-fifths additional year's | All building levels, but may take subject-area head to coordinate middle and high school implementation | Any academic area for which the grade-level curriculum has been taught in earlier grades or that is extremely basic in its first introduction; especially good for mathematics, |

| Option Choices | Student Attributes for Success in Option | Building Level | Curriculum Area |
|---|---|---|---|
| | growth in math and science and one-third additional year's growth in language arts and social studies. | | basic language arts, and reading |
| Multiage Classes | For gifted children, there is a need to be self-directed and motivated to work at own pace and to be learning new content and skills daily; can expect two-fifths additional year's growth in all academic areas. | Elementary and middle levels | For all academic areas at elementary level; for specific academic area at middle level |
| Combination Classes | For gifted children, there is a need to be self-directed and motivated to want to learn more, to work at own pace, and work with older children. The gifted children should be the younger children in the class; can expect two month's additional growth for all academic areas. | Elementary and middle levels | For all academic areas at elementary level; for specific academic area at middle level |
| Send-Out Program | Performing one grade level ahead in curriculum area covered by send-out; IQ one and a half (SDs) above average; can expect two month's additional growth in academic area studied or substantial improvement on test of critical or creative thinking if focus of send-out is on thinking skills over the course of a year. | All building levels, but more commonly offered at elementary level only | In younger years, should work on development of potential with thinking skills (higher-order, creative thinking, problem solving) In intermediate years and beyond, should focus on talent development in specific academic or other talent area, such as math, writing, visual arts, etc. |
| Regrouped Classes | Performing one to two grade levels ahead in specific subject area in which regrouping takes place, willing to be challenged on daily basis, high interest in subject area that is regrouped; can expect up to four-fifths year's additional growth in specific area that is regrouped. | All building levels | All academic areas in which there is wide diversity of performance in a building level; is imperative that children be placed in group according to their current performance levels. |

*(Continued)*

**Table 16.2** (Continued)

| Option Choices | Student Attributes for Success in Option | Building Level | Curriculum Area |
|---|---|---|---|
| Flexible Pacing | Performing one to two grade levels ahead in specific subject area in which flexible pacing is offered; can be expected to result in two year's growth in areas such as math for each year engaged in faster pacing. | All building levels, but increasingly important as grade levels progress | Faster pacing in math, science, world languages; depth/slower pacing for complexity in social studies, reading, humanities |
| Content Depth | One to two SDs above average, tendency to be a holistic or more global thinker/learner | All building levels, but increasingly important as grade levels progress | All academic areas |
| Independent Study Projects | Performing one to two grade levels ahead in specific subject areas, strong interest or passion in specific area | All building levels | All academic areas |
| Like Ability Within Class Group Projects | Performing one to two grade levels ahead or one to two SDs ahead on IQ score; can be expected to result in one-quarter year's additional growth in subject. | All building levels | All academic areas |
| Elimination of Excess Drill & Review | One to two SDs above average, one to two grade levels ahead in academic area; can be expected to eliminate about one-third year's drill efforts. | All building levels | Most academic areas, most especially math and science |

**Step 4:** Analyze all the existing documentation to identify trends and patterns in the district.

**Step 5:** Delineate the options and services the district will offer to gifted education students. As a part of this, identify which options will be implemented at what time in the succeeding years. You may need a multiyear plan of action for this, if the changes are great.

**Step 6:** Identify the current levels of teacher expertise related to the targeted options.

**Step 7:** Target new staff development initiatives that will be required in order for practitioners to deliver the targeted options.

**Step 8:** Provide input to the professional development committee about the nature of the new staff development initiatives.

**Step 9:** Gather evaluation data about the effectiveness of the strategies identified in the policy as they are implemented with students.

**Step 10:** Use data to systematically evaluate and modify the policies to ensure that they align with the learning needs of gifted education students.

---

*Timeline:* Months 1–2: convene a meeting of the Gifted Education Task Force to create or revise a policy document and study research-supported practices in identifying related service options from which to select.

Month 3: Send a working draft of document to the task force for review and edits. Make the revisions required.

Month 4: Send second working draft to building administrators for review and comments. Make the revisions required.

Month 5: Adopt final draft of policy document formally through school board and district leadership.

---

This timeline may change radically depending on the size of the task force, the number of actual changes the policy asks of the district and schools, and the diversity of opinions among stakeholders in this policy development.

## TEMPLATE FOR DISTRICT POLICY ASSESSMENT

No district policy decision is made in a vacuum—as mentioned previously, most district policies elaborate articulated state policies and are most effective when connected to a local comprehensive program design. The following template is designed to help a task

| Program & Service Options | Currently Codified | Needs to Be Codified | Barriers | Supports | Actions |
|---|---|---|---|---|---|
| Management Options | | | | | |
| Curriculum Modification Options | | | | | |
| Instructional Delivery Options | | | | | |

force or planning team consider existing school district policies regarding the program and service options for gifted learners, possible modifications that may need to be made, and the context in which the policies will be accepted and implemented. To help you identify and consider policies under the management, curriculum modification, and instructional delivery options, please refer to the definitions in Table 16.1.

## ADRICE FOR THE SOLE PRACTITIONER

The sole practitioner should identify those instructional management options that the district can reasonably offer and that he/she can oversee for the time allotted to the position. Regrouped classes, for example, which require little initial effort other than professional development for teachers and administrators, and help with resource collection by the practitioner, could be considered when a send-out program taught by the practitioner would be too laborintensive.

## MUST-READ RESOURCES

Gallagher, J. J. (2002). *Society's role in educating gifted students: The role of public policy* (RM02162). Storrs, CT: The National Research Center on the Gifted and Talented, University of Connecticut.

Passow, A. H., & Rudnitski, R. A. (1993). *State policies regarding education of the gifted in legislation and regulation.* Storrs, CT: The National Research Center on the Gifted and Talented, University of Connecticut.

Rogers, K. B. (1991). *The relationship of grouping practices to the education of the gifted and talented learner* (RBDM 9102). Storrs, CT: The National Research Center on the Gifted and Talented, University of Connecticut.

Rogers, K. B. (2002). *Re-forming gifted education: Helping parents and teachers to match the option to the child.* Scottsdale, AZ: Great Potential Press.

VanTassel-Baska, J. (2003). Curriculum policy development for gifted programs: Converting issues in the field to coherent practice. In J. Borland (Ed.), *Rethinking gifted education* (pp. 173–185). Danvers, MA: Teachers College Press.

Zirkel, P. A. (2003). *The law on gifted education* (RM03178). Storrs, CT: The National Research Center on the Gifted and Talented, University of Connecticut.

## REFERENCES

Gallagher, J. J. (2002). *Society's role in educating gifted students: The role of public policy* (RM02162). Storrs, CT: The National Research Center on the Gifted and Talented, University of Connecticut.

Passow, A. H., & Rudnitski, R. A. (1993). *State policies regarding education of the gifted in legislation and regulation.* Storrs, CT: The National Research Center on the Gifted and Talented, University of Connecticut.

Rogers, K. B. (1991). *The relationship of grouping practices to the education of the gifted and talented learner* (RBDM 9102). Storrs, CT: The National Research Center on the Gifted and Talented, University of Connecticut.

Rogers, K. B. (1998). Using current research to make "good" decisions about grouping. *National Association for Secondary School Principles Bulletin, 82*(595), 38–46.

Rogers, K. B. (2002). *Re-forming gifted education: Helping parents and teachers to match the option to the child.* Scottsdale, AZ: Great Potential Press.

Rogers, K. B. (in press). Lessons learned about educating the gifted and talented: A synthesis of the research on educational practice. *Gifted Child Quarterly.*

Zirkel, P. A. (2003). *The law on gifted education* (RM03178). Storrs, CT: The National Research Center on the Gifted and Talented, University of Connecticut.

# 17

# Aligning Gifted Education Services With General Education

*Carol Ann Tomlinson, Kristina J. Doubet,*
*and Marla Read Capper*

The significant problems we face cannot be solved at the same level of thinking we were at when we created them.

—Albert Einstein (1879–1955)

During his tenure as president of the National Association for Gifted Children 1993–1995, James Gallagher established a task force to explore the different ways the field of gifted education might interact effectively with general education. At that time, there were perceived tensions between the field of gifted education and regular education around a number of issues, including grouping practices, inclusion, the nature of the middle school philosophy and content, as well as the age-old tension between excellence and equity. In 1996, the task force published an article, "Interface Between Gifted Education and General Education: Toward Communication, Cooperation, and Collaboration" (Tomlinson, Coleman, Allan, Udall, & Landrum, 1996), that highlighted the benefits of collaboration, strategies for enhancing alliances between gifted education specialists and regular education teachers, and a general call for increased collaboration.

Since the mid-1990s, the context of education has changed. Currently, there is an increasingly diverse population of students in our schools and a pronounced emphasis on the need to close educational achievement gaps, especially between those students who have had all of life's advantages and those who have had less than their fair share. This current context should serve to alert us to Einstein's famous words that are quoted at the beginning of this chapter. Namely, we must augment our strategies for increasing collaboration between regular education and gifted education programs and services. We must redouble our efforts toward collaboration. Not only do gifted education professionals have much to offer in terms of instructional strategies to close the achievement gap, but we also have much to lose if we are not able to work with our colleagues to address another chronic gap: the underrepresentation of culturally diverse and low-income students in gifted education programs (Borland, 2003; National Research Council, 2002).

In this chapter, Carol Ann Tomlinson, Kristina Doubet, and Marla Read Capper take a closer look at collaboration as it might appear at the district level. They provide us with concrete examples to illustrate how collaboration can extend to the mission and planning aspects of schooling, instructional strategies, professional development, and curriculum. Not surprisingly, this section has strong linkages to the following chapters: Developing a Mission Statement on the Educational Needs of Gifted and Talented Students, 2, Designing a Professional Development Plan, 14, Curriculum for Gifted Education Students, 8, as well as Appendix A, on Establishing Gifted Education Advisory Committees.

## DEFINITION

Fostering alignment between gifted education and general education involves integrating—at natural points of intersection—the services of both programs to help meet the goals of each, as well as to increase schoolwide student achievement.

## RATIONALE

By joining forces, general education and gifted education programs will enhance opportunities to

- Help one another reach common or shared goals:

  Rich content, regular expectations for critical and creative thinking, development of meaningful products, establishing expectations for high quality and hard work are goals shared by both sets of educators (Tomlinson et al., 1996, p. 167).

- Learn from each other and improve the effectiveness of the school to better serve all: student populations:

  Both generalists and specialists have particular contributions to make to the success of education, and a symbiotic relationship would enhance the possibilities of both groups of educators—and the children whom they serve (Tomlinson et al., 1996, p. 167).

| *General Education Goals* | *Related Gifted Education Goals* |
|---|---|
| To advocate teaching for understanding, inquiry, and problem solving; to deemphasize strategies geared toward rote and passive learning (Darling-Hammond, 2000; Darling-Hammond, Ancess, & Falk, 1995; Eisner, 2003; National Research Council, 2000; Sizer, 1999) | To require students to use creative, complex, abstract, critical, and higher-order thinking skills (Feldhusen, VanTassel-Baska, & Seely, 1989; Maker & Nielson, 1996; Shore, Cornell, Robinson & Ward, 1991) |
| To promote authentic learning, real-world applications, and performance-driven tasks (Darling-Hammond, 2000; Darling-Hammond et al., 1995; Eisner, 1997; McDonald, 1999) | To provide students with the opportunity to deal with material through problem solving and authentic, real-world tasks (Shore et al., 1991; Gallagher, 2002; Tomlinson et al., 2002) |
| To provide students opportunity to discover their own strengths and passions; to develop curriculum that serves as a point of personal connection (National Research Council, 2000); and, as "a mirror held up to the student," to help the student discover what he or she "knows, understands, cares about, and uses" (Sizer, 1999, p. 164) | To allow students to discover connections among the disciplines, the world around them, and themselves, as well as to promote self-discovery (Shore et al., 1991; Tomlinson et al., 2002) |
| To shift emphasis away from an expansive, factual, standards focus to a "less is more" mentality—for example, the TIMMS Study (Eisner, 1997; Sapon-Shevin, 1996; Schmoker & Marzano, 2003)—and to use conceptual frameworks to organize content (National Research Council, 2000) | To make meaning from standards by organizing content around carefully selected concepts to unite discrete facts and skills into purposeful, connected, authentic learning experiences (Tomlinson et al., 2002) |
| To identify talent and maximize the capacity of each learner through escalating challenge and escalating support (National Research Council, 2000) | To identify talent and maximize the capacity of gifted learners by raising the achievement ceiling to provide appropriate degrees of challenge (Callahan & Tomlinson, 1997; Feldhusen et al., 1989; Maker & Nielson, 1996; Reis, 2003; Renzulli & Reis, 1997; Shore et al., 1991; Tomlinson, 1999, 2001; Tomlinson et al., 2002) |

| *Myth* | *Reality* |
|---|---|
| Gifted students possess unique learning needs that must be met regardless of the resulting effect on the rest of the school community. | "Gifted students are part of the developmental continuum of learners, all of whom have specialized needs, as well as shared needs" (Tomlinson, Coleman, Allan, Udall, & Landrum, 1996, p. 167). This continuum is interdependent; change to one part of the system affects all others. Focusing on needs shared by the gamut of learners will strengthen the entire continuum. |

| Myth | Reality |
|---|---|
| General education's reform goals are in opposition to the mission of gifted education. | General educators recognize the challenges facing our nation's educational system and seek to upgrade its curriculum and instruction according to many of the standards shared by gifted educators: "One hopes that the current American educational leadership, currently paralyzed by their belief in the need for One Best Standard, will have the courage to admit that our conventional ways of 'curriculum building' and the 'assessment' that follows from it are profoundly flawed" (Sizer, 1999, p. 165).<br><br>Both general and gifted educators recognize the value of curriculum and instruction that reveals and cultivates talent in students of diverse cultures (Darling-Hammond, 1997, 2000; Delpit, 1995; Ford, Harris, Tyson, & Trotman, 2002; Oakes, 2003; Passow & Frasier, 1996). |
| Gifted education is an entity unto itself. | "Educators of the gifted are one voice, in what should be a chorus of voices, seeking to help citizens and policymakers alike understand that a school system that does not pursue excellence for all students (even those from whom we have traditionally expected little) as well as equity for all students (even those whom we have seen as "ahead of the game") is doomed to fail all students and the society which supports it" (Tomlinson & Callahan, 1992, p. 185). |

- Gain strength through unity:

     Gifted education is part of a larger system; we must fix the whole system if we expect our part to get better (Tomlinson, 2003).

| General Education Contributions | Gifted Education Contributions |
|---|---|
| Familiarity with mandated curriculum material, resources, and standards (Darling-Hammond, 2000; Richardson & Roosevelt, 2004) | Using standards to achieve relevance and "instructional impact" (VanTassel-Baska & Avery, 2002, p. 3) |
| Expertise in the content areas (Darling-Hammond & Youngs, 2002; Interstate New Teacher Assessment & Support Consortium [INTASC], 1992; Richardson & Roosevelt, 2004) | Expertise in developing and applying instructional strategies to cultivate higher-level cognitive processes (Tomlinson & Callahan, 1992) |
| Experience using inclusion and collaboration models (INTASC, 1992). | Experience in developing instructional strategies that discover and develop talent (Tomlinson & Callahan, 1992) |

# GUIDING PRINCIPLES OR ASSUMPTIONS

- General educators and educators of the gifted share common goals.
- General educators and educators of the gifted can learn from each other.
- General education and gifted education programs gain strength through collaboration.
- Gifted educators, general educators, and specialists should work together as a team to appropriately meet the diverse needs of all students.
- Gifted educators should act as leaders in working with colleagues to meaningfully evaluate the effectiveness of services to learners with the goal of maximizing the capacity of a full range of learners—including those who are academically advanced.

# KEY COMPONENTS OF AN EFFECTIVE ALIGNMENT OF GIFTED EDUCATION AND GENERAL EDUCATION SERVICES

## Mission and Planning

- Gifted educators possess a comprehensive understanding of their school or districtwide mission.
- Gifted educators possess a comprehensive understanding of the strategic improvement plan in place for their school or district and play an active role in contributing to the development of this plan.
- Gifted educators identify components of the plan that overlap with the goals of serving gifted students and that would help to address the needs of all learners. They lend their expertise or leadership to the implementation of these components, as well as to the monitoring of their effectiveness.
- Gifted educators seek to understand the change process in schools and to promote change based on knowledge of what facilitates positive change.

## Collaboration

- Gifted educators seek administrative support and guidance for policies and practices that encourage sustained, consistent collaboration.
- The school or district administration initiates and encourages connections between gifted educators, general educators, and other specialists by providing opportunities for shared meeting and planning time.
- Gifted educators seek the content and curricular expertise of general education teachers and other specialists, including those who are already implementing models of inclusion or collaboration in their school or district.
- Gifted educators share instructional strategies regarding talent recognition, talent development, differentiating instruction, and authentic, performance-driven tasks with general educators.
- Gifted educators, general educators, and other specialists regularly plan together, observe one another's classrooms, and reflect on how they, as a team, can serve the wide range of students who have both overlapping and specialized needs.

- Gifted educators take a lead in establishing these collaborative teams while remaining sensitive to the concerns and challenges of general classroom teachers.

## Professional Development

- The school or district administration regards gifted educators as resources for staff development and training.
- Gifted educators take initiative to develop and provide inservice training and other learning opportunities for teachers in the areas of talent recognition, talent development, differentiation, providing support and challenge, and the creation and delivery of authentic, performance-driven tasks.
- Gifted educators act as a resource and/or support system for general educators and other specialists as they seek to implement these practices in their classrooms.
- Gifted educators continue to research and provide resource materials to assist general educators and other specialists in this process.
- Gifted educators seek opportunities to share staff development responsibilities with other educators and specialists to demonstrate shared goals and flexible use of strategies.

## Curricular and Instructional Integration

- Gifted and general education teachers seek to discover points of intersection between their curricula.
- Gifted and general education teachers use planning time to develop ways to integrate learning experiences around these points of intersection.
- Gifted educators, general educators, and specialists collaborate to develop learning experiences that will address the unique learning needs (mode, interest, readiness, level of support, degree of challenge, etc.) of students represented in all classrooms.
- Gifted educators develop an understanding of how to provide escalating challenge for a range of learners and help others develop an understanding of how to implement curriculum and instruction that provides this escalating challenge.

# AN EXAMPLE IN NEED OF REVISION

Joe Gonzales, principal of Forestville Middle School, returns from his beginning-of-the-year, districtwide administrative meeting regarding the system's performance on the previous spring's standardized proficiency tests. He e-mails his school's Strategic Planning Committee members to schedule a meeting for the following Monday.

At Monday afternoon's meeting, the four subject-area department heads, special education coordinator, and guidance counselor convene to begin drafting their school improvement plan for the year. Mr. Gonzales opens the meeting by sharing last year's test results with his committee. Hearts sink as they listen to the disappointing results—scores dropped in both English and math! The remainder of the meeting completely focuses on how to design the School Improvement Plan to ensure focus on boosting test scores in the jeopardized subject areas.

As Suzanne Rayford, gifted pull-out teacher, makes copies in the teacher work room, she hears the rumblings of concern over the recent news of the school's grim test results. She notes with dismay the announcement of the upcoming faculty meeting regarding the School Improvement Plan's goals to develop strategies aimed at improving the achievement of struggling students. Her emotions are mixed; although she feels relieved to be removed from the pressures associated with testing—all of her students passed—she is frustrated with the amount of attention this subject receives. "What about my students?" she muses, "I need to spend my time delving into ways to challenge my advanced learners—not sitting in a meeting that has nothing whatsoever to do with me!" She decides to bring work to the meeting—at least she can grade papers to make good use of the time.

At the faculty meeting, Mr. Jones, the special education teacher, joins Ms. Rayford at her table. He is bearing his typical paper load of Individualized Education Plan (IEP) documents and sinks into his chair with a frustrated sigh:

> "You know, Suzanne—I have a couple of students who are struggling with English and math, but who know more about history than I do! Sometimes I feel like I should send 'em on over to you! Of course, with all the remediation they need in the basics, there's no time for that."
>
> "I'd be happy to share some of my more challenging history materials with you, if you'd like," Ms. Rayford offers. "Just stop by my room when you get a chance."
>
> "Yeah, I may do that," Mr. Jones responds noncommittally, thinking to himself, "My kids wouldn't be able to read those materials!"

*Rating:*

| Component | 1<br>*No<br>Evidence* | 2<br>*Little<br>Evidence* | 3<br>*Some<br>Evidence* | 4<br>*Considerable<br>Evidence* | 5<br>*Exemplary<br>Powerful* |
|---|---|---|---|---|---|
| Mission & Planning | X | | | | |
| Collaboration | | X | | | |
| Professional Development | X | | | | |
| Curricular & Instructional Integration | X | | | | |

# PROCEDURES FOR ENHANCING OR IMPROVING THE QUALITY OF ALIGNMENT BETWEEN GIFTED EDUCATION SERVICES AND GENERAL EDUCATION

If alignment is rated low in terms of mission and planning,

- Gifted educators should take the initiative to become familiar with the school/districtwide mission and strategic improvement plan.

- Gifted educators and administrators should work together to ensure that gifted-education personnel are included as active participants in the planning process for developing the strategic improvement plan.
- Gifted educators should examine schoolwide goals and identify target areas which overlap with the goals of serving gifted students. They should lend their expertise and leadership to the implementation of these components while seeking to understand the change process in schools and to facilitate positive change.

If alignment is rated low in terms of collaboration,

- Gifted educators should seek administrative support and guidance for policies and practices that encourage sustained, consistent collaboration. Administrators should provide shared meeting or planning time. Gifted educators should take a lead in establishing collaborative teams while remaining sensitive to the concerns and challenges of general classroom teachers.
- Gifted educators should seek the expertise of general educators and other specialists regarding their content and curricular knowledge, as well as their experience with implementing models of inclusion/collaboration in their school/district.
- Gifted educators should work in the classrooms of general education teachers to develop materials, procedures, and processes that enhance challenge and quality of curriculum for all students—including those with high-performance and high-potential profiles. Gifted educators, general educators, and other specialists should regularly plan together, observe one another's classrooms, and reflect on how they, as a team, can serve the wide range of students who have both overlapping and specialized needs.

If alignment is rated low in terms of professional development,

- The school or district administration should use gifted educators as resources for staff development. Gifted educators should respond by developing and providing inservice training and other learning opportunities for teachers in the areas of talent recognition (especially in low economic and/or minority learners), talent development, differentiation of instruction, and the creation and delivery of authentic, performance-driven tasks.
- Gifted educators should avail themselves as resources/support systems for general educators who seek to implement these practices in their classrooms. Gifted educators should continue to research and provide resource materials to assist general educators in this process while seeking opportunities to share staff development responsibilities with other educators and specialists to demonstrate shared goals and flexible use of strategies.

If alignment is rated low in terms of curricular and instructional integration,

- Gifted educators, general educators, and other specialists should examine their respective curricula to discover points of intersection.
- Gifted educators, general educators, and other specialists should use planning time to develop ways to integrate learning experiences around these points of intersection, as well as to develop strategies that will address the unique learning needs (mode,

interest, readiness, level of support, degree of challenge, etc.) of students represented in all classrooms.

- Gifted educators should share methods of providing escalating challenge for a range of learners.

## MAKEOVER EXAMPLE

Joe Gonzales, principal of Forestville Middle School, returns from his beginning-of-the-year, districtwide administrative meeting regarding the system's performance on the previous spring's standardized proficiency tests. He e-mails his school's Strategic Planning Committee members to schedule a meeting for the following Monday and begins setting the meeting's agenda. After a first draft, he realizes that he has focused the meeting exclusively on how to address the drop in test scores. Going back to the top of the page, Mr. Gonzales types in his school's mission statement:

> Forestville Middle School is committed to developing students as individuals, calling on students, staff, and the community to work together to promote academic excellence, as well as to provide each student with the opportunity to cultivate his/her potential.

With this new focus, the principal is able to revise the agenda to allow time for each committee member to discuss his or her perceived areas of concern for the students and staff of Forestville Middle School.

At Monday afternoon's Strategic Planning Committee meeting, the four subject-area department heads, special education coordinator, gifted resource teacher, guidance counselor, and building-level administrators convene to begin drafting their School Improvement Plan for the year. Mr. Gonzales begins the meeting by sharing last year's test results with his committee. Hearts sink as they listen to the disappointing results—scores dropped significantly in both English and math! The committee notes this concern as top priority and collectively brainstorms initial plans for helping students who struggle in these areas. The list is narrowed to produce several action steps for their plan, and the group moves on to discussing the other areas of concern as perceived by committee members.

Suzanne Rayford, gifted resource teacher, listens intently to the concerns aired by her colleagues. When it is her turn to speak, she draws the committee's attention to the school's mission statement typed across the top of the agenda and notes that her concern overlaps with both the school's vision for its students and the school's concerns with testing. She wants to make sure that, not only are students' weaknesses addressed, but also that their strengths are developed, as well. "After all, our mission statement pledges 'to provide each student with the opportunity to cultivate his or her potential,'" she states. "Some of these students who are struggling with skills may possess talent in other areas. For example, I would hate to see a talented art student pulled out of that class to attend a standards-remediation class! I'm also wary of focusing exclusively on drill-and-practice methods of reteaching material. The research coming out of many fields of education suggests that authentic, performance-driven tasks are better motivators for students of all abilities."

Committee members respond to her concern with a mixture of agreement and frustration: "That *sounds* great in theory, but putting it into action isn't logistically possible!" many exclaim. Others argue that struggling students won't go for the types of tasks Suzanne has described. Still other committee members support her, including the science coordinator, who reflects that labs often draw the highest degree of participation from his students. Mr. Gonzales asks to hear more. Suzanne shares some of the research she has discovered on using flexible grouping and authentic assignments to address the various needs and diverse degrees of talent represented in the regular classroom. The principal asks if she would be willing to share this research; Suzanne agrees but suggests working with a smaller cadre of teachers first. This smaller cadre could then apply the ideas in their classrooms, as well as work with others on their teams or in their subject areas to share what they have learned. Mr. Gonzales suggests using the upcoming inservice day as an opportunity for the department heads, grade-level team leaders, special education coordinator, and Ms. Rayford to meet. They agree, realizing that they will need a concentrated period of time to examine curriculum and standards documents, discover areas in which the standards can be addressed through the performance-driven tasks, and find ways to integrate these practices into the general subject-area curricula. They acknowledge that this is merely the first step in an involved process, and they add Talent Development Cadres as an action step in their strategic plan.

In the teacher work room, Ms. Rayford hears the rumblings of concern over the recent news of the school's test results. She makes a mental note to make sure to acknowledge these concerns in her portion of the faculty meeting presentation. Although this year all of her students passed, she realizes she is not immune to these issues—students with gifts in certain areas often possess concomitant needs in others. She knows she must introduce the school's Talent Cadre project with a team mentality, knowing that improvement to the entire structure will ultimately benefit each part of the system—including highly able learners. She is invigorated by the prospect of her students' needs being more appropriately addressed in all of their classes—not just in special classes for gifted learners. She is also excited about the prospect of high-challenge curriculum and instruction becoming a catalyst for recognizing and developing abilities in a much broader range of students.

At the faculty meeting, Mr. Jones, a special education teacher, joins Ms. Rayford at her table. He is bearing his typical paper load of IEP documents, and sinks into his chair with a frustrated sigh:

> "You know, Suzanne—I have a couple of students who are struggling with English and math, but who know more about history than I do! Sometimes I feel like I should send 'em on over to you! Of course, with all the remediation they need in the basics, there's no time for that."

> "I can't wait for you to hear about the Talent Cadre project the Strategic Planning Committee is undertaking!" she replies. "I think that the students you've described will really benefit from it. In the meantime, I'd be happy to share some of my more challenging history materials with you, if you'd like," Ms. Rayford offers. "I think we can find ways to use those materials to build interest as well as to support student growth in areas of concern for them."

"Maybe I could use those materials with a small group during resource time—or even in my general history class inclusion time—especially if you could help me adapt them to my students' unique learning needs."

"Certainly," replies Ms. Rayford, adding, "You know, I'd like to learn more about how the inclusion program works," Mr. Jones. I think it would really help us implement our cadre. If I could watch you and your students at work, maybe I would have a clearer sense of how to ensure we attend to standards-based goals while we provide challenge for our kids."

Mr. Jones and Ms. Rayford agree to touch base during lunch the following day, just as Mr. Gonzales prepares to begin the meeting.

# A STRATEGIC PLAN TO ESTABLISH OR IMPROVE THE ALIGNMENT BETWEEN GENERAL AND GIFTED EDUCATION

| | |
|---|---|
| *Objective:* | To establish or improve the alignment between general education and gifted education. |
| *Evidence:* | Participation of gifted educators in school- or districtwide strategic planning committee and/or improvement plan, both of which address needs of *all* students; Collaboration between gifted educators and other faculty, administrators, and specialists, all working as a team to serve the wide range of students who demonstrate both overlapping and specialized needs. |
| *Tasks:* | Place gifted educators in collaborative or leadership roles within the school or district. |
| *Timeline:* | Ongoing |

# TEMPLATE FOR ALIGNING GIFTED AND GENERAL EDUCATION

### Trait #1: Mission and Planning

| *Focusing Question* | *Our Thinking* |
|---|---|
| Do gifted educators possess a comprehensive understanding of their school- or districtwide mission? | |
| Do gifted educators possess a comprehensive understanding of the Strategic Improvement Plan in place for the school or district and do they play an active role in the development of this plan? | |

| Focusing Question | Our Thinking |
|---|---|
| Do gifted educators identify components of the plan that overlap with the goals of serving gifted students and that would help to address the needs of all learners? Do they lend their expertise and leadership to the implementation of these components and to the monitoring of their effectiveness? | |
| Do gifted educators seek to understand the change process in schools and to promote change based on knowledge of what facilitates positive change? | |

## Trait #2: Collaboration

| Focusing Question | Our Thinking |
|---|---|
| Do gifted educators seek administrative support and guidance for policies and practices that encourage sustained, consistent collaboration? | |
| Does the school or district administration initiate and encourage connections between gifted educators, general educators, and specialists by providing opportunities for shared meeting and planning time? | |
| Do gifted educators seek the content and curricular expertise of general education teachers and other specialists, including those who are already implementing models of inclusion or collaboration in their school or district? | |
| Do gifted educators share instructional strategies regarding talent recognition, talent development, and differentiating instruction, as well as models of authentic, performance-driven tasks, with general educators? | |
| Do gifted educators, general educators, and other specialists regularly and deliberately plan together, observe one another's classrooms, and reflect on how they, as a team, can serve the wide range of students who have both overlapping and specialized needs? | |
| Do gifted educators take a lead in establishing these collaborative teams? In doing so, are they sensitive to the concerns and challenges of general classroom teachers? | |

### Trait #3: Professional Development

| Focusing Question | Our Thinking |
|---|---|
| Does the school/district administration use gifted educators as resources for staff development and training? | |
| Does the school or district administration initiate and encourage connections between gifted educators, general educators, and other specialists? | |
| Do gifted educators take initiative to develop and provide inservice training and other learning opportunities for teachers in the areas of talent recognition, talent development, differentiation of instruction, provision of support and challenge, and the creation and delivery of authentic, performance-driven tasks? | |
| Do gifted educators act as resources and/or a support system for general educators and other specialists as they seek to implement these practices in their classrooms? | |
| Do gifted educators continue to research and provide resource materials to assist general educators in this process? | |
| Do gifted educators seek opportunities to share staff development responsibilities with other educators and specialists to demonstrate shared goals and flexible use of strategies? | |

### Trait #4: Curricular and Instructional Integration

| Focusing Question | Our Thinking |
|---|---|
| Do gifted and general education teachers seek to discover points of intersection between their curricula? | |
| Do gifted and general education teachers use planning time to develop ways to integrate learning experiences around these points of intersection? | |
| Do gifted and general education teachers collaborate to develop learning experiences that will address the unique learning needs (mode, interest, readiness, level of support, degree of challenge, etc.) of students represented in all classrooms? | |
| Do gifted educators develop an understanding of how to provide escalating challenge for a range of learners and help others develop an understanding of how to implement curriculum and instruction that provides this escalating challenge? | |

# ADVICE FOR THE SOLE PRACTITIONER

Many gifted education teachers operate single handedly in school districts around the country. The most important task that this sole practitioner should do to ensure forward progress with respect to aligning gifted and regular education is to discover (1) the strengths of the gifted educators in his/her charge and (2) the school's or system's expressed areas of concern (e.g., from school improvement plan or school report card). Armed with an awareness of this information, the sole practitioner will be better equipped to recognize opportunities for collaboration when they naturally arise.

# MUST-READ RESOURCES

Borland, J. (Ed.). (2003). *Rethinking gifted education.* New York: Teachers College Press.

Council for Exceptional Children (1995). *Toward a common agenda: Linking gifted education and school reform.* Reston, VA: Author.

Tomlinson, C. A., Coleman, M. R., Allan, S., Udall, A., & Landrum, M. (1996). Interface between gifted education and general education: Toward communication, cooperation, and collaboration. *Gifted Child Quarterly, 40,* 165–171.

# REFERENCES

Borland, J. (Ed.). (2003). *Rethinking gifted education.* New York: Teachers College Press.

Callahan, C. M., & Tomlinson, C. A. (1997). *The gifted and talented learner: Myths and realities. ASCD curriculum handbook.* Alexandria, VA: Association for Supervision and Curriculum Development.

Darling-Hammond, L. (1997). School reform at the crossroads: Confronting the central issues of teaching. *Educational Policy, 11,* 151–166.

Darling-Hammond, L. (2000). New standards and old inequalities: School reform and the education of African American students. *Journal for Negro Education, 69,* 263–287.

Darling-Hammond, L., Ancess, J., & Falk, B. (1995). *Authentic assessment in action.* NY: Teachers College Press.

Darling-Hammond, L., & Youngs, P. (2002). Defining "highly qualified teachers": What does the "scientifically-based research" actually tell us? *Educational Researcher, 31(9)* 13–25.

Delpit, L. (1995). *Other people's children: Cultural conflict in the classroom.* New York: The New Press.

Eisner, E. W. (1997) Who decides what schools teach? In D. J. Flinders & S. J. Thorton (Eds.), *The curriculum studies reader.* (pp. 337–341). NY: Routledge.

Eisner, E. W. (2003). What does it mean to say that a school is doing well? In A. C. Ornstein, L. S. Behar-Hornstein, & F. P. Edward (Eds.), *Contemporary issues in curriculum* (3rd ed.). (pp. 239–247). Boston: Allyn & Bacon.

Feldhusen, J., VanTassel-Baska, J., & Seeley, K. (1989). *Excellence in educating the gifted.* Denver: Love.

Ford, D. Y., Harris, J. J. III, Tyson, C. A., & Trotman, M. F. (2002). Beyond deficit thinking: Providing access for gifted African American students [electronic version]. *Roeper Review, 24,* 52–58.

Gallagher, J. J. (2002). Gifted education in the 21st century. *Gifted Education International, 16,* 100–110.

Interstate New Teacher Assessment & Support Consortium. (1992). *Model standards for beginning teacher licensing, assessment, and development: A resource for state dialogue.* Washington, DC: Council of Chief State School Officers.

Maker, J. C., & Nielson, A. B. (1996). *Curriculum development and teaching strategies for gifted learners.* Austin, TX: Pro-Ed.

McDonald, J. P. (1999). Redesigning curriculum: New conceptions and tools. *Peabody Journal of Education, 74,* 12–28.

National Research Council. (2000). *How people learn: Brain, mind, experience, and school* (expanded edition). Washington, DC: National Academy Press.

National Research Council. (2002). *Minority students in special and gifted education.* Washington, DC: National Academy Press.

Oakes, J. S. (2003). Limiting students school success and life chances: The impact of tracking. In A. C. Ornstein, L. S. Behar-Hornstein, & F. P. Edward (Eds.), *Contemporary issues in curriculum* (3rd ed.), (pp. 394–400). Boston: Allyn & Bacon.

Passow, H. A., & Frasier, M. M. (1996). Toward improving identification of talent potential among minority and disadvantaged students [electronic version]. *Roeper Review, 18,* 198–202.

Reis, S. M. (2003). Reconsidering regular curriculum for high-achieving students, gifted under-achievers, and the relationship between gifted and regular education. In J. Borland (Ed.), *Rethinking gifted education.* (pp. 186–200). New York: Teachers College Press.

Renzulli, J. S., & Reis, S. M. (1997). The schoolwide enrichment model: New directions for developing high-end learning. In N. Colangelo & G. A. Davis (Eds.), *Handbook of gifted education* (2nd ed.), (pp. 136–154). Boston: Allyn & Bacon.

Richardson, V., & Roosevelt, D. (2004). The preparation of teachers and the improvement of teacher education. In M. A. Smylie & D. Miretzky (Eds.), *Developing the teacher workforce* (103:1–40). Chicago: NSSE Yearbook.

Sapon-Shevin, M. (1996). Beyond gifted education: Building a shared agenda for school reform. *Journal for the Education of the Gifted, 19,* 194–214.

Schmoker, M., & Marzano, R. (2003). Realizing the promise of standards-based education. In A. C. Ornstein, L. S. Behar-Hornstein, & F. P. Edward (Eds.), *Contemporary issues in curriculum* (3rd ed.) (pp. 394–400). Boston: Allyn & Bacon.

Shore, B. M., Cornell, D. G., Robinson, A., & Ward, V. G. (1991). *Recommended practices in gifted education: A critical analysis.* NY: Teachers College Press.

Sizer, T. R. (1999). That elusive curriculum. *Peabody Journal of Education, 74,* 161–165.

Tomlinson, C. A. (1999). *The differentiated classroom: Responding to the needs of all learners.* Alexandria, VA: Association for Supervision and Curriculum Development.

Tomlinson, C. A. (2001). *How to differentiate instruction in mixed-ability classrooms.* Alexandria, VA: Association for Supervision and Curriculum Development.

Tomlinson, C. A. (2003, November). *Past presidents' panel.* Symposium conducted at the National Association for Gifted Children 50th Annual Convention, Indianapolis, IN.

Tomlinson, C. A., & Callahan, C. M. (1992). Contributions of gifted education to general education in a time of change. *Gifted Child Quarterly, 36,* 183–189.

Tomlinson, C. A., Coleman, M. R., Allan, S., Udall, A., & Landrum, M. (1996). Interface between gifted education and general education: Toward communication, cooperation, and collaboration. *Gifted Child Quarterly, 40,* 165–171.

Tomlinson, C. A., Kaplan, S. N., Renzulli, J. S., Purcell, J., Leppien, J., & Burns, D. (2002). *The parallel curriculum: A design to develop high potential and challenge high-ability learners.* Thousand Oaks, CA: Corwin.

VanTassel-Baska, J., & Avery, L. D. (2002). *The application of instructional reform in classrooms: Benchmarking effective teacher behavior.* Washington, DC: ERIC Digest #ED467275.

# 18

# Planning for Advocacy

*Julia Link Roberts*

Never doubt that a small group of thoughtful committed people can change the world: indeed it is the only thing that ever has.

—Margaret Mead

The Marland Report, issued in 1972, was the first federal document that considered the educational needs of gifted education students, and its publication was a defining moment for the field in many respects. The report profiled the characteristics of gifted and talented children, characteristics of high-quality programs, offered case studies of programs, and outlined a series of recommendations to strengthen services to gifted and talented children (Marland, 1972).

A considerable part of the report was based on the testimony of individuals who attended public hearings. These public hearings were held in ten different regions of the country and were designed to solicit responses from constituents about the needs of high-achieving students. Half of the respondents in the regional hearings suggested that the general public required more information about the needs of gifted and talented students. "The present burden of education for the gifted and talented falls on parents who weep alone for their children" (Marland, 1972, p. 35).

We have come a long way since the 1970s. Today, many individuals who advocate for the needs of gifted education children at the local, state, and national levels. In this chapter, Julia Link Roberts walks us through the attributes of high-powered advocacy. The real-world examples she explains here—related to advocacy at the local and state levels—provide readers with a very clear idea of the nature and scope of efforts that are essential to lasting services to gifted education students. This chapter on advocacy contains strong linkages to Developing a Mission Statement on the Educational Needs of Gifted and Talented Students, 2; State Policies in Gifted Education, 19; and Managing a Communication Initiative in Gifted Education, 12. It is also linked to Appendix A, on Establishing Gifted Education Advisory Committees.

# DEFINITION

Advocacy is "the act of arguing in favor of something—an idea, cause, or policy" (National Association for Gifted Children, 2000, p. v). In this chapter, the discussion of advocacy will focus on getting decision makers at the school, school district, state, and national levels to support strategies, services, and policies to initiate, implement, and support gifted education. Advocacy may be a onetime event; however, advocacy is most effective when it is an ongoing process. Both individuals and groups may find this discussion of advocacy useful.

# RATIONALE

Why advocate? Informed and well-organized advocates can raise the level of awareness about the needs of children who are gifted and talented at the school, school district, state, and national levels. They can show that there is a positive impact on schools and communities when all children, including children who are gifted and talented, are provided opportunities to make continuous progress and to reach their potential. Advocates can influence the change of practices, policies, and laws that impact the education of gifted children. Without individuals and groups advocating on behalf of children who are gifted and talented, it is unlikely that decisions will be made to advance educational opportunities for gifted and talented young people.

An example of effective advocacy took place in a medium-size city without gifted education programs or services. A parent of a young gifted child knew that, as a newcomer in town, she would need to establish credibility before asking for accommodations for her daughter and other children who are gifted and talented. She spent the first year focused on schoolwide issues, including providing leadership for building a new playground. She also joined a small group of advocates for gifted education, and together they began to educate school and district administrators of the need to provide appropriate programming for gifted children. The next year the advocacy continued with a focus on educating members of the district school board. The goal was to have a gifted resource teacher at each school. The advocates were successful in reaching their goal. One person could not have done it alone. People without credibility or correct information could not have reached this goal. Well-informed advocates were able to achieve their goal because they had an agreed-upon message (their goal) and worked together to educate the decision makers who could make the goal a reality.

Another example of effective advocacy occurred at the national level in the late 1980s. The vote was going to be close to get legislation through the Appropriations and Revenue Committee in the U.S. House of Representatives. The legislative chair of the National Association for Gifted Children called a long-term supporter of gifted children whom she knew was a friend of the chair of the committee, a gentleman whose vote would likely make the difference on this issue. In turn, the friend called the committee chair to talk about the issue. The result was a vote of support for the legislation by the congressman. The rest is history. The Jacob K. Javits Gifted and Talented Students Education Act was passed. Knowing who in the organization has a long-term relationship with members of key committees is critical information. Having individuals follow up with decision makers is essential. Working together, advocates can make a difference for gifted children.

# GUIDING PRINCIPLES

Guiding principles need to be the subject of discussion among the leadership of the advocacy group. As the name implies, the principles will enhance the potential for successful advocacy if they are "front and center" in planning as well as in the implementation of the advocacy plan.

- A clear, focused message that is known and shared by advocates must be the centerpiece of an effective advocacy campaign.
- A well-developed plan is required to provide the blueprint for an effective advocacy campaign.
- Effective advocates should be well informed on gifted and general education issues and know where to locate answers they don't have.
- Advocacy is more likely to be successful when personal relationships are established with decision makers and communication is ongoing.
- Personalized communications, including hand-written letters, are more effective and preferred to mass, computer-generated letters or e-mail.
- The larger the number of advocates, the more likely the decision makers will respond positively to the advocates' message.
- A plan for speedy communication with advocates (for example, a Listserv) is an important component of effective advocacy, so there is a way to get quick action if needed.
- Advocates must understand that perseverance is a key to effective advocacy and that gifted children need individuals who will be lifetime spokespersons on behalf of gifted children.

# TRAITS OF A HIGH-QUALITY ADVOCACY PLAN

A high-quality plan for advocacy is characterized by clarity, inclusiveness, information, and specificity.

**Clarity:** The advocacy plan has a clear message.

- Does your group have parents or other advocates with public relations experience who could help craft the message?
- Does the message relate directly to the goal of the advocacy plan?
- Is the message carefully crafted to capture the interest of the audience?
- Is the message clear for a general audience as well as the targeted audience?
- Have you reviewed Chapter 12, on Managing a Communication Initiative in Gifted Education, in this book?

**Inclusiveness:** The advocacy plan involves interested parties.

- Which individuals and groups have similar goals?
- What groups share an interest in excellence and would join the advocacy effort?

Consider the following possibilities:

- Parents (parents of current students and of those who have graduated)
- Students (current and former students)
- Educators (active and retired)

- Representatives of business and industry
- The Chamber of Commerce
- University and college faculty
- Professional and education organizations at the local, state, and national levels
- Family members or close personal/professional friends of policymakers or other individuals of influence who can be very effective advocates
- Other potentially interested individuals or parties who share a belief in excellence and the development of potential talent

**Support Information:** The advocacy plan includes support information.

- What critical information do key individuals and groups need to know to provide support?
- What is the impact of this advocacy plan on children who are gifted and talented?
- What is the impact of the advocacy plan on other children?
- What policies at the school, district, state, and federal levels support (or negate) the point of advocacy?
- What research is available that will strengthen your message?

**Specificity:** The advocacy plan provides specifics for implementation.

- Who will carry out the plan? When? With whom?
- Who are the key individuals who will make the decisions or who will influence the persons who will make the decisions?
- Who will communicate with the key decision makers and with individuals who will influence decision makers?
- Who will coordinate the plan, and how will advocates report back? (This person or small group of individuals will be able to provide feedback based on responses from key decision makers. This coordinating individual or group will allow the advocacy plan to be responsive rather than fixed.)
- How will we fund our efforts? What resources will we need/use?
- If the decision makers have constituencies, who are the constituents (specific names) and who will communicate with them? Elected officials prefer to hear from those who vote in their districts.
- If the advocacy plan seeks action by a policymaking body (school board, state legislature, etc.), who are the leaders in the body (Speaker of the House, President of the Senate, Board President, etc.)? Who are the leaders of key committees (Education, Appropriations and Revenue, Curriculum and Instruction, etc.)? These people will be especially important in the process.
- Who will evaluate the implementation of the plan? When and how will it be evaluated? What can be learned to be increasingly effective with the next advocacy plan?

# PLANNING FOR AN ADVOCACY INITIATIVE

To ensure effectiveness, advocacy must be based on a plan. Individuals and/or organizations that are launching the advocacy plan must agree on its goal. Crafting the message is a key step in developing the advocacy plan because it is the cornerstone of the initiative. Soliciting feedback from others will help determine if the message will be clearly communicated to the individual(s) who will make the decision(s) concerning whether the advocacy initiative moves forward or is stopped. The individual(s) who have the authority to make the desired decisions must be identified so communication can be targeted to them and to individuals who influence them. Then the plan must specify who will communicate with each decision maker, how, what (the message), and when. The timeline may be established by the group or dictated by scheduled meetings of the decision-making body (legislature, school board, or school council). Review Table 18.1 for key questions that will help readers develop their own effective advocacy plan.

**Table 18.1**   Planning for an Advocacy Initiative

| | |
|---|---|
| **What is the goal?** | |
| **Who is the target audience?** | |
| **What is the specific message?** | |
| **When will the decision be made?** | |
| **Who will make the decision?** | |
| **Who are key individuals in and out of your organization to influence decision makers?** | |

## EXAMPLES OF ADVOCACY IN NEED OF PLANS

### Example 1

Two mothers are very interested in having teachers at the neighborhood middle school provide services for their children who are advanced in mathematics. These parents approach their children's teachers with concerns that the children were bored in class. One teacher was sympathetic and started providing different, more challenging work; but the other teacher reacted as though he were offended, saying that the child did not do well with the work that she was originally given.

*Comments:* This first example illustrates how people frequently act alone without the benefit of others and without a plan that contains a clear message. In the revised example that follows, not only did the mothers align themselves with others seeking the same services for their children, but they also collaboratively researched and crafted a message. Subsequently, they requested a forum with a targeted group of policymakers to share their message.

### Example 2

A half-dozen boys and girls at a summer camp for academically talented high school students are comparing opportunities for Advanced Placement classes that are offered at their high schools. One student has several AP classes that are offered regularly. Two young people have no Advanced Placement (AP) classes in their schools. Others have AP classes in their school's list of courses; however, they are seldom taught due to low enrollment. After talking, the students realize that opportunities for taking college-level classes are not equal for students in the state.

*Comments:* In this second example, the students did not realize the lack of equity in their respective school offerings. As a result, they lacked the wherewithal to act on their own behalf. In the revised example below, students organized and developed a clear message. They developed a Listserv to make their communication efficient. Finally, they capitalized on personal connections to enhance the likelihood that their state-level advocacy plan would succeed.

## MAKEOVER EXAMPLES

### Example 1

The goal of the two parents is to have their children receive instruction in mathematics that allows them to make continuous progress. The problem with only approaching each teacher individually as a need arises is that the situation may be repeated each year with different teachers. The two mothers identified other parents and educators at the school who shared their concerns for making math more challenging for students who demonstrate mastery on preassessments. The mothers were able to find several people who were very interested, including a group of professional engineers.

The newly organized group met and articulated the message in a recommendation: "Every learner who is advanced in math will become a mathematician, mastering challenging content to make continuous progress." Then the group developed a plan for presenting their recommendation. They gathered research, policies, and reports that supported their recommendation. They also included position statements from professional groups of middle school educators and an organization of mathematics educators that addressed the need to provide rigorous curriculum for middle school students, research on using preassessment to document mastery of math content and skills, and the *Road Map for National Security: Imperative for Change* (U.S. Commission on National Security/21st Century, 2001).

The group scheduled a time to present their recommendation to the school council. They discussed who would make the recommendation. They arranged for a large group of parents and educators to attend the meeting to show support. When members of the school council had questions, the spokesperson(s) provided additional information. The result was a schoolwide emphasis on continuous progress in mathematics.

## Example 2

The students at the summer camp asked the director if they could have an evening meeting of all campers who were interested in creating more AP opportunities for high school students in the state. They held a meeting and found that half of the campers came. They represented 35 school districts in the state. They gathered names and e-mail addresses to continue to communicate after the camp ended.

After returning home, several of the students set up meetings with their state representatives and senators. One of the students was from the governor's hometown, and she arranged a time to visit with the governor on the unevenness of the opportunity to take AP or other college-level classes across the state. The joint education committee of the State House of Representatives and Senate initiated a study of the situation. Three of the campers who had AP classes were asked to come to a joint House and Senate Education Committee meeting to talk about the advantages they had or didn't have with choices of AP classes in their high schools.

The e-mail addresses were essential in making contacts with the campers so they would have the needed information as the issue moved through the legislative process. The campers were encouraged to make personal contacts with decision makers and to talk with family members, their educators, and friends in the community to get others who shared their concern to make personal contacts with the legislators as well. Active involvement led to legislation requiring each high school to have a minimum of four AP classes, one in each of the core content areas.

## SOURCES OF MESSAGES AND INFORMATION

Where do you get the ideas for crafting the message and providing information to convince decision makers to support your advocacy initiative?

- Mission and vision statements of your local school, schools in the district, and the district.
- Articles in the current press (e.g., articles in the *Wall Street Journal* on the effect of federal legislation on gifted education).
- Results of research studies that may be found on Web sites, in journal articles, and in published studies. Two Web site's with information are the National Research Center for the Gifted and Talented (www.gifted.uconn.edu/nrcgt.html and NAGC www.nagc.org).
- Policies on gifted education that a local school board or the state has adopted. Policies are often printed in gifted education handbooks and are available on Web sites.

- Position statements from state and national educational and professional organizations (e.g., the National Middle School Association and the National Association for Gifted Children released a joint policy statement on gifted children in the middle school in 2004).
- State and national reports as well as reports released by foundations that discuss issues that impact the education of children who are gifted and talented. Examples include:

*A Nation Deceived: How Schools Hold Back America's Brightest Students*, The Templeton National Report on Acceleration, 2004, http://nationdeceived.org

*Prisoners of Time*, The Report of the National Commission on Time and Learning, 1994; www.ed.gov/pubs/PrisonersOfTime/PoTSchool/index.html

*Raising Our Sights*, The Report of the Commission on the Senior Year, 2001, www.c-b-e.org/PDF/Ncseniorrpt2001.pdf

*Roadmap for National Security: Imperative for Change*, U.S. Commission on National Security/21st Century, 2001, www.nssg.gov/PhaseIIIFR.pdf

Local, state, and national associations that advocate for gifted children are natural sources of information (e.g., visit the Web site of the National Association for Gifted Children at www.nagc.org).

Economic statistics for your state (e.g., visit the Web site www.neweconomy.index.org to see how your state ranks in the numbers of scientists and engineers and other indicators of potential success in the 21st-century economy).

## ADDITIONAL POINTS FOR BUILDING EFFECTIVE ADVOCACY NETWORKS

- Assumptions are dangerous. Mythology in gifted education is believed by educators, parents, and the public, so advocates for gifted children need to be prepared to educate.
- Effective advocates plan to be "in the room" when decisions are made.
- A central person or organization coordinates the advocacy initiatives so people will know whom to contact with current information.
- Personalized communications are the most effective. Spoken communication is important and needs to be followed up with the same message in writing.
- Ongoing communication is very important. Being known as an advocate for excellence in education and appropriate opportunities for all children, including children who are gifted and talented, can add credibility to advocacy initiatives.
- Providing accurate information is critical to establishing and maintaining credibility. If the advocate doesn't know the answer, then he or she should find the information and get back with the answer.
- Be recognized. Wear name badges or identification tags so that others become familiar with you and your organization.

# ADVICE FOR THE SOLE PRACTITIONER

Advice Advocacy cannot be conducted successfully by a single gifted education specialist. At a minimum, advocacy requires a small number of people to plan effectively and deliver messages to key stakeholders.

A few preliminary steps can be initiated by the sole practitioner, however, to jump-start advocacy in his or her respective district. In all likelihood, the single practitioner will form an advisory group. Although the purpose of the advisory group is to assist the gifted practitioner with all aspects of programming and service delivery, the environment of the group meetings will afford the practitioner an opportunity to pinpoint key individuals who might be interested and available to forward an advocacy initiative. A few conversations with prospective individuals will start the ball rolling.

Another helpful step that the single practitioner can take is to keep an ongoing list of local parents and significant adults who have an interest in gifted education. This list can be provided to those who step forward to help with advocacy. With a small set of names in hand, the advocacy group will grow the list and develop a network of people that can be connected through the Internet. E-mail proves invaluable during advocacy campaigns when it is crucial to get the word out about developing issues and events.

Another first step for the sole practitioner is to find out whether there is anyone at the state department of education charged with overseeing programs for the gifted and talented. Most states have at least part-time personnel charged with overseeing gifted education programs. If such personnel are available at the state department of education, they may be able to put the sole practitioner in touch with other advocate groups in the state, as well as put him or her on an electronic distribution list that provides updates on important issues related to gifted education and advocacy initiatives.

Once you've answered the questions, you are ready to assign specify tasks—who will do what and who will communicate with whom—and to establish a series of individual deadlines to implement your advocacy initiative.

---

### Collaboration Counts

  1 Parent  = A Fruit Cake
  2 Parents = Fruit Cake and Friend
  3 Parents = Troublemakers
  5 Parents = Let's Have a Meeting
 10 Parents = We'd Better Listen
 25 Parents = Our Dear Friends
 50 Parents = A Powerful Organization

---

Parent Leadership Associates

A Prichard Committee/KSA Communications collaboration

The Prichard Committee for Academic Excellence

## MUST-READ RESOURCES

California Association for the Gifted. (1998). *Advocacy in action: An advocacy handbook for gifted and talented education.* Whittier, CA: Author.

National Association for Gifted Children. (2000). *Advancing gifted and talented education in Congress.* Washington, DC: Author.

National Association for Gifted Children. (2003). Special issue on advocacy. *Gifted Child Quarterly, 47*(1).

National Association for Gifted Children. (March 2003). Special issue on advocacy. *Parenting for High Potential.*

## REFERENCES

Marland, S. P., Jr. (1972). *Education of the gifted and talented: Vol. 1, Report to the Congress of the United States by the U.S. Commissioner of Education* (Publication #72-502 O). Washington, DC: U.S. Government Printing Office.

National Association for Gifted Children. (2000). *Advancing gifted and talented education in Congress.* Washington, DC: Author.

U.S. Commission on National Security/21st Century. (2001). *Road Map for National Security: Imperative for Change.* Retrieved March 7, 2005, from the Air War College Web site: http://www.au.af.mil/au/awc/awcgate/nssg/

# 19

# State Policies in Gifted Education

*Joyce VanTassel-Baska*

Learning without thought is labor lost; thought without learning is perilous.

—Confucius

The field of gifted education has a long and interesting history since its inception in the mid-1800s. In addition to interesting twists and turns that run parallel with innovations in the fields of educational psychology and cognition, it also offers much to those who enjoy making connections between historical turning points (e.g., Sputnik) and the shifting American philosophies related to equity and excellence. At a deeper level, the history of gifted education offers very important and critical lessons to those interested in the future of the field.

One of the most critical lessons that the history of the field yields is that interest and support for gifted education programs and services fluctuates with the economic cycle. During times when states' economic indicators are depressed, provisions for the gifted ebb. Conversely, large investments in gifted education usually ride in on waves of economic prosperity and technological and ideological change.

In this groundbreaking chapter, Joyce VanTassel-Baska puts forward new notions about the way to reduce the ebb and flow of interest in providing programs and services for gifted education students at both the local and state level. Her recommendations for strengthening and aligning state policies to address cohesively the learning needs of highly able young people provide the latest thinking in the ever-changing field of gifted education. The idea driving this new work is that improved state-level policies will inform local district policies, which, in turn, will build a strong foundation for guiding and maintaining gifted program implementation. These ideas can provide insight to a wide range of stakeholders as they advocate for stronger state policies: members of state departments of education, professional organizations, advocacy groups, and parent and community members.

This chapter about policy revision is at the cutting edge of our field and is linked closely to other chapters in this guidebook that are connected to policymaking: Developing a Definition of Giftedness, 3; Constructing Identification Procedures, 5; Curriculum for Gifted Education students, 8; Connecting Program Design and District Policies, 16; Using Scientifically Based Research to Make Decisions About Gifted Education Programs, Services, and Resources, 20; and Planning for Advocacy, 18. Moreover, VanTassel-Baska's chapter is an introduction to a new action plan for strengthening gifted education—a movement that will surely expand and develop over time.

# DEFINITION

Educational policy is an adopted course of action by a governing board, motivated by the existence of an educational problem or issue. The substance of policy rests in a set of rules and standards by which educational agencies allocate resources to address the identified need (Gallagher, 2002, 2004). At the state level, gifted education policy is tied to the rules and regulations adopted by state legislatures that govern the administration of programs and control how funding is allocated (Zirkel, 2003). Aspects of program administration are also often captured in state publications on best practice guidelines in gifted education, but they do not carry the force of law. Ideally, policy in gifted education that is binding on local districts would address the areas of identification, program services, curriculum, instruction, and assessment of learning, program design and management, teacher preparation, and program evaluation (Gallagher, 2002; Landrum & Shaklee, 1998; Russo, Harris, & Ford, 1996; VanTassel-Baska, 2003).

State policy is a critical area that has not received the attention it deserves from advocates for gifted education services. Changing policy requires a long-term commitment to impact the educational opportunities for gifted education students. Yet it is a worthy endeavor because it will positively change the nature and quality of services for gifted students. The intent of this chapter is to create a more widely held vision for how we can garner increasing support for gifted students within state structures through the deliberate construction of relevant policies for program development.

# RATIONALE

The importance of coherent and comprehensive state policy in gifted education cannot be overstated. The history of the field suggests that the incentive for local program development is inextricably tied to state structures and related funding mechanisms for programs and services. Since the early 1960s, local districts have created programs based on state regulations and funding formulas (Baker & McIntire, 2003; Gallagher, 2002). Although the intent was always for local districts to increase and supplement state funding, we have reason to believe this situation never materialized in the majority of school districts across the country. Therefore, the structure that holds gifted programs together is nested in the policies that individual states have enacted. The direction and continuity of the field at the grassroots level, then, are heavily influenced by the state one resides in and the strength of the policy initiatives in that state.

Moreover, there are no federal laws or mandates governing gifted education programs and services, only guidelines published sporadically. In the 20th century, only two federal reports were issued about the needs of gifted and talented students. The first was the Marland Report (Marland, 1972). The second, National Excellence (U.S. Department of Education, 1993), was issued a full 20 years later. Federal attention to gifted education services is intermittent, at best. Consequently, state policy is the cornerstone of gifted programming in the United States. Therefore, an effort to evaluate current policies and determine how they can be strengthened to support the learning needs of gifted students is central to improving the field.

## GUIDING PRINCIPLES OR ASSUMPTIONS

The following general principles apply to all educational policies:

- Educational policy defines what educational institutions choose to do or not do about a perceived need.
- Educational policy controls how resources are allocated and used in a given program area.
- Educational policy defines the mechanisms and system by which opportunities for targeted students (e.g., gifted) will be offered.
- Educational policies should be comprehensive enough to ensure adequate impetus for program development and service delivery in an area.

The following specific principles apply to policy issues in gifted education:

- All states have legitimized gifted education through policies, rules, and/or guidelines regarding the education of gifted and talented students. (National Association for Gifted Children & Council of State Directors, 2003).
- The policies, rules, and/or guidelines differ from state to state in clarity, degree of detail or specificity, comprehensiveness of program elements addressed in regulations, and the types of rules and requirements (Gallagher, 2002, 2004; Passow & Rudnitski, 1993; Zirkel, 2003).
- States vary in the degree to which local education agencies may develop their own standards, policies, and procedures.
- Advocates for improved policies in gifted education must learn from other state policies in gifted education by investigating and borrowing ideas, language, and types of provisions.

## COMPONENTS OF A HIGH-QUALITY STATE POLICY

All states need to have comprehensive policies for educating gifted and talented students in the following areas: identification, program and service provisions, personnel preparation, and program management. Furthermore, supplemental state policies (e.g., monitoring of statewide proficiency data, support for Advanced Placement [AP] or International Baccalaureate [IB], etc.) that exist and affect gifted students need to be analyzed and linked to gifted education in some way. Existing policy should also be evaluated for its effectiveness regularly. In addition to the recommendations made by the National Association for Gifted Children (NAGC) *Pre-K–Grade 12 Gifted Program Standards* (Landrum & Shaklee, 1998), comprehensive, effective policies should address the areas that follow.

## Identification

Identification policy needs to address the following areas:

- An operational definition of giftedness should be constructed that acknowledges general and specific abilities.
- Clear specifications about identification for all categories of giftedness should be cited.
- Multiple criteria should be employed to identify students in each category of giftedness (e.g., general academic ability, specific academic aptitude, creativity, leadership, the visual and performing arts).
- Instruments sensitive to the inclusion of underrepresented groups, including low income, minority, twice exceptional, and ELLs (English language learners), should be used.
- A systematic process for the linking of identification procedures to appropriate program and service provisions should be articulated.
- A process for equitable decision making at screening, identification, selection, and placement stages, including an appeals process, should be delineated.

## Program and Service Provisions

Educational programs and services for the gifted must match the instruments and assessment procedures used to identify students. Thus, a careful delineation of program and service components must be included in state regulation. (See Landrum & Shaklee, 1998, for recommendations.)

The following components should be addressed in regulations:

- Grouping arrangements conducive to administering gifted programs and services include cluster, resource room, pull-out, special classes, or self-contained classrooms. At least one of these options should be employed to ensure adequate service delivery to gifted learners.
- Contact time for programs and services should constitute no less time than 150 minutes per week, with at least one hour per week of planning time for teachers (VanTassel-Baska, Brown, Worley, & Stambaugh, 2004).
- Curriculum should be modified in each relevant subject area for identified students according to the need for acceleration, complexity, depth, challenge, and creativity. Such curriculum differentiation is built upon and extends standards-based regular curriculum and requires the development and/or use of curriculum designed for the learning needs of gifted students.
- Assessment practices employed for gifted programs are matched to the demands of the specific curriculum objectives. Off-level standardized tests, performance-based tasks, and portfolio approaches are encouraged.
- A modified and extended program is articulated to accommodate at-risk and highly gifted populations.
- Acceleration in the learning rate of gifted learners should always be an option in a gifted education program. The following policies are central to such efforts:

- Students may enter kindergarten early, based on meeting the identification guidelines for general intellectual ability.

- Students may advance more than one grade based on review of performance and ability criteria.

- Students may be advanced in one subject area and accommodated flexibly by advanced curricular placement.

- Students may enter middle school, high school, or college early as determined by overall performance, demonstrated readiness, and relevant exit examination testing.

- Students may test out of state standards requirements early.

- Social-emotional support for student development is included as a part of the service delivery plan.
- Academic guidance and career counseling are available at Grades 6–12, emphasizing the need for advanced course-taking early and the use of student assessment data to counsel students on college and career alternatives.
- A state/local advisory council provides oversight to the state/local service delivery plan, which receives local board of education approval (see Appendix A).

## Supplemental Policies Linked to Program and Service Provisions

Because all states now have relatively new standards of learning in place for all students, there is a need to ensure that the differentiation of curriculum, instruction, and assessment for gifted learners is appropriately connected to these quality standards of learning. Specific regulations needed in this area are the alignment of gifted education curriculum to state standards of learning needs so that districts can see how gifted education addresses the standards but extends beyond them.

States should annually monitor statewide proficiency data to ensure that gifted students are reaching the proficiency levels desired (i.e., proficient or advanced) in each academic area relevant to their identification.

States need to monitor participation of gifted students in the hallmark secondary programs of AP, IB, and dual enrollment to ensure that gifted students in the state are participating in at least one of these options. Where state policies already exist to promote these programs, gifted education regulations should be linked to them; where state policy does not address these programs, gifted education regulations should encourage these service options at the secondary level.

## Personnel Preparation

Endorsement or certification of teachers in gifted education is a necessary provision to include in regulation regarding personnel preparation. The personnel preparation initiative should contain the following components, which are based on the preliminary recommendations of the National Council for Accreditation of Teacher Education (NCATE) standards for gifted program teacher preparation (National Association for Gifted Children, & Council for Exceptional Children, 2006 and the NAGC *Pre-K–Grade 12 Gifted Program Standards* (Landrum & Shaklee, 1998):

A minimum of 12 hours of coursework in gifted education should be required and linked to university-based programs with a statewide university collaborative network (VanTassel-Baska et al., 2004).

Frequent, regularly scheduled staff development opportunities for all program staff should be required. In addition, all classroom teachers, school counselors, and administrators should receive professional development about the nature and learning needs of gifted students.

Individuals who serve as gifted education program coordinators should be required to complete an additional 15 hours of coursework in educational administration, in addition to the requirements for endorsement or certification for working with gifted learners (VanTassel-Baska et al., 2004).

## Program Management

State leadership must exert quality control over programs at the local level. This may be accomplished through a five-pronged approach:

1. Each state should require an annual plan from school districts specifying how the districts intend to identify and serve gifted learners.

2. An annual state department review of district plans should be instituted. Local coordinators may be designated to work with state department personnel to carry out this task annually during a two- to three-day session.

3. An outline of major state plan components should be specified by regulation, including (1) screening, identification and referral processes; (2) program provisions employed at each grade level; (3) goals, student outcomes, and student assessment process for each specified program model; (4) student contact time for each model; (5) pupil-teacher ratios for each model; (6) a professional development plan; (7) counseling and guidance plan; and (8) a program evaluation design.

4. A State Education Agency (SEA) monitoring plan should be implemented to ensure local compliance. Onsite visits to local school districts should be undertaken annually, with all districts visited every five years.

5. A state system to require LEA evaluation of programs should be developed, requiring annual assessment and evaluation as a part of the documented plan submitted each year and tied to funding.

## Evaluation of Policies

Based on a careful review of several state policies (Brown, Avery, & VanTassel-Baska, 2003), it appears warranted to recommend that all states conduct an evaluation of any new regulations and policies. This evaluation should take place after three years from the date of enactment. Data from such an evaluation should reveal how well the mechanisms of identification, program, personnel preparation, program management, supplemental policies, and funding structure are working in tandem to benefit gifted children. Thus, states should consider studying the effects and impacts of policy on relevant stakeholders—districts, schools, teachers, students, and parents. Both quantitative and qualitative approaches should be employed to tease out the potential benefits and liabilities of policy enactment.

# ATTRIBUTES THAT DEFINE HIGH-QUALITY GIFTED EDUCATION STATE POLICY

The importance of self-assessment in developing sound state policy is a critical component of its chance for success. The following criteria are offered as guideposts for the policy evaluation process:

## Clarity

- Are the policies written in a clear and unambiguous way?
- Do the policies encourage a common understanding and interpretation?
- Can all stakeholders readily interpret each policy to determine (1) the extent to which their district complies with it and/or (2) how their practices can be strengthened in order to comply?

## Comprehensiveness

- Do the policies cover all the major components outlined?
- Is each component sufficiently explained to be interpreted for implementation?

## Connectedness

- Do the policies flow in a logical way from one component to the next? Are they internally consistent?
- Are policies linked, aligned, or compatible with one another (e.g., does the definition of gifted and talented align with the services?)?
- Do the policies in gifted education connect to general education policies in consistent and appropriate ways?

## Feasibility for Implementation

- Do the policies constitute a set of regulations that local districts could implement?
- Have the policies been implemented in other states successfully?

## Research-Based

- Are the policies grounded in research-based best practice?
- Are the policies congruent with new research in the field?

# AN EXAMPLE IN NEED OF REVISION

Using the attributes that define *high quality*, read and reflect on the following state policy excerpt copied from an existing gifted policy.

## Services for Children Who Are Gifted

### *Instruction*

The depth, breadth, and pace of instruction, based on the adopted course of study in appropriate content areas, shall be differentiated and may include

- (i) Differentiated curriculum related to
  - A. Replacement or extension of the regular curriculum
  - B. Broad-based issues
  - C. Themes or problems
  - D. Multidisciplinary study
  - E. Curriculum compacting

- (ii) Methods to simulate high-level thought, including critical thinking, divergent thinking, abstract thinking, logical reasoning, and problem solving

- (iii) Oral, written, and artistic expression

- (iv) Independent study and research methods

- (v) In-depth study of a topic through
  - A. Open-ended tasks
  - B. Products that reflect complex abstract, and/or higher level thinking skills

- (vi) Exploration of career options

- (vii) Accelerated coursework or content acceleration

- (viii) Mentorships

- (ix) Guidance

*Comments*: Based on the program and service recommendations provided, the following seven suggestions for changes in this policy should be considered:

1. The policy requires differentiation but includes the word "may" in the list of possible services. "May" is interpreted in policy as "optional." Therefore, there are no guaranteed specific services required or matched to the needs of gifted learners under this policy.

2. Section (i) lacks connectedness and parallelism regarding what constitutes differentiated curriculum because it lists strategies and procedural suggestions, rather than substantive curriculum options for gifted learners. Alignment to content standards is not stated.

3. Curriculum compacting (i)(E) and the inclusion of guidance (ix) are essential service provisions and should be required, not optional.

4. Section (i) is not explicit and could cause confusion in interpretation. For example, does (A) "Replacement or extension of the regular curriculum" imply that districts must align gifted content to curricular standards? Or does it mean something else?

5. Section (ii) includes abstract thinking. This is not a distinctive form of thinking from the rest of the listing.

6. Mentorships (Section viii) are optional program experiences that should be listed with "personalized" opportunities such as internships and tutorials.

7. Elements missing from the policy excerpt include contact time, assessment, accommodations for at-risk and highly gifted students, and more detailed information regarding acceleration and accelerative policies. Similarly, social-emotional support was unclear, although it could have been inferred under guidance. This section should be more explicit. Grouping options were not addressed.

## MAKEOVER EXAMPLE

After a careful preassessment of all areas for potential policy development using the attributes that define high quality, a policy template may be developed within each area for consideration. The following model template has been constructed in the area of programs and services as a revised example.

A flexible, comprehensive, and sequential system of program and service options is developed in each district that addresses the needs, strengths, and interests of gifted education learners in general intellectual and specific academic, artistic, leadership, and technical domains. This system is articulated in a local plan to be updated annually and revised every three years.

- Acceleration policies include provisions for early entrance and exit from school, early testing out, and Advanced Placement in relevant areas of the curriculum.
- Acceleration options are carefully delineated and shared with parents.
- Curriculum, instruction, and assessment meet the needs of gifted learners by modifying the pace, depth, complexity, creativity, and challenge level of the core program.
- Student progress in gifted programs is assessed annually, including proficiency levels on state tests.
- The gifted program coordinator monitors the implementation of gifted programs and the quality of instruction.
- A state/local advisory group oversees the implementation of plans and recommends areas for improvement.
- Special-needs gifted learners, including those who are minority, disabled, or from poverty circumstances, and the highly gifted receive value-added services, based on an assessed profile of learning needs.
- A counseling and guidance program is provided that addresses issues of social-emotional development and academic, college, and career counseling needs.
- Programs and services provided to gifted learners constitute a minimum of 200 minutes per week, are held during the school day, and occur in a grouped setting with intellectual peers.
- Opportunities are provided to students to address talent development in specialized areas through guided and independent work (e.g., mentorships, internships, independent research).
- A comprehensive program guide is provided to relevant stakeholders, describing the district's K–12 services for gifted learners.

# PROCEDURES FOR REVISING OR CREATING POLICY

To address flaws in state policies similar to those addressed in the previous example, the following four stages would need to occur.

1. The state coordinator for gifted education would convene a task force to examine the discrepancies between a model policy and the existing one.

2. The task force would assess the requirements for administrative implementation, including additional costs for mandated services.

3. The task force would assess the consequences of implementing such new policies in local districts, including selected interviews with local coordinators.

4. The task force and the state coordinator for the gifted would assess the political implications of strengthening the service delivery options in the ways suggested.

Figure 19.1 was designed to guide the reader through the four stages of state policy development. At each stage, focusing questions are provided to encourage reflection and discussion about the policy options being considered in your state.

**Figure 19.1**   The Four Stages of Policy Development

*Formulation of Policy Options*

- What policies exist currently at the state level?
- What are the different ways in which policy might be addressed for each of the following components?
  - Identification
  - Program and Service Provisions
  - Supplemental Policies Linked to Program and Service Provisions
  - Personnel Preparation
  - Program Management
  - Evaluation

*Assessment of Administrative Implementation*

- Where does this new policy fit within our organizational framework?
- Who will be responsible for designing the policy and its implementation strategy?
- What are the costs for implementing the policy option?

*Assessment of Consequences of Implementation*

- What are the implications and consequences of putting this new policy in place?
- What positive outcomes do we expect as a result of adopting this policy?
- Is it possible that enactment of this policy will lead to unintended consequences for districts, teachers, or individual students and will require revisions?

*Assessment of the Political Implications of Each Policy Option*

- How are the desires and interests of different stakeholder groups related to the new policy or the issue that the policy is designed to address?
- Are there links between these desires and interests and the potential consequences for each policy option?
- Does the policy option consider the unique needs of frequently underserved populations (e.g., low income, minority, twice exceptional, ELL)?

# PROCEDURES FOR TRANSLATING STATE POLICY INTO LOCAL EDUCATION ACTION PLANS

The components found in state policy should be mirrored in a local education plan. When local educational plans mirror state policy, there is a greater likelihood that all students will be provided with equal access to ongoing levels of challenge in their K–12 school experience.

One of the most effective ways to monitor state policy implementation is through the analysis of written local plans, coupled with administrative onsite review. Key questions to ask in the process of monitoring include the following:

- Who is responsible for the implementation of the gifted plan in a district? What evidence exists of their active management of the program?
- To what degree are the program components being implemented as they are stated, in compliance with state regulation?
- What is the district's process for monitoring the plan's implementation annually? What evidence exists that monitoring has occurred regularly?
- What documentation of value-added gifted student learning does the district have as a result of operating a gifted program?

# CONCLUSION

Developing and implementing state policies that govern the administration of gifted programs and services is the glue that holds this field together. Ensuring that these policies reflect up-to-date research is crucial to improving practice. Moreover, greater coherence among program policy elements will enhance the operation of gifted programs and ultimately benefit gifted learners.

# ADVICE FOR THE SOLE PRACTITIONER

Often only one person is responsible for gifted education in a district. Many times this person also has responsibilities beyond gifted education. Thus, the task necessary to effect policy development and revision may seem overwhelming. First, it is important to acknowledge that a discussion about and subsequent revision of state policies brings gifted education to the forefront and will lead to benefits for your students. However, this process also requires large investments of time and manpower. Several tasks can be undertaken to engage in this process as a sole practitioner. They are (1) participation in a task force to analyze current policies and determine issues and gaps, (2) collaboration with administrators responsible for enacting and overseeing policies, and (3) incorporation of onsite visits to other local programs to deepen your own understanding of what's working and what is not. The formulation of new policies to improve gifted programs and services in your state and community will surely follow.

# MUST-READ RESOURCES

Baker, B. D., & McIntire, J. (2003). Evaluating state funding for gifted education programs. *Roeper Review, 25*(4), 173–177.

Carnoy, M., & Loeb, S. (2002). Does external accountability affect student outcomes? A cross-state analysis. *Educational Evaluation and Policy Analysis, 24*(4), 305–331.

Gallagher, J. J. (2002). *Society's role in educating gifted students: The role of public policy* (RM02162). Storrs, CT: The National Research Center on the Gifted and Talented, University of Connecticut.

Kulik, J. A., & Kulik, C. L. C. (1992). Meta-analytic findings on grouping programs. *Gifted Child Quarterly, 36*(2) 73–77.

Landrum, M. S., Katsiyannis, A., & DeWard, J. (1998). A national survey of current legislative and policy trends in gifted education: Life after the National Excellence report. *Journal for the Education of the Gifted, 21*(3), 352–371.

National Association for Gifted Children. (2003). *Gifted education and the No Child Left Behind Act.* Retrieved January 4, 2004, from http://www.ncagt.org/nclb-gifted.shtml

Passow, A. H., & Rudnitski, R. A. (1993). *State policies regarding education of the gifted as reflected in legislation and regulation* (CRS93302). Storrs, CT: The National Research Center on the Gifted and Talented, University of Connecticut.

Purcell, J. (1995). Gifted education at a crossroads: The program status study. *Gifted Child Quarterly, 35*(1), 26–35.

Robinson, A., & Moon, S. M. (2003). A national study of local and state advocacy in gifted education. *Gifted Child Quarterly, 47*(1), 8–25.

Rogers, K. (1998). Using current research to make "good" decisions about grouping. *Education for the Gifted and Talented, 92*(595), 38–46.

Russo, C. J., Harris, J. J., & Ford, D. Y. (1996). Gifted education and law: A right, privilege, or superfluous? *Roeper Review, 18*(3), 179–182.

Shaunessy, E. (2003). State policies regarding gifted education. *Gifted Child Today, 26*(3), 16–21.

U.S. Department of Education, National Center for Education Statistics. (1997). *Pursuing excellence: A study of U.S. fourth grade mathematics and science achievement in international context* (NCES 97255). Washington, DC: Author.

VanTassel-Baska, J. (1992). Educational decision-making on acceleration and grouping. *Gifted Child Quarterly, 36,* 68–72.

VanTassel-Baska, J., Brown, E., Worley, B., & Stambaugh, T. (2004). An analysis of state policies in key program development components. Williamsburg, VA: Center for Gifted Education, College of William and Mary.

VanTassel-Baska, J. (2003). Curriculum policy development for gifted programs: Converting issues in the field to coherent practice. In J. Borland (Ed.), *Rethinking gifted education* (pp. 173–185). Danvers, MA: Teachers College Press.

## REFERENCES

Baker, B. D., & McIntire, J. (2003). Evaluating state funding for gifted education programs. *Roeper Review, 25*(4), 173–177.

Brown, E., Avery, L., & VanTassel-Baska, J. (2003). *Gifted policy analysis study for the Ohio Department of Education.* Williamsburg, VA: Center for Gifted Education.

Gallagher, J. J. (Vol. Ed.) (2004). Public policy in gifted education (Vol. 12). In S. M. Reis (Series Ed.), *Essential readings in gifted education.* Thousand Oaks, CA: Corwin.

Gallagher, J. J. (2002). *Society's role in educating gifted students: The role of public policy* (RM02162). Storrs, CT: The National Research Center on the Gifted and Talented, University of Connecticut.

Landrum, M. S., & Shaklee, B. (1998). *Pre-K–Grade 12 gifted program standards.* Washington, DC: National Association for Gifted Children.

Marland, S. P., Jr. (1972). Education of the gifted and talented. *Vol. 1: Report to the Congress of the United States by the U.S. Commissioner of Education.* Washington, DC: U.S. Government Printing Office.

National Association for Gifted Children, & Council for Exceptional Children (2006). *Initial NCATE standards for teacher preparation programs in gifted education.* Washington, DC: Author.

National Association for Gifted Children & Council of State Directors. (2003). *State of the states: Gifted and talented education report 2001–2002.* Washington, DC: Author.

Passow, A. H. & Rudnitski, R. A. (1993). *State policies regarding education of the gifted as reflected in legislation and regulation* (CRS93302). Storrs, CT: The National Research Center on the Gifted and Talented, University of Connecticut.

Russo, C. J., Harris, J. J., & Ford, D. Y. (1996). Gifted education and law: A right, privilege, or superfluous? *Roeper Review, 18*(3), 179–182.

U.S. Department of Education. (1993). *National excellence: A case for developing America's talent.* Washington, DC: Author.

VanTassel-Baska, J. (2003). Curriculum policy development for gifted programs: Converting issues in the field to coherent practice. In J. Borland (Ed.), *Rethinking gifted education* (pp. 173–185). Danvers, MA: Teachers College Press.

VanTassel-Baska, J., Brown, E., Worley, B., & Stambaugh, T. (2004). *An analysis of state policies in key program development components.* Williamsburg, VA: Center for Gifted Education, College of William and Mary.

Zirkel, P. A. (2003). *The law on gifted education* (RM03178). Storrs, CT: The National Research Center on the Gifted and Talented, University of Connecticut.

# 20

# Using Scientifically Based Research to Make Decisions About Gifted Education Programs, Services, and Resources

*Tonya R. Moon and Deborah E. Burns*

We cannot direct the wind, but we can adjust the sails.
—Bertha Calloway

Life used to be simple, the saying goes. In the past, our decisions about practices in gifted education were easily made. Sometimes, our decisions were based on tradition, "we've always done it this way." Other times, we used anecdotal evidence, sets of stories that happened to us or others to make decisions. Some call this the "folk wisdom of education." Finally, we based some of our decisions about identification techniques, program design, program models, and resources on the practices of those in the adjacent school district or state.

Now, however, life is more complicated. Consider this scenario: It is time to sit down to reflect on your gifted education program, its services, identification process and instruments, and curriculum resources. You have read a little about the No Child Left Behind Act of 2001 (NCLB), enough to know that the law requires knowledge and application of scientifically based research in the curricular areas of mathematics and science, instructional methods and strategies, parent involvement, professional development, extended learning, and language instruction. You also realize that your gifted program is a part of all the areas targeted by NLCB.

In this chapter, Deborah Burns and Tonya Moon collaborate to provide readers with insight about scientifically based research (SBR). The authors have a unique perspective because they ground the discussion about the need for SBR within the context of gifted education. The authors bring to this chapter a unique blend of two worlds that—some would argue—rarely meet: the university world and the practical world of the school district. Tonya Moon brings to this chapter her background as a university professor engaged in educational research, while Deborah Burns brings to the discussion her role as an assistant superintendent of a suburban school district in Connecticut.

This chapter has linkages with all the others that require careful, thoughtful decisions regarding student achievement: Constructing Identification Procedures, 5; Comprehensive Program Design, 7; Curriculum for Gifted Education Services, 8; Selecting Learning Resources in the Education of the Gifted, 11; Designing a Professional Development Plan, 14; and Developing a Plan for Evaluating a Program in Gifted Education, 15.

## DEFINITION

The educational community defines *scientifically based research* as the application of rigorous, systematic, and objective procedures to obtain reliable and valid knowledge about educational programs and services (Beghetto, 2003). Unfortunately, research that meets SBR standards for evaluating the effectiveness of programs and services is limited. In these cases, decision makers, including those responsible for gifted education services, need to rely on the best empirical evidence available and their professional judgment until such time that SBR evidence is available. The table at the end of this chapter illustrates the levels of quality that are commonly associated with various forms of evidence and research. The higher the level of evidence related to a model or service, the greater the likelihood that the model or services in question will deliver the intended impact. As the availability of SBR increases, stronger conclusions about the effect of program strategies, services, and learning of students in gifted programs can be drawn.

## RATIONALE

There are many reasons why decision making about gifted education services must be based on the strongest evidence possible. The first reason concerns professional responsibility. Specifically, the primary responsibility of professionals in charge of administering and coordinating gifted programs is to create a unified and comprehensive set of services and practices that promote student learning, emotional well-being, and the development of individual potential. To make the very best professional decisions about identification models, identification processes and instruments, curriculum, instructional resources, teaching and learning strategies, assessments, and related guidance services, gifted education specialists need sound evidence on which to base their judgments.

A second reason for careful, evidenced-based decision making concerns the vast number of resources available to decision makers. Since the mid-1970s, the number of books and articles that have been written about how to meet the needs of gifted education students and how to manage gifted education programs has expanded exponentially. Journal articles, publishers' catalogs, and texts written for gifted education specialists proclaim the benefits and advantages of various identification models and instruments, student services, programming models, instructional strategies, and learning materials. Although we welcome this bounty of publications, the sheer number has also resulted in a plethora of perspectives, techniques, tools, claims, and advertisements that must be reviewed, critically analyzed, and evaluated to determine their credibility and worth. On many occasions, practitioners share with us that this storehouse of materials also causes confusion, bewilderment, and, in the case of harried educators with scant support services and technical assistance, an all-too-frequent hasty rush to judgment and implementation.

The third reason for evidence-based decision making is related to accountability. Like our expectations for general education, gifted education programs and services are expected to increase student learning and be accountable for costs, quality, and equity of opportunity for all students. As decision makers for gifted education services, we must be able to explain to all stakeholders how our sound and scientifically based, decision-making process has led to the continuous improvement in all aspects of our programming.

Two additional reasons have fueled the need for SBR decision making. The federal government, using recommendations from the National Research Council (NRC), has created a Web-based information service that describes the criteria and standards used to evaluate articles, programs, materials, and research reports to support evidence-based decisions in the field of education. The NRC, the federal government, and leaders in the gifted education community have voiced agreement with the What Works Clearinghouse guiding principle that states that education programs, services, strategies, and resources should be based on a solid, justifiable foundation of students' unmet needs, national standards, and best practices based on available scientifically based research (SBR) (www.what works.ed.gov).

Quite simply, the most respected educational groups have provided us with criteria by which to make evidence-based decisions. These expectations are comparable to what we insist on from the medical, legal, and engineering professions. As clients of these professionals, we require our doctors, lawyers, and contractors to base their recommendations and practices on defensible evidence that demonstrates results; gifted education students should be treated no differently.

The NCLB Act is the reauthorization of the Elementary and Secondary Education Act, and it is the fifth and final reason for using evidenced-based decision making. NCLB requires knowledge and application of SBR in several areas: the curriculum areas of reading, mathematics, and science; instructional methods and strategies; parental involvement; and professional development, among others. Despite some educators' reservations and concerns about potential misconceptions and misuses of SBR, the federal government's insistence on using what works may ultimately lead to more effective teaching and student learning. Although the federal government does not specifically mention gifted education as a program that needs to adhere to SBR, having a gifted program based on evidence or SBR offers gifted education practitioners an unwavering foundation from which to defend their decisions, programs, and services.

## GUIDING PRINCIPLES AND ASSUMPTIONS

The following principles apply to the evidence (i.e., research) provided about particular programs or services. These principles should be used to make decisions about gifted education programs and services.

*Principle 1:* The program, identification process, resources, and service components of a gifted education program should be based on a specified and sound theoretical foundation.

*Principle 2:* A sound theoretical foundation should lead to the development, field-testing, and investigation of related and promising services, instructional strategies, resources, and programming practices for gifted education.

*Principle 3:* Significant questions should be asked and systematically investigated to study the effectiveness and appropriateness of specific program or service components and promising practices. Such questions should focus on the evidence that supports, refutes, or stipulates when, with whom, and under what conditions a promising practice promotes student learning.

*Principle 4:* The data collected to assess a promising practice should be appropriate to address the question(s) identified in Principle 3.

*Principle 5:* Evidence that supports a promising practice claim or hypothesis should be collected systematically and empirically.

*Principle 6:* The data collected as evidence to evaluate the effectiveness of a promising practice should be subjected to appropriate data analysis.

*Principle 7:* The methods used to assess the program and service components should allow for the direct investigation of the questions posed in Principle 3.

*Principle 8:* Evaluation and investigation procedures should be replicated at different times, in different places, and in different contexts to substantiate or modify the original evaluation conclusions and inferences.

*Principle 9:* Once an evidence-based program, service component or instructional practice is adopted and implemented, periodic evaluations of the related program or service components should be conducted to ensure that the component is still achieving its original goals and desired impact.

## CHARACTERISTICS OF HIGH-QUALITY RESEARCH PRACTICES

To gain an understanding of the potential usefulness of a particular program or service component(s), decision makers are advised to act as cautious consumers and test pilots who carefully examine the research about particular programs or services from three perspectives:

1. The theoretical base of the program or service. Does the program or service documentation contain a list of specific goals and clear and logical explanations about how and why each practice or service is expected to be effective with clearly identified target populations?

2. Information about the implementation and transferability of the program or service. Does accompanying documentation identify and describe the situations, conditions, student characteristics, and time frame under which the program or service has been effectively implemented?

3. The available evidence about the effects of identified and relevant student outcomes. Does the program or service have high-quality research studies that investigate and describe its outcomes and effects?

Particular questions that should be asked to address these three areas are listed next.

## Theoretical Base

- Is there a theoretical foundation for the program or service?
- What ideas and assumptions form the foundation for the program or service?
- Is there an operational definition of the term "gifted" that is tied to the identified goals of the program or service?
- Are there clear descriptions for each of the central aspects of the program (e.g., identification, curriculum) or service?
- Are the key features of the program well aligned with the stated goals and gifted definition?

## Application and Transferability

- Is there clear and detailed evidence that the program or service has been successfully implemented in the state? Nationally?
- How many other schools or districts have implemented the program or service component?
- In what settings has the program or service component been implemented?

## Evidence of Effectiveness

- Is there evidence that the program or service has a positive effect on identified outcomes (e.g., student achievement, increased number of underrepresented populations in gifted education programs)?
- Are there research studies investigating the effects on identified outcomes of the program or service?
- Are those studies of reasonable quality (i.e., systematic, empirical, and use of appropriate data analysis with reliable and valid data)?

  - *Who* conducted the research? Does the individual(s) or the organization have the necessary qualifications and resources to conduct research on the topic?

  - *What* is being investigated? Is the topic focused appropriately so that reliable and valid data could/can be gathered?

  - *When* was the research conducted? Seminal research has as much validity as recent research. However, the timing of the results is important and should influence how one uses the results. If the research is recent, does it acknowledge the previous research and findings?

- *Where* was the research done? Is the number of individuals involved in the study sufficient for the conclusions that are being made about the topic? Does the research cover students and schools like those in your community?

- *Why* was the research conducted?

- Is the *methodology* sound? That is, are there clearly identified research questions? Were the data gathered in a systematic way? Do the data gathering techniques correspond well to the research questions being asked?

- Are the *findings* connected to the research questions asked and the research methodology employed?

## AN EXAMPLE IN NEED OF REVISION

The coordinator of Rolling Hills School District's gifted program is also in charge of support services for students (e.g., guidance counseling) and afterschool programs. He has to appear before the district's school board to deliver the annual report about the gifted program and, in particular, information on the identification procedures, the population being served in the program, and the services that are implemented to address the population's needs.

For the last several years, the school board has attempted to increase the representation of minority students in the gifted program. To address the board's priority, the coordinator has attended numerous national and regional conferences and participated in regional gifted meetings with other coordinators. He has gathered information about the practices in other districts and the types of instruments they used to identify minority students. As a result of his attendance at these meetings, the coordinator and an appointed committee changed the identification process twice during the last three years.

Each year the coordinator is asked to explain these identification decisions and the effects these decisions have on the underrepresentation of particular student populations in the gifted program. Each year he shares the successes other school districts have experienced with similar strategies. He also shares the results that test developers shared with him about the test the gifted program is using to identify more minority students. Because of recent funding issues, the school district is facing increased expectations for fiscal accountability. The teachers that are responsible for implementing the ever-changing identification process have also voiced concerns, as have numerous parents. For this reason, the gifted education program coordinator is apprehensive about the upcoming school board meeting and the response he may receive to his report.

## IDENTIFYING CONCERNS AND ISSUES IN THE EXAMPLE

Many gifted education coordinators face a situation that is similar to the one explained in the preceding example. Making decisions based on what others are doing or what appears to be the latest trend means operating from the heart and not the head. The two specific concerns illuminated in this example are explained here.

1. The coordinator made significant program decisions without data related to his or her local program. In this case, he changed an identification process without considering the following three items:

   - Program philosophy
   - Program goals
   - The operational definition of gifted and talented used in the school district

2. The coordinator did not have access to or did not use longitudinal databases and data analysis software to review information (e.g., test scores, participation in special programs, grades, feeder schools, teachers, student demographic data) about students who did and did not receive gifted education services. To evaluate the effectiveness of an experimental identification procedure, the gifted education coordinator must be able to retrieve relevant data about students before and after the new procedures went into effect. In this case, without the longitudinal student database, decisions were made based on "gut" feelings rather than on systematic and empirically collected data about the effectiveness and impact of the identification instruments and process. With such data, the coordinator might have been able to evaluate the degree to which the instruments and the process aligned with the needs and strengths of underrepresented students and the program's definition of giftedness. This is dangerously close to selecting instruments on the basis of a convenient suggestion rather than a decision made with a sound rationale coupled with reliable and valid data to support decisions.

## REVISING THE EXAMPLE

Revising the lackluster example requires that we follow six easy-to-use steps, which are explained next. As you read through these steps, think back to a time when you made a weighty decision related to your gifted education program's model or services. Try to identify the steps you incorporated into your decision-making process. Which steps did you incorporate? Which ones might you have overlooked inadvertently?

### Step 1: Collect Data

The first task to resolve the problem illuminated in this example involves the development of a committee that represents the various stakeholders in the school district community who are vested in this question and problem. The committee should collect sufficient data to describe the context in which the gifted program operates. This information might include but is not limited to (1) funds available for the program's operation (e.g., salaries, resources, professional development opportunities); (2) community and districtwide perceptions of student needs, strengths, and services; (3) demographic data about student participants and nonparticipants (e.g., socioeconomic levels of students, needs, strengths, available services to address these needs, students' academic proficiency levels, numbers of students having dual or multiple classifications); and (4) professional development needs of the teachers responsible for the delivery of student services.

## Step 2: Analyzing the Data and Prioritizing Needs

The second item for this committee involves analyzing the information gathered in Step 1 and establishing priorities. In the earlier example, the committee might examine the district's philosophy, goals, and operational definition of gifted and talented to ensure alignment. Assuming that the alignment exists, the committee can prioritize the need to establish a defensible identification process within the context of the existing or revised program parameters. If there is no alignment of the philosophy, goals, and definition, the committee needs to address the necessary alignment before taking the next step.

## Step 3: Identifying a Research Base

Once the committee is confident about the alignment of the program's philosophy, goals, and definition, the next task is to gather relevant research about identification strategies for gifted and talented learners and related strategies to identify underrepresented gifted and talented minority students.

## Step 4: Discriminate Between Applicable and Nonapplicable Research and Information

After the latest research has been gathered, the next step is to discriminate potential and valuable sources of information from irrelevant sources. A review of each piece of information is critical to ensure that the research has a strong theoretical basis, that there is evidence of its potential usefulness for the district in terms of its identified priorities and context, and to determine if there is any evidence about the effects of particular identification procedures.

## Step 5: Critically Review Applicable Information Sources

If Step 4 suggests that some studies are applicable, the committee should review each relevant study. Specifically, the committee should verify that the evidence collected was done in a systematic way, that the evidence collected was reliable and valid for the purpose of the study, that the data were subjected to appropriate and rigorous data analysis, and that the study was replicated in different settings with different student populations, or has the potential for replication.

## Step 6: Implementing Changes Based on Sound Evidence

With the information obtained from Step 5, the committee can begin to establish a revised identification process that can be implemented in the district. The committee can also work with district personnel to establish a database to maintain data for use when making decisions. All information concerning students nominated, screened, and receiving services should be kept for five to seven years to ensure that the identification process is identifying the appropriate population of students for the services that are being delivered. This database is even more important when there are no research studies to use as a basis for decision making. With the use of a well-managed database, the coordinator can begin to collect and provide evidence about the impact of the decisions concerning the identification of students for services.

# A STRATEGIC PLAN FOR SELECTING AND EVALUATING PROGRAMS AND SERVICES BASED ON EVIDENCE

The following steps can be used to analyze claims made or evidence cited by a researcher, publisher, or developer related to a gifted education service, strategy, or practice. The same steps may also prove useful when developing a program or district plan to gather and analyze local evidence about the effectiveness of program services and strategies. There is no single timetable for conducting these activities. Instead, they can be used when needed.

| | |
|---|---|
| **Step 1:**<br>**Data Collection** | Collect data or information that gives an overall and accurate picture of the current context and situation in which the proposed program and/or services will be implemented. |
| **Step 2:**<br>**Data Analysis and Prioritization** | Analyze data or information to determine and prioritize the needs of the students or clients. |
| **Step 3:**<br>**Identifying the Research Base** | Gather literature to identify the research base for the potential programs or services being considered. (See the Must-Read Resources section of this chapter for potential sources for research.) |
| **Step 4:**<br>**Discriminating Relevant from Nonrelevant** | Use obtained results to determine (1) if there is a theoretical basis for a program or service, (2) if there are identified issues with the implementation of the program or service, (3) if there is evidence provided about the transferability of the program or service across different contexts, and (4) if there is evidence of the effects of the program or service on identified student outcomes. It is important to note that not all research will address all four areas, but more than one may be addressed in any given research study. |
| **Step 5:**<br>**Critical Review of Relevant Studies** | If the results indicate that the study is relevant to the identified needs in Step 2, each study should be further examined. Use the characteristics of high-quality research, outlined earlier in this chapter, to determine if the relevant research is of high quality, transferable to other contexts, and relevant to identified goals and needs. The examined research should meet the criteria for SBR. In some cases, there will be no, or little, high-quality evidence that the program or service will obtain the identified student outcomes. Refer to the Guiding Questions section when reviewing relevant studies. |
| **Step 6:**<br>**Making Changes** | Using the evidence provided in Step 5, defensible changes are made to the particular program/service under consideration. |
| **Step 7:**<br>**Ongoing Evaluation** | Continue to collect pertinent student data and research literature to support program decision making. |

## An Evidence-Based Hierarchy That Can Be Used to Assess the Trustworthiness of Educational Programs, Models, and Services

Educators make hundreds of decisions every year. When they make decisions that impact student learning and/or influence the implementation of services, models, practices, strategies, products, or tools, they must be mindful of students' learning needs. Specifically, children are best served when decisions regarding their educational program are based on solid evidence. In the context of NCLB, many call this process "evidenced-based decision making": the integration of professional wisdom with the best available empirical evidence in making decisions about how to deliver instruction (Whitehurst, 2002).

The quality of this evidence can be rated and ranked according to its fidelity, namely, its reliability and trustworthiness. When we apply the guiding principles from educational research, we can rank—from low to high—the trustworthiness and reliability of most gifted education services, models, practices, strategies, or tools.

Table 20.1 has been designed to help practitioners assess the fidelity of gifted education services, models, practices, strategies, and tools. It is divided into three columns. The left-hand column contains the Fidelity Ranking. Examples of models, program components, and products that are rated at the low end of the hierarchy have less evidence that can be used to support their effectiveness. Models, program components, and products rated at the upper end of this continuum hold great promise for delivering their intended impacts. The middle column, Evidence Sources, contains an increasingly rigorous set of research-related factors or conditions. The greater the number of research conditions that are met by a particular model, program component, or products, the more likely it is to be a trustworthy and reliable choice for decision makers. The right-hand column contains an example that may be associated with the rating and can be used to illustrate the Fidelity Ranking.

As you use this hierarchy, think of models, programs, program components, and products you have used. Try to determine each element's standing by locating it in the hierarchy and noting its Fidelity Ranking.

## Guiding Questions for the Analysis of Research Reports

Gifted education specialists, general education teachers, and school administrators usually rely on colleagues, regional service centers, their state department of education, local universities, conferences, journal articles, and Web sites as their primary sources of information about an educational practice, recommendation, or innovation. To assess the quality of the proposals, explanations, and recommendations provided by these sources, practitioners can use the criteria listed in Table 20.1. To evaluate the extent to which the description, evidence, claim, or recommendation meets the definition of SBR, practitioners should consider using the following questions as guidelines:

- Is the study systematic and empirical? High-quality research is conducted through the use of a discipline-based inquiry process. This means that the developer, researcher, and/or evaluator are able to provide evidence of careful planning and attention to details that is grounded in evidence drawn from observation or experimentation. Any findings from the research should be based on measurable evidence, and not on opinions or speculation.

- Does the research have a theoretical foundation?
- Were data collected using observation and/or experiment?
- Were data collected from appropriate groups? From multiple participants (students, teachers, etc.)?

- Are the findings supported by measurable evidence?
- Did the procedure allow for the collection of reliable and valid data? Reliable and valid data with appropriate data analysis produce credible findings. Reliable data provides assurance that the results could be replicated if the same individuals were tested again under similar circumstances. Valid data allow one to support particular types of inferences that are drawn.
- Was data collection consistent across all groups (e.g., training of data collectors, standardization of test administration)?
- Were the data collected appropriate for the research questions being investigated?
- Were appropriate data analysis procedures used to analyze the data? Appropriate data analysis is critical with failure to use such methods resulting in inaccurate or misleading findings.

- Does the research address the identified research question?
- Do the findings justify the conclusions that are drawn?
- Are sample sizes and methods of analysis (statistical procedures, qualitative techniques) fully described?
- Does the type of analysis employed address the research question?

- Are all procedures described in the research presented with sufficient detail to allow others to replicate the study?
- Are findings clearly described and reported?
- Are the findings presented objectively?
- Is the description of the methodology such that replicating the study is possible?
- Are limitations and/or issues concerning the research reported? Were explanations provided that contradicted the researcher's expectations?
- A high-quality study should be subjected to peer review. These peer reviewers provide quality control in the form of outside, objective, blind reviews of the research.
- Has the research been accepted and published by a scholarly journal or was it *only* reported in the media (newspapers, magazines, etc.)?
- If the research has not been published, is there evidence that it was reviewed by outside, objective reviewers? Is there evidence that the reviewers approved the study?

## ADVICE FOR THE SOLE PRACTITIONER

Being the only gifted education specialist in a district can be a lonely job, and it always helps to have friends. With respect to SBR, a critical friend is most valuable. Critical friends can help you evaluate the practices in your gifted education program and identify the evidence or research base that underlies each component. They can work cooperatively with you to help you decide which components may need to be examined, and possibly redefined, because no compelling evidence supports the efficacy of its practices. They can also help you decide if a research-based best practice is a good fit for the students in your particular school or district.

**Table 20.1**   An Evidence-Based Hierarchy

| Fidelity Ranking | Evidence Sources | Examples of Related Education Services or Strategies |
|---|---|---|
| 1 | A colleague's idea for curriculum, a service, identification, or grouping practice. *(No design; no empirical data have been gathered)* | Your colleague's curriculum unit that he or she recommended to you last year. It has no empirical evidence to support it. |
| 2 | Expert-developed services, models, practices, strategies, products, or tools that are accompanied by convenient sampling and teachers' subjective observations about effectiveness. *(Professionally developed materials + subjective reflections)* | An identification practice or way of handling professional development that has come from a credible source. |
| 3 | Theory-based, expert-developed services, models, practices, strategies, products, or tools accompanied by nonrandom sampling and student work that provides evidence of practical effectiveness. *(Convenience sampling + student work)* | A curriculum unit that has been field tested by a teacher. It includes the teacher's systematic observations about the effectiveness of the unit and samples of student work. |
| 4 | Theory-based, expert-developed services, models, practices, strategies, products, or tools accompanied by nonrandom sampling—treatment group only—and pre-and postassessment data that provide evidence of statistical effectiveness. *(Convenience sampling + pre- and postassessment)* | The conventional action research project conducted by a classroom teacher who used his or her own students in the study. |
| 5 | Theory-based, expert-developed services, models, practices, strategies, products, or tools accompanied by nonrandom sampling and treatment and control group data that provide evidence of statistical effectiveness. *(Convenience sampling + treatment and comparison group design)* | The conventional research study conducted, for example, within one district. Treatment and comparison groups are used to determine the effectiveness of an intervention. |

*(Continued)*

**Table 20.1** (Continued)

| Fidelity Ranking | Evidence Sources | Examples of Related Education Services or Strategies |
|---|---|---|
| 6 | Theory-based, expert developed services, models, practices, strategies, products, or tools accompanied by nonrandom stratified sampling and treatment and comparison group data that provide evidence of statistical effectiveness. *(Nonrandom, stratified sampling + treatment and comparison group design)* | A study that explores the effectiveness of an instructional strategy using a treatment and control design. The effectiveness of the instructional strategy is examined across subgroups of students, such as males and females, cultural groups, and/or income levels. |
| 7 | Theory-based, expert developed services, models, practices, strategies, products, or tools accompanied by random sampling and treatment and comparison group data that provide evidence of statistical effectiveness in one or more settings. *(Random sampling + treatment and comparison group design + more than one setting)* | • Early entrance to kindergarten as an organizational strategy to promote increased student achievement.<br>• Grade skipping as an organizational strategy to promote increased student achievement. |
| 8 | Theory-based, expert developed, services, models, practices, strategies, products, or tools that were implemented in multiple settings, accompanied by random sampling and treatment and comparison group data that were subjected to a meta-analysis that provides evidence of statistical and practical effectiveness. *(Random sampling + treatment and comparison group design + multiple settings + meta-analysis)* | The use of ability grouping with content modifications as a teaching and learning strategy to promote increased student achievement. |

Critical friends, however, don't always have to work with you in real time or space. Conducting a search of *Gifted Child Quarterly*—or other journals—for research articles that identify program components and characteristics that have a research or evidence base is one good way to start your hunt. Skimming Karen Rogers's latest book, *Re-Forming Gifted Education* (Rogers, 2002), provides another source for a meeting of the minds. The universities that make up the National Research Center on the Gifted and Talent also maintain Web sites that provide information on several research-based practices. Or, consider subscribing to the *Educational Research Newsletter*, PO Box 789, West Barnstable, MA 02668, for research reported in nontechnical language across a variety of subject areas and grade levels.

However you find your evidence-based best practices—through colleagues, research articles, or Web sites—please remember that it is up to you, the practitioner in a local school or district, to determine if these practices are relevant to your setting. Consider the demographics of your site, its student variables, and the needs and characteristics of your students and setting before deciding to investigate a promising practice. The effectiveness of a research-based replication project depends on a careful match.

## MUST-READ RESOURCES

What Works Clearinghouse (www.w-w-c.org). This Web site, sponsored by the U.S. Department of Education, helps educators make choices based on SBR. It is important to note that the site is continually updated.

Scholarly journals in the field of gifted education. Most of these journals have a peer review process for their published materials. Journals that specialize in the field of gifted education include *Gifted Child Quarterly, Journal for the Education of the Gifted, Roeper Review*, and *The Journal of Secondary Gifted Education. Gifted Child Today* is another resource that is more practical than the research-based journals listed earlier.

The National Research Center on the Gifted and Talented (University of Connecticut: www.gifted.uconn.edu/nrcgt; University of Virginia: http://curry.edschool.virginia.edu/gifted/projects/NRC/; Yale University: www.yale.edu/pace). The work of The National Research Center on the Gifted and Talented is guided by emerging research about the broadened conception of human potential and the need to develop "high-end learning" opportunities for all of America's students. Accordingly, the Center's research has applied the strategies of high-end learning to total school improvement and to focus that research on developing gifts and talents in young people based on a broad array of both traditional and emerging indicators of potential for high performance.

Buros Institute of Mental Measurement (www.unl.edu/buros). Buros is the publisher of the *Mental Measurement and Tests in Print* series, which provide critical reviews to support the informed selection of commercial tests.

Vogt, W. P. (1999). *Dictionary of statistics and methodology: A nontechnical guide for the social sciences* (2nd ed.). Thousand Oaks, CA: Sage.

Whitehurst, G. J. (2002). Evidenced-based education (slide presentation). Retrieved August 18, 2005, from http://www.ed.gov/nclb/methods/whatworks/eb/edlite-slide020.html

# REFERENCES

Beghetto, Ron. (2003). *Scientifically based research.* Retrieved August 18, 2005, from http://www.eric.ed.gov ED475107).

*No Child Left Behind Act of 2001,* Pub. L. No. 107–110, 115 Stat. 1425 (2002). http:// www.ed.gov/legislation/ESEA02/

Rogers, K. B. (2002). *Re-forming gifted education.* Scottsdale: AZ: Great Potential Press.

Whitehurst, G. J. (2002). *Evidenced-based education* (slide presentation). Retrieved August 18, 2005, from http://www.ed.gov/nclb/methods/whatworks/eb/edlite-slide020.html

# 21

# Strategic Planning and Gifted Programs

*Linda Smith*

Those who do not purposefully set strategy risk having their organization's momentum or direction developed implicitly, haphazardly, or by others.

—John Zimmerman & Benjamin Tregoe

What makes a plan strategic? The history of strategic planning begins with the military. Webster defines strategy as "the science of planning and directing large-scale military operations of maneuvering forces into the most advantageous position prior to actual engagement with the enemy." Although our use of the term strategic has surely been transformed over the years, one element remains key: the aim of strategic planning is to remain competitive in an age of rapid, often unpredictable change.

Today, strategic planning is used by a wide variety of organizations in business and education alike. Strategic planning examines an organization's values, beliefs, current status, and environment and relates these factors to the program's desired future state, usually expressed in 3- to 10-year time periods. The organization can be a program, a school, classroom, school district, or any other institution that wishes to control its future.

In spring 2004, the National Association for Gifted Children (NAGC) developed its own strategic plan with input from the membership at large. The rationale for the plan was clear: to help the organization identify its current status and seek new goals to increase its alignment within the political, social, economic, technological, and educational ecosystem, both internal and external to the organization.

Gifted education programs should be no exception. Teachers and program coordinators must be eager to engage in the strategic planning process to maintain agility in these times of rapidly shifting environments. However, even in times of great change, strategic planning must be constructed with the building blocks of the program's mission statement (Developing a Mission Statement on the Educational Needs of Gifted and Talented students, Chapter 2), a communication plan (Managing a Communications Initiative, Chapter 12), and its goals and objectives (Articulating Gifted Education Program Goals, Chapter 6).

In this chapter, Linda Smith leads us through the strategic planning process. The comprehensive process she explains is the one she used successfully as the coordinator of gifted programs in St. Louis County, Missouri.

## DEFINITION

Strategic planning is a process by which organizations plan for the future. The process entails examining belief, vision, and mission statements; gathering and analyzing information; discussing internal and external circumstances that potentially impact the organization's success; and proactively establishing and monitoring initiatives. If done well, the process results in a vivid description of what an organization is, what it does, and why it does it and generates a clear and ambitious statement of organizational goals. Leaders in both the business and public or nonprofit world have found strategic planning a valuable tool for charting future directions and strengthening and sustaining achievement of their organizations. Most strategic plans require three to five years to develop, implement, and evaluate.

## RATIONALE

For the purposes of this chapter, it is helpful to view gifted programs as a form of organization. They are, after all, an enterprise with a budget, defined staff, stated goals, a target audience, and accountability demands. In addition, gifted programs are in the marketplace of alternative services that are offered within a school district and community. The more valued the services and the more satisfied the "clientele," the greater the likelihood that program costs will be supported and that accomplishments will increase over time.

Gifted program personnel cannot be maximally effective without periodically examining their program's effectiveness and purposefully determining what enhancements are needed to improve performance. Thus, engaging in strategic planning is critical. The benefits of working methodically to plan for the future are many. Some of the key advantages are as follows:

- Strategic planning promotes thinking that is both critical and creative. Thinking strategically means establishing organizational priorities for action. To do that, one must systematically collect information, focus on analysis of data, facilitate team learning, and engage in problem-solving efforts. Those elements are all present in strategic planning efforts.
- Strategic planning improves decision making. If done successfully, the process generates useful information, taps a broad array of individuals to generate ideas, and provides clear assessment criteria to document the effectiveness of initiatives. These ingredients allow program personnel to be proactive in improving services, advocating for support, and enhancing student accomplishments.

- By its very nature, strategic planning enhances communication with key stakeholders. Engaging the public in planning efforts provides gifted program personnel with the opportunity to educate key stakeholders about the program and instill a sense of ownership and pride in the efforts and accomplishments of students and staff.

- Strategic planning helps programs deal with changing circumstances. Those changes might be financial, philosophical, or educational. Regardless of what the changes are or why the changes are occurring, proactive consideration of internal and external issues helps program personnel anticipate and address change in a productive fashion.

- Last, and perhaps most important, strategic planning provides the rationale for concentrating time, money, and people on moving a program forward in a purposeful and methodical fashion. All too often, leaders are distracted from achieving organizational goals by competing demands and the ongoing input from well-meaning colleagues, employees, and constituents. Although opportunities to modify the strategic plan are built into the planning process, the operating assumption is that all efforts, resources, and activities will be concentrated on the set of goals that have been approved.

## GUIDING PRINCIPLES

The gifted program's strategic planning process goals must be aligned with the district's mission, beliefs, and core values and must be consistent with state and federal mandates and standards, when applicable.

- The planning process should focus on continually improving services and opportunities for students. Those services and opportunities should be focused on enhancing student learning and increasing individual and group accomplishments.

- The planning process should be spearheaded by a steering committee and include representative stakeholders such as district administrators, building administrators, gifted teachers, regular classroom teachers, parents, and students.

- The planning process must be data driven and include an analysis of district, student, and stakeholder needs, demographics, and current performance levels.

- The process must result in a meaningful and manageable set of program goals.

- The strategic plan must establish specific timelines, milestones, and criteria for evaluating achievement of objectives.

- The strategic plan should identify staff development and communication efforts that are needed to successfully implement the plan.

- Resources needed to achieve the goals of the strategic plan must be clearly defined and supported by the district.

## ATTRIBUTES THAT DEFINE HIGH-QUALITY STRATEGIC PLANNING

One of the most widely implemented approaches to strategic planning was developed by William Cook, Jr. (Cook, 2001). He described two key components that define high-quality strategic planning efforts: (1) a comprehensive and clearly designed planning process (the *how* of strategic planning) and (2) a comprehensive, clearly designed strategic plan (the *what* of strategic planning). These components are then further divided into a variety of elements. (See Table 21.1) Where appropriate, some of the terminology has been modified in this listing to align with recommendations included elsewhere in this handbook.

In Tables 21.1 and 21.2, the components of strategic planning are described as they relate to gifted programs. A flowchart of how a strategic planning process works in a large, midwestern school district is also provided.

**Table 21.1**   The Strategic Planning Process

| Key Step | Description |
|---|---|
| Setting the Stage | A strategic planning process requires time, resources, and energy. Before embarking on such a process, it is important to receive approval and support from the central office, determine the overall parameters within which the planning team will operate, and communicate with key stakeholder groups. Also key is selecting an internal or external facilitator to guide the planning process. |
| Gathering and Analyzing Information | Planning team members will need information that enables them to take an objective look at the program. This information is best generated through a program evaluation or self-study. The information might include program history, demographics, identification procedures, program format, student accomplishments (including test score data), and prior strategic planning initiatives and successes. |
| Choosing the Strategic Planning Team | Participants who represent various stakeholders in the gifted program should be selected to participate on the planning team. Possible stakeholders include parents, teachers, administrators, students, community members, and possibly a board of education representative. |
| Building Consensus | In all likelihood, planning team members will have an interest in gifted education; however, they may also feel that they are serving as representatives of other school interests as well (e.g., school psychologists, math department) and need to express the concerns and interests of those groups if the plan is to be moved along and accepted. Conflicts will arise, but considering the need for consensus building with the facilitator in advance can serve to make discussions of differences of opinion or interests a productive activity that will garner critical feedback as the planning progresses. |
| First Planning Team Session | Team members review background information compiled by the gifted program, develop or revise mission and vision statements, analyze internal and external factors impacting the program, identify and prioritize areas for improvement, and formulate a preliminary set of program goals and objectives. (See the strategic planning flowchart in Figure 21.1.) |
| Communicating Results | The results from the strategic planning team's efforts are shared with key individuals and groups that have a stake in the gifted program and that might have feedback to offer. Those individuals include administrators, teachers, and parents. Once feedback from these groups is processed, the program's strategic goals should be shared and approved by the board of education. |

| Key Step | Description |
|---|---|
| Developing Action Plans | This step addresses the question, "How will the plan's strategic goals be achieved?" To answer this question, step-by-step action plans are needed. Action planning committees, which are formed for this purpose, generate the steps required to achieve the stated objectives. They also decide on criteria for assessing each plan's impact and determine the plan's costs and benefits. These committees are not responsible for implementing the plans that are created. |
| Second Planning Team Session | After the work of the action planning committees is complete, the strategic planning team reassembles to review the results. The team will decide to accept the plans, request specific modifications to be made to the plans, or reject the plans if the plans do not honor and advance the goals and objectives that were developed at the initial meeting of the strategic planning group. |
| Approval | Once action plans are approved by the strategic planning team, the central office and board of education should approve the program's strategic plan. Support from the district is important, since there will be resources needed to fund the strategic plan and significant staff time devoted to implementing changes in the program's format or offerings. |
| Organizing for Implementation | Implementation of the action plans requires leadership and committee work. An overall implementation chair is appointed, as well as a chair for each objective identified in the strategic plan. The chairs form individual committees and work to implement the action plans for which they are responsible. |
| Reviews of Progress | Reporting on the progress of action committees should take place every three to four months. Generally, the overall implementation chair and chairs of each action committee assemble to listen to updates and give feedback and suggestions as warranted. The focus of these meetings is on the specific action steps that have been taken and the use of stated criteria in assessing the committee's efforts. |
| Annual Updates | Each year, the strategic plan is reviewed and updated based on the progress that has been made, the results of assessment efforts, and any unforeseen challenges or opportunities that have occurred since the strategic planning process began. Participants in these updates should include key program personnel plus representatives from the original strategic planning team. |

**Table 21.2** The Strategic Plan

| Key Component | Description |
|---|---|
| Vision Statement | Vision statements are rooted in beliefs and are "from the heart" expressions of the program's hopes for the future. Vision statements are usually accompanied by mission statements. |
| Mission Statement | A mission statement is defined as a broad statement of the unique purpose for which the program exists and the specific function it serves. Mission statements are more practical than vision statements and focus on current efforts to develop the talents of gifted students. |

*(Continued)*

**Table 21.2** (Continued)

| Key Component | Description |
|---|---|
| Strategic Parameters | Strategic parameters refer to any limitations that are imposed on the strategic committee's work, such as the time frame for planning or that the committee is not charged with deciding if the district should have a gifted program. Likewise, a limitation might be that the basic structure of the program is not going to be changed or that increased funding will not be available. |
| Internal Analysis | Internal analysis involves the evaluation of issues or characteristics that either contribute to or limit the program's ability to achieve its mission. Generally, the focus is on identifying the program's strengths and weaknesses. |
| External Analysis | External analysis involves the evaluation of issues or forces in the external environment over which a program has little or no control. An external variable might be the state budget for gifted programs or changes in district demographics. |
| Strategic Issues | Strategic issues refer to the key issues that emerge from studying the program's current practices and factors related to the external environment. A strategic issue might be underrepresentation of culturally diverse students in the gifted program or inadequate differentiation for gifted students in the regular classroom. |
| Goals | Goals refer to broad statements of the desired outcomes of the strategic planning process. Goals should help achieve the program's mission and focus on enhancing program efforts and student accomplishments. |
| Objectives | Objectives are derived from program goals. Objectives are an expression of desired outcomes that are specific and measurable and help an organization achieve its goals. Often, objectives describe the key structures or elements that need to be created or addressed to achieve stated goals. |
| Action Plans | Action plans define the steps or outline of tasks required to implement an objective and achieve the desired results. Action plans include target dates for implementation, the person(s) responsible for each task, resources needed to support the effort, and procedures for assessing the impact of the plan's components. |

# AN EXAMPLE IN NEED OF REVISION

At the end of the year, Owenville's coordinator of Gifted Programs scheduled a whole day meeting with her staff. The purpose of the meeting was to plan the next steps for the gifted program. The coordinator engaged the staff in several activities, including brainstorming a list of changes that had been made to the program over the past three years, reviewing aspects of the program that they felt are most effective, and generating a list of areas that they believed should be addressed in the future.

Following that preliminary conversation, the coordinator asked staff members to work in groups to discuss the items listed as areas for improvement. Each group selected a leader to oversee the discussion and a recorder to keep track of the conversation. The task assigned to the groups was to rank order the ideas for improvement from highest to lowest priority.

**Figure 21.1** Strategic Planning Flowchart

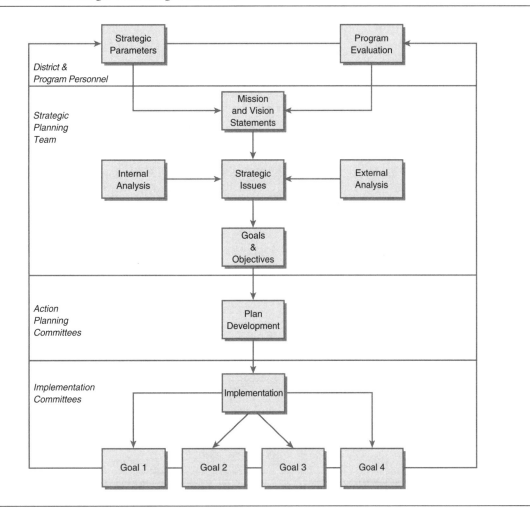

On completion of this task, the staff reassembled and listened to the outcome of each group's discussion. The coordinator entered the rank orders on an overhead transparency and asked the group to compare and contrast the rankings from each of the groups. Teachers were given the opportunity to advocate for the program goals they prioritized. After considerable discussion and some adjustment to the goal statements, the group agreed to target six items.

After a break for lunch, teachers were divided into a new set of groups and were assigned to work at one of six tables. Each table had poster paper with one of the six goals written on top. The teachers were asked to generate a list of steps the program might need to take to reach the agreed-upon goals. Each group spent 20 minutes at its assigned table before rotating to the next table. Within two hours, all groups were able to contribute to the list of implementation ideas related to each of the identified goals.

The final activity for the day was to have each teacher decide which goal he or she would like to work on beginning the following year. Rather than limit the response to just one interest area, the coordinator asked that each teacher rank the goals from one to six in terms of his or her work preference. The teachers were told that every effort would be made to assign them to the committee that they ranked first or second.

The meeting concluded after a date was set for a follow-up meeting in the fall. Before turning to the next section, pause for a moment to reflect on Owenville's planning process for program improvement. Jot down what you believe is noteworthy about their planning. What might be some of the limitations related to their planning? Read on, and compare your answers with the ratings in the next section.

## RATING THE STRATEGIC PLANNING PROCESS AND PRODUCT

As the ratings in Table 21.3 indicate, the strategic planning process described in the example falls short in most areas being assessed. These ratings highlight the fact that a strategic planning process should not be undertaken without a great deal of advanced organization and discussion. To assist in improving the strategic plan, two lists of questions are provided (Tables 21.4 and 21.5) to help the facilitator think through each step of the overall effort. A revised strategic plan is then offered that focuses on the specific tasks and general timeline that a comprehensive planning process requires.

**Table 21.3**   Evaluating a Strategic Plan and Process

| Strategic Process | (1) No Evidence | (2) Little Evidence | (3) Some Evidence | (4) Substantial Evidence | (5) Powerful |
|---|---|---|---|---|---|
| Setting the Stage | X | | | | |
| Gathering and Analyzing Information | | X | | | |
| Choosing the Planning Team | | X | | | |
| First Planning Team Session | | X | | | |
| Communicating Results | X | | | | |
| Developing Action Plans | | X | | | |
| Second Planning Team Session | X | | | | |

**Table 21.3** (Continued)

| Strategic Process | (1) No Evidence | (2) Little Evidence | (3) Some Evidence | (4) Substantial Evidence | (5) Powerful |
|---|---|---|---|---|---|
| Approval | X | | | | |
| Organizing for Implementation | | X | | | |
| Reviews of Progress | X | | | | |
| Annual Updates | X | | | | |

| Strategic Plan | (1) No Evidence | (2) Little Evidence | (3) Some Evidence | (4) Substantial Evidence | (5) Powerful |
|---|---|---|---|---|---|
| Beliefs/Vision Statement (Position Statement) | X | | | | |
| Mission Statement | X | | | | |
| Strategic Parameters | X | | | | |
| Internal Analysis | | X | | | |
| External Analysis | X | | | | |
| Critical Issues | | X | | | |
| Goals | | X | | | |
| Objectives | | X | | | |
| Action Plans | | X | | | |

## Questions to Ask About Strategic Planning Components

The answers to the questions in Tables 21.4 and 21.5 should be affirmative. As you work through the strategic planning process, if you find yourself answering no, it is an indication that more work has yet to be done before moving forward.

**Table 21.4**  Questions to Ask about the Strategic Process

| Key Step | Key Questions |
|---|---|
| Setting the Stage | • Did you properly plan for the strategic planning process?<br>• Was district-level support obtained?<br>• Did you establish strategic parameters for your work? |

*(Continued)*

**Table 21.4** (Continued)

| Key Step | Key Questions |
|---|---|
| Gathering and Analyzing Information | • Did you do your homework and assemble meaningful documentation about the gifted program?<br>• Was the documentation comprehensive, clear, and objective? |
| Choosing the Planning Team (See Appendix A) | • Did you select a representative group of individuals with different backgrounds and perspectives to offer?<br>• Is the group a manageable size (30 or fewer)?<br>• Is the group able to approach decision making in a collaborative fashion? |
| Building Consensus | • Which personnel support the plan? Which personnel oppose the plan due to principle or personal issues?<br>• How can we accommodate the plan to respond to individuals' concerns (e.g., territory, loss of status, limited resources, etc.)?<br>• Has there been a discussion to determine the point at which the group will move the planning forward because it represents a majority opinion? |
| First Planning Team Meeting(s) | • Did you adequately prepare for the planning meeting?<br>• Was there a facilitator selected to lead the planning group?<br>• Was the group's charge clearly explained?<br>• Did you keep on task and accomplish the meeting's goals? |
| Communicating Results | • Did you share the draft of the plan with key stakeholders?<br>• Was the plan shared in a timely fashion?<br>• Did you address questions and concerns that were raised?<br>• Was board of education approval received? |
| Developing Action Plans | • Did you appoint a leader for each action committee?<br>• Were the committees' charges clearly explained?<br>• Did you provide enough time to develop plans?<br>• Were assessment criteria included with each plan? |
| Second Planning Team Session | • Did the strategic committee receive copies of all plans?<br>• Was there adequate discussion of all plans?<br>• Did the committee set implementation dates and costs?<br>• Are meeting results shared with planning committees? |
| Approval | • Did you review the plan with your direct supervisor?<br>• Did you submit the plan for district and board approval? |
| Organizing for Implementation | • Was the program's strategic plan shared broadly?<br>• Were questions addressed and commitment built?<br>• Were implementation committees formed? |
| Progress Reviews | • Are there scheduled reviews of committee progress?<br>• Was the feedback at these reviews clear and helpful? |
| Annual Updates | • Were former strategic planning members involved in updating the strategic plan?<br>• Were necessary changes made in strategies, action plans, and assessments? |

**Table 21.5**  Questions to Ask About the Strategic Plan

| Key Component | Key Questions |
|---|---|
| Vision Statement | • Is your vision statement consistent with the district's belief or vision statement?<br>• Does the statement document the unique characteristics of your population and program? |
| Mission Statement | • Is the mission statement consistent with the district's overall mission?<br>• Does the mission clearly describe the purpose for the program's existence?<br>• Does it identify major goals and performance objectives? |
| Strategic Parameters | • Did you specify any givens, boundaries, or time frames within which the strategic planning committee needs to operate? |
| Internal Analysis | • Did you identify the program's strengths or positives?<br>• Did you identify the program's weaknesses or inadequacies? |
| External Analysis | • Did you identify external factors that might impact the program's future?<br>• Did you examine the assumptions you have related to those factors and how the factors might impact the program's future? |
| Goals | • Are the statements consistent with the program's mission?<br>• Do the statements focus on what the program will accomplish?<br>• Is the number of goals reasonable (three to five are recommended)? |
| Objectives | • Are the objectives related to how the goals will be met?<br>• Are the objectives measurable, observable, and specific?<br>• Will the objectives lead to achieving the stated goals? |
| Action Plans | • Are action plans consistent with the intent of the objectives?<br>• Are the action steps logically sequenced? Is there a completion date assigned to each action step?<br>• Did you identify the person(s) overseeing each action step?<br>• Did you identify resources needed for implementing each action plan?<br>• Did you specify criteria for evaluating the impact of each new initiative? |

# MAKEOVER EXAMPLE

| Month | Tasks |
|---|---|
| September | The individual(s) responsible for undertaking the gifted program strategic plan is authorized to begin work. Needed people, time, and resources are allocated to support the overall planning process. Background information, in the form of a self-study or program evaluation document, is prepared for use during the strategic planning process. |
| January | Members of the strategic planning team are identified and invited to participate in the process. (See sample notice requesting volunteers for the strategic planning team.) |
| February | The strategic planning team, composed of staff, administrators, parents, students, and other community members, meets to create strategic direction for the program. Strategic planning by this group is an open, collaborative examination of issues, challenges, and possibilities for future enhancements and/or modifications of the district's |

| Month | Tasks |
|-------|-------|
| | gifted program. Support for the strategic plan is obtained from the district and board of education. |
| March–May | The action team phase of the planning process begins. Teams of staff, parents, students, and other community members work to create operational plans to implement the objectives designated by the strategic planning team. (See Table 21.6) |
| June | The strategic planning team conducts its second and final session to consider the proposed action plans and reviews all components of the overall plan. |
| July | Central office and board of education receive a copy of the strategic plan for review and approval. |
| August Through End of Plan's Implementation (generally several years) | The individual(s) assigned responsibility for implementing each plan forms a working committee and initiates activities to achieve objectives. |
| Three- to Four-Month Intervals | Progress of working committees is documented and reviewed at meetings of committee chairs. Modifications of plans and assessment procedures are made as needed. |
| Annually through Duration of Strategic Plan | Progress of working committees is shared with original members of the strategic planning team and district-level administrators. Internal and external issues are examined and discussed. Modifications of plans and assessment procedures are made as needed. |

## Sample Communication and Action Plan

This section provides two items: an example of a strategic planning communication memo and a form that can be used to record specific action plans that an action planning committee might generate. These practical examples demonstrate how some features of a strategic plan are implemented.

---

Center for Advanced Learning

**GIFTED PROGRAM STRATEGIC PLANNING TEAM**

Call for Volunteers

The Center is engaging in a Strategic Planning Process and is now forming a committee of approximately 30 individuals to study issues related to the center and its programs. The committee will review our mission statement and descriptive data and help to define goals for the future. Strategic Planning Team membership requires attendance at a three-day planning session on February 22, 23, and 24, from 9:00 a.m. to 2:30 p.m., and a follow-up session in June. All meetings will be held in room A-12 at the Administrative Annex.

If you would like to be considered for participation in the gifted program's Strategic Planning Team, please complete and return the form provided below. If we have more volunteers than places available, we will keep names on file for possible participation on Action Teams that will be formed to develop step-by-step plans to implement each objective that is defined by the Strategic Planning Team.

Thank you for considering this request. Your participation is needed and will be greatly appreciated.

* * * * * * * * * * * * * * * * * * * * * * * * * * * * * * * * * * * * * * * * * * * * * * * * * * *

**GIFTED PROGRAM STRATEGIC PLANNING TEAM**

Volunteer Form

I am interested in volunteering to participate on the gifted program's Strategic Planning Team. I understand the group will meet on February 22, 23, and 24, from 9:00 a.m. to 2:30 p.m., and will hold a follow-up session in June.

Name_____

Address_____

Telephone (Home)_____ (Work)_____

E-mail Address _____

Connection to the Gifted Program_____

This form must be returned by December 15 to the Center for Advanced Learning via fax to (xxx) 222-2222. Selection of Strategic Planning Team members will be made no later than January 5, and you will be notified in writing.

Thank you.

\* \* \* \* \* \* \* \* \* \* \* \* \* \* \* \* \* \* \* \* \* \* \* \* \* \* \* \* \* \* \* \* \* \* \* \* \* \* \* \* \* \* \* \* \* \* \* \* \* \* \* \* \* \* \*

**Table 21.6**  Sample Action Plan

| | |
|---|---|
| Rockwood Gifted Program | Goal # 3 |
| St. Louis County, MO | Action Plan # 2 |

**ACTION PLAN**

GOAL: Expand participation of underrepresented students in the gifted program.

OBJECTIVE: Develop a case-study process for identifying culturally diverse students.

ASSESSMENT: Achieve a statistically significant increase in the number and percentage of culturally diverse students enrolled in the gifted program.

| Step | Action to be Taken | Costs/ Resources | Person Responsible | Start Date | Target Date | Date Completed |
|---|---|---|---|---|---|---|
| 1 | Review the literature on identification of culturally diverse gifted students. | Material Costs, Staff Time | D.J.B. | 4/05 | 12/05 | |
| 2 | Prepare a list of instruments that are recommended for identification of culturally diverse students. | Staff Time | D.J.B. | 10/05 | 12/05 | |

| Step | Action to be Taken | Costs/ Resources | Person Responsible | Start Date | Target Date | Date Completed |
|------|--------------------|--------------------|--------------------|------------|-------------|----------------|
| 3 | Develop a case-study identification system that incorporates research-based findings regarding characteristics of culturally diverse gifted students. | Staff Time, Use of Outside Expert | D.J.B. | 1/06 | 6/06 | |
| 4 | Field-test the identification system to determine its effectiveness. | Analysis Time | J.R.D. | 9/06 | 6/07 | |
| 5 | Provide staff development to district personnel on characteristics of culturally diverse gifted students and the case-study identification system. | Staff Time, Materials | C.S.P. | 9/06 | Ongoing | |

OUTCOME OF ASSESSMENT:

NAME:                              DATE:

# ADVICE FOR THE SOLE PRACTITIONER

District and community support is required for any gifted program to undertake a strategic planning process. In small districts with few staff members, it is essential to engage district-level administrators in making the decision to pursue a comprehensive planning process. Central office administrators must understand the need for such a process and be willing to invest the time and resources necessary for the gifted program to do the job well. Providing an experienced facilitator to oversee the process is a major contribution the district can make to this effort. Although an outside individual is highly desirable, the facilitator is often the in-house administrator who oversees strategic planning for the district as a whole. Collaboration with this individual will help you define a process that is tailored to the size and needs of your district. It is certainly possible to streamline the process to reduce the number of steps involved or the number of committees that will be involved. As long as quality is maintained, it is better to implement a modified planning process than to have no planning process at all. The key to success is to assemble quality information about the current program and to have a great team of people with whom to discuss the information. With these ingredients as your planning foundation, recommendations that will positively impact your district's gifted students are likely to emerge.

## MUST-READ RESOURCES

Bryson, J. M. (1995). *Strategic planning for public and non-profit organizations.* San Francisco, CA: Jossey-Bass.

Cook, W. J., Jr. (2001). *Strategic planning for America's schools.* Montgomery, AL: The Cambridge Management Group.

DuFour, R., & Eaker, R. (1998). *Professional learning communities at work.* Bloomington, IN: National Education Service.

Schmoker, M. (1996). *Results: The key to continuous school improvement.* Alexandria, VA: Association for Supervision and Curriculum Development.

Spain, C. A. (2000). *Chart your own course.* Seattle, WA: Applied Business Solutions.

## REFERENCE

Cook, W. J., Jr. (2001). *Strategic planning for America's schools.* Montgomery, AL: The Cambridge Management Group.

# Appendix A

## *Establishing Gifted Education Advisory Committees*

### *Jann H. Leppien and Karen L. Westberg*

## THE PURPOSE OF A GIFTED EDUCATION ADVISORY COMMITTEE

Members of a gifted education advisory committee play an important and necessary role in the development of successful gifted education services. This group of stakeholders offers perspective, expertise, time, and commitment to the implementation of a comprehensive gifted and talented program. By establishing a gifted education advisory committee, school districts create program ownership, increase the likelihood that a program will be of high quality, and ensure the program longevity.

A gifted education advisory committee is composed of volunteers who meet regularly on a long-term basis to provide advice and support to those responsible for the implementation of gifted education services. Advisory committees serve important functions, such as establishing an initial gifted education program, revising or expanding services, developing new identification guidelines; reviewing the extent to which a school district has implemented gifted education services, lobbying for appropriate funding, establishing public relations, disseminating information, and advocating for comprehensive gifted education services. Typically, the gifted education coordinator would take responsibility to staff the advisory committee. However, in the absence of a full-time coordinator, the central office should take the coordinating role, as the advisory committee will have the responsibility to steer the development and implementation of the gifted education program.

When establishing an advisory committee, a school district needs to consider the roles represented by the committee members and the processes and procedures that will guide their work. An advisory committee is more likely to be effective when the school district's administration genuinely desires the committee's input; therefore, decisions regarding the roles and responsibilities of this committee must be determined prior to its establishment. The committee members should be knowledgeable, committed individuals who are interested in volunteering their time to the support of the district's gifted education services. Procedures for governance should provide a sense of engagement and ownership and access to information about the program. Committee members must understand that they have no administrative policymaking or legislative authority and that meetings are a time to discuss and review the overall program, not individual students or personal concerns.

# FUNCTIONS OF A GIFTED EDUCATION ADVISORY COMMITTEE

The scope of the advisory committee's work will vary depending on the size of the school district, the stage of program development, and the provisions within a state legislative gifted education mandate. Regardless of unique contextual factors that may shape advisory committees, most effective committees

1. Meet regularly and work together to provide advice about the development or improvement of program services.
2. Evaluate the current gifted education services to determine if they are based on best practices in the field of gifted education.
3. Review features of the program, including design, goals, identification procedures, comprehensive services, and curriculum options.
4. Provide feedback about the effectiveness of the gifted education plan.
5. Advise the superintendent and the school board on the educational needs of all gifted students, including appropriate and effective services for identified gifted students.
6. Review annually the local plan for the education of gifted students, including any revisions that should be considered for implementation.
7. Help develop annual goals and establish program priorities.
8. Develop a collaborative relationship between school staff and the committee.
9. Become knowledgeable about current programs, research, and best practices in gifted education and its relationship with general education.
10. Focus attention on issues relative to improving the educational services for gifted students.
11. Assist in interpreting program survey data.
12. Submit program recommendations in writing to the superintendent and the school board.
13. Meet regularly, which may be as frequently as on a monthly basis.
14. Make suggestions to promote community awareness of gifted education.
15. Advocate initiatives designed to meet the needs of the gifted.
16. Promote dialogue between parents, students, school personnel, and community members on issues related to the needs of gifted students.
17. Support professional development training for staff.
18. Provide input and support for legislative funding for gifted education at the local, state, and federal levels.
19. Suggest and support local, state, and national action regarding gifted education programs; attend legislative meetings, write letters, and promote gifted education programs.

20. Secure financial assistance for gifted education programs by arranging for donations and establishing student scholarships and awards.

21. Help recruit volunteers to serve as judges for local awards and competitions for gifted learners.

22. Serve as a liaison to help the community understand and support gifted education services.

23. Encourage communication and a better understanding of gifted education issues among teachers, parents, and the general public.

## THE MEMBERSHIP OF THE ADVISORY COMMITTEE

The size and composition of the advisory committee will vary depending on the number of elementary, middle school, and high schools represented, as well as any state or local regulations that govern their existence. The members should represent parents of students in the gifted program, professional staff and community members for each school, business leaders, gifted education program directors or teachers, board of education representatives, and perhaps a student appointed by the administration. In addition, a school district curriculum and instruction representative and at least one principal should serve on the committee. Committee membership should reflect the ethnic and geographical composition of the school district. Members' terms should be determined prior to their appointment, staggered, and at least two to three years long.

## STEPS FOR ESTABLISHING AND IMPLEMENTING A GIFTED EDUCATION ADVISORY COMMITTEE

*Secure Approval*: Explain the function of an advisory committee to administrators. Point out the local need for, and advantages of, the advisory committee. Provide examples of schools where advisory committees are successfully operating. Explain how an advisory committee will be an asset to administrators, the school, and the gifted education personnel. If necessary, get approval from the school board for the establishment of a gifted education advisory committee.

*Select and Contact Committee Members:* Prepare a list of people from which committee members will be selected. Contact selected members to explain the role of the committee and determine their interest in serving.

*Call the First Meeting:* Avoid time conflicts as much as possible and stress the importance of attendance. Remind committee members by e-mail or telephone of the meeting date and time shortly before the first meeting. Establish an agenda for the meeting.

## EXAMPLE OF AN AGENDA FOR THE FIRST MEETING

1. Welcome and opening remarks by school personnel

2. Introduction of committee members

3.  Explanation of the role of the advisory committee

4.  Brief overview about the school district, its mission, and its goals for all students

5.  History and overview of the gifted education services in the district

6.  Review of the state's standards for gifted education, if any

7.  Organization of the committee, i.e., selection of chairperson and secretary, selection of dates and times for future meetings

8.  Discussion about future agenda items

## HELPFUL REMINDERS WHEN WORKING WITH EXISTING OR NEW ADVISORY COMMITTEES

- Provide biographical information about the chairperson and other members of the committee.
- Explain what is expected of committee members in terms of advice, assistance, cooperation, and time. Provide a written position description that can be based on the 23 descriptors listed earlier in Functions of a Gifted Education Advisory Committee.
- Communicate the gifted program's purpose and goals so committee members can provide appropriate advice and guidance. Familiarize committee members with the overall plan for the gifted program.
- Provide committee members with continuous information about educational developments in the field of gifted education at the local, state, and national levels.
- Invite committee members to attend school functions, board of education meetings, or special events sponsored by the gifted and talented program.
- Demonstrate enthusiasm for, and commitment to, the committee's role in improving gifted education services.
- Provide opportunities for representatives to meet with students throughout the school year.
- Establish subcommittees of three to four members to address specific issues and accomplish specific tasks when needed.
- Schedule meetings at a convenient time, and preferably host the meetings in a school.
- Notify committee members at least two weeks in advance of meetings.
- Keep meetings within a reasonable time limit. Before each meeting, provide members with an agenda containing a brief background statement of the issues to be discussed.
- Provide recognition to the service that this committee provides in newspaper articles, presentations, and the gifted and talented program's annual report.
- Always provide refreshments!

Advisory committees can have a direct, positive impact on the types of services that a school district provides to its gifted learners and to the overall improvement of a gifted education program. Committee members, by sharing their expertise and knowledge, support the quality and integrity of gifted education services, while ensuring that the needs of identified gifted students will be met in a school district.

# Appendix B

## NAGC Pre-K–Grade 12 Gifted Program Standards

## INTRODUCTION

This document delineates both *requisite* and *exemplary* standards for gifted education programming, and depicts pre-collegiate gifted programming standards for gifted education, representing a range of minimal, or requisite, and exemplary, or visionary, levels of performance. These standards may serve as benchmarks for measuring programming effectiveness, criteria for program evaluation; guidelines for program development, and recommendations for minimal requirements for high-quality gifted education programming.

Several **organizing principles** guided the work of the task force, including:

- Standards should encourage but not dictate approaches of high quality.
- Standards represent both requisite program outcomes and standards for excellence.
- Standards establish the level of performance to which all educational school districts and agencies should aspire.
- Standards represent professional consensus on critical practice in gifted education that most everyone is likely to find acceptable.
- Standards are observable aspects of educational programming and are directly connected to the continuous growth and development of gifted learners.

**Definitions** of some terms may be found on the back cover.

## DEFINITIONS

***Gifted education programming*** is a coordinated and comprehensive structure of informal and formal services provided on a continuing basis intended to effectively nurture gifted learners.

***A standard*** is a designated level of performance that programming must achieve for the criteria to be deemed a success (Worthen, Sanders, & Fitzpatrick, 1997).

***Gifted learners*** are "children and youth with outstanding talent who perform or show the potential for performing at remarkably high levels of accomplishment when compared with others of their age, experience, or environment" (U.S. Department of Education, 1993, p. 3).

***Minimum standards*** include requisite conditions for acceptable gifted education programming practice.

***Exemplary standards*** designate desirable and visionary conditions for excellence in gifted education programming practice.

## Task Force Membership

Mary S. Landrum & Beverly Shaklee, Editors

*Contributing Authors*

Tim Burke, Gloria Cox, Jan DeWaard, Susan Hansford, Tom Hays, Marta Montjoy, Carol Reid, Anne Slanina

*Other Task Force Members*

Sally Beisser, Sally Dobyns, Coleen Ehreshmann, Michael Hall, Frank Rainey, Julia Roberts, Sue Vogel, Joanne Welch

# REFERENCES

Texas Education Agency. (1996). *Texas state plan for the education of gifted/talented students.* Austin, TX: Author.

U.S. Department of Education. (1993). *National excellence: A case for developing America's talent.* Washington, D. C.: Author.

Worthen, B. R., Sanders, J. R., & Fitzpatrick, J. L. (1997). *Program evaluation: Alternative approaches and practical guidelines* (2nd ed.). New York: Longman.

## Gifted Education Programming Criterion: Curriculum and Instruction

Description: Gifted education services must include curricular and instructional opportunities directed to the unique needs of the gifted learner.

| Guiding Principles | Minimum Standards | Exemplary Standards |
|---|---|---|
| 1. Differentiated curricula for the gifted learner must span grades pre-K–12. | 1.0M Differentiated curriculum (curricular and instructional adaptations that address the unique learning needs of gifted learners) for gifted learners must be integrated and articulated throughout the district. | 1.0E A well-defined and implemented curriculum scope and sequence should be articulated for all grade levels and all subject areas. |
| 2. Regular classroom curricula and instruction must be adapted, modified, or replaced to meet the unique needs of gifted learners. | 2.0M Instruction, objectives, and strategies provided to gifted learners must be systematically differentiated from those in the regular classroom. | 2.0E District curriculum plans should include objectives, content, and resources that challenge gifted learners in the regular classroom. |
| | 2.1M Teachers must differentiate, replace, supplement, or modify curricula to facilitate higher level learning goals. | 2.1E Teachers should be responsible for developing plans to differentiate the curriculum in every discipline for gifted learners. |
| | 2.2M Means for demonstrating proficiency in essential regular curriculum concepts and processes must be established to facilitate appropriate academic acceleration. | 2.2E Documentation of instruction for assessing level(s) of learning and accelerated rates of learning should demonstrate plans for gifted learners based on specific needs of individual learners. |
| | 2.3M Gifted learners must be assessed for proficiency in basic skills and knowledge and provided with alternative challenging educational opportunities when proficiency is demonstrated. | 2.3E Gifted learners should be assessed for proficiency in all standard courses of study and subsequently provided with more challenging educational opportunities. |

| Guiding Principles | | Minimum Standards | | Exemplary Standards |
|---|---|---|---|---|
| 3. | Instructional pace must be flexible to allow for the accelerated learning of gifted learners as appropriate. | 3.0M | A program of instruction must consist of advanced content and appropriately differentiated teaching strategies to reflect the accelerative learning pace and advanced intellectual processes of gifted learners. | 3.0E When warranted, continual opportunities for curricular acceleration should be provided in gifted learners' areas of strength and interest while allowing a sufficient ceiling for optimal learning. |
| 4. | Educational opportunities for subject and grade skipping must be provided to gifted learners. | 4.0M | Decisions to proceed or limit the acceleration of content and grade acceleration must only be considered after a thorough assessment. | 4.0E Possibilities for partial or full acceleration of content and grade levels should be available to any student presenting such needs. |
| 5. | Learning opportunities for gifted learners must consist of a continuum of differentiated curricular options, instructional approaches, and resource materials. | 5.0M | Diverse and appropriate learning experiences must consist of a variety of curricular options, instructional strategies, and materials. | 5.0E Appropriate service options for each student to work at assessed level(s) and advanced rates of learning should be available. |
| | | 5.1M | Flexible instructional arrangements (e.g., special classes, seminars, resource rooms, mentorships, independent study, and research projects) must be available. | 5.1E Differentiated educational program curricula for students pre-K–Grade 12 should be modified to provide learning experiences matched to students' interests, readiness, and learning styles. |

**Gifted Education Programming Criterion: Program Administration and Management**

Description: Appropriate gifted education programming must include the establishment of a systematic means of developing, implementing, and managing services.

| Guiding Principles | Minimum Standards | Exemplary Standards |
|---|---|---|
| 1. Appropriately qualified personnel must direct services for the education of gifted learners. | 1.0M The designated coordinator of gifted education programming must have completed coursework or staff development in gifted education and display leadership ability to be deemed appropriately qualified. | 1.0E The designated gifted programming coordinator must have completed a certification program or advanced degree program in gifted education. |
| 2. Gifted education programming must be integrated into the general education program. | 2.0M The gifted education program must create linkages between general education and gifted education at all levels. | 2.0E Responsibility for the education of gifted learners is a shared one requiring strong relationships between the gifted education program and general education school wide. |
| 3. Gifted education programming must include positive working relationships with constituency and advocacy groups, as well as with compliance agencies. | 3.0M Gifted programming staff must establish ongoing parent communication. | 3.0E The gifted education programming staff should facilitate the dissemination of information regarding major policies and practices in gifted education (e.g., student referral and screening, appeals, informed consent, student progress, etc.) to school personnel, parents, community members, etc. |
|  | 3.1M Gifted programs must establish and use an advisory committee that reflects the cultural and socioeconomic diversity of the school or school district's total student population and includes parents, community members, students, and school staff members. | 3.1E Parents of gifted learners should have regular opportunities to share input and make recommendations about program operations with the gifted programming coordinator. |

| Guiding Principles | Minimum Standards | Exemplary Standards |
|---|---|---|
| | 3.2M Gifted education programming staff must communicate with other on-site departments as well as other educational agencies vested in the education of gifted learners (e.g., other school districts, school board members, state departments of education, intermediate educational agencies, etc.). | 3.2E The gifted education program should consider current issues and concerns from other educational fields and agencies regarding gifted programming decision making on a regular basis. |
| 4. Requisite resources and materials must be provided to support the efforts of gifted education programming. | 4.0M Resources must be provided to support program operations. | 4.0E A diversity of resources (e.g., parent, community, vocational, etc.) should be available to support program operations. |
| | 4.1M Technological support must be provided for gifted education programming services. | 4.1E Gifted education programming should provide state-of-the-art technology to support appropriate services. |
| | 4.2M The library selections must reflect a range of materials, including those appropriate for gifted learners. | 4.2E The acquisition plan for purchasing new materials for the school should reflect the needs of gifted learners. |

## Gifted Education Programming Criterion: Program Design

Description: The development of appropriate gifted education programming requires comprehensive services based on sound philosophical, theoretical, and empirical support.

| Guiding Principles | Minimum Standards | Exemplary Standards |
|---|---|---|
| 1. Rather than any single gifted program, a continuum of programming services must exist for gifted learners. | 1.0M Gifted programming services must be accessible to all gifted learners. | 1.0E Levels of services should be matched to the needs of gifted learners by providing a full continuum of options. |
| 2. Gifted education must be adequately funded. | 2.0M Gifted education funding should be equitable compared to the funding of other local programming. | 2.0E Gifted education programming must receive funding consistent with the program goals and sufficient to adequately meet them. |
| 3. Gifted education programming must evolve from a comprehensive and sound base. | 3.0M Gifted education programming must be submitted for outside review on a regular basis. | 3.0E Gifted education programming should be planned as a result of consultation with informed experts. |
| | 3.1M Gifted programming must be guided by a clearly articulated philosophy statement and accompanying goals and objectives. | 3.1E The school or school district should have a mission/philosophy statement that addresses the need for gifted education programming. |
| | 3.2M A continuum of services must be provided across grades pre-K–12. | 3.2E A comprehensive pre-K–Grade 12 program plan should include policies and procedures for identification, curriculum and instruction, service delivery, teacher preparation, formative and summative evaluation, support services, and parent involvement. |
| 4. Gifted education programming services must be an integral part of the general education school day. | 4.0M Gifted education programming should be articulated with the general education program. | 4.0E Gifted services must be designed to supplement and build on the basic academic skills and knowledge learned in regular |

| Guiding Principles | | Minimum Standards | | Exemplary Standards |
|---|---|---|---|---|
| | | | | classrooms at all grade levels to ensure continuity as students progress through the program. |
| | | 4.1M Appropriate educational opportunities must be provided in the regular classroom, resource classroom, separate, or optional voluntary environments. | | 4.1E Local school districts should offer multiple service delivery options, as no single service should stand alone. |
| 5. Flexible groupings of students must be developed in order to facilitate differentiated instruction and curriculum. | | 5.0M The use of flexible grouping of gifted learners must be an integral part of gifted education programming. | | 5.0E Gifted learners should be included in flexible grouping arrangements in all content areas and grade levels to ensure that gifted students learn with and from intellectual peers. |
| 6. Policies specific to adapting and adding to the nature and operations of the general education program are necessary for gifted education. | | 6.0M Existing and future school policies must include provisions for the needs of gifted learners. | | 6.0E Gifted education policies should exist for at least the following areas: early entrance, grade skipping, ability grouping, and dual enrollment. |

**Gifted Education Programming Criterion: Program Evaluation**

Description: Program evaluation is the systematic study of the value and impact of services provided.

| Guiding Principles | Minimum Standards | Exemplary Standards |
|---|---|---|
| 1. An evaluation must be purposeful. | 1.0M Information collected must reflect the interests and needs of most of the constituency groups. | 1.0E Information collected should address pertinent questions raised by all constituency groups and should be responsive to the needs of all stakeholders. |
| 2. An evaluation must be efficient and economic. | 2.0M School districts must provide sufficient resources for program evaluation. | 2.0E School districts should allocate adequate time, financial support, and personnel to conduct systematic program evaluation. |
| 3. An evaluation must be conducted competently and ethically. | 3.0M Persons conducting the evaluation must be competent and trustworthy. | 3.0E Persons conducting the evaluation should possess an expertise in program evaluation in gifted education. |
| | 3.1M The program evaluation design must address whether or not services have reached intended goals. | 3.1E The evaluation design should report the strengths and weaknesses found in the program, as well as critical issues that might influence program services. |
| | 3.2M Instruments and procedures used for data collection must be valid and reliable for their intended use. | 3.2E Care should be taken to ensure that instruments with sufficient evidence of reliability and validity are used, and that they are appropriate for varying age, developmental levels, gender, and diversity of the target population. |

| Guiding Principles | Minimum Standards | Exemplary Standards |
|---|---|---|
| | 3.3M Ongoing formative and summative evaluation strategies must be used for substantive program improvement and development. | 3.3E Formative evaluations should be conducted regularly, with summative evaluations occurring minimally every five years or more often as specified by state or local district policies. |
| | 3.4M Individual data must be held confidential. | 3.4E All individuals who are involved in the evaluation process should be given the opportunity to verify information and the resulting interpretation. |
| 4. The evaluation results must be made available through a written report. | 4.0M Evaluation reports must present the evaluation results in a clear and cohesive format. | 4.0E Evaluation reports should be designed to present results and encourage follow-through by stakeholders. |

## Gifted Education Programming Criterion: Professional Development

Description: Gifted learners are entitled to be served by professionals who have specialized preparation in gifted education, expertise in appropriate differentiated content and instructional methods, involvement in ongoing professional development, and who possess exemplary personal and professional traits.

| Guiding Principles | Minimum Standards | Exemplary Standards |
|---|---|---|
| 1. A comprehensive staff development program must be provided for all school staff involved in the education of gifted learners. | 1.0M All school staff must be made aware of the nature and needs of gifted students. | 1.0E All school staff should be provided ongoing staff development in the nature and needs of gifted learners and appropriate instructional strategies. |
| | 1.1M Teachers of gifted students must attend each year at least one professional development activity designed specifically for teaching gifted learners. | 1.1E All teachers of gifted learners should continue to be actively engaged in the study of gifted education through staff development or graduate degree programs. |
| 2. Only qualified personnel should be involved in the education of gifted learners. | 2.0M All personnel working with gifted learners must be certified to teach in the areas to which they are assigned and must be aware of the unique learning differences and needs of gifted learners at the grade level at which they are teaching. | 2.0E All personnel working with gifted learners should participate in regular staff development programs. |
| | 2.1M All specialist teachers in gifted education must hold or be actively working toward a certification (or the equivalent) in gifted education in the state in which they teach. | 2.1E All specialist teachers in gifted education should possess a certification/specialization or degree in gifted education. |
| | 2.2M Any teacher whose primary responsibility for teaching includes gifted learners must have extensive expertise in gifted education. | 2.2E Only teachers with advanced expertise in gifted education should have primary responsibility for the education of gifted learners. |

| Guiding Principles | Minimum Standards | Exemplary Standards |
|---|---|---|
| 3. School personnel require support for their specific efforts related to the education of gifted learners. | 3.0M School personnel must be released from their professional duties to participate in staff development efforts in gifted education. | 3.0E Approved staff development activities in gifted education should be funded at least in part by school districts or educational agencies. |
| 4. The educational staff must be provided with time and other support for the preparation and development of the differentiated education plans, materials, curriculum. | 4.0M School personnel must be allotted planning time to prepare for the differentiated education of gifted learners. | 4.0E Regularly scheduled planning time (e.g., release time, summer pay, etc.) should be allotted to teachers for the development of differentiated educational programs and related resources. |

**Gifted Education Programming Criterion: Student Identification**

Description: Gifted learners must be assessed to determine appropriate educational services.

| Guiding Principles | | Minimum Standards | | Exemplary Standards |
|---|---|---|---|---|
| 1. A comprehensive and cohesive process for student nomination must be coordinated in order to determine eligibility for gifted education services. | 1.0M | Information regarding the characteristics of gifted students in areas served by the district must be annually disseminated to all appropriate staff members. | 1.0E | The school district should provide information annually, in a variety of languages, regarding the process for nominating students for gifted education programming services. |
| | 1.1M | All students must comprise the initial screening pool of potential recipients of gifted education services. | 1.1E | The nomination process should be ongoing, and screening of any student should occur at any time. |
| | 1.2M | Nominations for services must be accepted from any source (e.g., teachers, parents, community members, peers, etc.). | 1.2E | Nomination procedures and forms should be available in a variety of languages. |
| | 1.3M | Parents must be provided with information regarding an understanding of giftedness and student characteristics. | 1.3E | Parents should be provided with special workshops or seminars to gain a full meaning of giftedness. |
| 2. Instruments used for student assessment to determine eligibility for gifted education services must measure diverse abilities, talents, strengths, and needs in order to provide students an opportunity to demonstrate any strengths. | 2.0M | Assessment instruments must measure the capabilities of students with provisions for the language in which the student is most fluent, when available. | 2.0E | Assessments should be provided in a language in which the student in most fluent, if available. |
| | 2.1M | Assessments must be culturally fair. | 2.1E | Assessment should be responsive to students' economic conditions, gender, developmental differences, handicapping conditions, and other factors that mitigate against fair assessment practices. |
| | 2.2M | The purpose(s) of student assessments must be consistently articulated across all grade levels. | 2.2E | Students identified in all designated areas of giftedness within a school district should be assessed consistently across grade levels. |
| | 2.3M | Student assessments must be sensitive to the current stage of talent development. | 2.3E | Student assessments should be sensitive to all stages of talent development. |

| Guiding Principles | | Minimum Standards | | Exemplary Standards |
|---|---|---|---|---|
| 3. A student assessment profile of individual strengths and needs must be developed to plan appropriate intervention. | 3.0M | An assessment profile must be developed for each child to evaluate eligibility for gifted education programming services. | 3.0E | Individual assessment plans should be developed for all gifted learners who need gifted education. |
| | 3.1M | An assessment profile must reflect the unique learning characteristics and potential and performance levels. | 3.1E | An assessment profile should reflect the gifted learner's interests, learning style, and educational needs. |
| 4. All student identification procedures and instruments must be based on current theory and research. | 4.0M | No single assessment instrument or its results deny student eligibility for gifted programming services. | 4.0E | Student assessment data should come from multiple sources and include multiple assessment methods. |
| | 4.1M | All assessment instruments must provide evidence of reliability and validity for the intended purposes and target students. | 4.1E | Student assessment data should represent an appropriate balance of reliable and valid quantitative and qualitative measures. |
| 5. Written procedures for student identification must include, at the very least, provisions for informed consent, student retention, student reassessment, student exiting, and appeals procedures. | 5.0M | District gifted programming guidelines must contain specific procedures for student assessment at least once during the elementary, middle, and secondary levels. | 5.0E | Student placement data should be collected using an appropriate balance of quantitative and qualitative measures with adequate evidence of reliability and validity for the purposes of identification. |
| | 5.1M | District guidelines must provide specific procedures for student retention and exiting, as well as guidelines for parent appeals. | 5.1E | District guidelines and procedures should be reviewed and revised when necessary. |

**Gifted Education Programming Criterion: Socio-Emotional Guidance and Counseling**

Description: Gifted education programming must establish a plan to recognize and nurture the unique socio-emotional development of gifted learners.

| Guiding Principles | Minimum Standards | Exemplary Standards |
|---|---|---|
| 1. Gifted learners must be provided with differentiated guidance efforts to meet their unique socio-emotional development. | 1.0M Gifted learners, because of their unique socio-emotional development, must be provided with guidance and counseling services by a counselor who is familiar with the characteristics and socio-emotional needs of gifted learners. | 1.0E Counseling services should be provided by a counselor familiar with specific training in the characteristics and socio-emotional needs (i.e., underachievement, multipotentiality, etc.) of diverse gifted learners. |
| 2. Gifted learners must be provided with career guidance services especially designed for their unique needs. | 2.0M Gifted learners must be provided with career guidance consistent with their unique strengths. | 2.0E Gifted learners should be provided with college and career guidance that is appropriately different and delivered earlier than typical programs. |
| 3. Gifted at-risk students must be provided with guidance and counseling to help them reach their potential. | 3.0M Gifted at-risk students must have special attention, counseling, and support to help them realize their full potential. | 3.0E Gifted learners who do not demonstrate satisfactory performance in regular and/or gifted education classes should be provided with specialized intervention services. |
| 4. Gifted learners must be provided with affective curriculum in addition to differentiated guidance and counseling services. | 4.0M Gifted learners must be provided with affective curriculum as part of differentiated curriculum and instructional services. | 4.0E A well-defined and implemented affective curriculum scope and sequence containing personal/social awareness and adjustment, academic planning, and vocational and career awareness should be provided to gifted learners. |
| 5. Underachieving gifted learners must be served rather than omitted from differentiated services. | 5.0M Gifted students who are underachieving must not be exited from gifted programs because of related problems. | 5.0E Underachieving gifted learners should be provided with specific guidance and counseling services that address the issues and problems related to underachievement. |

# Index

## CORWIN
## PRESS

The Corwin Press logo—a raven striding across an open book—represents the union of courage and learning. Corwin Press is committed to improving education for all learners by publishing books and other professional development resources for those serving the field of PreK–12 education. By providing practical, hands-on materials, Corwin Press continues to carry out the promise of its motto: **"Helping Educators Do Their Work Better."**

## MISSION STATEMENT

The National Association for Gifted Children (NAGC) is an organization of parents, teachers, educators, other professionals, and community leaders who unite to address the unique needs of children and youth with demonstrated gifts and talents as well as those children who may be able to develop their talent potential with appropriate educational experiences. We support and develop policies and practices that encourage and respond to the diverse expressions of gifts and talents in children and youth from all cultures, racial and ethnic backgrounds, and socioeconomic groups. NAGC supports and engages in research and development, staff development, advocacy, communication, and collaboration with other organizations and agencies who strive to improve the quality of education for all students.